Laos

China
Burma
Hanoi
Sam Neua
Houei Sai
Luang Prabang
Xieng Khaouang
Vang Vieng
Phone Hong
Vientiane
Nongkhai
Vietnam
Laos
Thailand
Hue
Da Nang
Pakse
Cambodia
Bangkok
Phnom-Penh
Saigon

Laos

A Personal Portrait from the Mid–1970s

by
JUDY AUSTIN RANTALA

McFarland & Company, Inc., Publishers
Jefferson, North Carolina, and London

British Library Cataloguing-in-Publication data are available

Library of Congress Cataloguing-in-Publication Data

Rantala, Judy Austin, 1922–
Laos : a personal portrait from the mid–1970s / by Judy Austin Rantala.
p. cm.
Includes bibliographical references and index.
ISBN 0-89950-939-8 (lib. bdg. : 50# alk. paper) ♾
1. Laos—Description and travel. 2. Laos—Politics and government. 3. Laos—Politics and government—1975– 4. Refugees—United States. 5. Laotian Americans—Cultural assimilation.
6. Rantala, Judy Austin, 1992– . I. Title.
DS555.8.R35 1994
959.404—dc20 93-38746
CIP

Manufactured in the United States of America

McFarland & Company, Inc., Publishers
Box 611, Jefferson, North Carolina 28640

To the memory of my husband,
John W. Rantala,
who, believing that "without risk
there is no adventure," led me into
the wonderful adventure that was Laos

CONTENTS

ACKNOWLEDGMENTS

In many parts of the United States, as well as in France, there are expatriates of Laos who have had a hand in helping me put together this book. To Khampheng and Souvanh, Bounliane, Chanboumny and the entire Sivongsay family, I extend thanks for their continuing friendship and the privilege of being one of the *mee taows* (grandmothers) in their families.

To the writers and writing groups in Hawaii, especially Jane, Judy and Karen, who critiqued, listened, suggested and encouraged, I am deeply grateful. I am grateful also to Iris, who gave me invaluable tips on how to rewrite. To those who read parts or all of the manuscript, some more than once, thank you for your time and encouragement: Kikue, Iris, Jean, Jo, June, Pat, Amanda, Chuck, Mary Ann, and especially my teacher of autobiographical writing, Lorna Hershinow.

Thanks also are due a variety of computer users, who nursed me through a change of programs and answered my calls when I could not retrieve a chapter, or figure out how to perform a particular function.

And to Linda, who suffered the grinding repetition of my ancient printer's jarring noise in our small apartment: thank you for your patience and forbearance.

But most of all, to the people of Laos, who have shown the world how to bear adversity without rancor, and hardship with a smile, I acknowledge a dimension in my life that I covet for all people, an ability to laugh at misfortune and to live with what one has. They continue to enrich my life beyond anything I deserve or expect, and I am deeply grateful.

PREFACE

The writing of this account of the years I lived in Laos began following my husband's fatal heart attack in 1989. I found that recalling and recording these memories helped me work through the loneliness and grief. I first wrote mainly about Khamnouy, the young man we sponsored to an American university, and about the views and customs of the Lao people that we came to know thanks to his presence in our lives.

In the midst of this a cousin sent me a box of all the letters I had written to various family members between 1970 and 1975. Carefully saved by her mother, the box included long accounts written in lieu of a personal diary. Rereading this astonishing complete record of those five years overseas jolted me into a new vision of where my writing might take me. I had a strong desire to share my personal perception of the American presence in Laos and to honor the promises John and I had made to each other to represent an average American's view of events in this part of Indochina.

The writing progressed from an anecdotal account of our experiences to an attempt to interpret and evaluate the complex military and political events that had happened all around us.

I need to emphasize that the opinions expressed in this book are my own. Many who read it will take issue with my interpretations. I also need to say that I have risked expressing them because I am convinced that ordinary Americans often are exposed only to the information that powerful forces in government and in the economic sphere want us to hear and that seldom do the newspapers or television newscasts provide enough information to enable us to see a whole picture. This certainly became apparent in Laos, making me both angry and sad.

The editors at McFarland asked me to document my facts and opinions and only then did I search for materials that had been written about Laos.

This research, relying primarily on books found in the Honolulu Public Library and the library of the University of Minnesota, not only corroborated my statements but moreover proved what I had suspected. Only in segments of Christopher Robbins' book *The Ravens* had anything been written about the 1970s in Laos.

A friend who was a newspaper editor read my manuscript and called me to ask if the chapter "Naïveté Abroad" was written tongue in cheek. "Surely you are not serious," he said. "Everyone knows American presidents lie."

I contend that in the pre–Watergate year 1971 everyone did *not* know the extent of either domestic or foreign policy omission – or sheer misinformation – engineered by our government. My systematic and persistent questioning of a succession of friends confirmed that many still could not locate Laos on a map and to a person they professed ignorance of the extent and nature of the U.S. military presence in Laos in the 1950s, 1960s and 1970s.

A further motive for writing this account was my desire to help Americans learn about and appreciate the Lao people. More than 10 percent of the population fled as refugees in the late 1970s; many of them relocated in the United States. They now live from Miami to Seattle, Honolulu to Boston. My research had revealed that few books have been written about Laos, and almost none in which individual Lao are featured or their lives and customs described in personal terms.

Finally, I hope readers will enjoy the information this book provides about one of the least known countries on earth. I know of no one who lived and worked in Laos who does not still speak with warmth and affection about the people. The country is miserably poor and the economic base nearly nonexistent. Yet the people are gentle, friendly, fun-loving and universally generous and hospitable. If my effort sparks an appreciation of the unique Laotian culture, I will be amply rewarded.

1
The End

The bell kept ringing and ringing. Even after I turned off the alarm it rang. The phone! Who could be calling at this hour of the morning?

Stumbling from bed, I roused myself enough to reach the telephone in the living room. I lifted the receiver to hear the chief of party for our University of Hawaii team ask crisply for John.

"He'll be right here. Is something wrong?"

"The Pathet Lao have taken over the USAID compound."

Turning from the brief call, John added that the Pathet Lao had also surrounded our living area, Km6, and that we were instructed not to attempt to leave. Aghast, I looked at him, hardly comprehending the implications of this news, even as I heard myself whisper, "It's the end, isn't it? It's all over."

The entire scenario of an evening social gathering only four days earlier flooded my thoughts. The imminent takeover of the American consular and AID facilities by the Pathet Lao, predicted so nonchalantly by a Pathet Lao sympathizer that evening, had proceeded on schedule, almost to the minute.

We had naïvely brushed off his comments about what was about to happen in Laos as fiction or wishful thinking. Now it had all caught up with us.

How could we have been so unprepared for this? I thought of the postcard that was in the mail to my brother in New Hampshire: "Don't believe everything you read in the papers. We are not in any danger. Our contract has been renewed, and we expect to be here until December of 1976."

I thought of Khampheng, my Lao "daughter" who, with her small son, had departed from the airport on a flight to Paris barely two hours prior to the Pathet Lao takeover last night. I remembered the morning coffee gathering I had driven to a week ago, in a Lao home, only to find it canceled because on the previous day the whole family had fled to Thailand. I thought of the Thai Dam tribal group which had just crossed the Mekong River, refusing, for the third time in three decades, to live in a Communist-dominated area.

Numbly I looked at John, ever the pragmatist, getting into his work clothes.

"What are we going to do?"

"We're going to start packing."

Tears blurring my eyes, I stumbled toward the cupboards, memories flooding in as I began to sort and fill the boxes. I recalled the day our lift vans arrived, nine months after they had been packed in Hawaii, and the joy of once more having our own household effects. I thought of our Lao friends in the villages—would we ever see them again? Were they in danger? I stroked the *baci* strings on my wrist, reminders of Khampheng's farewell party. How would we ever contact her now?

Taking myself in hand, I began methodically to make decisions, forming piles of related articles, and as I sorted, I recalled the circumstances that had brought us to Laos, four and one-half years earlier.

2
Arriving in Laos

Peering through the plane window I tried to envision the country in which we were to spend the first half of the 1970s. Half a world away from our home in Hawaii, would Laos, country of our destination, resemble the flat brown fields of central Thailand below us? Would Vientiane, the capital city, be anything like Bangkok where we had just spent twenty-four hours?

My husband and I had flown into Thailand from East Pakistan and had been assailed by cultural contrasts. The noise, the frantic human activity, the exotic aura provided by brilliantly colored temples, the trauma of suicidal taxi drivers all had been compressed into a very brief glimpse of this sensual Southeast Asian city.

The ride from the airport to the hotel had been classic Bangkok. Vehicles on the roadways were six abreast, separated only by a stripe of paint. We caught glimpses of upwardly curving, bright orange and green pagoda roofs, watched sidewalk vendors thrusting their wares towards camera-toting tourists, marveled at canals, known as klongs, jammed with shore to shore sampans.

The abundance confronting us was mind-boggling. It was immediately obvious that we had left behind us the austerity of Pakistan, that country where we had just completed a six-month assignment for the U.S. State Department. We were eager to look around and, leaving unopened bags in the hotel, soon found ourselves in streets awash with taxis. We gawked at neon signs designed to lure us into nightclubs and restaurants and, giving in to a wave of homesickness, availed ourselves of the opportunity to view an American movie.

After the show we strolled along the sidewalks, noting the mixture of cultures reflected in passing faces, staring at the excess of consumer goods offered in stores. We had repeatedly delighted the street children by responding with, "Hello. How are you?" and, "What's your name?" to their giggling attempts at English.

On our way back to our hotel we stopped to eat small hot coconut cakes cooked over a portable brazier set up on a street corner. Tucked into my bag was some fruit from a sidewalk stand, ready for the next morning.

Our early start on the following day produced only frustration. Officials dispensing visas to Laos were insensitive to our eagerness to move on, causing us to spend most of the day filling out forms and waiting in line. Grateful at last to be airborne, I gazed out of the plane window where below us I could see a two-lane highway down which toy trucks appeared to be racing in slow motion.

Did this highway connect with Laos? Perhaps figuratively, but I reminded myself that the Mekong River was a boundary between the two countries. Was Laos a country suffering from the severe economic restrictions we knew in Karachi, or would it be more likely to reflect the sights and sounds of Bangkok?

Neither of us knew a great deal about the small, landlocked country we were approaching, and John responded to my questions with, "I'm quite sure it will not be as economically advanced as Thailand—and probably less sophisticated."

"What about roads?" I asked. "The one we can see under us looks pretty impressive."

"Not surprising. Unless I'm mistaken, it was built primarily with American money in order to facilitate the movement of military vehicles from south to north. I don't know that American foreign policy has set that kind of priority in Laos." His answer was my initial clue toward the intricate interconnection between American foreign aid through the United States Agency for International Development (USAID) and the political ramifications of American foreign policy in this part of the world.

"I understand that our University of Hawaii team members usually fly from one point to another since many of the roads are in the hands of insurgents and too dangerous to use, even when they exist." (Much later I learned from Martin Stuart-Fox in *Laos: Politics, Economics and Society*, that in all of Laos there were less than six thousand kilometers of highways and two of these roads in the Laotian panhandle connected Lao communities directly with Vietnamese ports and were, thus, constant targets of both American and North Vietnamese military action [16, 122].)

Further questioning was interrupted by the proffering of a drink by our cabin attendant who was wearing what she informed me was traditional Lao dress. Her stunning calf-length woven silk skirt was matched by a *pa peh* or shoulder sash. Gold thread formed intricate patterns in both the skirt and sash. Was this everyday dress for Lao women? Did anyone wear slacks in public? Would all Lao women have the fresh complexion and delicate features of this attractive stewardess? Was hers a coveted job?

As we neared our destination I became acutely aware of how little I knew about this small country and recalled my astonishment when John had asked me what I would think about living in Laos. "What's Laos?" I had countered triggering his explanation that it was a country in Southeast Asia where the University of Hawaii had a team of education specialists in place and was seeking an experienced vocational education specialist with his skills in welding, machine shop and blueprint reading. He would supplement the team's practical arts curriculum development efforts, help to install equipment and also train teachers in the use of both the equipment and the curriculum materials. The University was pressuring him for a reply, and he was obviously eager to accept.

Sensitive to the enormity of the changes that were about to take place in my life, for a marriage proposal was attached to this career change, he offered me the USAID Post Report for Laos and suggested that some of my questions, at least about Laos, if not about marriage, would be answered in this document.

I turned to the government-produced report to learn how it might separate the lure of travel from the risks of marriage. The Post Report was helpful about Laos and answered questions I didn't yet know enough to ask. Laos nestles in the midst of Vietnam and Thailand, Burma, China and Cambodia. The Kingdom of Lan Xang claimed three million inhabitants (and according to legend, one million elephants). The report indicated that the United States had a very extensive presence in Laos. In fact, the USAID contingent—more than two thousand people—was second in size only to the USAID program in Vietnam.

What would it be like to live there?

I tried to visualize the climate (both rainy and humidly hot) and the accommodations:

> The Vientiane plain is located in a bend of the Mekong River.
>
> Most Americans live in a compound six kilometers from the center of Vientiane.
>
> The homes have modern American conveniences.
>
> You may ship one vehicle in addition to four thousand pounds of household goods.

The report explained that the United States was providing aid in the form of road construction, public safety training, agricultural assistance and, of course, education. I was introduced to the fact that some USAID programs were contracted to nongovernmental agencies, such as the University of Hawaii, while others were under the direct supervision of our government and staffed by foreign service officers. Because of the large number of families accompanying the employed American workers the post had an American school offering all grades through high school.

"What do Americans who live in Laos and who are not government employees do?" I wondered.

With my husband I examined the Post Report and concluded that teaching in the American school, or possibly teaching English to Lao nationals were both options. The American Women's Club was active and ran a small library as well as a thrift shop. I saw several ways to fill my time during John's working hours, and the intrigue of living in a hitherto unknown country piqued my adventurous nature.

I had traveled to Japan, Thailand and India in the previous ten years and was eager to go again to Southeast Asia. Indochina was unknown territory, although all of us were deluged with conflicting opinions about America's role in South Vietnam. With a minimum of time to wrap up my job as a student activities advisor in a community college, I had no chance to research the country of Laos and its relations to its neighbors.

June 6 was our marriage date, and four days later we were on our way overseas. Our diversion to Pakistan, where John had previously served on a University of Hawaii/USAID sponsored team, allowed him to complete some unfinished tasks of that effort and delayed our arrival in Laos by six months.

The "Fasten Seat Belt" sign interrupted my reveries, and the musings melded into the excitement of touching down in a country promising new experiences. Several members of the Hawaii team greeted us at the gate and sped us through customs. We were then ushered into a car from which I gazed eagerly as we drove slowly through the streets.

The air was soft and warm, encouraging people to enjoy this twilight pause in the day. Such a contrast to the chilly January weather we had left behind in Peshawar! There were many people out strolling along the roads, all of them smiling and relaxed. I had a strong impression of happy people, friendly and in good spirits.

My second impression was that not only were the streets full of people but that they also were full of litter—cast-off plastic bags and paper trash—another sharp contrast to our recent Pakistani experiences where scarce packaging materials had caused children's school papers to be recycled as wrapping for store purchases.

As we headed toward the American Club in the USAID compound we passed large stucco buildings built, I surmised, in a style reflecting the nearly seventy years of French colonial presence. These huge homes were painted pink, light green or pale yellow and exhibited the genteel decadence of minor disrepair. Next to some of them and in sharp contrast were small square bamboo and thatched huts, raised above the ground on wooden posts. I had a glimpse of wooden looms under the houses where children were playing in the packed dirt yards.

"Typical Lao houses," I was told by our driver. "Houses on stilts and sticky rice are characteristic of the Lao." It was several days before I had a chance to clarify this remark, for not far from the center of town we passed through an imposing chain link fence and entered the USAID compound, characterized by solid concrete buildings that proclaimed American affluence and design.

"We expected you a couple of days ago," remarked the chief of party as he ushered us into the dining area.

"We were misinformed about where and how to get visas into Laos," John explained. "We were told we could get them at the airport, but it turned out we had to go into the city, and the officials took their time examining the papers that proved we were authorized to become long-term workers in Laos."

"Not unusual." Exchanged glances around the table indicated others had experienced similar delays.

"You'll get used to it. Even with two-year contracts negotiated by the Lao government we still have to leave the country every six months and obtain a re-entry stamp in our passports in order to renew our visas."

I reflected on my growing suspicion that such minor red-tape obstacles and snafus were ways a so-called developing country could exercise control over some of its own procedures and functions. How else could the leaders of a small country maintain "face" when confronting foreign "expert advice"? How else parry the arrogant assumptions of superiority that accompany the presence of people from large industrialized countries: those latter-day colonizers who often have moved in for military and economic purposes of their own?

We were both eager to meet the team members, and I was more than ready to join them in the dining room. I divided my attention between a fine roast beef dinner and becoming acquainted with these Americans who were to be our colleagues and closest friends. John had served in Pakistan with one of the couples, Ah Chong and Tootie Zane, and they greeted one another with hearty familiarity. I had known DWane and Myrtle Collins from my own associations at the University of Hawaii, and DWane was currently the team's chief of party. Introductions around the table confirmed that the other team members were also UH faculty members. Seated next to me, Myrtle provided a running commentary on the team members.

The men and women who were team members immediately began to respond to John's inquiries about the Fa Ngum schools, while I listened attentively to comments from the accompanying family members about household details and how they were managing in this culture.

I was ecstatic to hear that by sheer good luck a house had been vacated only that week and we were going to be able to move directly into it, avoiding yet another stay in a USAID guest facility. We had lived in one for the six months in Pakistan with only a small bedroom to call our own.

Dinner over, our friends drove us to the American housing compound known as Km6, a designation referring to its location six kilometers out the Thadeua Road from the center of Vientiane. Although we had read the Post Report with care, John and I were surprised when we turned through a chain link fence into an American suburban village. Our reading of the report had not conjured up visions of carports attached to unimaginatively spaced houses on streets complete with light poles and stop signs. It was such a contrast to the poorly maintained, unlit roads we had traversed in Vientiane itself only minutes earlier!

Our neighborhood reflected nothing of the culture and charm, nor of the economic stress of this developing Asian country of which it was a part. We glanced at each other in dismay. We were glad to have a home but distressed to find it in a sterile moderate-income American housing development.

No one seemed to detect our consternation, and Myrtle continued her orientation by noting, "You will need to be prepared to have Lao coming to your door applying to be your servants."

"Servants?" I gasped. "To do what?"

The temporary furnishings stacked in the center of the room included a table and four chairs, place settings for four, three cooking pots, a bed and one set of linens. Our personal possessions were contained in the three pieces of luggage at our feet. Our household shipment would only now leave Hawaii and would probably take three months to reach us.

"What in the world is a servant going to do?" I had struggled to keep out of the way of the sixteen servants in our Pakistan guest house where they had cooked, made beds, dusted, chauffeured, carried bundles, shined our shoes and tended the lawn. I had hoped that I had left all this behind and would now be able to take charge of my own house. I was not eager to supervise a cook and gardener.

Lao people live in houses on stilts (Thadeua Road, 1971).

Homes of the poor in Vientiane are made from scrap lumber and corrugated roofing sheets.

"You will need servants soon enough. Don't even think about not hiring someone."

"The word of your arrival will spread quickly. Call any one of us if you need help with your interviewing."

On that note our colleagues bade us goodnight and left us to examine our quarters. We surveyed the L-shaped room which combined the living and dining areas and the adjacent kitchen which also had an outside door. The appliances were the usual American stove and electric refrigerator. Through and beyond the living room were two bedrooms, each with an air conditioner, and a shared bathroom.

We found another door that led to a surprisingly extensive outside area.

"How wonderful to have a yard." I peered through the dusk at a well-kept lawn and a variety of shrubs. This very adequate house with its large surrounding area dispelled my earlier mental images of making do with primitive facilities and cramped quarters. There was obviously a lot to be learned about being an American living overseas, and it was pretty clear that Americans in Laos had no expectations or requirements of living on the local economy. So much for roughing it in Indochina!

"Do you suppose there is any problem about Lao coming to visit us in these quarters?" We had not come here to restrict ourselves to knowing Americans. John echoed my eagerness to get to know Lao people and stated firmly that we would do whatever was necessary to find our way into the lives of the Lao people. Comforted by his reassurances but plagued by the specter of a line of applicants showing up at the door the next morning, seeking to be our cook, I confessed, "I'd rather not have servants at all."

"Nonsense! You will find them useful, and it will free you to do other things. Besides, we will be expected to do a lot of entertaining. Someone has to buy food, and right now you don't even know what is available or where to get it! You can't be a rich American and not have servants. It just isn't done." I responded with astonished laughter.

"Rich American!" It was not a classification that had ever described me. This introduction into an economic category in which I had never pictured myself led me to examine more carefully the role of Americans who live in a foreign country, especially a very poor foreign country. In high-cost Hawaii my social worker salary had been stretched to the limit to pay rent and basic living costs. We had borrowed money in order to purchase tickets which allowed us to travel across the United States and Europe on our way to Asia. On the other hand, we would no longer be living on the American economy; we had no rent to pay, no utility bills and would not be subject to paying income tax. It slowly dawned on me that it was very probable that in Lao terms we were, indeed, extremely wealthy.

The Rantalas' Km6 home, Vientiane, Laos. Judy on porch.

How did one reconcile having so many benefits while surrounded with people whose yearly cash income could be as little as the equivalent of twenty-five American dollars? Did other Americans struggle with this kind of ethical issue?

"Okay," I conceded, "We 'rich Americans' will hire servants, but you'll have to help me interview and choose. This is all very new to me."

I picked up the linens that were on temporary loan to us and headed for the bedroom, grateful for the promise of a well-deserved night's rest.

It was a good thing we had been forewarned about job applicants. We were barely finished with our breakfast the next morning when there was a knock on the door and a slender, smiling young Lao greeted us, references in hand.

"Madame, you are needing a cook?" He thrust a sheaf of papers toward me as I backed into the living room, glancing at the affidavits that proclaimed him to be neat, trustworthy, and experienced.

I wanted to find out how he had known so quickly about the new folks who had just moved in, but what I said was, "How is it that you do not now have a job?"

He shrugged. "Mister gone from Laos. Left last week, so I looking for new job."

As if to clinch his qualifications he added, "Mister no married. *Very* good cook. Teach me everything."

I had to ask the young man several times how to pronounce his name, Synouane (Sin-wan), and had barely finished talking with him before another applicant appeared. I interviewed four that morning, all of whom had documentation of prior experience cooking for American families. I needed to make up my mind quickly, or I would be deluged with qualified candidates.

We chose Synouane, who could start immediately. He was married, the proud father of a baby girl, and he did not expect to live with us. He would come to work in time for a 6:30 breakfast and would remain until the evening dinner dishes were done. He was expected to clean the house, wash clothes, and do the ironing as well as go to market daily. We agreed on his having Sunday afternoons off, unless we needed him for a party, in which case another time would be substituted.

All this was ours for twenty-two dollars a month. The gardener, whom we hired a few days later, received twelve dollars. Even at these prices Americans were constantly being accused of grossly inflating the market and spoiling the servant pool for the French and the third-world nationals like the Indians and the Vietnamese.

Lao were less vocal in their complaints over our inflated salaries, but I understood their concern more clearly when a Lao friend with the equivalent of two years of college education explained that my cook's salary was higher than the salary she received as a full-time bank employee. She and her husband required a twenty-four-hour nursemaid for their baby and paid her the equivalent of eight American dollars, plus room and board.

If we had been given a choice, we would have preferred to respect the economic conditions and opinions of our Lao friends. We knew that the higher wages paid by Americans inflicted hardships on other employers and that it siphoned off the cream of the available workers. Nevertheless, we had not come to initiate dissention within our own ranks. We decided that for the time being we had little choice but to conform to the hiring standards of our American neighbors.

I often worked along with the cook in the kitchen in order to learn the Lao names of various foods.

"Mister," I learned to my delight, had indeed been an extraordinary cook. He had passed along some superb recipes with a hint of New Orleans in the seasoning. In addition, working along with Synouane gave me the chance to quiz him about his life and family. I learned that schooling in Laos was pretty haphazard and that finishing the third grade was as far as many

Synouane (the Rantalas' first cook) and his wife and baby girl.

went. A sixth-grade education often qualified one to become a teacher in a rural school.

Synouane was curious about where we came from, and I spent one disastrous morning attempting to explain where Hawaii was. He had no concept of the earth as round, and I made the mistake of saying to him that when the sun was out in Laos, it was night in Hawaii.

A quizzical look shot in my direction as he said, flatly, "Madame, if the sun is shining here, it is shining where you come from, Hawaii."

Aha, I thought, time for a geography lesson. I picked up an egg (we didn't have oranges or apples), and I tried to indicate that there was land on all sides of this object which I represented as the earth. I even rotated it around a second egg which I labeled "the sun."

"If this were true," he courteously corrected me, "people in Hawaii would fall off."

I avoided the trap of trying to discuss gravity and returned to the presence of the sun and the moon, daylight and dark.

It became very clear that I was not going to convince my cook about rotating planets and time zones. He politely took the eggs away from me and replaced them in the refrigerator. Now and again I caught him darting puzzled looks in my direction, as if debating my sanity.

We never discussed geography again.

3
Market Manners

Having a cook in Laos soon became addictive. At first I sent him to the market alone while I bought food staples at the American commissary. My curiosity, however, got the best of me, and soon I accompanied Synouane to see how he did things and to pick up "market Lao" so I, too, could bargain.

Bargain. Now there's an activity few Americans are trained for! From the moment we stepped into the market it was clear that we were fair game for any enterprising vendor.

"*Sabaidee,* madame, *chow yak sue nyang*?" Good morning, madame, what is it that you want to buy?

Fresh vegetables would be thrust at us, and the bargaining would begin. Synouane advised me that one never bought at the first stall. We needed to get some indication of today's offerings as well as the going price.

We walked down narrow rows crammed with small tables loaded with fruits and vegetables, eggs, tofu, marijuana, clothing—Whoa! marijuana? I glanced at Synouane, who obviously did not see anything strange about open sales of this weed, and lowered my eyebrows, vowing to inquire about its use later.

We progressed further along the market and saw nonedibles such as jewelry, clothing and imported ceramics. There were so many people pushing their way through the narrow aisles that I glanced down at my feet to be sure that I was not stepping on anything—and gasped. I had nearly put my foot into a container full of wriggling worm-like creatures, slithering around in a big aluminum pan.

"What are those?" I gingerly stepped back, bumping into Synouane.

Before he could answer a small group of grinning folk gathered around, laughing at the discomfort of the *farang* and waiting to see what I would do next.

Synouane smiled broadly. "Those are *paa,* fish."

They looked incredibly slimy to me.

"Do people eat these things?"

"Oh yes, Madame, *saap lay.*" They are delicious.

I would not give the local people the satisfaction of seeing me grimace. "Interesting, what else is there to see?"

We moved into the produce area, and I was enchanted with the variety of vegetables and the wonderful colors. I saw purple, white and green onions, brown potatoes, orangy carrots and a variety of greens in the cucumbers, sweet pea pods, green beans and cabbages. Round chop suey potatoes were displayed next to oblong red, purple and orange yams, and there were large and small chili peppers heaped in colorful mounds.

There were a dozen kinds of papaya. The Thai variety was as large as a football and the meat very orange; some were long and thin, others short and fat. In some the flesh was quite yellow, and in others it was very orangy red. And the mangoes! Every variety one could wish for. More exotic were custard apples, resembling boiled custard inside, and purple mangosteens with their sectional wedges that taste a little like lychee. Abundant were longen, rambutan (looking quite like porcupine eggs), and huge, yellow pomelo, like a grapefruit but sweeter and easier to peel and section. Fruits that required a temperate climate, such as apples or strawberries, were noticeably absent.

Chunks of bean curd or tofu were stacked, uncovered, in two-foot-high blocks on the corner of a table. Here also were water chestnuts in their black skins. The hardy could purchase live frogs and those eel-like squirming creatures I had nearly stepped into.

Synouane by now was busy discussing prices with the vendors. He had already checked with a couple of other cooks from our neighborhood who were also shopping, to determine today's price for some of the items we needed. I watched him with fascination.

Holding up a handful of green onions he offered:

"Saow kip." Twenty kip, a ridiculously low price, barely three cents.

"Baw die." Cannot sell for that price! *"Sam see kip."* Three hundred kip, about sixty cents.

"Pheng lai!" Too expensive. *"Haa sip kip."* Twenty cents.

"Tuk lai!" Too cheap. The vendor feigned indignation that such a small price would be offered for such a fine bunch of onions.

Back and forth the bargaining would go until either the vendor came to the price that Synouane felt was reasonable, or a stalemate was reached, and we would turn away and go on to another stall.

Bargaining was a game, each person seeking to read the mind of the other and negotiate the best deal. It is a major outdoor sport in many parts of the world and especially in open markets. My American expectations of fixed prices (which I knew were often a result of price fixing) made me reluctant to bargain. I felt I was cheating the vendor if I did not accept his offered price.

I couldn't have been more wrong. Many vendors took advantage of timid Americans who didn't know that any initial price offer was at least double the value of the merchandise, maybe more. No vendor would submit to being cheated, and on the other hand, for a buyer to refuse to bargain often meant totally losing the interest of the seller. It was a tricky game to play and took determination and skill.

It was clear to me that marketing was not only a household chore but also a social outing for our servants. To deprive my cook of a chance to go to the market was to incur his injured countenance for the rest of the day. I learned to trade off with him and to invent purchases that only he could negotiate. In this way, we would both head for *talat saow* on those days when I craved the challenges and the cultural lessons to be learned there in the morning market.

After a few weeks I suggested to a neighbor that she accompany me on a trip to the market and was startled at her sharply incredulous refusal. "Go to the market? Why? Doesn't your boy do this?"

"Of course he markets, but it's such fun, and I am constantly seeing things I wouldn't otherwise know were available in Laos."

Her obvious discomfort led me to try another friend who gladly accompanied me on my weekly olfactory experience in the rice market. The wonderful aroma of fresh bagged rice lured me through this aisle whenever I had the chance.

"What kinds of rice do you buy?" I innocently asked her, casting my eyes over the Pakistani Basmadi rice, Vietnamese sweet rice, *caow niow* the Lao sticky rice and the Chinese *caow chow,* or plain short-grained white rice.

"Heavens, I don't buy rice here. Not when I can get Uncle Ben's instant rice in the commissary."

What an insult to a rice-growing culture, I thought. How sad that this woman, and many of my other American friends knew nothing of these wonderfully aromatic varieties of rice that could be purchased so cheaply.

Most Lao families who lived outside of Vientiane came in monthly to purchase a one-hundred-kilo bag of rice, two hundred and twenty pounds!

Everyone flocked to the morning market in Vientiane, 1971.

This and other purchases would be tied onto the back of a rickety taxi, and when the shopping trip was over the family would head back for the countryside. It was the sticky rice they most often purchased since regular rice was grown in this part of Laos and many of them had rice paddies of their own.

I apologetically purchased ten kilos of rice at a time and quickly learned to savor the *caow niow* that is the staple of every Lao diet. There were special pots used for the steaming of this rice which was washed and placed over hot water in woven conical plaited baskets. The rice was filling and often the sole ingredient of a laborer's lunch. The rice was carried in *tip caow,* special woven containers. We often saw men and women walking to work, or riding their bicycles, with rice baskets slung over their shoulders to be opened for their midday meal.

The Lao economy afforded a minimum of protein for most people, and they leaned heavily on the small fish they could catch in the streams. The market, however, did offer both meat and fish in great variety, purchased mainly by wealthy Lao families and foreigners like us. Fresh ocean fish came in daily from the Gulf of Thailand. Pork was plentiful and excellent, but the beef was mainly from the Asian water buffalo—a very red flesh and usually tough. Pot roast with lots of herbs was the only way we really found to make a tasty dish of this.

There was one kind of meat that was unfamiliar to me, and I turned to Synouane. "What is this?" I pointed to a chunk suitable for roasting.

"Sin guang." His hand gestures indicated an animal with slender legs and a body about the size of a calf. In response to my puzzled looks he made horns of his fingers. Goat? No, deer meat, I surmised.

"Where does it come from?"

"People bring in from up there." He gestured off-handedly toward the hills we could barely see from the Vientiane plains and explained that local hunters who bagged a deer often brought it to market in order to get cash to purchase other items. This meat was always tender, not gamey, and became a prized dish for our table whenever we could find it.

Food was not all that the market held. One vendor who caught my eye was selling heavy silver jewelry which I later recognized as coming from some of the indigenous tribal groups—people who had no knowledge of or use for a bank and so displayed their wealth in stunning bracelets and heavy hand-crafted neck pieces. In the market also were treasures from many other countries: jewelry, cloth, ceramic jars and glazed pots, silk blouses and woven stoles. It took me months to even identify some of the things one could find when there was time to browse around in these displays.

Talat saow closed up by ten in the morning, and many of the vendors reopened about four in the afternoon at another location, known as *talat leng*, or the evening market. In the center of town, however, were some permanent shops with fixed daily hours, their proprietors mainly Vietnamese or Indian. The latter tended to sell clothing and yard goods and were skilled tailors. Jewelry shopping in the Vietnamese-owned stores captured the interest of many of the Americans, and why not? Settings were invariably twenty-two-carat gold for rubies, sapphires and imperial jade, and prices were considerably lower than they would have been back home or even in Hong Kong.

These town shops were small, dingy and seldom displayed their wares in any attractive form. Window displays were rare, and every night the shops were barred with wooden or metal shutters. Shoppers in this part of town were also attracted by the colorful Hmong tribeswomen who lined the sidewalks placidly embroidering their incredibly intricate petit point handwork.

It was a scene of intriguing contrast. The women sat directly on a packed dirt sidewalk not more than a few feet from paved streets bustling with Renaults, American General Motors cars, Vespas and bicycles. We tall, fair-skinned Americans would pause, intently watching the dark-haired, dark-eyed Hmong, whose features reflect Chinese heritage. The Hmong always wore their traditional dress, identified by the red, green and yellow colors in their headgear and the bright red and green sashes with long, black, baggy pants or skirts. Casual passers-by and we who tarried were dressed in Western shirts and trousers or cotton dresses or shorts. Seated crosslegged in a row, the Hmong women chatted animatedly with each other while their gnarled hands delicately threaded needles with colorful silk thread. Only occasionally did they look up, peering intently over small gold-rimmed glasses to acknowledge our interest in their handiwork.

"What does one do with these square pieces?" I asked a friend who gave me a ride into town during my first week in Laos. We had stopped to watch the women who eagerly began the bargaining process.

"If you are coming to the ambassador's reception for newcomers tomorrow," she answered, "you'll see. I'm wearing a long gown into which I've incorporated some of this work. I think it quite stunning." I also learned from my friend that people made these pieces into large pillow covers, tablecloths and even framed some of the more intricate work as wall hangings.

"But the petit point?" I pressed. "Surely this is not indigenous to the hills of Laos!" She laughed and reminded me of the long history of French colonial presence and said it was her guess that some of the nuns had taught this art and supplied the original needles and thread from which a very substantial cottage industry had now grown.

I was too new in the country to trust myself to dicker for one of the pieces at this time, but I returned many times during the years I was in Vientiane to admire and purchase their work.

As we continued to walk along the street I noticed that all of the foreign women looked exceptionally well groomed and asked, "Where do you get your hair done?"

"Clever of you to ask," she replied. "I'm on my way to make an appointment at the beauty parlor." We turned the corner and walked a short block to a traffic circle with a dry fountain in the center. On one side of the circle was the former French cultural center, now the home of the Lao-American Association, where English was taught to any Lao wishing to learn "to speak American." Three beauty parlors ringed the rest of the circle, and I was ushered into one run by a tiny, bright-eyed young woman named Saysamone.

When we walked into the shop every one of the six operators was engaged with a customer, and there were Lao, American, Japanese and Filipino women in the shop that particular morning. Obviously this was an affordable luxury.

Ninety cents, American, paid for a complete wash, dry and set, plus a manicure. For twenty cents more, a total of six hundred kip, one could also get a pedicure. It was a deal none of us passed up, and it became a weekly ritual for me.

On my third trip to have my hair done Saysamone said, "My sister runs the tailor shop. You need clothes? Go see her." I had walked through the shop that adjoined the beauty parlor without knowing the relationship and soon began to have all of the new clothes I needed fashioned by this very clever seamstress for a fraction of what similar clothes would have cost me at home.

The acquisition of a new outfit became the excuse to celebrate by going out for Sunday brunch with other members of the Hawaii team. Sunday brunch at Tan Dao Vien meant excellent *dim sum,* as long as you got there by ten o'clock and before they began to run out of their very popular offerings. We also found French and Indian restaurants in town, but I knew of only one small shop serving Lao food, possibly because most Lao could afford only very simple ingredients.

A small percentage of wealthy Lao had attended French schools and along with learning the French language had acquired a cosmopolitan appetite for a varied menu. In their homes they incorporated Vietnamese spring rolls and Thai curries into very appetizing meals.

We soon discovered a wonderful bakery, patronized by Lao and foreigner alike, famous for its crisp French baguettes. This bread is a major legacy of colonial days which all the peoples of Indochina, including the Lao, have adopted as their own, although the richer French pastries and tarts, while sometimes available, have not been as popular.

The Lan Xang Hotel was the other major discovery of this first trip around town. Situated on the banks of the Mekong River, it was a gathering place for most visitors. Foreign correspondents, however, preferred the bar at the Constellation, a hotel in the middle of town. Within a few months I discovered that when I craved to learn more about rumored political unrest or present military action, I could satisfy my curiosity by ordering a beer at the bar in this hotel and eavesdropping on the most recent travels of the journalists gathered there.

An equally reliable source of news, and a faster one, was the thrift shop run by the American Women's Club. This astonishingly busy enterprise incorporated a payment system that satisfied everyone in town. Foreigners such as third-country nationals as well as the Lao were free to shop there for an incredible array of goods that ranged from clothing and jewelry to small appliances, bedding and even furniture. The seller retained 40 percent of the sale, and the thrift shop reaped 60 percent. With no overhead and all employees volunteers, it was a thriving business.

By volunteering there on a regular basis I was able to meet women I otherwise would not have seen since only some of the Americans lived in Km6 and the military families as well as families of the Air America pilots lived in houses scattered throughout Vientiane.

The failure of a regular volunteer to appear on her appointed day was nearly always a clue to some major political or military event. If the wife of a consular officer or a high-ranking USAID official was absent, it could mean that some very important person was visiting Laos: U.S. senators, a British official, or maybe His Royal Highness was in Vientiane for a special meeting. If the wife of an Air America pilot was absent, it often meant that someone had not returned from the previous day's flight. Rumors, backed with reliable facts, flew around the thrift shop, and I can't think of a time that John came home with news of a downed flier that I had not only already known about but about which I could fill in many more details than he. The tacit understanding in the thrift shop about not sharing this information beyond our own walls kept me from divulging my sources even to John, who could never fathom how I knew so much about supposedly very hush, hush happenings.

4
Learning About Laos

The city of Vientiane is located in the center of the country, along a major bend in the Mekong River in an area of flat land and uninteresting landscape. Only on very clear days could we glimpse the hills in the extremely far distance. In January, the month we arrived, the fields were dry, parched and dusty, but it was not yet unbearably hot. That was to come.

The people of Laos were friendly and relaxed. They had an honest sense of self-worth and a dignity we respected and admired. They loved jokes and laughed a great deal of the time. Laughter, in fact, seemed to be the antidote for nearly every situation, especially those incidents that were either embarrassing or frightening. I was driving home to Km6 one day and found myself just behind my husband on his Honda motorcycle, returning from work. As he turned the corner his tires skidded, and he flew over the handlebars, lunch bucket, briefcase and all. Instantly he was surrounded by Lao who were obviously distressed but also somewhat uncertain as to how to help this portly American sprawled on the road.

Stopping the car I pried my way into the circle. Had he broken anything? Was he all right? A few of the spectators worked in Km6 and recognized us both, which seemed to be a trigger that released nervous laughter into loud giggles. My impulse was to lash out at them for their unfeeling mirth at the plight of this poor injured man, until I recognized that they were covering up their concern in the way they knew best, laughter. All of them knew only too well what being thrown from a motorcycle was like, and once we had determined that the injuries were more to his pride than to his limbs, I too conceded that he had looked pretty funny. A neighbor's cook offered to wheel the bike up to our house, and once home, we dug gravel out of several scrapes and applied plenty of salve and bandages as I attempted to soothe his oozing elbows and wounded pride.

How does one describe the Lao? I start by saying that they are gentle. I find that to be the most telling description of a Lao person. Gentle. Their Mahayana Buddhism gives them a clear bond with all of creation, animate or inanimate, and as a result they revere the world they live in. The Lao always put relationships first and are most solicitous of guests, making sure they are comfortable and have a cool drink before any conversation starts.

This hospitable gesture was nearly my undoing while visiting in a small village where, in hut after hut, a glass of freshly opened coconut water was offered to me. After six or more glasses my innards rebelled.

"Khampheng," I hissed to my Lao friend, "I've *got* to find a bathroom. I have terrible cramps."

Masking her amusement until she extricated me from my hostess, she burst into laughter as she led me to the primitive latrine, a facility I remained close to for the rest of the afternoon. I wondered why she wasn't having the same trouble until I thought back over our sequence of visits and recalled that after one sip she would put the glass down and not drink again. I consoled myself by reflecting that the kindly and gentle women we had been visiting simply didn't think about the possibility that others had also cracked open a coconut in order to provide a refreshing, pure drink.

It was the Lao reverence for life, their courtesy to their elders and their loving, gentle guidance of their children that made John and me wonder if perhaps the Lao had something more precious to teach us than we had to teach them. Technical know-how would never be a substitute for their responsiveness to nature or their concern and care for each other. We often pondered what we Americans really had to offer these people, this country.

I especially appreciated the opportunities I had to learn about Laos and the Lao people through talking with Khampheng, her husband, Souvanh, and our servants. The cook and the gardener, proud and adaptable, shared bits and snatches of their life apart from Km6 even as they learned with quick grace the ways in which we wanted our food prepared or guests entertained. They told me about their children, or the kind of work their wives did, and when the gardener revealed that he and several other men were building a fish pond for themselves in order to increase their own food supplies, John and I found an acceptable way to make a contribution toward the purchase of concrete with which to line a portion of the pool.

The servants also were quick to learn and to accept practices required of Americans which would also improve their own living standards. Almost the first order we were given upon arrival was that water must be both boiled

Traditional Lao dress, young woman on left carrying a *baci* bowl, on right a Lao rice basket, *tip caow.*

and filtered. Each American house had a large ceramic container through which the boiled water could be poured.

"Why are we doing this, Madame?" Synouane inquired.

"Because we can get sick from drinking the water. There are small bugs in it that can make us very ill."

Synouane held the water up to the light, his already familiar question-mark forehead wrinkle prominent. "I don't see any bugs."

"No, of course not, they are invisible." Brightly, "Have you ever seen, or heard of a microscope? It's an instrument that makes what you are looking at become very large. You can see the bacteria through a microscope." Synouane was silent for a few moments and then shrugged his shoulders. I could see that this lesson was headed toward the debacle of the geography lesson about Hawaii, and I shifted the topic to an inquiry about where he got water to use in his home. Noting his evasiveness I silently feared that instead of a well it might be only a stagnant pool.

"Never mind. In this house, just remember to always boil the water and keep the filter full, and use this water when you cook anything."

Although my attempt to explain that disease could be caused by invisible organisms was greeted with polite skepticism, the cook did begin to boil the water he used at home and within a month volunteered that sickness in his household had dropped dramatically. This basic sanitation lesson triggered a fervent wish, expressed often between John and me, that the American USAID administrators seriously consider putting our money into simpler, less spectacular, but more practical efforts that would contribute to the quality of life and increased economic capabilities of the Lao. Big money spawned big projects which often seemed to lead to big graft and big failure. Personally we wished we had the wisdom and influence to convince American planners to design projects and programs that would more nearly touch and enhance the lives of the simple, nonpolitical people in that country.

Soon after our arrival in Laos I had an opportunity to travel to Luang Prabang where we met a farmer who pleaded, "*Seun,* Madame," please, "can you help for me to get *ha sip* American dollar?"

"How would you use fifty American dollars?" I countered.

With gestures and halting English he indicated that it would be enough capital to allow him to begin a small trading venture that could support his entire family.

"Why not?" I asked John. A bit of informal research had uncovered that a small loan program of amounts of as little as fifty dollars was desperately needed and would aid dozens of families. American bureaucrats, however, could think only in hundreds of thousands. A loan program on this much-needed and very practical reduced scale was not even considered.

Khampheng, one of our closest friends with whom we shared lasting ties, proved to be another major source of information about Laos and the Lao. Newly arrived Americans were required by USAID to learn the language, and she taught the class for which both John and I signed up. Khampheng told me that she taught English not only to earn extra money, but because she appreciated the fact that Americans really wanted to be able to talk with the Lao. "In all the years they were here, the French never learned our language. We had to speak French." The bitterness with which she said this needed no further amplification. It also helped to explain the extraordinary willingness with which the Lao cooperated with Americans. They appreciated our sincere efforts to understand their language and culture and to respect their way of life. They liked us.

Khampheng was petite, willowy and had what I came to learn were classic Lao Loum features. Women from the lowlands of Laos had high cheekbones, a broad forehead and firm chin. Their eyes were set wide apart, and they seemed to have an innate serenity. Khampheng was always polite and gracious and displayed a wonderful sense of humor. She was in her early twenties and agreed to tutor us on weekends to help us keep up with the class. We were not very apt pupils, even though I fairly soon was able to bargain with the vendors in the market. Speaking pidgin Lao was not exactly the same as being able to hold an intelligent conversation in a group.

Every Saturday morning our teacher arrived in a white Volkswagen bug, driven by an attractive young man who returned for her two hours later.

"He's my cousin," she explained when I asked.

"Would he like to come in for some cookies and a cool drink before you leave?"

She at first demurred, then shyly introduced us to Souvanh who, once he discovered chocolate chip cookies, often stayed for the entire lesson. There was something in their relationship that indicated to me that here was a suitor, and after I got to know her better I gently challenged, "I don't believe this is your cousin. He seems more like a boyfriend." She blushed prettily and confessed that it was not always seemly to be out in public unchaperoned and she felt more comfortable pretending a family connection rather than risking shocking my puritan sensibilities. They were, she said, to be married in November.

As the weeks passed our Lao proficiency improved haltingly but our personal relationship grew to the extent that Khampheng and I developed a mother-daughter bond. As the date for the wedding approached John and I accepted with delight an invitation to participate in the ceremony which would join Souvanh and Khampheng in matrimony. We not only wanted to be a part of this most important day in their lives, but also looked forward to the opportunity it would give us to meet the members of both their families. And there was the added attraction of participation in a traditional Lao celebration with all of its local variations.

A Lao bride exhibits a rare, classic composure and beauty. For her wedding Khampheng was dressed in green and gold. Her traditional calf-length narrow Lao skirt was made of silk with gold threads woven into it. Her blouse was pale green with a wide, gold encrusted green *pa peh* crossing from one shoulder to below her waist. All brides sculpt their hair into a top-knot around which are wrapped as many chains of twenty-two-carat gold as can be placed there. I marveled that 'Pheng's neck didn't snap under the weight of all that gold, so carefully placed to show to the best advantage. She wore gold bangles on both arms, dangling gold earrings and a gold pin fastened on her shoulder. The groom's costume, also traditionally Lao, featured pantaloon-styled silk trousers and a white silk jacket with a Nehru-like collar. His clothing matched the green worn by his bride, and they were a stunning couple.

A wedding in any country has unique customs attached to it, and in Laos the ceremony begins with the bridegroom, accompanied by several boisterous friends, noisily approaching the bride's home, demanding to see his intended. The girl's family playfully turns them away, and there is considerable physical and verbal sparring until the bride's family "gives in" and allows him to enter the home. There the two families "bargain" for the bride price (long since agreed upon), and when an acceptable compromise is reached, the bride appears and a *baci* is held. This traditional Lao ceremony invokes benign spirits and gives all the guests an opportunity to wish the couple good health and many children. A revered elder from the village (and even in a city like Vientiane there are clear village designations) conducts the *baci*, chanting many phrases of advice and experience as each of the guests ties a white yarn string on the wrists of bride and groom, wishing them good luck. We didn't have to understand the language to pick up the tone of bawdy comments and good-natured jokes.

At the close of the wedding festivities there is a great to-do surrounding the ushering of the bridal couple into an elaborately furnished bedroom where, after very suggestive gestures and comments they are left behind closed doors to consummate the marriage and, hopefully, to start their family. With loud singing and joking the guests continue to party until long into the evening.

Through these two young people we gradually learned about family life in Vientiane. Khampheng lived with her father and mother, and her earnings went into sustaining the household which included several nephews and nieces who had been sent to Vientiane to attend school. Souvanh's parents lived in the south of Laos, but cousins of his were pupils at the Fa Ngum school where John taught. We felt privileged to become acquainted with the cousins' parents who often invited us to family gatherings at their home. Their mother was Lao, their father a prosperous Chinese merchant. It was a close and hospitable family and a strong marriage. We had no way of judging to what extent, if any, the marriage had been dictated by expediency, but we learned years later that one reason for the large number of mixed marriages was that a Chinese, indeed every non–Lao person, was forbidden to own property in Laos. This family was prospering and the family loving and cohesive.

John and the cousins' father, Boun Hom, shared a two-word vocabulary and a common activity. They would sit on the family porch after dinner, each firmly grasping a tumbler of Scotch, smiling broadly and periodically uttering loudly, "Very good, very good!" as they belted down the Scotch. I can see them to this day.

5
Naïveté Abroad

Lying in bed I could hear the rumble of huge planes flying overhead. In January of 1971 we had been in Vientiane just a week, but I had already picked up vibrations of increased security from tight-lipped political officers in the American post. I felt sure I was hearing American B-52s and turned to my husband, who reconfirmed my worst fears.

"Why are there American planes flying overhead? I've understood that there is no U.S. military presence in Laos. Surely the Lao air force doesn't fly American B-52s."

Long into the night the muffled roar filtered into our house as we lay there pondering the significance of this latest discovery about life in Laos. Where did bombing raids fit into the educational assignment of the USAID-sponsored Hawaii contract team that was in Laos at the request of the Lao government to build, equip and staff six comprehensive high schools? Two of the schools were already in place—in Vientiane and Phone Hong. Classes also were in session in a temporary building in Savannakhet where construction was being started on the third school. Soon there would also be a school in Luang Prabang and also in the plan were Fa Ngum schools for Pakse and Paksane. My husband's role was to develop curricula within the industrial arts component as well as to train teachers, demonstrate the practical workings of a variety of shop machines and oversee basic construction of the shops. The development of these schools, named for a former king of Laos, was a major undertaking and one we were confident would further the desire of the Lao people to move more quickly into the current Asian economic and political scene.

A few days after we first noted the bombers, an issue of *Stars and*

Stripes, the semi-official newspaper for GIs, declared in black letters three inches high, "NIXON VOWS NO TROOPS IN LAOS."

I was bewildered and incensed. Surely my own ears did not deceive me. I had been hearing the planes every night. Was I so naïve that it hadn't occurred to me that the president of the United States might flatly lie about our actions abroad? Could it be possible that under the façade of altruistic humanitarian aid there was a military and political agenda far more complex than providing educational assistance? Were projects like the Fa Ngum schools merely a veneer covering a more deadly program about which we were not being informed? Our introductory briefing should have clued me in.

"I want you to be clear about one thing," our chief of party had admonished us the day after we arrived. "We are here in Laos to protect American turf."

"What do you mean, protect American turf?" I blurted.

"We are here protecting San Francisco: to guarantee that the commies will never land on American shores."

John jabbed me in the ribs before I could expostulate further on this outrageous statement, and I listened in mute disbelief during the remainder of the briefing.

"Protect American turf by building a school in Laos? Is he serious?" I stormed when we were finally excused from the interview. Although this attitude directly contradicted my understanding of what a prosperous "first-world" nation ought to be doing in a country like Laos, I was forced to come to terms with the fact that there certainly were a number of Americans, at home and abroad, who firmly endorsed that viewpoint and who, indeed, believed that this was our proper mission in Laos.

The influence of John Foster Dulles on American foreign policy lingered long after his death. Raised by Christian missionary parents in China, his fear of Chinese communism was phobic and pervaded all of the decisions he made on behalf of the U.S. government in relation to Southeast Asia. Many Americans subscribed to Dulles' "Domino Theory" and honestly feared an eventual invasion of the United States by China.*

What gives America the right to fight its battles on Lao soil, I stormed? "How did we get mixed up in this?" Later we examined in earnest this

**John Foster Dulles' Indochina strategy is documented in Adams and McCoy, eds.,* Laos: War and Revolution, *by several authors, notably Marek Thee, "Background Notes on the 1954 Geneva Agreements on Laos and the Vientiane Agreements of 1956–1957," pp. 121–28; also by Mirsky and Stonefield, "The Nam Tha Crisis: Kennedy and the New Frontier on the Brink," pp. 155–78.*

distressing revelation of the hidden American agenda in Laos and together we discussed the very real possibility that John had accepted an assignment that was so antithetical to our own convictions that we would be unable to stay.

I knew that there had been a very close examination of my political activism by the U.S. State Department before permission was given for me to accompany John to Laos. In the fall of 1969 I had been deeply involved with a sanctuary for Vietnam War protesters, a sanctuary which had been declared and supported by my Honolulu church. I had very strong feelings against the kind and volume of U.S. presence in Vietnam and no knowledge of how Laos fit into this conflict.

John did not believe that the words spoken by our chief of party reflected majority opinion either of our team members or of the American people, and in April 1971 he wrote my parents a long letter in which he said:

> I do not know whether I fit the definition of a liberal, but I do hope I can call myself a humanist and a realist. . . . What we are doing out here is wrong and inhumane, even from the point of view of a realist. The sooner we halt the military effort and put the shackles on our uncontrolled CIA, the better. The consideration of people and how they are affected by military decisions that stem from an intelligence system that sees only the objective of taking a hill, a road or valley is something the CIA does not take time or care to consider. I fear our nation will yet hang its head in shame when the whole story of this Indochina war is written.

How prophetic those 1971 words were, and how reassuring to me, this reaffirmation of my husband's value system and deep sense of justice. He made it very clear that he had joined the University of Hawaii contract team in order to share his technical and teaching skills with the people of Laos. "When American political activity interferes with that, I'll leave," he said. We would do whatever was necessary to avoid being duped into becoming rubber stamps for American foreign policy in Asia.

Clearly, when we had agreed to join the Hawaii USAID contract team we had known too little about the politics of Laos. I was determined to rectify this as quickly as I could, but discovered it was not going to be easy. There was no such thing as a public library in Laos, and the few political analyses that had so far appeared were all written in French. As contract workers rather than foreign service officers employed directly by the American government, we were on the fringes of the information channels. We were alerted to the escalation of fighting in Laos not by any internal news system, but through letters from New England quoting headlines that claimed "South Vietnam Is Invading Laos." "What is going on out there?" my father wanted to know. "Are you safe?"

"Why is he asking this?" I brandished the letter before my husband as soon as he came home from work.

"I don't know much except that security is much tighter, and right now Ah Chong and George are being flown by helicopter the thirty kilcks to Phone Hong. They've been told that possible insurgent action on the road makes it unwise to go there by car."

I shuddered when I heard this and called Tootie, Ah Chong's wife. "Oh, not to worry," she assured me, "this often happens. It's not very clear just who the insurgents are, or who they might attack, so the mission protects the men by flying them in. It's no big thing." Maybe not for her. She had been here nearly three years and was used to these military flurries.

I turned back to John. "Why do we have to depend on the Thai newspaper and letters from home to let us know what is going on right here? Don't we count?" I answered my own questions with the less than satisfactory conclusion that American officials were busy with the running of the war and were looking after those Americans who were most closely involved. The rest of us could just sit tight and get on with our lives.

It was obvious from the anxiety expressed by some of our Lao compatriots that we were not the only ones struggling to understand this country's status. Something very serious was happening in February of 1971: the Americans and the Vietnamese were jockeying for control of the Ho Chi Minh Trail, and American bombs were raining down on Lao villagers. I became aware of this through the journalistic efforts of a young photographer from Australia. He had visited a small tribal village situated on a hill in the northern part of Laos and photographed it, showing the small bamboo huts, the skimpily cultivated fields. A few weeks later, knowing there had been some kind of military action in this area, he wangled permission to go again to this spot, and took another picture. Both pictures appeared on the front page of the Sunday supplement of a foreign newspaper. In the second photo the hill was entirely bare of huts, trees and, indeed, life of any kind. It was as if the village had never been there at all.

The furor over his photo earned the young journalistic photographer a one-way ticket out of Laos and frantic attempts at cover-up from the Americans. I now understood why such a large part of the USAID budget was devoted to refugee resettlement and why the USAID personnel assigned to this duty were scrambling so fiercely to find space and goods to accommodate the hundreds of Lao who were being bombed out—by our own planes.

What I did not understand was why the Lao permitted their country to be so thoroughly taken over by Americans. It was years before I came across sources which detailed the intricate maneuvers of Prime Minister Souvanna Phouma's dogged attempts to keep Laos a neutral country when the North Vietnamese totally ignored their own promises (reported in detail by D. Gareth Porter's chapter in *Laos: War and Revolution* 179–212, essentially pointing out that neither the Vietnamese nor the Americans held to the agreements of 1962 or 1973 to remove all troops from the country). I sought out what few written materials there were about Laos, talked with my Lao friends, and through considerable speculation, deduced that Laos was so newly put together that the people themselves hardly knew what it meant to be a nation. For many, foreign domination was the only thing they had ever known, and for most Lao the Americans were currently preferable to the French, if only because we offered lots of money and munitions. To some we appeared to be more friendly, and it is true that the Americans made honest efforts to learn the Lao language and honor Lao customs.

Laos had been formed from three separate kingdoms and, in the words of Bernard B. Fall *(Anatomy of a Crisis: The Laotian Crisis of 1960–1961)* was

> neither a geographical, nor an ethnic or social entity, but merely a political convenience. Its 91,000 square miles (about the size of Oregon in the United States) is a geographer's nightmare of small deep valleys surrounded by saw-toothed mountains covered with jungle almost to the tips. With its mountain villages inhabited by semi-nomads who displace their whole habitat lock, stock and barrel every four or five years, taking the name of the village along with them, Laos, seen from the air, gives one the impression of a lunar landscape that had suddenly developed a luxuriant carpet of vegetation. [23]

Fall also told us that Laos has "at least forty-two different tribal clusters which can be grouped into at least five major linguistic families" (24). There had been little or no opportunity, and perhaps little inclination, to practice cooperative self-determination in governance. They were a country carved out of Thailand by the decision of a succession of colonial powers, most recently the French.*

**Arthur J. Dommen,* Laos: Keystone of Indochina, *would dispute this statement. Writing on the pre-colonial period in Laos (p. 19) he points out that Laos, unified by King Fa Ngum in 1353, remained a unified monarchy with "a distinct Lao race* (Sua Sat Lao), *a Lao nation* (Sat Lao), *a Lao country* (Muong Lao), *and Lao State* (Pathet Lao) *until the early 1700's." Dommen thus concludes, "We may safely reject the notion, fashionable among apologists for a colonial enterprise of a later day, that Laos was a creation of French colonial policy and administration." In fact, Laos became divided into three parts by 1713 and remained so until the late eighteenth century.*

The surrender of Japan in 1945 had resulted in the removal of Japanese occupying troops from Indochina and again opened the way for French dominance. The French by-passed the small group of Lao who attempted to create a free Lao government and instead established a constitutional monarchy, discrediting the fledgling Lao Issara whose leaders then fled to Thailand. The ineffectiveness of this exiled band of former officials and military officers gave rise to another group who sought freedom and independence for Laos, the Pathet Lao.

The growing strength of this second independence-seeking group attracted the intervention of additional outside powers. The Vietnamese, under Ho Chi Minh, infiltrated the Pathet Lao and offered aid in organizing and recruiting members. The millions of dollars worth of military aid channeled through the CIA to the faltering French army virtually forced the Pathet Lao to accept Ho Chi Minh's help. Commenting on a 1955 report by John Foster Dulles, Marek Thee, formerly the Polish representative to the International Control Commission in Laos and Vietnam, confirms this opinion in a chapter in *Laos: War and Revolution:* "To some extent, emphasis on a military solution played into the hands of the Hanoi-supported Pathet Lao. It allowed them to buy time, to dig in deeper in the northern provinces [of Laos], and to strengthen their forces for a vigorous political comeback" (130). The 1953 treaty making Laos fully independent within the French Union seemed to give further backbone to the political forces opposing this move.

America's strong support of the Royal Lao forces and the abysmal lack of reliable channels of communication within the country meant that during the 1971 crisis those of us who were not full-time foreign service officers or otherwise directly employed by the American government had little or no access to information about what was happening in the country. It confused me to discover that within a seemingly homogeneous group of Lao I could detect considerable difference of opinion toward the current Lao government. Loyalty was apparently directly tied to economic advantage and subsequent reading has confirmed that there were many political figures who made it a point to change political sides whenever it seemed expedient in order to remain on the "winning" side. If you had a pipeline into the money that Americans doled out, you supported the RLG forces and the king. If you did not have access to this seemingly endless cornucopia, you tended to applaud efforts that would rid the country of all foreign domination—except that here too, there was a distinct split. To some "foreign domination" meant Western or European influence and did not include the Vietnamese. To others it meant anyone who was not Lao.

There was little political sophistication or ambition among the majority of Lao people. They had few expectations, or indeed few standards of performance by which to measure the achievements of their own leaders. In *Laos: War and Revolution,* Fred Branfman identifies politicians—meaning those related to one of the Lao princes, plus the wealthy merchants and military officers—as, "elitist, urban-centered and riddled with corruption from top to bottom," pointing out that they were all French educated and trained, and that, "RLG officials generally do not venture more than 10 or 20 kilometers from the provincial and district capitals" (223). Many of these men were primarily interested in preserving their relatively high standard of living and continuing to siphon foreign aid into their own pockets. Those who worked for a free and independent Laos and who protested the actions of some of their leaders were conveniently labeled "Communist."

What might have happened had other nations kept their hands off Laos? Would the people who sought self-rule have been able to defeat officials who relied first on French support and soon switched to embracing military and economic aid from the United States? Had we not bolstered the French efforts at Dien Bien Phu, would the Lao's long-standing animosity toward the Vietnamese have helped them band together to stave off the opportunistic Vietcong? There was division on these issues even within Lao families.

Khampheng revealed, "In the early sixties one of my brothers supported the coalition government that tried to establish a policy of neutrality. They were working to stabilize Laos' position in the region." Her parents, on the other hand, supported the Royal Lao Government forces and at this time moved from Vang Vieng, headquarters of the neutralists, taking the twelve-year-old Khampheng with them into Vientiane.

I better understood the confusion in loyalties once I learned that after the defeat of the French the high-level talks which attempted to determine how Laos should be governed were held in Moscow, London and Washington. No wonder the Pathet Lao had protested this very pro–Western coalition and called for a reconvening of the Geneva Conference. Instead of a cease fire, the Lao people were subjected almost immediately to daily American reconnaissance and bombing raids over the mountain areas of Laos because at this same time the Vietnamese stepped up the flow of materiel over the Ho Chi Minh Trail.

I associated the Ho Chi Minh Trail with the Vietnam War and finally had to corner one of our military adviser friends to ask him what the Ho Chi Minh Trail had to do with Laos. His withering reply reinforced how little I knew about this country in which I now lived. He confirmed that this was the Vietcong's major supply route, adding, "But much of it is actually in Laos."

In Laos? I felt paralyzed both by outrage and by helplessness. How could we Americans pretend to be the great hope of the Lao people when they were caught in a dilemma created largely by our own military and political efforts? I pictured them being squeezed in a gigantic vise: Americans obliterating innocent people in a country most of us couldn't even locate on a map, people in the path of Vietcong supplies being moved through Lao jungles: Vietcong claiming to support Lao freedom efforts yet jeopardizing the innocent villagers who had the misfortune to live along the Ho Chi Minh Trail: American dollars shoring up and supporting an outdated, corrupt regime run by French-educated Lao officials. It was mind-boggling.

Americans were not aware of the magnitude of American military involvement in Laos. We were still reeling from the tragic killings of Jack and Robert Kennedy and of Martin Luther King. We were engaged in a national soul searching following the Kent State tragedy and violent campus anti–Vietnam protests. We had never heard of the Meo, more correctly known as Hmong, let alone discovered that thousands of these tribal men formed the bulk of the CIA-directed forces in Laos, far outnumbering the Royal Lao Army. Old-timers in the American community in Laos professed to be surprised at our innocence about the CIA presence. It startled me whenever a member of the overall USAID education team was discreetly pointed out as a probable CIA man. It appeared that career foreign service officers who had long served overseas really were out of touch with mainstream America and seldom shared or explained the intricacies of foreign policy. I protested that it wasn't my fault that I was so naïve about the inner workings of our government abroad. We weren't being told. The desire to represent an ordinary civilian American point of view became my justification for wanting to stay in Laos—to be able to observe and interpret for myself what we Americans were doing there.

Living overseas in the midst of political and economic upheaval can be like living in the eye of a hurricane. All around us on the fringes there were explosive and earth shattering military encounters. Whenever an American air sortie appeared to be successful, the Pathet Lao would simply work around the devastation or, more often, repair the damage and keep right on going. The guerilla warfare was fierce and effective. We in Vientiane, however, continued to pursue our low-key routines: checking out a few books at the American library, picking up laundry at the cleaners, making a coffee cake for a morning gathering, attending an American movie at the ACA.

Because the war made travel by car dangerous and curbed our movements, we entertained ourselves and each other by hosting dinner parties.

We easily accepted being cared for by servants who cleaned, cooked, chopped and waited on us. Some American women were content with daily bridge games, while others sought ways to learn more about the people and the culture of Laos. I wanted to meet the Lao people and if possible visit the areas my husband worked in up north or down south in Savannakhet and Pakse. Many of us had professional skills which we utilized as teachers, in a library, or by managing the American Women's Club thrift shop. As a social worker I was curious to know what I could do in this adopted country and found a niche in a most unexpected place, the American Women's Club.

"Madame, you have a phone call." Synouane handed me the receiver.

"Mrs. Rantala, this is Sally Mann." I recognized her as the wife of the director of all USAID operations on the post, a position second only to the ambassador of Laos, Mr. Godley. "I want to be sure that you will attend our reception for newcomers." Having already sent in my acceptance, I was curious about receiving this follow-up call, but assured her I would be there.

The reason for her call became clear the following Monday when she drew me aside during the evening and said, "We in the American Women's Club want to nominate you for president." Surprise must surely have been evident in my reaction. I had been in Laos barely a month and was shocked to be approached for a position I felt ill suited to take on without being more familiar with the programs of this group and the women who had already contributed their time and interest.

"You are very kind to ask and I am flattered, but I really don't feel I'm ready for such an honor."

Mrs. Mann conceded that it was a bit early and justified the request by pointing out that several qualified women had recently left the post earlier than anticipated, creating a leadership gap in the American Women's Club. We compromised on my accepting the vice-presidency for the following year.

Being in the Women's Club was a very new setting for me. Many of the women were wives of career foreign service officers and had spent years living on American posts overseas. Through the AWC I had my first opportunity to be in close touch with a large number of military families and soon discovered that officers' wives were expected to be active in the Women's Club as a support to their husbands' careers, whether or not the activities really interested them. As I met and worked with some of these women they quickly briefed me on the necessity to be extremely careful to observe all of the protocol demanded by the wife of the ambassador, who invited John and me to a social gathering in their home shortly after my encounter with Mrs. Mann.

"Do you realize that we have been here four and one-half years and have never been invited to the embassy?" The wife of one of the Hawaii team members seemed more than a little miffed when she learned of our summons.

"Not my doing," I assured her. "I haven't the faintest idea how this came about, and I'm more than a little nervous. I'm told this amounts to a command performance." The only reason for being asked was, I felt sure, because my name had come up in the Women's Club nominating committee and Mrs. Godley, as a somewhat imperious honorary chairperson, was curious to know who this upstart newcomer was that so quickly received a nomination.

I was not anxious to get involved with the politics and protocol of *Sama Kum Pu Nying Amelican,* the Lao name for the AWC, but others convinced me that I had little choice and pointed out that it could be an avenue for learning more about Laos. Formal American activities in Laos were reviewed and chartered by the Royal Lao Government with the proviso that if they generated income, a maximum of one thousand dollars could be used for the purposes of the club and the remainder had to be spent on the Lao people themselves. It was a very clever proscription and led to the formation of a social service component of the Women's Club to which I quickly attached myself.

The American women in Laos were energetic and creative and generated a number of yearly projects which inevitably earned money. Making a profit on a project ran in our blood, and the AWC thrift shop, a thriving enterprise patronized by everyone in town, was the major source of the twenty thousand dollars we had to work with. This astonishingly large sum of money we were given to allocate meant that the social service group kept very busy. We sifted requests from villages and individuals who brought proposals and sought new areas of service. When I could arrange transportation I hitched a ride with a USAID truck or flew courtesy of Air Support to another town to assess first hand the merit of some of the requests we received.

Exploring the validity of requests for aid was a task I eagerly accepted, especially after I discovered that several of the women really were not interested in subjecting themselves to hot, dusty, bumpy inspection trips into small villages where we viewed run-down schools or met with local villagers to discuss the needs of their village. For me, this was a great treat, and fortunately there were some other women who shared my intense interest. Together we examined leaky school roofs and looked at potential locations for playfields needing equipment. We noted the absence of shelters to house the families who accompanied and cared for sick persons who were confined to a rural hospital and negotiated for lumber.

We had the opportunity to supplement the extension of the UNESCO nutrition programs which provided powdered milk for undernourished babies and then discovered that these villages had no provisions for sterilizing the water used. I understood more clearly the powdered formula boycott that some women in America so ardently supported. Contaminated river water that flowed through the village was used in reconstituting the milk, and women who had no knowledge of this danger fed it to their children, who then began to die. We began to provide "milk kitchens" with special equipment for guaranteeing that reconstituted milk would be safe for babies.

We also received endless requests for volleyballs.

One morning I received a call asking if I would like to join the other members of our social service committee and fly into an area which was noted for its large number of refugees. Quickly changing into sturdy shoes and slacks I drove out to Wattay, the Vientiane airport. Air America, the former Claire Chennault Flying Tiger outfit was the airborne CIA arm servicing American operations in Laos. Air Support was the title given the section of the USAID mission which decided day by day when it was safe for dependents, those of us who were family members of American employees, to fly into remote villages or to visit towns outside of Vientiane. Today we had their go-ahead.

Off we flew to Luang Prabang, forty minutes away, where we were transferred to one of the huge green army helicopters known throughout Indochina as the Jolly Green Giant. Crouched in bucket seats flanking the open door, we flew for a few minutes over increasingly heavy, uninhabited jungle until suddenly we saw a river flowing directly beneath us.

Drifting down the river were dozens of very small boats crowded with people. We circled the spot where these boats were landing at river's edge and were shortly standing with huddled groups of newly arrived refugees. These were hill tribe people: Kha or Leu. All were dressed in black cotton shirts and pants, tattered and grubby with wear. A few clutched personal belongings in small cloth bundles, but most carried nothing at all. Fear and dazed looks were reflected on their brown, sad faces. Women tried to keep their children close to them; men dragged their small boats up on the shore or stood in mute inaction.

We looked aghast at this collection of several hundred displaced people, recognizing that we were in the midst of the making of a new refugee village. No common language enabled us to talk with them or to offer comfort. Indeed, what we did provide was diversion. What must they be thinking about five white-skinned, light-haired women who literally dropped out of the sky? I provided considerable merriment for youngsters who dashed over to measure their small stature against my near six-foot height, backing up to me in comparison and scampering off, giggling and poking each other. Some of the bolder women stroked the hair on our arms and rubbed our skin to see if the whiteness would come off.

These men, women and children from further north kept drifting to shore from their distant bombed villages. Tired, bereft and hungry, they crouched in small, dispirited groups until word reached them of supplies to be secured. One person was then selected to go down the slope to a huge pile of tarps, plastic sheeting, rice pots and bags of rice. Each family received enough plastic to shelter them and enough rice to begin to feed them. There was no meat and no vegetables. And there was no telling when there would be.

"How often does this happen?" we asked the USAID refugee worker on the site. "Too often," he wearily replied. "Right now we are setting up almost one new village a day."

"Would there be a way to fly vegetables in to these people if we can make the arrangements?"

"Yes, it would be a big help. They aren't used to eating just rice. Vegetables will be scarce until they can plant and harvest, and that will be weeks from now." We felt embarrassed by the smallness of this stop-gap measure of aid, but we were determined to do something, *anything*, to indicate our desire to alleviate some of the pain. It was such a small gesture in the face of such massive upheaval.

We were sobered by our short journey, and it was a chastened group of American women who returned to the airfield and our homes. What must it be like to move, perhaps forever, from your own village? What would these people have for homes? How soon would houses be built for them? How well would hastily erected bamboo structures hold up in the coming rainy season? Did they have any notion of why all this was happening? Did we? As time went on we found answers to some of our questions in visits to other, more established refugee villages and in sharing with each other concern and explanations for the upheaval that gripped this country.

Our trip to this riverside was the first of several I made that introduced me to the relocation of the thousands of refugees in Laos. In the south I visited a well-laid-out temporary village where typical Lao stilt houses had been erected, side by side. It was an area that housed hundreds of fugitives from the Boulevans plains, the villages through which the Ho Chi Minh Trail wound. The site was treeless, flat and hot. But the people were invariably courteous, friendly and cheerful and the children curious and eager to attach themselves to visitors. In every village I visited a trail of youngsters tagged along, recorded in photos shared with committee members causing them to ask where this Pied Piper was going next.

I marveled at the resilience of the refugees even as I raged at the disruption and misery being caused by what I reluctantly acknowledged as "The Hidden War." Figures on the number of refugees at any one time vary, but former IVS'er Fred Branfman, in a chapter in *Laos: War and Revolution* reported that in 1965, 25,000–30,000 refugees were relocated; in 1967 there were 200,000; and in 1969, 230,000 (223). This corresponds roughly to figures reported in the same volume by Peter Dale Scott who in 1969 said, "The country is today a battlefield where U.S. bombings, with some 400 to 500 sorties a day, have generated 400,000 refugees" (315).

There was much to learn, and I was rapidly being educated into a much more comprehensive awareness of the complexity of the American presence in Laos and the intricacies of the problems posed by the Vietnam War and its effect on its neighbors.

6
AID May Not Mean Help

I was very nervous. The DC-6 plane on which I had hitched a ride was illegally loaded. At my elbow, in the aisle of the plane, was a barrel of raw gasoline, loosely secured to some arm rests. We had just been advised that the plane was to make an unscheduled landing and the "Fasten Seat Belt" order was given, but I felt I would have more chance of fleeing a disaster if I were not belted in. Nevertheless, I buckled up and looked out of my small window.

I was on my way to Ban Houei Sai, seat of the Golden Triangle. It was my first opportunity to visit this area where Burma, Thailand and Laos converge at the Mekong River. The reading matter I had taken with me that morning included a recent USAID publication which featured Southeast Asia. On the cover was a bright color photograph of an irrigation project which was the showpiece of Laos. This project was reported to be providing irrigation for an entire section of the country, and the article glowed with artful pictures and self-congratulations.

I had just finished reading this piece when we were warned to prepare for an unscheduled landing. As we lurched onto an earthen airstrip I exhaled a sigh of relief, grateful that the barrel of gasoline was still upright and intact. Through the window I could see the town in which the miraculous irrigation project had been developed. What I saw was sand and desolation.

We were literally sitting in the midst of irrigation channels which were plugged with debris and weeds. There was no water anywhere, and the earth was parched and sere: no rice, no vegetables, not even a few scrubby bushes.

I looked at the cover picture in my lap and looked back through the window. The irrigation project on which close to half a million American dollars had been lavished was in ruins. I had no clue as to why it had been abandoned. Bitterly I wondered if perhaps the direction of the war had changed so that it was no longer important to win the hearts and minds of the people of this village. Was this another example of American technology that was too complex, too sophisticated, too expensive for village farmers to maintain? I thought back to Lederer and Burdick's pleas for simple devices that could utilize a bicycle wheel to lift water up to terraced paddies. Their *Ugly American* (219ff.) had been a folk hero for Asians, but we had come to misuse the term to let it reflect our lack of real sympathy with and understanding of third-world peoples; ugly Americans indeed.

Stunned, I compared the elaborateness of this failed effort with the achievements of a friend who worked in Laos for the American Friends Service Committee. In his job he took simple, mechanical pumps with Volkswagen motors into villages where their installation would provide needed irrigation. He taught the farmers to install, maintain and repair these pumps. Volkswagen parts were easy to find in Vientiane, and the entire mechanism cost only a few hundred dollars. The pumps could harness small streams and create storage ponds that were used in the dry season. The cost of the pump was borne by the service committee, but the added economic capability it gave the farmer allowed him to finance repair parts. A remarkably practical gift to the people of Laos, these pumps continue to operate to this day.

Learning about American foreign aid from the inside became a very sobering process. Millions of Americans, I am convinced, at one time believed that there were genuine altruistic motives behind the foreign aid voted each year by the United States Congress. As a nation we have been sympathetic to the struggle of others. Many of us, at least in the sixties and seventies, assumed that foreign aid was a channel through which help went to underdeveloped countries which needed health, education, agricultural and social welfare assistance.

It was a rude awakening to discover that foreign aid seemed to mean primarily aid to American businesses. It appeared that what made it "foreign" aid was that American money purchased American goods and equipment which were then shipped to foreign countries in American ships. No matter that our shipping rates were often double those of other carriers, or the material three and four times more costly than similar items already available in Asian markets. Again, Branfman confirms the arrangements in *Laos: War and Revolution,* reporting, "By an act of Congress, moreover, all USAID commodities must be imported from the United States, although such goods are often inappropriate, hard to get, and overly expensive to maintain" (263). When these goods reached their destination, American technicians earning American-scale salaries then installed the equipment. Their local counterpart workers most often were paid according to local rates. I was curious to know what happened when equipment like this breaks down.

"It depends on whether American foreign aid is still being offered to that country," my husband volunteered.

I didn't understand. "What do you mean? Can't people go to the market to find replacement parts?"

"Many small, poor countries cannot afford to import American spare parts. Their cost is prohibitive."

"But there are Japanese and European things all over the market," I pointed out. "Surely needed parts are available from these sources."

"Not if they are threaded parts, like screws, nuts and bolts."

I pondered this and asked, "Are you saying that a French-made screw will not fit into an American-made machine?"

"That's what I'm saying."

"But how stupid! Why don't manufacturers get their act together? What kind of monkey business is this?" I had never had to look for spare parts in anything other than an American hardware store, and it shocked me to discover that there were no agreed-upon international standards for equipment that was marketed and used worldwide. This certainly explained the fierce competition to have aid accepted by foreign countries and opened my eyes to the lack of altruism in these multi-million-dollar programs.

Another experience reinforced our understanding of the intricacies of American foreign policy and foreign aid. Shortly after John arrived his job assignment had been changed from the development of an industrial arts curriculum for each school to supervision of the logistics related to the actual construction of the schools. The third Fa Ngum school was behind schedule, and a fourth one was about to be started. John was expected to requisition materials, arrange to transport them to the proper sites and check that the items were received, stored and actually used for the school.

It was the practice of making the requisitioning officer responsible for all supplies that became my husband's nemesis. The assignment was a nightmare. Despite careful surveillance much of the material was siphoned off and sold on the open market, and more often than not it was the school officials themselves who spirited away lumber, cement, even electrical equipment. In one location there were dozens of local families bootlegging electricity off the Fa Ngum construction line using materials meant for the school itself. Often shipments of materials arrived with only a fraction of the

Fa Ngum school, May 1991.

goods still intact. We were at this time unaware of the blatant AID acknowledgment, even support, of the corruption practiced by so many RLG officials. Branfman speaks of "the *de facto* arrangement between the U.S. military and the Lao elite, which guaranteed that *aid programs would work through and around the elitism and corruption and not change it*" (italics mine) (261).

Even though this kind of major pilferage was frustrating, we could understand why it happened. A few sheets of plywood were worth several months' salary, and the undercover sale of an office machine could provide necessities for a whole family for close to a year. The salaries of the school principals were higher than those of many others in Laos, but at thirty to a hundred dollars a month they couldn't begin to match the thirty- to forty-thousand dollars earned by their American mentors. The temptations were many and continuous, and members of the Hawaii team flew the length and breadth of Laos continually following up on shipments and trying to locate missing cargo.

Most of the members of our Hawaii team had assignments in each of the Fa Ngum schools, which meant continuous and frequent travel, often with absences of several days at a time, north to Luang Prabang or south to Savannakhet or Pakse. Listening to tales of visiting in these places whetted my desire to see them too, and I quizzed my husband at length after each trip to learn what I could about these areas. Dealing with losses of material, delays, procrastination and lack of building experience and expertise often caused him to be irritable and discouraged when he returned home, but a good dinner usually worked wonders and led to new tales of recent experiences.

I was, therefore, startled when he came in from a trip to Luang Prabang looking very uneasy and saying almost nothing. I found it difficult to read his face and asked, "Did something go wrong on this trip? What's bothering you?"

He hesitated, and then shared, "I boarded my scheduled flight back to Vientiane as usual. Part way into the flight I could see from my window a well-developed, fully paved road beneath us in the jungle. There was no one on the road."

I stiffened, as memories hearing about the "China Road" flashed to mind. Dommen in *Conflict in Laos* corroborates that by agreement with Souvanna Phouma's coalition government, "Chinese Army Engineers constructed roads in northern Laos to link the Kingdom with southern China. These roads had little bearing on the war in Laos but had great strategic importance for China's relations with guerillas operating in Thailand" (126).

John made discreet inquiries of others on board and learned that they were, indeed, following a supposedly secret road that was being built from the border of China across Laos into Thailand. The road, according to Christopher Robbins in *The Ravens*, was agreed to by Souvanna Phouma in Peking in April 1961 and was reported to be "protected by formidable batteries of antiaircraft guns." Robbins claims a "force of twenty thousand combat engineers" was in Laos, constructing this road. Ample grounds for my husband's apprehension.

"It's dangerous to be anywhere near there, isn't it?"

"Of course it is! I couldn't figure out why we were there at all until it occurred to me that it was possible that the pilot was lost and was following the only landmark he could identify in his effort to reach the Thai border." We both knew that navigating in Laos was difficult at best, with no radar, few landmarks and the continual shifting of guerilla lines, making it very hard to know where one was safe and where in danger.

As John continued to ponder the possible cause for having deviated from the usual flight path, he was suddenly advised to tighten his seat belt to prepare to land. The fact that they were still over dense jungle and had seen no villages for several minutes strengthened his misgivings.

"When we landed we were in the middle of a full-blown American military installation."

I gasped. I was well aware of the hundreds of U.S. troops stationed in Udorn, Thailand, and had seen some of them in the south of Laos during the day, but was told by the Lao people that the soldiers always went back across the river at night. I had reluctantly acknowledged America's involvement in what I was beginning to call the little war that isn't here. But a full-blown military installation inside the country? "Are you sure you were still in Laos?"

"Absolutely. All around us were GIs in fatigues as well as tanks and ordnance of all kinds. There was no identifying insignia on anyone, so I couldn't tell if I was seeing privates or generals." Welcome to Laos, land in which there is no U.S. military presence!

"What was so urgent that you, a civilian employee, were allowed to land in an armed camp full of American soldiers?" I kept hoping he would tell me this whole story was a fabrication, his idea of a joke.

He said he had no idea why the plane stopped there, where they were, or why he was not allowed out of the plane. There were a couple of passengers who did disembark, and after a few minutes a military person came into the plane and barked, "You have not been here. You have not seen anything and you will not talk about this to anyone." No questions were asked and no information volunteered. It was clear that my husband felt he should not be telling me, but that he was so startled by the entire episode he had to talk with someone. I never shared his revelation with anyone during our entire stay in Laos. Recalling this incident, I still wondered if I had made it all up until Christopher Robbins, writing in *The Ravens*, reports over and over again that men without identifying insignia of any kind flew hundreds of sorties out of Long Cheng, often landing Thai mercenaries, camouflaged in Lao uniforms, into battle (27, 126).

John's distress over this incident recalled the dilemma of another team member who ran into a different kind of problem with the political arm of the American mission in Laos. George worked in Phone Hong, an area surrounded by active Pathet Lao cadres. It was approximately thirty miles from Vientiane, and the men who were developing the Fa Ngum school there often remarked on the makeup of the student body. "I'm sure that more than 50 percent of our students are Pathet Lao sympathizers," Ah Chong had volunteered recently. "That's why they don't bother us as we work. Everyone knows the completion of this school will benefit all of the kids. The PL aren't going to disrupt our work because they want education too."

This delicate balance of power was very tenuous, and it was, therefore, shocking to have one of the team members who worked there pressured by the American area coordinator to inform on the activities of the local people.

George steamed into the Vientiane USAID education office to announce, "I'm through. You can send me back to Hawaii."

Unaware of the cause for this outburst the chief of party suggested he calm down and explain himself.

"I'm getting the arm to become an informer for the CIA."

"But that's impossible, a breach of our contract. We have a clear agreement that no USAID Hawaii team member is expected to become a spy."

Bitterly George continued, "Someone out there doesn't know about this provision or else doesn't care. For three days some CIA types have been asking me questions and suggesting that it's my duty to supply them with answers." George was livid. "Don't they realize that it's because the people know I am *not* an informer that they don't shoot me outright?"

He was not being overdramatic. Team members assigned to Phone Hong often discussed the very real possibility that one day someone might doubt their sincerity, or just take a notion to wipe out the Americans. It required considerable nerve to work at this particular site.

George paced up and down the office. "The Pathet Lao are all around us, but they never touch us. It's because their kids go to our school and because we don't report their activities. In no way am I going to change that."

It took several cables and finally a phone call from Hawaii to Washington to reconfirm what every team member counted on: immunity from providing intelligence. There were no more coercive advances toward any of the team members.

Listening to George and Ah Chong talk about the delicate relationship between them and the Pathet Lao sympathizers in the village, I wondered why the embassy would be so callous as to even suggest asking members of the education team to assume this risk. Were they so expendable?

John's eyewitness account of American troops inside the country, which recalled this other brush with the clandestine military presence, caused us both to think long and hard about what the real intent of the USAID operation was. It had a huge budget, something over $50 million, which was listed as foreign aid to Laos. Yet the budget for our Fa Ngum schools during our first year there was something like $300,000, and even projects which seemed humanitarian had a military undercurrent. Road building, so desperately needed in this country where there were no means of shifting produce, lumber and people from one area to another was designed for military transportation and went to the borders where the heavy fighting took place and in and out of the Long Cheng area, seat of the CIA forces. The common people still depended on rutted paths and muddy tracks to lead them from the markets to their homes. The USAID agricultural assistants were experienced teachers and practitioners who devoted the majority of their efforts to a futile attempt to persuade the hill tribes to switch from growing opium, which brought high returns, to growing fruits and vegetables, which spoiled on the way to the markets that needed them because of poor transportation and no refrigeration. It was a losing game.

Observations about the hidden war, the use of foreign aid to bolster American political ends, and the gross denial of events we ourselves experienced helped us to conclude that we might not be the only Americans who were being misled as to the real American agenda abroad. The longer we stayed in Laos, the more opportunities might arise to share our firsthand observations about what was happening here. Through us friends and family back in the States, less aware even than we of the turmoil in Indochina, might begin to learn about this part of the world. We nurtured the hope that we could in some small way shed light on the ways in which U.S. foreign policy was operating in this part of Southeast Asia.

7
Khamnouy

Khamnouy was a Lao teenager we each met under quite separate circumstances soon after we arrived in Laos. My husband spoke often of a student of his at the Fa Ngum High School who helped him on weekends. The young man soaked up information about motors and machines and enjoyed helping with the set-up of demonstrations that required early preparation. He was markedly different from most of the others in my husband's class. "Other students volunteer to help me, but the minute my back is turned, off they go and I never see them again. This one hangs around and watches and asks questions and is very quick to pick up on ideas and skills."

I would have expected the Lao instructors to be called upon for this kind of preparation since, after all, they were the ones being trained to become more skilled in the teaching of practical arts.

My innocent mentioning of this opinion unleashed a fury of frustration as John rolled his eyes. "The instructors don't do anything. They come to class in white shirts and suit jackets and are afraid to get their hands dirty. Trouble is, they often know less than the students about some of the things we are working on."

I found myself rising to the defense of the teachers who were being castigated. "Do you suppose this business of not getting their hands dirty has something to do with their role as upper grade teachers?" I knew they had received advanced training in Thai technical institutes, and I also knew many of them had received their own education in one-room schools with dirt floors from teachers who had themselves gone only through the sixth grade. We Americans often found it hard to realize that our Puritan work ethic just didn't fit the circumstances of developing countries. High school teachers were *somebody* and messing around with oily machines or engaging in strenuous manual labor jeopardized their expectations of being treated with respect and deference.

"Well," I rushed on, "then it's a good thing that you have at least one eager helper." During all of our conversations about this person, if I had heard the young man's name, it hadn't stuck in my memory.

I remember very clearly the day I met Khamnouy. As a volunteer at the American Teen Club of Laos, set up in a USAID dwelling that had been recently allocated for this purpose, I had been watching a group of Ameican boys in a lively game of pool. At the sound of my name, I turned somewhat absently toward the voice that asked, "Are you Mrs. Rantala?"

Surprised to see a Lao teenager, I switched my attention at once. What had caused him to venture into this spot? Surely he wasn't expecting to join the pool game. American kids didn't mix with Lao kids, and there was a real chance that this particular group would be hostile toward this young man. We had formed this teen center for the more troubled and troublesome American teenagers on the post, boys who reflected the anxiety created in families where the fathers sometimes failed to return from the missions they flew to drop rice to hungry Lao and Hmong hill tribes. The tribal people were cut off from food supplies by the war and often fled to valleys encircled by steep, jagged mountain peaks. Casualties were high and sudden among this group of fliers, and it was often the teenagers who suffered most because of absentee fathers and anxious mothers.

"I'm Khamnouy. I think American Women's Club must help to me." His question, delivered in a statement that sounded like a demand, was apparently going to reveal a request for money. He did not seem the least in awe of the noisy gang in the adjoining room. He also had done some research in order to discover that I was chairing the social outreach committee of the AWC, and that I could be found at the Teen Club.

"How can the American Women's Club help you?" I inquired.

"My friends say you help Lao people. You must give me seventy thousand kip for Sam Neua students."

"Let's go to a quieter spot and talk about this." I was finding the rattle of the pool cues and accompanying shouts of disgust or triumph distracting. We moved to another room, and as I sat down I urged him to also take a seat.

His response was to perch gingerly on the edge of a chair.

"Tell me your name again."

The reply sounded like "Kanooy." "Could you write that down for me?"

Too late I caught myself wondering if he could write in English. He rescued me by taking the offered pencil as he spelled out K-H-A-M-N-O-U-Y, and as he did so he flashed a dazzling smile that set his eyes to dancing. His entire face sparkled, the corners of his eyes crinkling and his white, even teeth showing in a wide smile that captured my heart.

The whole encounter appeared to be a big lark for Khamnouy. His relaxed stance and ready smile confirmed that he was not apprehensive about coming into this very American teen center. Courteously, he repeated his request.

"I need money for Sam Neua students. My friends said American Women's Club must help." (Using "must" instead of "might" or "could" was a common Lao misuse of our complicated language.)

"What's this about Sam Neua students?" I leaned forward. Khamnouy's face sobered, and his eyes darkened to reflect his seriousness. "I'm the president of Sam Neua Student's Association."

"Yes? Tell me about these students."

"You know where is Sam Neua?" Doubt was clearly audible in his voice.

"Oh yes. It's 'way up north of Vientiane, and it's where the Pathet Lao headquarters are." It was common knowledge that the Communist-inspired nationalist party, the Pathet Lao, had settled into this northern area of Laos and operated from there with considerable backing from the North Vietnamese.

"I'm Sam Neua boy." He squared his shoulders, making me poignantly aware of being close to something terribly basic and important to Khamnouy. "I'm *openyoke.* Refugee. Three times I'm refugee."

"Three times!" I gasped. "But you are so young."

"We don't like Communists." I acknowledged the contempt in his voice with a nod. "There are two hundred of us in Vientiane."

"Two hundred Communists?"

I was treated to a scathing look. "*Baw,* no. Sam Neua refugee students." He was much too courteous to verbalize the look that indicated he was trying to be patient with a very slow learner. I pushed for further elaboration.

"They go to high school. Some go to the *lycée,* some to Dong Dok, others to Fa Ngum." He listed the three major secondary schools in Laos and flashed his famous smile. "Fa Ngum, that's my school. Some also go to French Technical School, the Law School, even Medical School." He expanded the list, shrugging his shoulders, in an eloquent gesture of inclusiveness. Obviously Sam Neua students were furthering their education through every available means.

"Do you want scholarships?" I ventured, denial of this possibility clearly in my voice. The Women's Club granted scholarships only in very special cases.

"No, no. They just need little help. Soap to wash clothes, notebooks, pencils."

"Pencils? You want seventy thousand kip for soap and pencils?"

The value of the Lao kip varied from time to time, and although Americans could receive an artificially supported value of two hundred and fifty kip for one dollar, one had to consider the current market value of the kip to the Lao, more like six hundred to one, when calculating requests such as this. The money he was asking for at that time represented about one hundred and forty dollars, not a large sum for the Social Action Committee of the American Women's Club to grant.

Because the AWC was required, under the terms of its charter, to spend everything over earnings of one thousand dollars on activities that would benefit the Lao people, it was not unusual for me to receive such requests. As chair of the Social Action Committee I was accustomed to being asked for money and presenting to the committee requests for ways in which to use our twenty-thousand-dollar yearly allocation. It was the smallness of the amount Khamnouy requested and its even smaller-sounding purpose that startled me.

Noting my confusion Khamnouy began to describe his Sam Neua students. They were, he said, living apart from their families and parents who were in refugee camps in remote mid-country areas of Laos. Few Sam Neua refugee families had connections that offered the relatively luxurious living of this major Lao city. Further, school hours were long, and jobs were scarce. The students were unable to support themselves. As he spoke it occurred to me that working while attending school was not something a Lao would normally have to do. As in many developing countries, the educated person was not expected to perform any menial work, and only menial work would be offered these days to high school students.

"You need money to buy supplies for your friends."

A brilliant smile rewarded me for reaching this conclusion. "I am the president of the Sam Neua Association."

"Ah, and it is your responsibility to take care of these students because they have no relatives in Vientiane." Dancing eyes rewarded my belated insight as to the nature of his request as he explained to me the close ties among these students. It became obvious that they were Khamnouy's "family," and in Laos family obligations take precedence over everything. By elected right he had assumed the family obligations relative to these two hundred young men. They were in need; he would get help.

As we talked further about his very specific request and the costs to be incurred I could see that he was asking for a bare minimum. It also became clear that there was another item on his agenda.

"Many students have gone to stay with the Buddhist monks in their living areas." I knew that he was referring to the monks in the Buddhist *wats* and the obligation they assumed for housing and feeding needy people. "The students leave for school early in the morning while the *Bonze* are out seeking food." My mind flashed to the silent line of orange-clad Buddhist monks who could be seen just at dawn each morning, walking barefoot through the streets, accepting gifts of food offered as merit by kneeling men and women who waited for them in front of their homes. With bowed heads they would place cooked rice into the monks' silver bowls.

"The monks eat their only meal of the day at eleven in the morning. Often there is no food left over for the students who return to the *wat* in the late afternoon after school."

"Are you saying that they go all day and often to the next day with nothing at all to eat?"

"Yes," he replied. "They don't get anything to eat. Maybe you can help me get some bread for them. They don't have any kip."

What he was saying was that they lacked the equivalent of ten cents with which to purchase the hot noodle soup offered each morning from huge kettles yoked across the shoulders of a vendor who walked the streets, filling bowls brought from the houses by children and adults who paid fifty kip for a steaming bowl of soup.

"I think American Women's Club must help us."

"Indeed," I mused, "I do think we must." We agreed on another day to meet since I had additional duties to attend to that afternoon.

Khamnouy left, thanking me profusely for my promised help. *"Koop chai, lai, lai. Puok en mai."* Thank you very much, see you again.

"Baw pen nyan. Pai dee." Don't mention it. Go well.

Khamnouy showed up the following Tuesday armed with a detailed list of the number of bars of soap, pencils, notebooks and boxes of soap powder he would need. I looked over the list and then suggested that we talk about the bread. Together we figured out how many loaves of French bread would be needed to give the boys living in *wats* half a loaf each morning. Apparently young men from the hills of Laos were as familiar with French bread as people in the city.

I had been searching for another agency which might be better equipped than we were to give this help and suggested that World Vision Laos might help with providing the bread.

Khamnouy's eyes danced. "Yes, yes." His nods were vigorous. "Very good idea."

No wonder he had a mischievous look! He had already been negotiating a deal with the director of the local World Vision team. When I spoke to him he immediately knew of Khamnouy, and as we talked we each agreed to do what we could to cooperate in aiding this group of Sam Neua students.

Because I had already had some experience in allocating money to needy projects I had also learned that it was most unwise to give cash directly to any individual. It was a temptation few could resist and too often the money would disappear and the project for which it was solicited never came into being. I had gone many times to the lumber yard and the hardware store to purchase awarded supplies and arrange for their delivery to a village by USAID truck. Direct funding was often too tempting for the receiver who pocketed the money or bought the materials and then sold them to someone else and failed to complete the project for which the money was intended. How much risk would there be if we gave seventy thousand kip to this penniless young Lao?

At our committee meeting I felt constrained to point out that possession of a large amount of kip might be overwhelmingly tempting to Khamnouy. The committee voted to take the risk.

On the following Saturday morning Khamnouy appeared at the door of our house in Km6. John and I reached him at the same moment and expressed in unison our surprise at seeing him. We all spoke at once.

"Mr. Rantala, I didn't know you lived here!"

"Sivongsay, how did you know where to find me? Come in."

"Khamnouy, I'm glad to see you, is there something I can do for you?"

"Mrs. Rantala, I have an invitation for you."

"This is the young student I've been telling you about. The one who comes on Saturdays to help me," John hastened to interject.

"No, no John, this is Khamnouy, the young man from Sam Neua who is helping his fellow students."

"But he is my student."

By this time Khamnouy was doubled over with laughter, his eyes dancing with glee at the consternation expressed on our faces. For days we had both been extolling the virtue of the same person, Khamnouy Sivongsay, who was now standing with us in our home. Our uncontrolled hilarity brought the cook running out to see what was happening. 'Nouy provided an explanation in Lao, and I suggested that cold drinks and cookies be brought out to fuel the sorting out of circumstances that had brought us together.

"I've come to invite you." Khamnouy turned to me, an envelope extended. "You must come next Thursday to Dong Dok at 3:30." Dong Dok was a high school located at Km9, beyond our living area, a school in which English and Lao were both used as a teaching medium. Several Sam

Neua students were enrolled there. "You must come on Thursday," Khamnouy repeated.

"I don't understand," I countered. "What's going on?"

With a flourish he presented a written invitation to attend the ceremony at which he would parcel out the items purchased with AWC monies. He wanted to be sure it was witnessed by someone from the club itself. "You must come," he repeated.

I was there. It was a scene so contrary to every other experience I had had in the allocation of money that it is indelibly etched in my memory. Twelve students were lined up outside the Dong Dok administration building, on the grass, motor scooters and bicycles parked neatly to one side. Also lined up were twelve cartons containing pencils, notebooks, bars of soap and small boxes of the Thai equivalent of Duz detergent. Each young man was prepared with a piece of paper on which were the names of the students to whom they would deliver the goods. Beside each name were the needs of that particular student.

Khamnouy signaled each person to present his list for verification, a double check prior to taking the allotment. Each leader received the exact items as requested. At the end of the ceremony I was presented with a receipted bill for every item dispensed. It totaled seventy thousand kip. Almost in chorus the young men expressed thanks to the American Women's Club. I thought of the pitiful amount of money, so carefully expended, and as I absorbed their lavish gratitude I was too moved to speak. The fairness of the distribution, the care with which it had been cost accounted, the democratic way in which it had been distributed all left a lasting impression. I managed to mumble a few Lao phrases of good wishes: *"Suen pai dee."* Go well. *"Puok en mai."* Until next time.

The young men strapped the boxes on their bikes and scooters and roared off in a flurry of dust and exhaust. I turned to Khamnouy. "Thanks for inviting me. I'll tell the American Women's Club members about this. I wouldn't have missed it for the world." A careful search of each brief accounting revealed the Khamnouy had not placed himself on any one of the lists. Surely his needs were as urgent as those of his fellow students for I knew that his family was in a refugee camp and had no means to support him with even token gifts. Well, he might not be on one of those Sam Neua student lists, but he surely was now on mine!

8
Growing Up in Laos

Khamnouy was eight the day he and three young friends went together after school down to the river with their water buckets. The path from the village skirted several bamboo huts, ran along through a banana patch and fell steeply toward the water. The descending path was well worn but narrow and the boys picked their way carefully, laughing as they balanced the pails on their heads in this familiar thrice-daily ritual. Their country, Laos, had been at war for all of their young lives, and the boys had been warned about buried land mines, so they looked carefully as they jumped over roots and skirted roots. Sometimes they found discarded treasures left by a careless soldier, and when one of the boys spied a strange metallic object on the path he picked it up saying, "I'll take this to my father. He'll make a knife."

"No," screamed Khamnouy, recognizing the grenade. Too late. The pin had been jarred loose, and as his pal frantically tossed the grenade away, two of the boys were blown to bits and Khamnouy was knocked unconscious by the blast. The villagers found him lying on the path, bits of red, raw flesh clinging to his own shredded back and legs and the fourth boy also badly injured. Khamnouy told me this story to explain the ugly twisted scars on his legs and also to justify his eating only well-done meat. He still carried terrible memories of the river bank and the red chunks of flesh that were his playmates.

Sam Neua, Khamnouy's birthplace, is both a province and a town in northeastern Laos—an area that had been in political contention among the French, the Vietnamese, the Lao Freedom Party (Pathet Lao) and the Royal Lao Government since the early fifties. Airplane raids and bombings had always been a part of his family's life.

Early in these years the Sivongsay family lived in Hua Mouang, a four-day walk from the town of Sam Neua. Souk, the oldest child, was born in 1942. The second child was Mai, a daughter. The father, Piavong, had been the village chief or *nai ban* and often had to leave his family in order to act as a guide for the Royal Lao soldiers who were desperately trying to hang onto the territory but were often unfamiliar with the terrain. Piavong was not a soldier, but as a village official, and a strong supporter of the king, it was his duty to serve as a scout whenever his knowledge and experience were needed. When the Communists came the rest of the family hid in the jungle and lived in makeshift huts or caves, often for weeks at a time. His wife, Tai, and her children at times found themselves trapped on the Communist side of the fighting lines and had to be extremely careful and clever to avoid exposing Piavong's alliance with the Royal Lao Government and his sympathy with the loyalist forces.

Life in the jungle had two facets: hiding from the French, and later the American bombs and searching for food. Fish from local streams and rice grown in paddies which they hoped would escape the bombings were their source of daily food. There were only four or five families in each small jungle grouping. Fear and hunger were constant companions.*

Souk remembers these years in the jungle very clearly: "When my sister Mai was very little and I was only ten, we lived for half a year in a small hut made out of twigs and branches while my dad was helping to defeat the Communists. By the time he came to take us back to the village, one of my brothers had died."

On the day Khamnouy was born, Souk and his mother were home alone, for his father had been out all night deer hunting. The baby came about five o'clock in the morning. Upon the father's return shortly after dawn, he was asked by Souk, "Dad, did you catch any deer?"

"Yes, we got two. Two large ones, over six hundred pounds."

"Well, Mom caught something too. A baby boy."

There were no doctors to assist with a pregnancy, and women in the village came to help. They boiled some roots and gave the birthing woman this bitter liquid to drink. It was horrid-tasting but purported to make her strong. Pregnant women also drank boiling hot water, lots of it, prior to giving birth. Water that failed to burn your finger when tested wasn't hot enough!

**For readers who want to understand more fully the terrible impact of the American saturation bombing of Laos, see* Voices from the Plain of Jars, *by Fred Branfman (New York: Harper Row Colophon Book, 1972). These translated stories told by villagers from the Plain of Jars in the Xieng Khouang area, illustrated often by young Lao children, are compiled by Branfman to document the devastation and horror that rained from the skies and the American military planes.*

Building a small fire under the delivery bed was another practice observed not only in this village, but by all Lao during childbirth. The neighbor women tended it. Fred Branfman, writing in *Voices from the Plain of Jars,* records "After child birth, a Lao mother traditionally sleeps over or near a bed of hot coals, drinking hot liquids and keeping to a very strict diet" (64 fn. 6).

"Isn't this dangerous? Won't you start a fire this way? What's the purpose?" I had asked Khampheng after the birth of her first son.

"It's just what we do, and no, it doesn't start any fire, it warms the bed." I gave her a hard look, to which she defensively responded, "I don't know why we do it, it's our custom."

In the late fifties and the sixties babies were born in those makeshift huts and caves in the jungle between air raids. If there were complications the women died, and many of the children could not survive the rigors of primitive jungle life. Commenting on the aftermath of bombing raids, Branfman reports that a Lao villager wrote, "We felt most sorry for the young mothers of new born babies who couldn't sleep near the fire warming their beds. If we made a fire, the planes could come" (64). Of the nine children Khamnouy's mother bore, four died in early childhood.

Many Lao children died from disease and especially from malnutrition within one or two years of birth. As long as a mother could breast-feed the child developed normally. The major cause of infant mortality was lack of milk and digestible food for the very small children whose mothers, once they again became pregnant, could no longer nurse them and for whom there was little in the villages on which to subsist. There were no milking animals in Laos as far as I could determine. Although there were caribou or water buffalo, these animals were not used for milk. Why, I have never found out, since they can produce up to thirty gallons of rich milk a day and are coveted for this purpose in both India and the Philippines. Cows struggled to survive in the hot, humid Lao climate, and no one seemed to know about goat milk. Many children were given sweetened condensed milk which rotted their teeth and created other nutritional problems.

I once made the mistake of engaging our cook in a conversation about the source of the evaporated milk that we bought in cans. We were talking about what children drank once their mothers could no longer nurse them, and I asked Synouane if he knew where milk came from.

He looked very puzzled, brightened, rushed into the pantry and came out holding aloft a can of evaporated milk and pointing to it said, "Here." I let that pass but pressed him further, hoping to elicit a more generic answer. He contemplated the can and then, acknowledging the source of nearly all foodstuffs in Laos, said, "Thailand." Still I pressed on.

"But how does the milk get in the cans? Where does the milk itself come from?" There was a long silence while he looked first at me, then at the can, and suddenly gave me a triumphant smile, pointed to the "Three Goats" brand name, with picture, on the can and shouted, *"These!"*

If I who had traveled the length of Laos had yet to see a goat in that country, the chances were good that he had not seen one either, but I admitted defeat, gently accepted the can of Three Goats brand evaporated milk from his hands and left him to his triumph.

Khamnouy's birth was followed by his father's long absence in service to the army, thus providing time before the arrival of the next sibling, giving him a better chance to take hold of life. As a youngster he was active and creative. He tried everything he saw others do; he was fearless. Sometimes in Hua Muong a makeshift outdoor movie theater was set up under the trees, a sheet stretched out for a screen upon which they all viewed an American Western with cowboys and horses. Searching for him the morning after viewing one of these shows, his family found this determined small boy astride a huge water buffalo, trying to herd him into the water. Khamnouy thought he could do anything, and he tried everything. When the adult men were gathered in a small group, exchanging news of the day, pondering their circumstances, the youngster, far from being in awe of his elders, would curl up in a ball near enough to them to be able to overhear the conversation. He wanted to know what was being said, and he often gave free rein to his well-developed sense of curiosity.

Piavong and Tai grew rice in a small plot some distance from their village. They worked hard in it, bending over to plant and weed and cultivate the tender green shoots, carefully guarding their life-source of food. The oldest girl, Mai, could not attend school on the days both of the parents were tending the rice because there was a small brother, Khamnai, who needed to be cared for. When Khamnouy returned from school she would attempt to enlist his assistance in the chores, but he would immediately claim he just had to go for a swim and dash off to the river with his friends.

In a small, makeshift hut preparing for a meal included gathering wood, chopping ingredients, hauling water from the river and tending the fire with care so as not to waste fuel. Only a child herself, Mai recalls, "I was so angry with him for going off to *ap nam* (take a swim), that when he came back I hit him. Khamnouy cried and told me 'don't you do that again to me.'" Mai's face softened in the retelling of this incident, years later. Her eyes said she wished it were possible to retract the sharp cuff she had administered to this bright, energetic small boy—to apologize for causing the tears.

Schooling for these children was a very hit-or-miss affair. Souk was for a while sent to school at Mouang Phoun, a two-day walk from his small jungle village. There, at the age of thirteen, he enrolled at the third-grade level. He remained in this school for four years until, in 1959, the family sent him to Vientiane to attend the *lycée,* the one French school of higher education that existed in the entire country. A *lycée* offers the equivalent not only of high school, but of two years into post–high school learning. Souk struggled to adapt from jungle village life to the city and to having all of his subjects taught in the French language.

For the next five years life for the family in Sam Neua was a succession of moves and feints—fleeing into the jungle to avoid the Communists, moving back to the village for a few weeks, only to flee again. If people were able to stay in one place for as long as six months a small school would be started for the children, but there had to be at least thirty people in a location to justify a school, and these standards were hard to meet. A young boy, whose account of these years is translated by Branfman in *Voices from the Plain of Jars,* writes, "Schools were only in places where a great many people lived. There was no school in my village. To go to school, it was necessary to leave in the morning, taking rice along because it was so far away. As a result children in the six-year-old category could not go to school, only those over ten could go. And then almost no one went to school, and everyone followed in the path of the old traditions" (83).

During the sixties Piavong was almost never with his family, and in spite of the army's frantic efforts to hold the land for the loyalist forces, by the end of 1965 all supporters of the king were forced to flee to Na Khang, and shortly afterward to a Hmong village in Sam Pra Kha.

It is unusual for a Lao Loum, an ethnic Lao from the lowlands, to live in the mountains with a tribal group, but this episode in the Sivongsay family explained to me why, years later, in a refugee camp in Thailand, Souk chose to stay in the portion of the camp that held the Hmong people. He was comfortable with them, had fought with them during this difficult period in the history of Laos, and identified more with them than with others.

At the time the family fled to the mountain Hmong village the Royal Lao Army was barely surviving. In Xieng Khaouang province army trucks drove through villages picking up boys ten and over to conscript them into the army. Fearing that Khamnouy would be snatched, his mother made an arrangement with local Buddhist monks to smuggle him out on a plane which took him first to Sam Thong and then into Vientiane.

Khamnouy entered the fourth grade in 1965 in Vientiane. He studied at the Chou Anou military school and lived with his brother's wife and her family. He too had adjustments to make in this move to the city, not the least of which was trying to accept the authority of an older brother he had not seen for six years and whom he scarcely knew. It was hard on them both and created frictions they were still trying to work out when we met Khamnouy in March of 1971. Khamnouy was then a student at the Fa Ngum schools, living with his aunt and a cousin who was the same age. Somehow he managed to support his basic needs for food and clothing, fuel for his motorbike and school supplies. When we first met him we didn't know enough to ask him how he managed.

Loth, the cousin Khamnouy lived with, was a most attractive young man who also came regularly to our Km6 home and became addicted to the banana bread I regularly made to use up the never-ending supply of over-ripe fruit. He confided that the bread provided him with his breakfast; and following our weekly conversations, he left with a loaf tucked under his arm. His political leanings were very different from those of other members of the Sivongsay family in that he was not averse to accepting assistance from the Pathet Lao and was awarded a scholarship to attend school in Czechoslovakia. The elder Sivongsay, Piavong, was so disgusted and angry he refused to speak to the young man directly and referred to him only in the most derogatory terms. Khamnouy was upset about Loth's expedient assessment of how the political winds were blowing but was not so scathingly contemptuous. He did not, however, hide his conviction that Loth was casting his fortunes with those who were betraying and destroying all that others in the family had been fighting for during the past twenty years.

The tension between Loth and the rest of the family alerted us to the need to be very careful about criticizing the actions and activities of the incumbent government in the presence of Khamnouy's parents. We often were critical of what we judged to be blatant unconcern for the common people of Laos, among whom we would have classified the Sivongsay family in those days. We saw greed and corruption and ineptness of governance in the fawning acquiescence to the power of foreign assistance. At best the administration's vision for the country was obscure. Their goals appeared to be to milk the American government of as much as they could, pocketing any benefits they could extract through favoritism and mismanagement.

I was at this time totally unaware of the way in which the neutralist position, held so firmly and so long by Souvanna Phouma, had been subverted by extreme pressure from the United States in spite of strong support from other third-world countries. Dommen in *Laos: War and Revolution,* reports lengthy and exhausting negotiations held in Paris during the late sixties, during which the prime minister warded off all suggestions that the tripartite coalition among the far right, the neutralists and the Pathet Lao be altered. All during his regime, Souvanna had kept open positions that were slated to be held by Pathet Lao, who scorned the offer as they continued to be under the influence of the Vietnamese Communists. American presidents Lyndon Johnson and Richard Nixon had little sympathy for the careful neutrality so torturously preserved by this head of state who sought no personal glory or reward for his efforts to preserve the nonviolent nature of his small country (chapters 4 and 5, 49–117).

The Vietnamese soldiers had never left Laos, in spite of signing agreements to do so at the same time as the French and Americans agreed to leave in the early sixties. It was the pressure exerted by the United States, despite opposition from their own ambassador, William Sullivan, that altered the makeup of the Lao government to a 50 percent Royalist and 50 percent Pathet Lao configuration. It was the tocsin sounding the death knell of the neutralist effort.

While well-fed and sometimes well-meaning politicians on all sides of the Indochinese conflict gathered to hammer out the fate of Laos, the thousands of refugees in the country lived in limbo—jobless, often moving because of additional fighting, dependent upon foreign aid for food and existing in makeshift dwellings. Under the new coalition in Vientiane a few well-heeled and ineffective officials lived in luxury. Perala Ratnam, ambassador to Laos from India in this period, observes in *Laos and the Superpowers*, the "scramble for favors and wealth within the officer corps was not the least of the reasons for the military ineffectiveness of the opposition to the Pathet Lao. Instead of being used to finance rural economic development U.S. money never got out of Vientiane. The leading families of the city developed discriminating tastes in German cars, scotch whiskey, caviar, and air conditioning equipment" (12).

Admirers of the Pathet Lao seemed equally obsequious toward their Vietnamese mentors, and neither major political body in the country appeared any longer to be in touch with their people.

We were not eager to have Vietnamese Communism take over Laos and increasingly also felt that the Royal Lao Government lacked the insight and the strength to govern the country. The Lao factions which attempted to remain free of both American and Vietnamese financial and military support lacked the experience and sophistication needed to compete with either the insurgents or the incumbents. They were pointedly ignored by American foreign policy personnel. It was a lose-lose situation.

A few months after Khamnouy was sent to Vientiane by his parents the entire family was forced to leave Na Khang for a new refugee village which was being set up with American money. The village of Phone Xay was situated about twenty miles from the seat of the CIA military activity in Sam Thong, and about forty-five miles from Vientiane. All inhabitants of this new village were strong supporters of the Royal Lao Government, and once they were settled in, Piavong was able to journey in Vientiane to connect with his sons, where he found Khamnouy living with his uncle, Lanoi.

Lanoi and Piavong bore so little physical resemblance to each other that John and I could not help but be puzzled about the relationship. The Lao easily refer to close associates as "cousin," "brother," and "sister," and one never knows who are the bona fide family members and who are merely good friends. There was a third brother in this generation of Sivongsays who was, in turn, different in physical traits from the other two. I was mystified by the lack of similarity and searched in vain for common identifying features.

Piavong, tall, lean and the source of the flashing brown eyes that were a trademark for each of his children, had been orphaned when quite young. He was taken in by Lanoi's father, who accepted him as his own son, *luke liang*. Lanoi was short, round and had a very smooth, shiny face. The third sibling, Senthama, also an orphan, was of medium height and had a square face, thick bushy hair and a rugged, lined face. Knowing that these three had been raised as blood brothers further confounded our efforts to identify similar physical characteristics. John and I had learned of the practice of taking in orphaned children when we visited the mother of another young Lao friend and found that she, long widowed, was caring for a whole brood of young children whom she had simply incorporated into her family after their parents were killed in the war. To discover that Khamnouy's uncles were not blood related to each other relieved us of our fruitless search for similarities of looks or action that would link him to cousins that were the same age, and it released us from looking for family traits where none existed.

The mischievous, sparkling brown eyes that danced with laughter in each of Piavong's children were a genetic stamp of unique identity traceable directly to their father, an undeniable trademark that has carried into the next generation.

9
Chocolate Soup for Breakfast

Khamnouy's knowledge and use of English were surprisingly good and facilitated our getting to know him better. It was clear, however, that he was eager to improve his understanding of the language, and we felt, correctly, that he would accept our underwriting of the cost of courses at the Lao American Association. Shortly after my arrival in Laos, as I cast around for ways to fill the unaccustomed free hours acquired as a benefit of employing a cook and houseman, I had discovered there was a need for teachers of English. With no experience in teaching ESL, English as a second language, I was nevertheless encouraged to join the faculty since I am a native English speaker, a rarity in most of Laos. It was a challenge that provided an endless series of surprises and was not without its moments!

For one thing, I quickly learned which of the tongue-twisting American phrases were next to impossible for the Lao to pronounce. As with some other Asians, "l's" and "r's" were interchangeable. I had in fact already noticed this in the young members of the rock band that played now and then at the American Club where the popular song "Yellow River" was belted out into a swinging "Yerrow Liver."

Our efforts at the LAA included not only helping our students learn English, but also drilling them on difficult pronunciation. How we labored over "Malaria and cholera are really rare in Little Rock!" Mostly it came out sounding like "Marraria and chorerra ah leely lare in rittle lock." I couldn't help but wonder what quirk of fate had singled out Little Rock for all of this agonizing attention.

Khamnouy was a good student, had less than the usual difficulty with pronunciation, and learned quickly. He practiced his English on us at every possible occasion and was in our house daily for various reasons. He was always smiling, cheerful and helpful, and John soon began to conscript him as a helper on his current projects.

John was a great one for "projects" wherever he was, and Laos was no exception. Shortly after our arrival he designed a small but adequate sauna which fitted neatly across the back wall of our carport and still left parking space for the car. The building of this sauna occupied him for several months after which work began on construction of a bricked terrace outside the dining room French doors. 'Nouy assisted by trundling aggregate, mixing cement and laying bricks, the two of them laughing and talking in a mixture of Lao and English.

Our cook, Synouane, was not so proficient in English. Although we also sent him to classes at the Lao American Association, he had a much harder time assimilating the drills. We used to practice as we worked together in the house, but with diminishing returns. Once when we were in the market together he was talking to me about something being near as against something being far. We also had just purchased a chicken. All of those words, near, far and chicken, sounded like "Khai" to me and I could not distinguish one from the other. Suddenly Synouane stopped in his tracks, looked at me and triumphantly crowed, "Khai, khai, khai! Same same as 'Mararia and chorerera are rearry rare in rittle lock!'" With that he took off for home leaving me doubled over with laughter, remembering the exuberant toss of his head at this evidence that even I, his teacher, had problems with pronunciation.

Khamnouy was soon enjoying free run of our home, although he seldom spent the night. I had the impression that he shared quarters with his cousin, Loth, but he never offered to show us the place where he lived in Vientiane. He often stayed for meals with us, helped "Dad" with chores around the house, and talked with the servants as they went about their daily rounds. Everyone in the household liked Khamnouy, whose ready smile and cheerful offers of help provided a *joie de vivre* that gave all of us a lift. He made friends easily, wasn't afraid of hard work and always carried his share of chores around the house. He would come roaring up the driveway on his motorcycle, park it under a tree and stop to play a moment with the dog while calling, "*Sabaidee!* Hello! Anybody home?" Sometimes I would find him at the dining room table working on his studies when I came back from a meeting or my teaching at the Lao American Association.

In December of 1973 John and I decided to return to the States to meet with our sons. We had family business to discuss that required face-to-face exploration, and although we were not entitled to a home leave, we did have accumulated vacation time. We flew to London for Christmas and then on to my niece's New Hampshire house where there was bed space for us all.

In our absence we asked Khamnouy to stay in our Vientiane home. The post discouraged having Lao live in American quarters, but we were already so used to having 'Nouy around we never thought of him as anything but an adopted son. He got along well with the recently acquired new cook, now a young man named Sakhorn, and it seemed wise to have someone in the house nights and weekends. We took off for Europe and America leaving them in charge.

In New Hampshire a letter arrived from Khamnouy that sent us all into gales of laughter. He said Vientiane was very cold, adding, "I put a lot of blankets on my bed. I also cook my own food in the morning before Sakhorn arrives. Usually I fix an egg and some toast. Best of all, I make chocolate soup for breakfast."

We all gagged. Chocolate soup? For breakfast? What in the world was he drinking? We all shortly adopted this new designation for instant cocoa finding it much more tantalizing than the prosaic hot chocolate—we chose chocolate soup.

Khamnouy seldom imposed upon our hospitality, but he did feel free to bring his close friends by, and this was how we met Boonpheng. He too soon began to make our house his headquarters. Shorter than 'Nouy, quick to laugh and an obvious entrepreneur, Boonpheng always had many activities to attend to. In the midst of it all he constantly referred to his mother, and we learned that she lived in a refugee village near Nam Ngum Dam. A trip to this area, about fifty miles from Vientiane, was a prized outing, for this huge hydroelectric dam had an artificial lake behind it that was producing mammoth catfish and other edible fish. The dam had been a project of the World Bank and was funded by the United States, Japan, Netherlands, Canada, Thailand, Australia, Denmark, France and New Zealand. It had only recently begun operations, selling electricity to Thailand, one of the few exportable commodities to be found in Laos. The reservoir was a coveted fishing place, and the anticipation of accompanying us there to fish produced near religious ecstasy in Boot, our faithful gardener.

We prevailed upon busy Boonpheng to set a day aside and accompany us to the village to meet his mother. We chose a typical Lao day and endured a typical Lao drive, hot and sunny, with dirt roads boiling up clouds of dust. We arrived in the village parched, dusty and thankful to be out of the hot car. Dozens of small children clustered around us, jabbering, pointing, rubbing our skins, marveling at John's hairy arms.

Lao refugee villages never seemed to be located where there were trees or greenery. Perhaps these had once been there but had been chopped up for cooking fuel and firewood. Rough huts were made of bamboo and rose on stilts, providing space under the house for a hammock in which to place a young child, room for a wooden loom and space out of the hot sun for pigs, chickens and occasionally a buffalo. Water was lugged from a nearby parched stream which served as the laundry and bathing area as well. There were no visible sanitary facilities, and most small children ran around clad only in t-shirts, facilitating the performance of natural functions.

Boonpheng had disappeared into the village as we were looking around and soon returned and presented to us a tall, smiling woman, his mother. I was captivated by the serenity in her face. Around her skirts were clustered several small children, and she was carrying one in her arms. They were many years younger than Boonpheng, a real surprise, for we knew from what Boonpheng had told us that both his father and his older brother had been killed in the fighting in Laos. He was now the head of the family. He explained this unexpected collection of young children by saying that his mother, when they had left their previous refugee village because of the encroaching military action, had simply gathered up the children whose parents had been killed or who had disappeared and had taken them with her to the new location. Now they were her children.

John and I were dumbfounded. That this woman, mourning the loss of her husband and oldest son and alone in life, would simply take on half a dozen unrelated children was mind-boggling. We liked her immediately. She was very gracious and poised in spite of the incredible paucity of belongings. She offered us a cool drink and a mat to sit on in the shade. We had no language in common, but as we gestured and Boonpheng translated, she rose, went into her hut and returned with a pile of woven cloths. Her loom was under the house, and her son told us that she wove these cloths in order to take them to Vientiane to sell so that she could get enough money to buy rice to feed her young family.

A healthy Lao person eats from one to two pounds of glutinous rice a day. This family of six might well need two one-hundred-kilo bags of rice a month. Going into Vientiane to buy it and hiring a taxi to carry it back to the village were costly.

The weavings helped her pay for the rice. I was charmed by the imagination in the designs and the use of everyday objects such as deer, chickens and elephants as major themes. On a black or white background she used bright threads and depicted all sorts of scenes which included birds, buffalo and children. All of the designs had that peculiar kind of angularity their looms produce. I was struck by their similarity to Guatemalan and other South American patterns. Some weavings had the words

"Laos" or "Vientiane" in them. Some were approximately a yard square, while others might be fifty or sixty inches long.

"I'm sure I can help your mom sell these," I said impulsively to Boonpheng. "Give her directions on how to get to where we live. Ask her if I can take these with me today and sell them. She can come to my house for the money when she next comes to town." We struck a deal, and I returned home with a stack of weavings through which I would be able to help this indomitable Lao mother without damaging her sense of pride or self-sufficiency. We were both pleased with the arrangement.

Boonpheng's mother came monthly to our Km6 home. We used Lao terms of respect when we addressed each other. She referred to me as *Mee Tow* or grandmother and I simply called her *Mee* Boonpheng, Boonpheng's mother. My servants came to know her well, and we all looked forward to her visits. The cook would help me with translations if we got really stuck in our conversations. Once she was detained at the entrance to our American living compound, and it was only when a neighbor returning from town saw her and told me she was at the gate that I understood why she had not arrived at her usual time. I rushed down to get her and later called the USAID headquarters to inform them that they were never again to deny a Lao person entry to our compound. In my anger I demanded, "Do you need to be reminded that it is *their* country? How dare you arbitrarily decide to detain Lao at the gate!" Fortunately, there was no move to restrict entry to Americans only.

After selling several piles of weavings and establishing a monthly time to meet, it was an easy progression to decide to take our Thanksgiving dinner that year up to Boonpheng's village. We ordered a huge turkey. The few traditional foods which were not available in the local market, such as cranberry sauce, could be found in the American commissary. All we needed to make this a real American Thanksgiving dinner was a large family. Boonpheng's family seemed to be the right answer.

Some of our neighbors must have thought we were more than a little crazy when on Thanksgiving morning Boonpheng and Khamnouy arrived to help us load boxes and kettles into our car in preparation for the trek toward Nam Ngum Dam. I was sure that none of the villagers would have ever seen a pumpkin pie, but that didn't prevent me from baking four of them. My American mental picture of a carved turkey on a huge platter made me wonder how they would cope with this very large bird in a culture that didn't use table knives or forks or chopsticks. I needn't have worried, they reduced the turkey to bite-sized pieces easily handled by fingers or spoons and picked the bones clean.

Our arrival was celebrated by the entire village, old and young, children and grownups. Everyone knew we were coming and that we were bringing a feast. The food was carried up the rickety ladder-like steps into the small bamboo house with a sway-backed floor. The turkey, dressing, sweet potatoes, onions, salad and pies became the focus of excited chattering and exclamations by the women who crowded into the tiny partitioned area used as a kitchen. I was banned from further food preparation and included in a round of welcoming drinks.

The Lao make a rice wine called *lau lau* which we branded "white lightning." It was aged in twelve-inch-high earthen pots and made from a sugared concoction of rice mash that had been sealed with mud and left to ferment. The cover was knocked off with a machete or sharp-pointed stick when the wine was ready to be consumed, and buffalo horns of water were emptied into the opened jar. The action of the water with the fermented mash bubbled up into a potent wine. The villagers took great delight in egging visitors on to see how many buffalo horns of water could be emptied into the jug while you drank through long, reed straws.

Our Thanksgiving party was not my first encounter with this lethal drink called *lau lau*. The first time I had tried it had been followed by near unconsciousness and a blinding headache. I was not about to ruin my Thanksgiving dinner, and I looked around wildly for Khamnouy. In anticipation of such an occasion he and I had a deal. We would both drink from the same jug, but I would fake drinking it, and he would consume those horn measurements. This was his native drink, and he could take it! Two-foot-long reed straws were inserted into the jug, and together we fulfilled the expectations of our hosts.

There was one minor disaster in our dinner arrangement. I had bottled the gravy when it was hot, and the ride up through the countryside had soured it. After pouring a quantity of it over my dinner and discovering its sour taste I looked in alarm at the dozens of others happily gobbling up our shared dinner. I was the only one who even noticed. Either they were used to fermented food, or they liked it, or both. Probably their stomach enzymes were far more able to cope with it than mine! It was our first Thanksgiving in which *caow niow*, sticky rice, was given preference over mashed potatoes and turned out to be a most agreeable substitute. And everyone enjoyed the first taste of pumpkin pie, all in all, a great success.

Late that afternoon, tired, certainly not hungry, glowing from the smiles, the *wais*, or clasped-hand bows, and the look of satisfaction on the face of Boonpheng's mother as she surveyed her home and family, we climbed into our blue Datsun and headed for home, satisfied with our effort to introduce Thanksgiving into the Lao culture.

Driving home that afternoon Boonpheng and Khamnouy talked about

Khamnouy Sivongsay and Judy Rantala preparing the village Thanksgiving feast in Boonpheng's mother's Lao house.

their friendship and how they had met through their school activities. This led us to quiz Khamnouy more closely about his family, where he was born and how he got to Vientiane. We knew his parents were in a village about sixty miles from Vientiane and that they were rice farmers. He had once brought his brother Khamnai to our home, and we knew there were other siblings. Now that we had met Boonpheng's family, we were curious to know more about Khamnouy's.

10
Village Visit and a Rescue

Seated in the plane, I white-knuckled the arm rests as I peered out at a fog so dense I could hardly see the wing tips. I was on my way to visit Khamnouy's parents in Phone Xay, airborne in one of Air America's trusty DC-6 planes. I knew that the pilot was making slow circles for I could occasionally see sharp peaks through the clouds. The side of a mountain loomed only inches from my window as the plane slowly curved away from it.

I had observed two helicopters taking off in Vientiane just before we did and knew that they too were circling in this space hoping the clouds would lift and allow them to find the pass that leads to the Ban Xon airfield. I trusted our pilot and the safety of the plane, but I was very nervous about there being so many aircraft flying in such a small space.

We banked to the left, and a sudden breach in the clouds showed me, hundreds of feet below, a lovely green valley. I could see the winding river and the rice paddies. The clouds closed in again, and I took a deep breath as I tried to convince myself that we would soon find our way to the airfield.

I was in this plane because USAID officials, in their wisdom, had decided it would not be safe for me, a dependent on this large military-economic aid post in Laos, to travel the road between Vientiane and Ban Xon. Of course they had allowed my husband to travel over the road in our blue Datsun, but the logic of which of us was more expendable escaped me. As I sat in presumed safety, trapped in this small plane "somewhere in Laos," I envied him the opportunity to see the Lao countryside and prayed that we would rendezvous as scheduled.

The village for which we were headed was the third that Khamnouy's parents had lived in as refugees and was approximately seventy miles from

Vientiane. All of the inhabitants were Sam Neua people who had been forced to migrate to this location where they again established their homes, grubbing out paddy fields with back-breaking exertion as they reconstructed their lives. For quite some time 'Nouy had been reminding us that his parents wanted us to visit them, and we were grateful to be able to accept the invitation.

John's job requirements and, more crucial, the current security status had kept us from leaving Vientiane for some months, but we had received the okay for this Saturday, and Khamnouy was guiding them on the road, even as I was being flown to meet them at the airstrip.

Suddenly the awaited break in the clouds materialized, and I could see the pass through which our pilot skillfully maneuvered the plane. Scanning the ground I saw a vehicle working its way up the narrow dirt road, and as we began our descent I identified a blue car. Despite distance and clouds, we were going to connect with near perfect precision. A smile broke over my face as I happily relinquished the puckery feelings encountered while circling in the clouds. I tightened the seat belt for the landing.

I had been at this airstrip before, and my first trip had also included a number of hair-raisers. At that time a Thai member of our American Women's Club Social Assistance Committee and I had brought eleven hundred sweatshirts to distribute to the children of the Hmong tribal groups who lived on nearby mountain peaks. This descent had none of the trauma of that previous helicopter landing on an area that had seemed about the size of a postage stamp.

No time now to reflect further on that expedition. As we came to a stop, there were John and Khamnouy, driving up to the apron. 'Nouy's sparkling smile beamed in my direction, excitement dancing in his eyes as I jumped down and transferred to the waiting Datsun.

"My village is about ten kilometers from here," 'Nouy explained as he directed us through the small village, past an active open market. As we crossed a creek he added, "This is where my father and I come to fish."

"Are there big fish?" I hoped to hear that the tiny river fish I sometimes saw in the market were not the only size the rivers afforded. Hands opened wide in the typical exaggeration of the proud fisherman, 'Nouy assured us that sizeable fish were here for the taking. I mused briefly on the wonders of nature and the wisdom of the Almighty, to provide this protein-poor country with abundant fish as well as soil that was especially right for the rice crops.

Fish is the major protein staple of the Lao. The bonier the fish, the better they seem to like it. A fishing trip was a day's excursion of pleasure second to none. In the Vientiane markets you could buy ocean fish, shipped

Sivongsay family in Phone Xay village, with neighbors, 1972 (Chanbounmy and Mai on left with children; Piavong and Tai next; Khamnouy standing behind and to right of Mai).

up from Thailand, but the Lao preferred river fish whenever they could get it. I dragged my thoughts back to the increasingly muddy road. It had been raining gently for some time, and now there was a steady downpour.

As I surveyed the gooey muck impeding our progress, I indulged in a few unkind thoughts about all of the American road building that was underway in this small, landlocked country and wished that this road had assumed some sort of strategic importance. American road graders and civil engineering expertise were applied liberally to roads of military importance. Perhaps it was just as well this was not one of them. A grinding of gears and our jolting stop informed me that we had gone as far as the car would take us.

"*Baw pen nyang.* Don't worry," Khamnouy said, assuring us that when we were ready to leave the people in his village would get us out. For now we would walk the quarter-mile remainder of the way.

The floor of the car was level with the mud as I clambered out, hiking up my shin-length Lao skirt to keep it clean, worn because I knew that seeing me in typical Lao dress would please my hosts. We sloshed down the road and then took to the side of a ravine in what Khamnouy assured us was a short cut.

We scrambled down a rocky, narrow trail and up the other side, all three of us by now soaking wet. My hair hung in limp strands, and I noticed orange rivulets coursing down my legs. The dye on my handwoven skirt material was bleeding!

The village was at the top of the other side of the ravine, achieved with considerable squishing and sliding. Folks came rushing to greet us, smiling and clasping their hands in the traditional *wai* before tugging us along the slick village paths. We were in the midst of approximately thirty stilt houses built of split bamboo, and at the far end of the village was a two-room building we learned was a school. A few scrawny chickens pecked aimlessly around the houses which were barren of grass and trees and even shrubs. It was still pouring rain, and the paths were treacherously slippery. I was ashamed to enter the family house with muddy feet, but they brushed aside my protestations and ushered me up the steps onto the verandah. At least I could shed the offending sandals at the door.

As I entered, my first impression was the starkness. There was absolutely no furniture, not even stools or mats. I was shocked at the barrenness of this home, and my eyes circled the bare walls until they rested on two young Caucasian men half reclining on the floor under a glassless window.

I could hardly believe my eyes. Who were they, and what were they doing here? We were introduced and urged to sit down on hastily brought mats by Khamnouy's mother, who smiled and bobbed and disappeared.

"Where in the world did you come from?" My astonishment replaced my manners.

The young men, one Norwegian, the other French, had met in Europe and had continued to travel together. In slightly accented English they explained that they had hoped to see the Plain of Jars, the scene of great archeological mystery as well as the seat of much of the recent fighting in Laos. "We were on our way to Sam Thong, hoping to see for ourselves those huge, ancient pottery jars."

The presence and purpose of huge containers in this area, some taller than the average man and several feet in diameter, remain a mystery to this day. Robbins' fliers in *The Ravens* support the common supposition that they were burial jars, but the fact that they are carved out of "a gray stone found nowhere in the region" (140) in an area that lacks a culture with a record of the use of such burial customs, leaves many questions still to be answered.

The young men grinned engagingly and continued to explain: "The military police stopped us, explaining that we must stop, because this area was off limits, so we came back down into the Ban Xon market. We were browsing around, wondering what to do next when Khamnouy spoke to us and invited us to come to stay with his parents." The young man's eyes were smiling and both of them seemed quite at home in this sparse refugee house.

They had been in Phone Xay for three days, guests of the Sivongsay family. They were humbled by the generous hospitality of these grimly poor villagers. Whatever there was was shared, and they had been made to feel thoroughly at ease. The graciousness of the welcome by this Lao family far exceeded anything they felt they might have learned or seen had they actually reached Sam Thong.

What, they asked me, could they do to show their appreciation? They suspected that if they offered money the family might feel insulted. They understood that the Sivongsays expected no payment and were merely behaving in a time-honored expression of Lao hospitality. I was gratified to realize that they seemed also to be fully aware of how rare an experience Khamnouy's friendliness had afforded them. Through him they had learned that their hosts lived in a barter economy where twenty-five dollars was probably their total yearly cash income.

I pondered the ticklish question of a material gift of thanks to their hosts and ventured, "I think you can give money to Khamnouy. He will not be offended, and he will see that it gets to his parents."

They were enormously relieved, and as we drank the orange soda offered as refreshment they said that this was by far the most gracious hospitality they had received in their months of travel across Europe and Asia. To be so received was also a tribute to their own sensitivities, for "world travelers" were now common all across Asia, and many of these young people offended people like the Lao, who are meticulously clean and well groomed, and who were shocked by the unkempt appearance of young people who were careless of their personal hygiene.

Gradually other village members came to meet and greet us. Never comfortable on the floor with crossed legs, I was offered a low six-inch stool to relieve my aching knees. My skirt was beginning to dry, and I had managed to comb and fix my hair, but my legs remained an interesting shade of orange.

John was happily talking with some of the men in the village, aided by Chanbounmy, the village school teacher and husband of Khamnouy's older sister, Mai. As I looked around it was easy to identify Khamnouy's siblings. The distinctive feature was their flashing brown eyes, inherited from their father. When they were excited their eyes danced with laughter and mischief. It was the first thing I had noticed when I met Khamnouy.

We knew that the Sivongsays would prepare a *baci,* and we were eagerly anticipating the traditional Lao foods that were served on such occasions: chicken with long rice and green onions, basil and other herbs; strips of beef which had been marinated and then dried and *lap* made with chopped chicken or fish, bean sprouts, hot peppers, long rice, cilantro and herbs I didn't know the names of. There would, of course, be sticky rice, *caow niow*, and all this would be washed down by the local rice wine I had already learned to imbibe with considerable caution.

What surprised us both was the realization that the preparations for our visit involved the entire village. Each family had contributed something to the feast, and everyone was there: giggling, active youngsters and older folks gnarled with arthritis, mothers with babes in arms and small children tending smaller children who were slung on their hips. Anticipation of the party shone in their faces. We met them all. How do I know? Because of the picture.

While there we took advantage of the opportunity to gather people together in the center of the village in order to take a photograph. Once the film was developed we gave a copy to Khamnouy and forgot about it, but that picture, taken to Minnesota by Khamnouy, has served to verify the kinship of each Sivongsay refugee family that has reached America. Every Minnesota Sivongsay home proudly exhibits a copy of this photo in a prominent place today.

In the picture John is standing next to Khamnouy, who is behind his brothers, as well as his parents and two uncles. Mai is holding a small infant with another little girl tugging at her skirt. Beside her stands her brown-haired school-principal husband, who in soft-spoken Lao and English had been translating questions and answers all afternoon. That photograph, reverently displayed in refugee homes in the United States, documents the success of the twelve-year struggle to reunite this family scattered because of the fall of Laos to the Pathet Lao and their Vietnamese Communist partners.

We enjoyed the *baci*, the feasting, the dancing and singing. A highlight was entertainment on the *khene* by Piavong, Khamnouy's father. The *khene* is an indigenous Lao musical instrument that is best described as a giant vertical pipe organ. Piavong's instrument was made of sixteen bamboo pipes or tubes the size of an index finger arranged back to back and about six inches in width. The pipes are mounted in a wooden windchest or "gourd" located in the midsection of the instrument. The instrument is slightly over three feet in length, and Piavong held it vertically by cupping his hands around the windchest and blowing into holes in the center.

Our host not only played this instrument, he demonstrated his skill by simultaneously performing a Lao dance. He began with solo steps, playing while turning inside his own arms and stepping over the held instrument while continuing to provide his own accompaniment. It was an amazing display of agility, skill and humor. Other Lao in the room were keeping time by beating their hands on the floor, and Khamnouy brought a metal pot from the kitchen with which he provided a drum accompaniment. All of us were swaying and tapping our feet, caught up in the exuberance of the moment.

Following Piavong's dance, the young people formed a double circle of couples, women in the center, for the *lamvong*, a gentle Lao dance in which the dancers moved forward to the beat of the music. The accompaniment was a simple, rhythmic melody with the *khene*, now supplemented with a tambourine-like instrument as people began to sing and clap. The dancers pivoted in place, turning in a small circle away from each other and moving their feet in time to the music, using a flexed and then straightened knee motion. As they moved they extended their arms away from their bodies and moved their wrists, hands and arms in a graceful, twisting motion. The *lamvong* is a slow-motion dance in which the circle moves counter-clockwise. It is also a very sociable dance during which the men and women flirt, joke and laugh and obviously enjoy themselves. It was not long before both John and I were ushered into the circle by Lao partners and instructed on the proper manipulation of our hands as we too became a part of the dance circle.

The party ended too soon, and we regretfully made preparations to return to our car and the mud. It was too late for an airlift back to Vientiane, which meant I would join John and Khamnouy in the Datsun. The men from the village cheerfully accompanied us back to our mired blue Datsun and with careful strategy, lots of joking and one mighty heave they picked up the car and put it on solid ground. We clambered in and began our journey home.

We left Khamnouy's village with an additional passenger, a young woman whose parents had asked if we would be willing to give her a ride into Vientiane where she would stay with relatives. She spoke no English and was very shy. Beyond a few murmured words with Khamnouy, she shrank into a corner and was silent. She seemed to be in awe of these loud, enthusiastic foreigners and grateful for a reassuring word now and then from a fellow Lao.

There were no villages along our route. We realized that the warnings about insurgents might well be accurate and knew we would be an easy target if someone wanted to stop us.

We bolstered our spirits with a few songs and rehashed the high points of the *baci*. I was still trying to figure out which of the people we had met were Khamnouy's relatives and which merely other Sam Neua refugees.

Kinship is a very flexible matter to the Lao who often seem to rely more on proximity and obligation than on blood ties.

As we traveled along the dusty road and negotiated a curve, I thought I caught a glimpse of a house with people on the porch. A large van was parked in front. We passed by so quickly that I was afforded only a brief glance, and it was such an unlikely place to see anyone that I was still pondering the possibility of it being a mirage when catastrophe struck.

Smoke began to pour from under the hood of our car.

"We're on fire! Get out!" John yelled as he slammed on the brakes.

We opened the doors and dove for the side of the road. Peering from the bushes we waited for the car to explode. The silence of the surrounding jungle magnified the pounding of our hearts. Suddenly flames began to snake out of the cracks and lick the edges of the hood.

Khamnouy chose this moment to break out and race to the car.

"I'm going to get the keys. I need to open the hood."

Before we could stop him he reached through the driver's side, grabbed the keys and dove back into the bushes.

The fire continued to burn. Still no explosion.

Khamnouy went gingerly to the trunk of the car and opened it with the key. I held my breath in horror.

In the trunk we kept a small hatchet, which Khamnouy grasped and then tiptoed around to the front of the car. Using the hatchet as an extension of his arm, he lay flat on the ground as he attempted to trigger the hood latch. The rest of us were paralyzed with fear. What if the whole thing blew up?

Regarding all this as just another lark, Khamnouy, eyes dancing with the excitement and danger of it all, kept calling to me, "Don't worry, Mom, don't worry."

Finally we heard the faint click of the latch. Pushing up the hood with the hatchet blade we could see, even from a distance, that smoldering wires were the cause of this carburetor fire. Scooping sand from the road, Khamnouy frantically dumped it on the motor and smothered the flames.

John, the young village girl and I were just emerging from the bushes when around the corner came a large white van. The driver skidded to a halt, and out tumbled an entire collection of good friends from Vientiane. Five adults, four children. It is hard to say who was more surprised. We had barely had time to even contemplate the predicament we were in—miles from a village—no way to communicate our plight to anyone—nearly dark—no other travelers on the road. The arrival of our friends seemed nothing short of a miracle.

We stared at each other in astonishment. The van belonged to

Puongpun Sananikone, and he had not only his wife and children with him, but two American USAID workers, one a member of the Hawaii contract team, and another Lao and his children.

Puongpun got in the first words. "What's going on? What's the matter with the car? What on earth are you doing way up here?"

"Where have *you* been?" I countered.

"Where did you guys come from?" John echoed my astonished query.

"How come you got here right now?" Khamnouy wanted to know.

Puongpun finally managed to break into the frenzy by saying, "We've been up here for a weekend outing. Fishing, camping, just having a good time. We saw your car go by a few minutes ago. "I told these guys. 'That was the Rantalas who just went by,' but they refused to believe me."

"What would they be doing here?" Art had challenged. He was a co-worker of John's in the Fa Ngum schools. Others had accused Puongpun of "seeing things."

"No, I tell you, it was the Rantalas. Let's go see."

Persuaded, they headed down the road to arrive just as Khamnouy had succeeded in putting out the fire.

"What are we going to do?" I asked. "The car is a disaster, and we're miles from Vientiane."

I glanced at our young Lao guest whose frightened eyes darted from one face to another. I could not imagine what she must be thinking about her chances of ever reaching her relatives in Vientiane.

Art Crisfield, a member of our Hawaii contract team, and his friend Bob were both USAID employees. They had been together in the Peace Corps in Thailand prior to coming to Laos. Their fluency in the Lao language and their identification with the Lao culture bonded them to their two Lao companions. Further, both Puongpun and his wife had attended the University of Hawaii on USIS scholarships during the 1960s and had known Art there.

Our other rescuer, Somsanith, also had been to America on a scholarship. He quickly took charge, assuring us that we were not very far from the village of Phone Hong.

We agreed that Khamnouy was the logical candidate to remain with the car. Someone venturing upon an unattended automobile might find the means to remove it, even in its crippled state, before we could ourselves arrive with assistance.

I had indulged in some fleeting fears that there might be some insurgents near us in that stretch of lonely road. If so, they must have been so astonished at the whole scene that they failed to attack. An automobile would be a fine consolation prize. Khamnouy thought it might be possible to get a tow from a passing truck, should one happen along. Not having seen either a bus or a truck during the entire return trip, I thought him unduly optimistic. *"Baw pen nyang,"* he said. It would all work out.

The rest of us were shoe-horned into the already loaded van, and we took off for Phone Hong. Once we reached the town, John and Puongpun agreed that they would try to find a means of getting back up the road to rescue the car and Khamnouy. The rest of us would continue on into Vientiane, deliver our extra passenger to her family, and be available for back-up help. The three men would have to seek their own accommodations in the village.

I reluctantly agreed to the plan, although I seriously doubted that they would find a tow in Phone Hong. Somsanith drove the van into Vientiane, following pointed fingers and hand signs from the girl in an effort to locate her relatives' house. She knew where the *pinong* lived, but had no idea about street names or locations. We wound through a series of alleys and small passageways at the end of which beaming smiles of welcome proved she had, indeed, found her waiting family. If they were surprised to see the mixture of Lao and Americans who delivered their niece, they were too polite to show it. We offered a brief explanation of who we were and where we had come from and left her to recount the lurid tale of trying to get to Vientiane from her village, Phone Xay.

I extracted promises from the Americans who dropped me off in Km6 to keep in touch, and late the next morning, John and the car appeared in the driveway. Still under tow, they had succeeded in finding help in Phone Hong but had waited until daylight to negotiate this leg of the trip. Examination showed that damage was minimal, and spare parts were available locally. The fire seemed to have been mostly electrical.

Within a few days the car repairs were completed, and we were sufficiently recovered to welcome the next opportunity to travel.

11
Close Ties with the Lao

During the 1960s and 1970s thousands of Americans were in Laos because of the incredibly tangled web of involvement spun by the U.S. State Department, the CIA and the U.S. Agency for International Development. Historians may explain our presence in Laos during those years in terms of military imperialism and twentieth-century colonialism.

A socialist, however, might refer to the deep personal attachments between individual Lao and individual Americans as characterizing this period. Respect, surprise, concern, discovery and genuine affection all describe our emotions as the Lao shyly invited us into their lives and their hearts. Experienced foreign service officers affirm that they formed deeper and more lasting relationships with the Lao than in any other overseas post. There was a uniqueness to the reciprocal generosity, the friendliness and the resulting bonding between Lao and American which has had a lasting effect on all of us who were there.

Perry Stieglitz speaks for many of us, writing of several years he spent in Laos in a book entitled *In a Little Kingdom.* He refers to a 1968 meeting of ten high-ranking Lao, including two ministers, and reflects:

> Being with them, listening to them, observing the manner in which they conduct themselves, made me again aware of the qualities that are so evident and so admirable among the inhabitants of this little kingdom: a quiet dignity, a sense of devoutness that comes through with no superficial or hypocritical piousness, a rich sense of humor that indicates a profound understanding and acceptance of life. Compassion is there but not flaunted, and sentimentality is avoided. [135]

Less than a week after our arrival in Laos we received an invitation to attend a social gathering at the home of the principal of the Fa Ngum school in Vientiane. Other team members said it would include a meal and that it would be an opportunity to meet most of the school staff. We were delighted with the prospect of going to a Lao home and upon our arrival at Somsak's house joined an already noisy and relaxed group.

This was our first visit to a Lao home, and while we felt quite sure he did not live in a bamboo stilt house, neither had anyone pointed out to us any Lao homes that reflected the colonial French architecture of the many houses occupied by Americans. We were, therefore, pleasantly surprised to be greeted at the doorway of a large stucco home with spacious rooms opening into each other on the first floor. A succession of Fa Ngum teachers was introduced, and the tongue-twisting Lao names rolled over us as we mingled with the guests, drinks in hand.

Dinner was served buffet style, and several friends hovered over me solicitously as I peered into pots and surveyed platters, attempting to determine the ingredients of various dishes. Hot chili peppers can send me into paroxysms of hiccuping, so I attempt to avoid them when I can. I was especially urged to try a "*baw si pet*—not too spicy-hot" chicken curry in which small eggplants, potatoes and carrots were easy to recognize. It was such a delicious concoction that I went for a second helping, especially appreciative of the delicate mixture of herbs including lemon grass and basil. There was, however, another herb I could not identify.

My host took particular interest in my enjoyment of this curry. Cocking his head with a mischievous grin on his face he gleefully suggested, "You probably are enjoying this so much, Mrs. Rantala, because it is cooked with marijuana." I looked at him in frozen surprise, to see if he was jesting. He in turn searched my face for the look of shock he fully anticipated. For a split second we stared at each other while I mentally digested the import of his announcement, my mind careening wildly through a kaleidoscope of thoughts: Would I begin to experience some euphoria? Did everyone use this herb in cooking? A chicken in every pot I knew about, but pot in every chicken? I began to giggle at my own cleverness.

"Aha, you see Mrs. Rantala, you must be careful about what you eat in foreign countries." His elfin grin indicated that he thought I was already slightly out of control.

A newspaper editor friend in Honolulu with whom I shared this incident in a letter passed the remark along to one of the columnists, causing the incident to become a quotable item in Honolulu for some time to come.

The friendliness of that evening gathering, and the eagerness of the teachers from Fa Ngum school to meet and get to know us were typical of most of the Lao. It was very clear that Americans and Lao liked each other and treated each other with great respect. The Lao hosted wonderful parties at which we danced and sang and enjoyed stories. We quickly learned that almost any slightly celebrative event would trigger such an evening of partying and gaiety.

Many of the Lao were eager to improve their English and were willing to attend classes at the Lao American Association where I and many others taught basic courses in English as a second language. Many Americans paid the English class tuition fee for our cooks and gardeners, as well as for students we knew whose careers would be enhanced by knowing better English. We saw it as a means of improving relationships all around and considered it a small but important gesture of support.

The men and women we employed quickly became our friends. We seldom thought of them as servants, and nearly all of us worked side-by-side in the kitchen with our cooks, learning from them how to prepare uniquely Lao vegetables and herbs while they in turn picked up clues from us about baking and American tastes in food.

I had arrived in Laos with a couple of packages of chocolate chips in my luggage and before testing my cook's baking expertise had made cookies that Souvanh and Khamnouy both enjoyed in great quantity. They begged and begged for more, but there was a long gap in the supply of these morsels in the commissary, so when some arrived in a box from home I triumphantly bore them into the kitchen and asked the cook to make a batch of cookies. He was good at reading recipes, and I happily went off to teach my afternoon LAA class with thoughts of fresh cookies urging me to return quickly.

Coming up the driveway several hours later I could smell the newly baked cookies and entered through the kitchen door, delighted to see them cooling on racks. I snatched one, munching as I took my books into the living room and dumped them in a chair, stopping in mid-stride.

Something was missing! Where were the chocolate chips? Had I picked up a cookie that somehow had been slighted? I went back for a second and had the same disappointment. No soft, chocolatey morsel around which to wrap my taste buds.

"Synouane," I called. "What happened to the chocolate chips?" He regarded me with astonishment. "Madame, they are *in* there."

"In *where*?" I held up three cookies. "I can't see any chips at all."

"*See*, them, madame?" He couldn't have looked more pained if I had physically struck him. "*See* them? When I mixed up the cookies there were all those big lumps and it took me more than an hour to crush them so that the batter would be smooth." He rubbed his aching arm.

In my haste to sample the cookies it had not occurred to me that my excellent cook had not watched me bake the earlier batch, and, having never seen a chocolate chip, he was blissfully unaware that the morsels were not meant to be smoothed out. The chips were in those cookies, all right, as tiny chocolate flecks that flavored the cookie, but they lacked the gustatory satisfaction that biting into a chocolate chip can give.

I did my best to soothe Synouane's injured feelings and vowed to be more attentive to my instructions and to any other cultural differences that might become major emotional crises.

Sakhorn, the cook who replaced Synouane two years later, was equally easy to work with, and about six months after coming to us he asked me if we could lend him enough money to help him set up an income-producing project that his wife could manage. They wanted to grow straw mushrooms, a "must" for nearly every Lao dish and in great demand in the market. He asked if he might borrow the initial needed capital from us, explaining how much he could set aside each month from his salary as repayment.

That evening I spoke to my husband about the request for a loan. None of our other employees had made such a request, and we were not quite sure if it was a wise move. We consulted with other team members and learned that most of them had loaned small amounts of money from time to time to pay the medical bills for a child, or to buy repair parts for a motorcycle, and even to fund the digging of a community fish pond to supply food fish for several families. We were told that very few Lao have credit with banks or money lenders, and that except for very unscrupulous usurers who charged exorbitant interest an ordinary citizen had no source of financial aid for family needs or small entrepreneurial efforts.

It was clear that to lend Sakhorn the money would be a wise and compassionate investment, and we negotiated a one-hundred-dollar loan which he promptly put to work in his straw mushroom effort. As soon as Ah Chong Zane and Iwao Kumabe, knowledgeable agriculturalists on the Hawaii team, heard about this project they went with Sakhorn to his home and pitched in to construct the straw mounds, offering both advice and sweat equity, which Sakhorn accepted with enthusiasm.

In the yard of his house they mounded straw to a height of about two and one-half feet, and into this they placed the mushroom spores purchased in the market. It seemed nothing short of miraculous that within a few weeks Sakhorn's wife had a flourishing business, reaping up to three kilograms of mushrooms a day to sell in the morning market. It was a very welcome supplement to his salary and was used to pay the fees required to send his children to school. Universal free education was not available in Laos, but this family was determined to make the necessary sacrifices to educate their three children.

Sakhorn repaid us a specified amount each month until the debt was canceled. We were delighted to have this small part in supporting his goal of educating his children and grateful to be able to do it in a manner which was dignified and acceptable, smacking neither of charity nor of a handout. It seemed very short-sighted of American USAID efforts that similar small loans could not be offered. The USAID considered them too small to bother with and so effectively cut off 90 percent of the population from pursuing individual farming and business efforts which might well have defused the appeal of the Communists.

Myrtle Collins advanced the education of Lao children in another equally important way. Each year several Lao children were admitted to the American school on a space-available basis, and as the end of the Royal Lao Government came nearer, Myrtle, the principal of this school, worked day and night to collect the scholastic records of each Lao child who had attended. Wherever possible, she also wrote letters of recommendation to schools outside of Laos in order to help these youngsters escape the almost certain repressive influence of the new Communist-oriented government. Dozens of young people were saved from work details and re-education camps by the tireless efforts of the American school personnel.

Another avenue of financial aid to education for the Lao came from the American Women's Club Social Assistance Committee, which often received requests for scholarships to aid youngsters seeking to study abroad. We gave special consideration to the young people who came from families of very moderate means and gave several substantial grants over a period of several years.

"What about Khamnouy?" one of the members of the committee inquired one day, referring to our efforts to send him to Wisconsin to pursue a curriculum in industrial arts education.

I reported, "We are doing all we can—you know his parents have no money at all." But I was grateful that the group was aware of the financial burden his education would place on us.

"I suppose you wouldn't ask us for a scholarship yourself, since you are a committee member."

I had to admit that it didn't seem proper, and had so far kept silent.

"Ask Khamnouy to come to meet with us next week. You just stay away and let us determine if he deserves a scholarship. Help him fill out our usual request forms and insert all costs for both travel and the university fees."

It was with considerable suspense that I awaited news from Khamnouy the evening of his interview. We were fairly well set to cover his tuition and college fees, but had of necessity been searching for the lowest available direct travel routes between Vientiane and Wisconsin. The members of the

AWC Social Assistance Committee reviewed his application and granted him an eleven-hundred-dollar travel scholarship, allowing him to see other parts of the United States before he settled down in the Midwest. It was a generous offer that rewarded Khamnouy's scholastic efforts and recognized his potential. We were delighted that he now would have an opportunity to stop off on the West Coast as well as be able to travel through several national parks on his way to college. It was mind-boggling to try to imagine what a young man who had never traveled more than a hundred miles from his birth village in a landlocked mountain kingdom would think about as he experienced flying for hours over an ocean he had never before seen, discovered how terribly far Laos is from the United States and encountered the vastness and variety of terrain in this country to which we were sending him.

There were many ways in which Americans bonded with the Lao. Marge and Jack Huxtable both spoke fluent Lao and formally adopted two orphaned Lao children while they were still living in Laos. Although John and I did not formally adopt Khamnouy, by Lao custom and due to the deep personal ties formed with him and between his family and ours, we have always thought of him as a son. Every family on our Hawaii team took a great interest in the Lao who worked for and with them. It was not uncommon to have a mixture of Lao and Americans at social events, and we were invited to countless functions that marked important passages in Lao family life—births, marriages, even death.

Khampheng had become our friend, indeed as a daughter to us, shortly after she began to instruct us in the Lao language. It was a comfortable next step to accompany her to her home where her parents incorporated us into their household with quiet graciousness. We used sign language to communicate with her mother and father but found them always welcoming and pleased to see us when we visited. We were, therefore, most distraught to learn of her father's illness which very quickly resulted in his untimely death.

Khampheng insisted that we join the family for the observance of his funeral rites, gently communicating that she needed us there for personal support and that her family would fully expect us, as adjunct family members, to be present. On the day of the final ceremony the first thing I noticed after arriving at her house was that Khampheng was dressed wholly in white, in a rough, plain cotton shift that had no belt and an uneven hem, giving it an unkempt, ragged appearance. She wore no makeup and had little white rags tied into her hair.

"The women do the mourning at a Lao funeral. I cannot make myself look attractive in any way, and I cannot touch or be touched by any man—

not even my little boy, Nono." She had informed us of this custom as she stopped by our Km6 home to tell us about the death and what the next days would hold for her. At that moment she had not only been grieving the passing of her gentle father, but she also was terribly worried about the expenses connected with the traditional observances conducted in the home prior to the cremation.

Following a death, a Lao family keeps open house twenty-four hours a day, and neighbors, friends and relatives drop in at any hour. "When do you sleep?" I asked her, noting, "You look exhausted now, and this all sounds so terribly demanding."

Khampheng indicated that there really was little she could do to avoid the rigors of the next three days of mourning by shrugging her shoulders in the familiar Lao *baw pen nyang* (not to worry) gesture. "We are expected to provide drinks and food for all of the guests as they come to pay respects, and it is not the custom for others to bring such items with them."

Khampheng didn't need to explain further—I could see she was desperate for cash, and I emptied my purse, fortunately having the equivalent of about two hundred dollars available to give her. With this money she purchased endless cases of soft drinks, expensive in Laos, but expected by the visiting neighbors, family and friends.

John and I went to her home on the third day following the death where it was immediately apparent to us that her one-year-old child, Nono, did not comprehend the restriction that forbade his mother to touch any male, including him. Nono ran from one woman to another, holding out his arms to his grandmother, his aunt, the young girl who was his live-in nursemaid, but none of them would hold him. He reacted to the rejection with loud wails and screams which his father did his best to comfort, but with only sporadic success. I found the prohibition against his being comforted by any woman both distressing and incomprehensible, but I was a guest in another culture and I needed to keep my observations to myself.

As the home ceremonies drew to a close, and the more formal ceremonies were about to begin, John and I joined the other mourners who surrounded a wooden coffin, which was elevated in the center of the living room and was surrounded with flowers. In Laos and in Thailand, *dok champa,* plumeria, are flowers symbolic of death, and they were everywhere in this room.

Sitting in a row at the head of the coffin were three monks clad in saffron robes, their posture the lotus position, intoning endless chants. By custom the family had been obligated to supply them with gifts such as a new robe, a rice bowl, or bedding, all of which were resting in piles on the floor next to the monks. On the opposite side of the room the women, designated mourners according to Lao custom, were dressed in white and were kneeling or sitting with legs tucked under their bodies, crying and wailing. Those of us who were friends and neighbors shuffled into the room in a crouching position to avoid the insult of allowing our heads to be higher than those of the monks, and seated ourselves on the straw mats on the floor to the left of the women.

There is no such thing as embalming in this hot country, so that already there was some odor of decaying flesh. From our position between these two groups, John and I looked back and forth from Souvanh to Khampheng, trying to pick up clues as to what was expected of us. Fortunately we could detect no special requirements, so we knelt and observed and sweltered.

At a signal from the head monk we all rose, and the coffin was carried out of the house and placed on a wooden cart along with many of the father's possessions which were to accompany him into the next world. All of us followed this heavy cart, pulled by a succession of men for over a quarter of a mile through small dirt alleyways that were rutted and bumpy, to the large temple where a very tall funeral pyre had been readied. With an increasing crescendo of wailing and chants, the coffin was hoisted to the top of the pyre, the fire lit, and the entire conflagration surrounded by the mourners.

I tried to see Khampheng's face across on the other side of the pyre where she sat with the women. The fire roared and crackled and mesmerized me with the mixture of symbolism and reality. I had only the most superficial knowledge of the Buddhist teachings about individual death, so I silently applied my Christian teachings to the scene. "Dust to dust, ashes to ashes." "Lord, into thy hands we commend his spirit." How much merit toward Nirvana, I wondered, had this gentle man accumulated, or was that even a proper question to ask? I was aware that probably neither Khampheng nor Souvanh would be able to answer my many questions, not just because of language differences, but, and more importantly, because of our cultural differences. From my past efforts to glean explanations for why certain rituals were followed, I had learned that they seldom had a clearly articulated explanation for why certain funeral rites and customs were followed, or what, indeed, they expected after death. Intense philosophical musing and even current political observations and deductions are a luxury that people who have limited access to written language and even less access to spare time can ill afford. These two young people were both bright and educated, but their life-style was a basically hand-to-mouth continuous effort to supply the daily needs of a large, extended family and did not allow them to spend time to ponder obscure philosophical or theological questions.

We sat through the intense heat of the flames that was so searing we occasionally had to move quickly as the wind shifted, sending ashes and flames too close to be endured. We watched the flames slowly consume first the coffin and then its swaddled contents, until at last the pyre collapsed in on itself. We knew the monks would later collect the cooled ashes of the deceased which would then be preserved in an urn. In a few minutes Khampheng's second brother would enter the monkhood for a period of three months, a practice usually expected of the eldest son, who in this family was unable to be at the ceremony because of his obligations toward the currently stepped-up military actions in other parts of the country.

After the cremation we accompanied everyone back to the house for more food and drinks, but soon took our leave, feeling both grateful and slightly guilty to be able to retreat to the coolness of our Km6 air conditioning.

Our very comfortable American-style homes were easy to entertain in, and within a few months of our arrival John and I faced the fact that we were long overdue in returning the many invitations we had received to other people's homes and parties. We talked with the cook and planned a large evening gathering to which at least seventy-five people were invited. On the afternoon of the party, as I was dashing around, checking on the myriad details connected with such an event, I was astonished to find several Lao in the kitchen busily helping my cook. Here was the girl from next door, as well as the Zanes' cook and several others I recognized from the neighborhood, chopping, brewing, making spring rolls, laughing and having a great time.

I stopped in my tracks, astounded to see all this unsolicited assistance so cheerfully employed.

"What in the world . . ." I began.

"Oh Madame, *baw pen nyang,* not to worry. They will not have to cook at home tonight, so they have come to help me." Synouane grinned happily at this turn of events and waved me out of the kitchen. I was delighted at the influx of this gratuitous labor, although I fully intended to slip them some extra cash to thank them for their help. "Not necessary," I was advised by one neighbor, whom I ignored, since these men and women could just as easily have taken the evening off leaving Synouane to fend for himself. It was heartwarming confirmation of the generous and self-giving nature of the Lao and touched me deeply.

Just as the Lao could make the chores of cooking for a large group of people into an evening of laughter and cooperation and celebration, so also they exhibited a special affinity for festivals of all kinds. They loved parties, and as guests in their country, we were welcomed into every feast day and festival held throughout the year.

We first participated in the *Loy Krathong* festival during a visit to Ban Houie Sai. I remember it as one of the most charming evenings of my life. Called *Lai Heua Fai* (Drifting Boats of Fire) in Laos, it observes a custom in which little boats carrying a candle or a lamp are released on the water at night. Falling on the full moon of the twelfth lunar month, it is a late fall festival, the evening tending to be slightly crisp and cool.

The Mekong River divides Laos from Thailand in this corner of the country which provides the festival with a double complement of participants as both Thai and Lao ready their boats for the evening.

We walked through the town in the afternoon, marveling at the intricate construction of many of the boats, not all of them small—in fact some several feet long—with dragons painted on the sides and sails of colored tissue paper held by bamboo poles. These craft were lovingly decorated with great care and intensity, and we were astounded to realize how many boats were being prepared.

The launching of these small boats began at dusk. Those who send them off may have one of several explanations for why they are doing it. Some feel the boats represent the footprints of the Lord Buddha on the banks of the Yamuna River in India. The Japanese who follow this custom believe that it is time for the souls of the dead who have been visiting on earth to return to heaven, and that these small, lighted boats will show them the way. The Lao who joined us that evening believed they could place their bad luck in the boat, depending on the current to sweep it away and in its place bring new hope and good luck to the family. Whatever the motive or the mythology, the effect was magical.

We sat on a bank high above the swift-flowing Mekong as thousands of fairy lights bobbled and danced along below us. We could identify the few large dragon boats we had seen under construction earlier in the day as they rounded a bend above us and blazed down on the swift current. Tiny, but just as brave, were hundreds of miniature craft, each candle cleverly shielded so that the light continued to gleam until the boat disappeared far down the river.

What can describe the fairyland quality of this sight? I was transported far beyond myself, beyond Laos, away from anything I had ever known before, lost in the mystery and the ethereal translucence of these tiny expressions of hope for the living and the dead. These fairy craft were fashioned with reverence and love and sent off with the conviction of better days to come, and we spectators sat in hushed contemplation, silently launching our own failures and acknowledging our own hopes and dreams, joining in spirit these glowing symbols as they mingled and drifted away into an unknown future.

Nights of fairy-lit boats and memories of days of earlier races on the rivers came to an abrupt end in May of 1975, but the most telling proof of the strength of the relationship between Americans and the Lao was played out in the aftermath of the fall of the country to the Communists. Any Lao who had in any way been connected to Americans was suspect, whether cook or professional counterpart, student or teacher. Hundreds and thousands of Lao, eventually 10 percent of the population, fled across the Mekong River to avoid punishment, incarceration in re-education camps and death.

Within a few months following our own precipitous return to the United States, even before we settled into our new routines, we began to receive heart-rending messages from former employees, counterparts and good friends who were now crowded into refugee camps and who turned to us asking for asylum. They were not turned away. From Maine to Texas, Hawaii to Minnesota, Florida to Oregon, those of us who had lived in Laos responded by sponsoring Lao in order to enable them to reach freedom and start a new life. We lobbied the U.S. Immigration and Naturalization Service through our congressional representatives seeking liberalized immigration rules in order to make provisions for the men and women who had supported American efforts in Laos. We talked to church groups, hounded landlords to find reasonably priced apartments, set up language and job training programs and met endless special refugee flights from Bangkok.

One of the most poignant resettlement stories involves the Thai Dam people, who days before the fall of Laos poured into Vientiane and tried to cross the river. We accompanied Marge Huxtable by driving out the Thadeua Road to a makeshift staging area in which the Huxtables' long-time cook, nanny and friend, Ba Lai, was awaiting transport. Tears coursing down her lined face, we clutched each other through the fencing. "We have fled three times from the Communists, starting at the Chinese border. We will never live in a Communist country. We *must* leave, please don't forget me." Eyes blinded by our own tears, we stumbled back to the car, uncertainty, anguish and despair mingled with our respect for this strong, principled woman we might never see again.

All of the Thai Dam went to the same refugee camp in Thailand from which they began a letter-writing campaign. They wrote to every governor of every state in the Union, asking to be taken as a group so that they would not have to be split up as a people. Individuals such as Ba Lai, who might have been sponsored by a single family, turned down the offer in order to preserve the tribal coherence. Art Crisfield from our Hawaii team helped immeasurably in this tortuous writing and waiting process by assisting with the wording and mailing of letters. The governor of Iowa was so touched by their story that he made it possible for the Thai Dam to emigrate to Des Moines and its environs. The governor's actions enabled this tribal group to remain together and preserve their identity.

The drama of this story caught media attention and was told in a number of news articles and TV clips. For those of us who had poignant and positive memories of our years in Laos, it confirmed that at least some Americans were aware of their interconnections with the Lao and recognized an obligation to help relocate those people who had rallied to what became *our* cause in Laos. That they were not turned away reflects not only years of Lao hospitality and the surfacing of an American conscience, but the depth of the relationships with these very special people.

12
Sweatshirts and Lepers

The mountain peaks stood out sharp and clear in the morning sunlight as the helicopter circled around in preparation for our descent.

"That's our landing site."

Craning my neck to look several hundred feet down I was shocked to see what a small area the pilot was pointing out. From where I sat this mountaintop space appeared to be the size of a small handkerchief.

My companion, a Thai woman married to an American employee of the USAID mission in Laos, gulped, and we pulled our seat belts tighter. Boon was a diminutive woman, carefully groomed and with a ready smile. She had agreed to accompany me on this trip when I convinced her that it would be helpful to have a Lao-speaking person along. It was only on the site that we realized these people spoke only their own language, which wasn't Lao, and by that time she couldn't turn back.

Nearing the ground we could see people scattering into the bushes as our rotors kicked up dust and grasses. Crouching, we disembarked and ducked under the blades. Men and women filtered out of the bushes to help with unloading, smiling their greeting. Our interpreter said we would radio when we wanted him to return, and the pilot then took off while we also ducked into the bushes to avoid the whirlwind.

Boon and I were members of the Social Assistance Committee of the American Women's Club of Laos. We had been authorized to spend a thousand dollars to buy warm clothing for the ill-clad children who lived in Pung Moh, a village that could only be reached by footpath or helicopter. Through shrewd bargaining at Talat Saow, the morning market, Boon had secured eleven hundred sweatshirts in small sizes. These, and the interpreter loaned to us by USAID, had been stashed behind our seats in the tiny bubble helicopter which had flown us from the Ban Xon airfield to this Hmong village high up in central Laos.

The Hmong are hill tribesmen from southern China who began to arrive in Xieng Khouang in the late 1850s. They developed a slash-and-burn style of agriculture, cutting trees and burning them and then planting among the stumps. Within three to five years the land was no longer agriculturally productive and they would move. In *Voices from the Plain of Jars,* Branfman documents a familiar phrase, "Seven times around the mountain" which is descriptive of this swidden agricultural lifestyle (8). Only recently had Christian missionaries begun to provide a written form of the Hmong language, and most villages were both extremely isolated and extremely poor.

Once we had unloaded our goods from the helicopter, the first item on the agenda was hospitality. Following the Hmong village chief, we picked our way down a narrow dirt path to his home. Their poverty was evident in the ragged clothes of the people who crowded around us. A lack of iodine in their diet showed in the large goiters many of them had on their necks. On this stark, windy mountaintop food for an adequate diet must have indeed been hard to find. Edgar "Pop" Buell, a former Indiana farmer who had volunteered for International Voluntary Service and then became the most ardent champion of USAID to the Hmong, estimated that by 1970 somewhere between fifty- and a hundred-thousand Hmong had been relocated to similar isolated mountaintops.* It was he who had recommended to the American Women's Club that we choose this village as a recipient of our assistance.

A five-minute trek down the path behind our nimble leader brought us to a small hut. Several women and children were squatting in the doorway, and inside the low-ceilinged room a small graying woman quickly put a kettle on to boil over open coals on a floor fireplace. Soon tea was brewed and offered to us in cups encrusted with dirt and grime. Rolling my eyes at my companion I inwardly prayed that the boiling liquid would dispatch some of the bacteria that must surely be living on those cups.

Simultaneously I began to be aware of sharp, stinging bites around my midsection and legs. Fleas! They obviously were inhabiting the ancient couch I had been surprised to find in this room. As I sat on its greasy, infested blankets, I tried not to scratch. We nodded, drank our tea, talked

**A more detailed account of the relocation of the Meo from the Long Cheng-Sam Thong area is found in the chapter "Presidential War in Laos, 1964–1970," by Fred Branfman in Adams and McCoy,* Laos: War and Revolution, *pp. 251–53.*

Lao hill tribal people in native dress.

with our hands, smiled, and itched! Gratefully we sprang to our feet when our host indicated we could now return to the business of giving out our precious cargo.

Back up the path we went, to find the entire child and female population of the village patiently awaiting our reappearance. The long queue in which they were standing seemed oddly out of place in this windy, untamed setting. We set the men to opening boxes and a procession of small children paraded past us. Some were stark naked. Others wore a ragged t-shirt. Few seemed dressed warmly enough for the brisk temperature of this four-thousand-foot elevation. Brown, shy eyes looked at us, small grubby hands reached out. We placed a sweatshirt in each proffered set. The designs with frogs, fish and other animals, all in bright colors, brought smiles of delight to the children's faces as they solemnly filed by. Each child grasped his or her prize firmly and ran to mother.

Finally the last child straggled by. To our astonishment, a line of pregnant women now filed past, each expectant mother smiling and pointing to her swollen belly. The coming child would also need warmth. We grinned our understanding and gave out additional sweatshirts.

When everyone had received something, we found ourselves still with two hundred garments undistributed. Our interpreter suggested we call in

Black Tai tribal dress.

the helicopter and visit a second village. In another flurry of dust and noise and confusion we boarded the whirlybird and flew for about ten minutes to a second mountaintop. These folks were Black Tai, and they could not possibly have expected us, so we surmised that their very elaborate and distinctive clothing was everyday wear. Each woman wore a colorful red and black pleated skirt which reached just below the knee and a red and black turban-like headdress. The skirt material was hand-loomed and very intricate, and there was also embroidery on the borders. Their clothing reminded me of Scottish kilts.

Our arrival brought out a crowd of curious villagers, all of them dressed in their elaborate tribal clothes. Once our mission was described we were again treated to a line of eager children as we happily gave away the remainder of our goods. As we looked around this site I was struck by the airstrip. Arriving in a helicopter, we had not needed a runway, yet there was obviously a landing strip for conventional planes. But what a strip! Its landing edge was at the top of a two-thousand-foot cliff that was a sheer drop to the jungle below. The runway was like a ski jump on which the plane landed at the bottom, roared up the hill, and was grabbed by an agile ground crew who literally prevented it from crashing into the trees.

We looked at all this with great interest because the helicopter pilot had told us that we would not have to return to Ban Xon because an Air America plane would come for us and fly us straight back to Vientiane. Well maybe, I thought with considerable apprehension; the take-off looked pretty iffy to me! We were in this village less than an hour when the conventional plane did, indeed, land on that incredible runway, inches from a cliff, roared up the rocky approach to be arrested and turned around by many willing hands. Within minutes the plane catapulted down again with us as passengers. Thirty minutes later the level Wattay airfield in Vientiane was a most welcome sight.

I recalled all of this several months later when I had gone to the airport to meet my husband, who had spent the week in Luang Prabang. When his plane failed to arrive I made inquiries and learned that he had left Luang Prabang. Where was he, then? To tell the truth, Air Support didn't know! For more than three hours I fretted, visions of plane crashes filling my head. Nearly every week planes got shot down or slammed into cliffs. Accidents were common in Laos.

When the LP plane finally arrived I was greeted with, "You'll never guess where I've been. We left Luang Prabang with instructions to drop a load of medicine off at a tribal village, and you should see the runway! We landed on something that looked like a ski jump, hit a rock, blew a tire, and ended up hanging half way over a cliff. It's the closest call I've had here in Laos. Fortunately the local folk saved us from disaster."

The pilot had threatened to quit on the spot when a box he was unloading was inadvertently damaged revealing that it did not contain medicine but was a case of liquor. The pilot was furious at the risks he had been ordered to take, pacing back and forth while they waited for a rescue plane to bring in a new tire and replace the blown one. The delay provided them with plenty of time to anticipate the wonderful ski-jump effect of gunning down the steep hill, hoping to gain enough air speed to avoid just dropping off the cliff.

I listened with increasing recognition until my husband finally paused for breath whereupon I grinned at him and said, "Ah, but I *do* know where you have been. I've been there myself! I delivered a more acceptable cargo, sweatshirts."

John's oft-repeated phrase "without risk there is no adventure" took on added meaning as we compared notes about our visits to this mountain village. Our adventures not only helped us learn something of the isolation, customs and hospitality of tribal groups, but through them we also became more fully aware of the devious political influences at work in this beautiful, beleaguered country.

A quite different village visit came when we had the opportunity to travel together to Ban Houei Sai, in northeastern Laos. There, a chance question to the fathers in the local Catholic Mission School led to an invitation to attend a *baci* for the *nai ban*, or chief of a remote village. As we approached the area we found the village nestled in a lush, sloping valley fronting on a narrow stretch of the Mekong River.

Strategically built into the sunny hillside were approximately twenty new, spacious Lao bamboo houses. They were larger than many of the Lao village homes we had previously seen and were designed to allow for maximum air circulation. The houses were designed for ease of access, and the entire village was attractive, neat and well kept—noteworthy because it was so new. A gush of clear mountain water rushed out of a two-inch pipe in the very center of the village. Serving as a place for securing water for each family, it also doubled as a watering place for animals and a shower for a hot, dusty worker. As I looked at this unusual central and safe source of water I recalled that the American Women's Club had granted a request to finance a project to pipe water into a village and a quick question confirmed that this was the village. It had been money well spent.

The uniqueness of this village stemmed from its inhabitants. Forty of them were lepers* and the other sixty were members of their families. None of them had originally lived in this area. They had moved here approximately eighteen months before our visit, and since that time a phenomenon of faith, trust and love had created not just a group of houses but a true community. "When the people came," reminisced Father Tony in soft-spoken Lao, "they kept saying, *'Koi baw me khon.'* I'm not a person." The ravages of their disease, their ostracism by others in their home village and general feelings of hopelessness had slowly led to a state of almost total apathy. They could hardly do anything for themselves. They were sullen, depressed, dirty; indeed, they had sunk close to being nonpersons.

To learn the depth of the villagers' original negative self-image after experiencing their cheerful, bustling activity in the several hours since we had arrived in this newly created village heightened our wonder at the transformation. We had been escorted by five of the eight Catholic priests in the area and joined by two nuns. All were Italian Roman Catholic missionaries. The village had organized itself into a community that boasted both a male and a female *nai ban* as well as an assistant. It was the first time we had seen a woman acting as a village official, and we were impressed with the manner in which her participation as a leader of the *baci* ceremony was accepted. All three of these individuals suffered from leprosy, but they were on medication that would eventually arrest its progress.

All of us, priests, nuns, guests and villagers, sat in the cool *sala* to participate in the *baci.* We learned that some of the badly disfigured members were ashamed to come into the open while we *farangs* were present. The priests assured us that it was better to have us participate with those who were there than to leave in order to accommodate the absent members. Our departure might easily be misinterpreted as rejection.

The *baci* was both solemn and festive, and the supplies of *lau hai* and *lau lau* were pressed on all participants with typical good humor and insistence. Father Tony's heartwarming speech in Lao congratulated the two new *nai bans* and wished them luck, with a sprinkling of the humor only good friends can share. It was a testimony to the mutual respect and comradeship that existed between the villagers and their Italian mentor.

Two things intrigued and touched us deeply: the growing self-sufficiency of the villagers, and the quiet dedication of the priests. Neither group asked us for anything. The villagers were learning to do all the tasks their

**Only Tom Dooley in* The Edge of Tomorrow, *p. 149, mentions the ravages of leprosy among the Lao. It seems strange that this disease is not mentioned in other materials which have extolled the setting up of dispensaries both by the Pathet Lao and by the Royal Lao Government, and, more recently, the Lao People's Democratic Republic.*

bodies would allow them to perform including the maintenance of all aspects of living. This village was as totally self-help as it could be. Garden areas were soon to be cleared, and within a few months they would begin to build a school. In the meantime, USAID and the Royal Lao Government were aiding the village with food and clothing. The healthy children were going to school in a neighboring village. The residents fished in the river and indicated with widely stretched arms the size of a large fish caught just the previous day.

After many toasts and expressions of goodwill we were invited by our new Italian friends to join them for a meal in Fr. Tony's house. This house had been provided by the RLG which had also built a dispensary and was constructing a small store. There was a Lao medic on duty in the village, and he, too, would soon have his own quarters. Medicines which arrest leprosy were provided by the Royal Lao Government, but the materials for those sturdy Lao houses had been purchased with money sent from Italian parishes. Each house bore the name of the parish and the village from which the money had come.

Our delicious lunch, topped off with real Italian espresso, was cooked by a young Lao girl who had been trained by Sister Patricia, the lone nun in Ban Houei Sai. Our other female companion had come for the occasion from her post in Chiang Rai, Thailand. The deep spiritual commitment and camaraderie of this group of men and women were to be envied.

I was deeply touched by everything we had seen and done this day, and one small incident indicated to me that my feelings were shared. During lunch there had been difficulty in opening a bottle, and John had whipped out his trusty boy scout knife to deal with the offending cap. He must have caught the look of wistfulness on Father Tony's face. He certainly had observed the spartan accommodations and the lack of even bare essentials in the priest's quarters. He finished his task, took the knife, and handed it to Father Tony. "I would like to leave this with you. Perhaps you can find a use for it." Fr. Tony's face lit up in pure joy, and thanking John profusely he reverently took the knife and laid it beside his missal. I knew what the knife meant to John, who never left the house without it securely in his pocket. I also knew that these two men were communicating at a level deeper than words about life and caring and sharing. I bit my lip to stem the quick tears that stung my eyelids.

Our visit had a profound effect on us both. As we departed from this oasis of laughter and caring and mercy hidden in the far mountains of Laos, we contrasted it with the villages in which the war was creating bitter divisions and untold suffering. We acknowledged the dedicated service of an obscure priest, thousands of miles from home and country, and knew we too had benefitted from his selfless ministry.

13
Forest Creatures and Festivals

My husband's job often took him away for several days at a time, either north to Luang Prabang, or south to Pakse or Savannakhet, areas which I at first visited vicariously during evenings when he would regale me with stories of what he had seen and done. A phone call from the area coordinator telling me when his flight was expected would alert me to drive to the airport to pick him up. Delayed planes were always a cause for some anxiety, and on a day I recall very clearly I had been hanging around the airport for an hour, relieved when his plane landed and he appeared at the debarkation steps.

In his hands were his briefcase and a crudely woven basket which he held out to me as he strode across the tarmac. In it was a tiny, perfect deer with soft brown eyes, velvety ears and a moist brown nose. It was small enough to fit into my cupped hands. "Where on earth did you get this? Will it survive? Is it a he? Can we keep it?" The questions tumbled out.

Lifting him gently from the basket I held him close to my chest, hoping the warmth would be reassuring enough to calm his violent shivering. He was so small and so beautiful, and his huge, brown liquid eyes pleaded for gentleness.

The story was simple. John had been eating lunch in a small noodle shop in Luang Prabang when a Lao approached offering him this captive baby deer. "Five thousand kip."

"Baw peng lai." Too expensive. "Two thousand kip." John's bargaining response had become automatic.

"Baw dai!" Can*not!* *"Tuk lai."* Too cheap. The man left, indignant at not being able to persuade this foreign victim of the worth of his prize.

John and Judy Rantala with Herky, a barking deer.

John, with no intention of buying a deer, returned his attention to his plate of noodles. Five minutes later the same man returned. Thrusting the basket into John's hand he announced, "Yours."

Too astonished to demur, John fished out two thousand kip (approximately four American dollars), and the man left. Since there was still work for him to do in Luang Prabang he persuaded the wife of a colleague to assume custody of the deer until he departed the next day.

As soon as we arrived home I fixed a basket and placed a hot water bottle in it to give the still quaking deer the assurance of being close to a warm body. I had now learned that our newcomer was a little girl deer, and although I offered her milk from the bottle that John had worn in his shirt pocket, it was clear that she was not yet able to master the baby bottle. I spooned milk into her from a teaspoon for several days and was relieved when she began to gain strength.

Now that she had a home and was settling into our Km6 routine, she needed a name. Before we knew she was a girl, John had started to call her Herkimer. We failed to find a more feminine name and so shortened this to Herky, a name she seemed to begin to recognize, for when we called she would respond with appreciative squeaks. I found myself responding with what I tried to fashion as similar squeaks, and Herky and I began to communicate through this apparently mutual language.

We had no idea what kind of deer she was nor how big she would grow. One of the Lao identified her as a barking deer, a species that when fully grown is not much bigger than a good-sized dog. He assured us she would be no taller than three and a half feet high. Herky thrived on milk, which she soon learned to take from the baby bottle, and after about six weeks began to strip the reachable leaves off our fruit trees in the yard. We began to supplement her diet with leaves and grasses we foraged from other areas.

She was truly the most unusual pet we ever owned and a real charmer. Nocturnal, these animals come to life at dusk. Every evening during dinner she would streak past the dining room windows as she charged around and around our house. The children in the neighborhood begged to come in to pet and play with her. She in turn developed a form of tag that sent the kids into ecstasy. One day the woman across the street came over with her two-year-old, who was well acquainted with the deer. The tot ran toward Herky, who dug in her hooves and charged straight at the little boy. Just as a collision seemed unavoidable the deer soared over the head of the laughing youngster who had played this game before. His mother fainted dead away, and it was several days before she allowed the boy to return again to play tag with Herky.

Herky became *my* deer through our feeding routine. She had been found as a baby beside her dead mother, a victim of Lao hunters. As soon as she could stand on her spindly legs she developed a pattern of butting her head into my thigh before she would nurse. Black and blue from this treatment, I nevertheless became used to it and thought nothing of it until John and I went to Bangkok for three days, leaving Synouane, our servant, in charge of feeding Herky in our absence.

We returned to find a frantic cook and a weak deer. Herky had refused to take a bottle from Synouane, who was beside himself with worry. "She won't drink the milk. I've tried everything." His voice and eyes pleaded with me to believe him and not to become angry. As soon as I took the bottle Herky trotted to me, butted my leg for a minute and greedily devoured the milk.

Synouane directed a venomous look first at Herky and then at me, while it gradually dawned on me that a deer—perhaps every nursing animal—stimulates the flow of the mother's milk by kneading the udders or flanks. Herky's butting of my thigh was her instinctive action that was a prelude to obtaining milk. Synouane was not her mother, so there was no possibility of milk from him! Even seeing the bottle didn't help. I was Herky's mother, at least in her experience, and she knew I had to be present for milk to be available to her. Fortunately when she got onto solid food this was no longer a problem, but the bond between me and this small woodland creature remained very close.

Herky lived with us seven months, and we still debate the cause of her fatal illness. We came home one day to find her listless and feverish, her nose hot and dry. She refused to eat. There was a sore on her neck causing us to wonder if a poisonous animal or insect from our yard had stung or bitten her. We also wondered if someone had tried to lasso her from the other side of our five-foot chain link fence.

Lacking anything like a vet, I called the American medical unit and explained Herky's symptoms to a sympathetic neighbor who was also our doctor. On the off chance that the deer had some sort of bacterial infection, the doctor came to our house with a hefty antibiotic shot. It didn't help. Herky became weaker. I sat on our porch floor, Herky's hot twitching body beside me, her head in my lap, stroking her ears and nose. When she died the following afternoon my gulping sobs reflected the wrenching loss of this family member.

The servants, who usually viewed our American addiction to pets with considerable skepticism, were also shaken by Herky's death. We were aware that few Lao kept pets of any kind and that the American penchant for adopting and pampering animals generated considerable discussion among the men and women who worked for us. We surmised that the marginal living conditions under which most Lao lived prohibited them from keeping a tame animal as a pet. We also knew that many Asian cultures do not approve of pets being kept inside the house, a possible explanation for my failure to see domesticated cats and dogs in other than American homes. Our servants had been very tolerant of our acquisition of pets and were themselves fond of Herky.

Sadly I reconciled myself to the death of our little girl deer and called for Boot, our gardener. He was a diligent, good-hearted man who worked for a minimal salary and who had often eyed Herky with some venison steaks in mind. I lifted my tear-stained face to him, seated on the floor, Herky's lifeless head in my hands. "Boot, will you please take Herky and find a nice place in the woods and bury her. I don't know what made her sick, but I don't think it is safe to try to eat her. It might make you sick too."

Boot's brown, deeply lined face expressed genuine sympathy for me, but also a mixture of skepticism and disappointment about my reasons for pointing out to him why he must forgo enjoying some fresh venison. In deference to my devotion to this gentle creature he knelt, lifted the warm body from my lap, and bore her off to her final resting place.

Herky had come from Luang Prabang, home of the king and a town I was itching to visit. Others had told me of its beautiful setting, the unique temples and the particularly fine crafts. The Fa Ngum school that was being built there claimed a good deal of John's time, and it was with great delight that I received a phone call one morning from our Hawaii team counterpart in Luang Prabang.

"There has been a cancellation by someone who was coming to the king's ball and the area coordinator, Lou Connick, said it would be okay to call you folks to see if you want to come." Want to come! I would have walked the distance to have a chance to participate in the annual festival which included boat races on the Nam Khan River and culminated in a formal ball at the king's palace. His Royal Highness, King Savang Vatthana, was enthroned in 1959, the successor to Sisavangvong, who at his death had been the oldest reigning monarch in the world. The new king, less flamboyant and more austere, immediately ran into political troubles. Dommen, writing in *Conflict in Laos,* states that by 1970 the king was reigning in name only in a country being buffeted by outside powers beyond his control (146). Nevertheless, there were a number of yearly official functions to which an invitation was highly prized by Americans.

The number of USAID members permitted by the mission to attend the boat races and the ball was limited each year in order not to overload the guest list with Americans. I gleefully announced the invitation to my surprised husband when he returned from work that evening, and we set about making the necessary arrangements, checking with neighbors who had attended in former years, brushing up on royal protocol.

Boun sooung heua, the boat racing festival held the afternoon of the ball, occurs in September or October, toward the end of the rainy season, and is a festival of general rejoicing. Races are held in many Lao communities, but the first races of the season begin in the royal capital.

Our first challenge in Vientiane was to get John outfitted properly. This is not a casual affair, and it is imperative that the men sitting near the king wear white suits. We made a quick trip to the tailor to acquire a pair of trousers that would match the white jacket we had earlier acquired for five dollars at the AWC thrift shop. It was also necessary to take dark tuxedo pants to wear at the ball. Fortunately, John could still fit into his tux, and having borrowed a bow tie from a neighbor, he was ready to go.

Although glass slippers might have been appropriate garb, I decided to wear a Lao silk *sinh* and matching blouse and sash. For the boat races I would wear a white cotton skirt and blouse. Even though it had been raining steadily for a month, I remembered to toss in sunburn lotion, since part of the celebration was to honor the end of the rainy season.

We flew to Luang Prabang on Monday morning, arriving in time to climb the hill in the center of town to visit *Wat Puu Si* and the other stunning temples situated high above the town. Resplendent in red and gold, they reigned over this seat of royalty with a protective presence and benign calm.

Tuesday morning, the day of the boat races, was hot and humid. Our hosts took us to the river to watch the preparations for the races. Each boat is sponsored by a *wat* or other organization and is a long, narrow dugout, or pirogue with barely width enough for one person to man an oar. Crews of young men, paddles over their shoulders, sing as they march in cadence to the riverside and their waiting boats. There are usually twenty men per boat in addition to the coxswain who perches precariously on the upwardly sloping stern. Those of us gathered on the banks were entertained by the chanting crews, dressed in colorful costumes and head scarves, who awaited their turns with impromptu dancing and acrobatic antics. Spirits ran high, and the chants and songs were often bawdy, eliciting much laughter from the Lao spectators. Because there were sixty boats in this race, heats were run with the winners of each heat designated to enter the final race. Colorful banners fluttered along the banks of the rivers, and on an occasion such as this the boats were painted with bright colors and festooned with colorful streamers.

The day we arrived there had been a violent rain storm, and the Nam Khan River was a raging torrent. Huge trees careened through roiling, muddy water. The visible whirlpools and rapids caused us to wonder if it would be possible for the frail boats to race at all. Luckily by the next morning the rain had stopped, and although the river was very wide and very swift, it was not deemed to be dangerous. The races were on!

His Royal Highness, King Savang Vatthana, was already seated in the special pavilion built on the side of the river for him and his guests when we arrived. Those seated around him appeared to be relatives and a sprinkling of foreign diplomats and high officials of the Lao government. With gold braid decorations on his spotless white uniform, the king, erect in posture, calm and handsome, was a focal point in the crowd. Directly across the river from him were hundreds of Lao who had gathered to cheer their teams. Some had signs, others had colorful banners, and all of them were in high spirits, laughing and roughhousing as they awaited the start of the races.

The crowd was more sedate on our side of the river, possibly because many of us were foreigners who had no idea of how the races were conducted or, indeed, who the favored teams might be. For our comfort there were rows of folding chairs, but only those seated close to the king had the luxury of an overhead canopy and protection from the sun.

The width and swiftness of the river allowed six boats to race in one heat. The competition was keen, and the skill of each steersman masterful.

We were quickly caught up in the drama of near collisions, evenly matched crews, the treachery of the currents and the excitement of the crowds. Since few of the spectators on our side of the river knew one entry from another, our participation was considerably more subdued than the supportive antics of the Lao, who yelled and cheered, pounded each other on the back, splashed water and in general whooped it up.

John and I became restless and were glad not to be seated so close to the king that we would be forbidden to get up or to move around. He sat ramrod straight during the entire occasion, his wife, a tiny, smiling woman sat at his side, and the crown prince was next to them, talking and gesturing with his companions. As it was, we could wander in the crowd, take pictures from different angles and relieve the tedium of sitting in one place for a long time. The races lasted until nearly dusk, but we retreated after four hours in order to prepare for that evening's festivities.

As we dressed for the banquet and dance, both to be held at the palace, I felt a bit like Cinderella. Here we were in an exotic foreign country, attending a ball given by the king! On arrival at the palace we were greeted by the crown prince and princess, and I curtsied, as expected. When the king arrived he went around the circle of people who were in the first line of folks in the entry hall, shaking hands with the men while we ladies again curtsied.

Standing in the rear of the guests, I had an opportunity to admire the gold and brocade throne, the rich hangings and the stately staircase that led to the second floor. It was a disappointingly modest palace, yet one that did indeed reflect royalty. Ascending the wide staircase to the second floor I noted the cut glass chandeliers and the gilt and brocade chairs lining the perimeter of the room.

In the center of the large ballroom were two enormously long tables laden with tureens, platters, samovars and all manner of dishes heaped with food. To the side were French doors leading to a series of tiny balconies, each with a miniscule table around which several chairs were clustered. The banquet was a buffet, and we were invited to help ourselves.

Among the dishes I chose was a curry which I ladled over the traditional *khaophoun* one is always served at Lao functions. I helped myself also to *lap,* fried chicken, dried meat strips called *sin heng* and rice. Clutching dessert spoons, the only eating utensil offered, and balancing our plates as we threaded between the guests, we joined four others around one of the small balcony tables. I seated myself, raised my spoon and stared into the two beady black eyes of a fat, white grub, or larva, complete with six tiny curled legs.

I muffled a cry and nudged John. "What *is* it?" I hissed. I was acquainted enough with Lao food to know that this had not fallen into the food by mistake, but that didn't reduce my surprise.

"Looks like a white grub to me." John refused to acknowledge my shock.

"Well, *I'm* not going to eat it; *you* eat it! I flipped it onto John's plate and watched with fascinated horror as he casually picked up the offending creature and popped it into his mouth.

"Tastes all right, but it's quite aromatic," he murmured, pinching his nose to indicate the effect of the pungency. Minding our manners, our small table group continued to eat, conversing in hushed tones about the fact that the grub was not due to carelessness in the kitchen, but was a delicacy, and that the scarcity of protein foods in Laos caused the people to eat any form of protein they could find.

Sitting there in the royal palace hoping I would not encounter any further surprises in my food triggered recollection of an instance involving our yard man, Boot, who used a powered lawnmower to care for our fairly large yard. As he swept back and forth across the lawn grasshoppers sprang out of the grass and onto the machine. He would quickly grab them, sizzle their heads on the hot motor and pop them into his mouth, hardly missing a step.

The other foods on our plates were less bizarre and included shrimp, sliced pork, fried noodles and cold fish mayonnaise. Following dinner the food tables were cleared away and we waited for the ball to begin. The king, we were informed, didn't dance. He sat instead in a far corner talking to a progression of ambassadors and foreign dignitaries. The crown prince, who was then in his late forties, danced very well, and it was he who started the evening off and obviously enjoyed each dance with a succession of attractive partners.

The party picked up considerable momentum after the king left at one o'clock. The Lao military officers, who by now had consumed large quantities of alcohol, began to sing and dance, and the demure Lao ladies, who until this time had been sitting with lowered eyes on the sidelines, also entered into the festivities. While the king had been present the dancing had been either the *lamvong* or slow Western-style dances using American music of the thirties and forties. Now the stately Lao *lamvong* was transformed into the gyrations of the sixties as activity on the floor became frenzied. John and I lasted until about two-thirty, when we noticed that the dancing was degenerating into lurching, and the once-soft smiles were becoming glazed stares. We paid our respects to the crown prince and retired to our guest quarters.

The following morning we reviewed a conversation held toward the end of the evening with one of the Lao generals. He had, to our surprise, waxed philosophical, expressing his belief that concepts of God embraced Christians as well as Buddhists. He also told us that all people are meant to live together in peace, and although his mixture of Lao and English and his less than sober condition produced a somewhat garbled conversation, there was something compellingly earnest about his sharing of both his own and his country's basic philosophical stance. He confirmed observations that we ourselves had made concerning this beleaguered country. The irony was that only after many drinks could a Lao general share these views with civilian representatives of the American presence in his country.

Reliving our banquet experience on the way home, especially our encounter with the grub, recalled the first time we experienced the termite swarming in Laos. We knew from living in Hawaii that at certain times of year winged termites appear in great clouds—they swarm. They are attracted to light, and even in Hawaii we had seen them flutter around lamps, lose their wings and fall, wriggling and helpless.

In Laos the termites were big—often at least one inch long—and they were formidable when in flight. On the outside of our Km6 house was a work sink over which we kept a night light. The morning after the termites swarmed, our cook, eyes alight with excitement, dashed out to that sink, a plastic bag clutched in his hand. Helpless in the depths of the sink were masses of wingless termites, perhaps two or three inches deep. Grinning from ear to ear at this wonderful haul, Sakhorn scooped up the termites into his plastic bag, announcing that his family would have a great feast of stir-fried termites for dinner that evening.

If we had been served termites at the king's banquet, I had mercifully not known it.

14
Pi Mai: Pakse

Bordered by the Mekong River and nearly two hundred and fifty miles northwest of Saigon, the city of Pakse in southern Laos was the site of one of the Fa Ngum schools. My husband had several opportunities to go there on business, filling me in on his return with descriptions that made me long to visit this part of Laos. I was, therefore, very pleased to accept on our behalf an invitation from Souvanh, Khampheng's husband, to spend *Pi Mai* in Pakse.

It would be a rare treat to spend this most traditional of all festivals with a Lao extended family. Souvanh would visit his parents, who lived a few kilometers out of Pakse, and we would stay with his aunt. All work stops in Laos during the New Year celebration, held on the first full moon after the vernal equinox, similar to the Christian Easter. It wasn't the New Year that Americans celebrated, but nearly all of Laos would be on holiday, and a trip to Pakse might also enable us to see some of the ancient temples in the Champassak area, just a few kilometers from the Cambodian border.

Souvanh's uncle and aunt from Vientiane would also be going, a couple we were as well acquainted with as sign language and lots of hand gestures allowed. Although we studied weekly with Souvanh's wife, Khampheng, our Lao language capabilities were still woefully inadequate.

Twelve of us converged on Pakse at the end of the week. As usual, we were required for security reasons to fly on Royal Air Lao while Lao members of the party went by bus.

Ai Siphong greeted us warmly with a big smile and a hearty "*Sabaidee.*" *Ai* is the Lao word for aunt, and the Lao language assigns every member of the family with a title appropriate to his or her age and placement in the family structure. We too would refer to her as *Ai* in recognition of her position as the older sister of Souvanh's father. John and I were designated as honorary grandparents and while *Poh Tow* seemed to fit John nicely, I cringed when I was given the additional *Nya Mee*, roughly translated "most honored elder mother" title.

We were shown into a high ceilinged room with a rotating fan, one of several bedrooms in a huge house. I judged that the house was built when the French were also living in Saigon and Phnom Penh. An entire family usually lived in this room, displaced by our coming, but no one seemed to mind. I lost count of who it was that usually lived in this extended family, aware only that there were several young families in addition to Ai Siphong and her husband, Colonel Thoune.

That he was a high-ranking military officer was another surprise. We had not known that the man of the family was a colonel in the Royal Lao Army, and apparently one with considerable influence. There seemed to be endless food and liquor supplies, jeeps for transportation and Lao Army trucks to take sixty of us out to a picnic area two days later. The appropriation and use of military goods and transport by the families of Lao officers were apparently so normal that they were never remarked on. Observing the private use of American-supplied goods in all areas I had visited caused me to wonder about the nature of American support of the Vietnamese incursion in Laos and who was benefitting most from our presence.

I was too new to the country to know that Laos was sectioned into five military regions whose generals were powerful, rich and, according to an article by Fred Branfman which I read many years later, were benefitting from American support by maneuvering funds into businesses, land and arms trade, and even into the opium trade. Branfman, in *Laos: War and Revolution*, categorized military region four, with headquarters in Pakse, as being commanded "by the toughest of the Lao Commanders" (224), and continued, "The colonels who control each district capital regard these posts as opportunities for personal enrichment and jealously guard their domains, which they rule with an iron hand" (225).

Pakse was a bustling town almost due west of Da Nang, a city often in the news during the Vietnam War. It was a military center for American and mercenary troops who were billeted in Thailand, but who spent their days in Laos. We were unprepared for the number of army trucks and men in jungle camouflage dress in that town. Since United States foreign policy persisted in sticking to the "no military presence in Laos" charade, local Lao referred to these soldiers as "ghosts." Perhaps they were expressing that common Southeast Asian euphemism for white-skinned people or strangers. In conversations they constantly referred to "the men who are not here," a recognition of the eerie kind of self-deception being played out by Lao and American alike in this conflict no one would admit was a war.

Our first dinner was a foretaste of things to come during the entire weekend. Foods were produced magically from a small kitchen with a toe-level fire and no shelves, few utensils, and wonderful aromas. Curry, Lao sticky rice, a soup with green spinach-like vegetables, dried strips of meat known as *sin heng,* and orange pop and beer. Everyone, including the guests, dipped into common dishes throughout the meal. At our insistence *Ai* Siphong joined us. We ate until we were stuffed and then went out into the evening breeze where we watched a magenta and gold sunset blaze and fade into twilight and darkness. The mosquito hour sent us to our room early, where netting draped over the bed protected us while we slept.

Saturday was *Pi Mai,* a spring festival embracing the new growing season. It heralds the anticipated onset of the rains which will restore crops to a land parched and brown from the previous dry months. To be wished *"Sabaidee Pi Mai"* is to be wished a Happy New Year.

The Buddhist customs from which *Pi Mai* originates are gentle, sane and charming. Water scented with pikake or plumeria is sprinkled as a blessing on the Buddha image and on guests and friends. A *baci* is held to restore one to the good graces of the spirits or *phis* whom one may have offended. Good wishes and benign spirits are entreated to come into your life and are secured by bits of string tied to your wrists. Then there are feasting and drinking and dancing and a great party for all. The old man who chants the proper phrases in the *baci* is a revered village elder or wise person. He is not a Buddhist monk.

The *baci* ceremony is not solemn. Participants kneel or sit with legs tucked decorously under them on mats placed around a large silver vase of flowers and leaves. Whole cooked chickens, eggs, sweets and drink are also placed around the base of the *baci* bowl. Ten-inch slender bamboo sticks around which lengths of white string or yarn have been placed are inserted among the flowers in the arrangement. Participants make comments and expound on what the elder says as he chants in his singsong voice. My arthritic knees ached and I thought I might embarrass everyone by having to stand up. I shifted to a "side saddle" position, hoping I would not offend by pointing my feet at anyone's head, an unforgivable insult.

Finally the chanting ended and strings were tied on our wrists by the chanter and then by others, each person who crowded around placing fruit, a cookie or an egg into the recipient's hand while a white string was tied around the wrist of the other arm. Mischievous well-wishers entreated the spirits to give us many children and lots of money or, *"Sok dee, yu dee me heng,"* good health, long life.

Following the ceremony the serious partying began. Platters and trays of food were laid out on trestle tables. Neighbors and colleagues began to gather, but as guests we were urged to go first. Still fairly new to Lao cuisine, we proceeded down the buffet line, eyeing an array of foods we were only beginning to recognize. There was *lap,* meat chopped fine with mint, red peppers, basil, and bean sprouts. The meat is traditionally raw and has been known to give foreigners serious intestinal problems, but the Lao seem to have cast-iron stomachs and suffer no ill effects. We too liked the delicate herbal mixtures in *lap* and served ourselves, hoping to avoid later consequences. It was a lavish buffet: smoked fish; dried fish; *sin heng* (dried meat); white rice; sticky rice; sauces of red pepper and tomato; papaya salad; platters of mint and basil; meat curries; fish curries; vegetable curries with tiny, round eggplant; hot curries; hotter curries; seasonal fruits; and the large plate of chocolate chip cookies I had brought, knowing Souvanh's addiction to these very American treats.

Some of the men spent most of their time drinking. I watched in horror as tumbler after tumbler of undiluted Scotch was tossed down with a toast. I stuck to orange pop, but, as an honored guest, John was a sought-after drinking companion. He and Boun Hom, our Chinese-Lao friend from Vientiane, already had an established drinking friendship. Round-faced and smiling, this friendly gentleman and my husband sat together in Pakse as they did on the porch of Boun Hom's Vientiane home, drinking Scotch, beaming and nodding, reinforcing each other periodically with bursts of, "Very Good!"—the only two words they had in common. This phrase was uttered with increasing abandon as the afternoon wore on, and at five o'clock I looked around and failed to see either John or Boun Hom. Concerned, I made inquiries and was directed to a first-floor room. Peeking in I saw them stretched out on their backs, a gentle smile on each face and benign snores emanating from their prostrate bodies. Out cold, both of them! I mentally checked my aspirin supply for future application and rejoined the others.

The festivities became increasingly noisy and soon developed into boisterous water games. No gentle sprinkling this! The young folks were heaving buckets of water at anyone within range, and I was soon a target. It was refreshing to let the water evaporate in the very hot late afternoon sun, and since I'd had the foresight to wear a simple cotton dress, I relaxed and entered into the melee with abandon. The partying went on into the late evening, but pleading age and a need to be ready for the morrow, I rescued John and retired to our mosquito-netted haven to drift into memory-filled slumber.

The next day's activities came as a real surprise. We were told we would be going on a picnic: our hosts wanted to take us to a riverside picnic area for an outing. At least three army trucks were in the house compound, two of them for passengers, the third being loaded with a seemingly endless succession of boxes, hampers, tubs and pots. Low-ranking army personnel were being pressed into service to load the mats and necessary accompanying equipment. As guests, we were expected to ride in a car.

Our first stop was a large dam where hundreds of people were celebrating the holiday. We dutifully walked around and made the right kinds of exclamations, feeling increasingly hot and dusty. I was greatly relieved when we were encouraged to drive on to the shady site of the picnic. There we thankfully plunged into the river, blissfully ignoring all we had heard about how contaminated such rivers usually were and how easy it was to acquire things like liver flukes and other unnamed parasites from an innocent swim.

In the meantime the feast was being prepared. I use the word feast advisedly. We had, frankly, never been on a Lao picnic anywhere, and thinking about the usual scarcity of food, not to mention picnic sites, I was unprepared for the abundance of food that was spread before us. Fried chicken, cucumbers, basil, *caow niow*—the Lao sticky rice which is always served in round, woven, covered baskets that are identifiable anywhere in the world as coming from Laos—French bread, noodles, or *khaophun*, the dishes were nearly as lavish as the *Pi Mai* banquet had been, yet here we were in an area approaching near wilderness.

This wilderness, however, was inhabited by nearly two hundred people who were refugees, having arrived literally the night before. (Their presence explained, at least in part, the flurry of activity and comings and goings of vehicles that John and I had heard in the wee hours of the previous night. As the ranking Lao officer in the area, Colonel Thoune had sent trucks out to pick up and assist the refugees and bring them to a temporary place of refuge.) They came from the Boulevans plateau and Attopeu, east of us, between Pakse and the Vietnam border, where fighting was heavy and from which they had fled. Some had been lucky to catch rides on government or army transport. Others had walked, carrying what little they could salvage. It all seemed so incongruous. Here we were, with an overabundance of food and a military support system. Here they were with nothing but their lives. I was touched and relieved to observe that although when we began to eat men and women had separated into two groups, the men in our party had gathered the elders and officials of the refugee group to join them and were hunkering down with them around platters of food. This picnic was like the biblical loaves and fishes: the more we ate the more we had.

There were at least seventy-five of us from *Ai* Siphong and Souvanh's family. Children, parents, older men and women, John and me. Covertly watching us were over a hundred hungry refugees who were polite enough not to even seem to notice us as we ate. When we finished, Ai Siphong called them over and gave them everything that was left. It was more than enough to feed them all. This was some impressive woman! Belatedly I realized that she had already known about these refugees and had made it her business to see that we brought enough food for everyone in that new refugee encampment: just a casual picnic that took care of nearly two hundred people!

After lunch we all stretched out on mats and snoozed. Some played the *khene* and sang. The children enjoyed a variety of games including tag, hide-and-seek, and a Lao game with sticks and small stones. It could have been Old Home Day anywhere in rural America.

Naps and games ended, it was time to go. The refugee families shyly thanked us with hands clasped in the traditional *wai* greeting. John and I climbed into the back seat of the car, with *Ai* Siphong and Colonel Thoune in front, but we were not permitted to leave. As we started to move down the dirt-track road, an old man came toward the car, holding in his hands a small glass jar with water and plumeria blossoms in it. Stopping the car, he reached through the rolled-down window space and gently emptied half of the jar of water over my head. He then trotted around to the other side of the car and blessed John with the other half-jar of water.

"Sabaidee Pi Mai." A beatific smile spread over his leathery, wrinkled face.

"Sabaidee Pi Mai," we answered back, clasping our hands in front of our faces to return the traditional greeting. Oblivious to the small puddles of water in which we were now sitting, I turned to John whose eyes glistened with tears as he took my hand and said, "To think that this homeless man, a refugee who has lost everything he ever owned, would come to bless and anoint *us* with water. . . ." John's voice trailed off, choked with emotion as he squeezed my hand and added, "The Lao are such beautiful people, such *beautiful* people."

We celebrated five *Pi Mai*s in Laos and more in America, but none have held the poignancy of that bittersweet New Year blessing.

The next morning we were scheduled to return to Vientiane, but before we left we discovered a second source of breakfasts. Until our trip to Pakse I had not stayed in a Lao home and had not given much thought to what the Lao ate for breakfast. Looking out of my window early on Saturday morning I had seen an old lady with yoked kettles on either side, moving down the street. Soon she was approached by people carrying bowls, and as she dipped into her steaming kettles, money changed hands. It occurred to me that this was breakfast. Sure enough, for fifty kip, about ten cents, you could buy a steaming bowl of noodle and vegetable soup. So much easier than stirring up a fire and trying to produce something in your own kitchen.

That final morning in Pakse our hosts took us to a local restaurant where *pho,* Vietnamese noodle soup with meat and fresh vegetables, was served. We learned that adding some coarse sugar granules and a squeeze of lime gave considerable zip to this tasty bowl of broth, flat noodles, bean sprouts, mint, basil and thin slices of beef. You could add as much hotness as you wanted from a red pepper sauce. It was a delicious and filling dish that we have continued to be fond of, grateful that the new immigrants who have come to live in America have opened restaurants where this kind of *pho* can be purchased in virtually every city.

15
Phi Pops

Pi Mai was just one of many celebrations in Laos. Because nearly every occasion warranted a *baci* it seemed as if there was always a special observance going on. We were *"bacied"* when we went on a trip and when we returned as well as on anniversaries and birthdays. Weddings occasioned a *baci* and also recovery from an illness. We became very proficient at repeating the correct good luck phrases as we cheerily tied white strings on the wrists of the person for whom the *baci* was being given.

The Lao cautioned us that *baci* strings were meant to stay on until they rotted off. Considering that we often had fifteen or twenty on one arm, that seemed excessive. We did, however, keep some strings on for three days, a compromise some Lao considered to be acceptable. The exception was when we went on trips. On those occasions we were careful not to remove the strings until we reached our destination, deplaning in Frankfurt or Hong Kong, Barcelona or Boston, grubby white strings still on our wrists, confirmation that the good luck stayed with us.

Rotting *baci* strings were merely an introduction to a whole culture full of customs that both fascinated and bewildered us. Early on we had learned of the practice of placing glowing coals under the beds of women who were about to give birth. Although we quizzed Khampheng closely for an explanation of this practice, "it's just what we do" was the best she could offer.

She had married Souvanh in the late fall of 1971. By the next spring she was pregnant, and when I asked her if she would have the baby in a hospital, she gave an embarrassed giggle and attempted to sidetrack my question.

Pressing the point I asked, "Will you have the baby at home?"

A nervous nod.

"Will the doctor come to your home?" The ensuing silence told me that there was something in this issue she was loath to address.

"Does someone else deliver babies?" Hesitantly venturing into this apparently touchy dialog, Khampheng brightened. "Yes, an older woman comes to help me have my baby. My mother and sister will also be assisting."

"Ah, in America we call these women midwives."

It was after I reassured her that we shared a common birthing practice that she felt free to discuss in more detail the hot rocks routine, and that was when it became clear to me that for Khampheng, a logical explanation for these customs was not necessary.

Living as she did between her mother's world of superstitions and tradition and the scientific discoveries her French-based *lycée* education provided, she welcomed an opportunity to air with me her many questions and doubts. Since I had not belittled the Lao birthing customs and had often participated with her in Lao celebrations, it was easy for us to talk about other customs. Our sharing helped her to recognize and more readily accept tradition as a valuable part of her own heritage. It also freed her to be critical of customs which modern medicine, education and practice proved to be outmoded. Together we worked through which of her parents' traditional behaviors were to be acknowledged and followed, and those areas in which she and Souvanh could be firm in pursuing their own best judgment.

This was how we had come to discuss the birth customs of the Lao which she had, at first, been reluctant to reveal. It also explained why she took a different tack when her small son became very ill. She wanted to call in a Western-trained doctor but her mother was busy applying home remedies. A servant had been sent to the Chinese herbalist for some special ingredients and a Buddhist monk was also called to offer appropriate prayers.

Khampheng was aware that many people in the place where she worked and around the city were showing the same symptoms as her son and that Western medicine had helped them. She felt that more was needed than her mother's efforts could provide. I encouraged her to follow her instincts to consult a doctor but not to ignore totally the folk remedies her mother offered. In the end both her mother and the doctor could claim that they had brought the child safely through his crisis.

Khamnouy, on the other hand, was much less tolerant of some of the folk ways and superstitions of his people. "They are very backward," he would say scornfully.

"What do you expect them to do, 'Nouy, with so few hospitals, no doctors outside of the cities, and few places to buy medicine?" Where, I might have added, would they find the money to fill prescriptions even if the drugs had been available?

Hardly anyone beyond the few who had attended the *lycée* or Fa Ngum schools understood germs or microbes. That cholera might result from drinking a cup of water would have never occurred to the average person.

When I encountered practices or events I did not fully understand I talked to both young people about them. I called on help from Khampheng after Synouane, the cook, had come rushing in one morning, late for our breakfast. In obvious distress, he was too distraught to speak coherently, but he mentioned his daughter and said he could not stay.

I had the impression that something terrible had happened to the little girl, causing him to be frantic with anxiety and fear. Because I had not had a chance to ask what was wrong, I made it a point to try to find his home later that morning, to see if I might help.

In his small village I found both men and women gathered in somber clumps, looking extremely serious. In halting Lao I inquired about the child. Was she ill? Did she need to go to a doctor? Was it a problem of no money for the doctor? Was there anything I could do?

Whitefaced, Synouane told me that he did not want a doctor. His little girl, he said, had been hexed by a *be bop.* If he hadn't been so deadly serious, I would have laughed.

"A *be bop?* What on earth are you talking about?"

"She is paralyzed and cannot move. I am afraid she will die."

"Paralyzed? From what? What is going on?"

Slowly he put the story together. The previous afternoon an old woman unknown to anyone in the village had come through selling iced goodies. The little girl had begged some kip from her mother and bought one of these treats. Shortly after she started to eat it, she had had a seizure and become rigid.

"How can that be?" I asked. "The kind of treat she bought is merely frozen water and coloring." I felt reasonably sure that even if the water had been contaminated one didn't normally get instant seizures from it or become immobile. Did cholera come on like this? I didn't think so.

"Synouane, let's take her to the hospital," I begged. "There the doctors can help her."

"No, no, you don't understand. She is possessed. That old woman has cast a spell. She was a *be bop.*"

In vain I pleaded with him to let me take the child to a medical center. Ashen-faced, her father told me that what he needed to do was to get a monk to come. The bad spirit must be cast out.

Knowing Synouane's penchant for gambling, I suspected he had little ready money with which to persuade anyone to come to the aid of the family, so I gave him all the kip I had before I left.

I could hardly wait for Khampheng to drop in after work. She barely got in the door when I demanded to know about *be bops.* She burst into laughter and said, "Not *be bop,* it's *phi-pop.*" Suddenly noticing that there was no servant in the kitchen and that I was rustling up dinner, she asked, "Who is talking about them?"

"Synouane. His little girl is—well I don't know how to say it. She's a victim of a *phi-pop.* At least that's what he said." I quickly recounted my experiences of the morning.

Khampheng was clearly upset. "A *phi-pop* is a person possessed by an evil spirit."

"Come on, Khampheng, a demon? A genuine witch?" I had not expected her to confirm my cook's superstitious beliefs.

"Yes, Mom. This is serious." With that she headed for the door to go see Synouane, leaving me to face my own doubts and confusion as I tried to comprehend the possibility that a spell had been cast on the child. I respected Khampheng's credibility and acknowledged that she shared Synouane's real fear for this small girl, confirmed when she returned and verified what I had gathered in my own brief trip to the village. A strange woman had come into the area selling some sort of iced treat. The little girl had bought one, taken a few bites and become rigid. Everyone was convinced that she had been placed under a spell. It was very serious. Furthermore, there was nothing that I, an outsider, could possibly do to help.

"Do you believe in these things?" I waited to see what Khampheng would say.

Her reply was cautious. "Well, let's say that I know the belief in them is strong, and, frankly, I don't see any other explanation for this little girl's becoming so sick." We discussed the potential outcome of the ministrations of the monk, or bonze, who had come to exorcise the demon and the fact that it would be hard for him to be effective because, contrary to many other cases, this *phi-pop* was unknown to the villagers, giving the holy man few clues for his work of healing. There was no question but that the villagers believed in the power of the monk, a position verified by an article in Donald Whitaker's *Laos: A Country Study,* "A bonze may be called into a household in which one of the members is sick in order to participate in the ceremonies and music-making designed to exorcise the malevolent *phi* from the body of the victim. Many bonzes are thought to have a special knowledge of the *phi*" (117). I was terribly concerned for Synouane, for his wife, and of course for the small girl, but I found it hard seriously to accept what I was being told. I waited and prayed, relieved on the following day to be told that the little girl had recovered movement in her limbs and was able to swallow.

I treated this entire incident with considerably more credibility after finding this additional support for the belief in *phi-pops* in this book researched by American University scholars:

> Demons called *ho* sometimes take possession of people, according to a widespread belief, and these people, *phi-pop,* are greatly feared for their power to cast spells and work magic. In addition to their ability to kill by incantations or an evil eye, *phi-pop* supposedly have the power to reduce a buffalo hide to the size of a grain of rice, which when swallowed by the victim swells to its original size, bursting his stomach.
>
> A *phi-pop* is believed to inherit his power from a parent or relative, but a victim of a *phi-pop* may sometimes become another *phi-pop.* Sometimes a *phi-pop* may be persuaded to cure his victim. In other instances, a practitioner is asked to effect a cure, usually by removing the foreign object from the victim's body. Formerly, a person believed to be a *phi-pop* was sometimes put to death by villagers. Even now he (more often, she) may be ostracized and forced to wander. [118–19]

Dommen, in *Conflict in Laos,* also says in relation to the *phi,*

> Even for many Lao today, the jungle is peopled with powerful spirits called *phi,* which must be propitiated with sacrifices, exorcised by complicated rites, and never wantonly abused or angered.
>
> The *phi* of those who died violent deaths roam the earth tormenting people. Certain living persons contain malevolent *phi* and must be kept away from the village. Visitors to a village, ignorant of local custom, are liable to anger *phi* by stopping in the wrong places, failing to make proper obeisance or speaking forbidden words. [15–16]

Within two days Synouane came back to work. He was still shaky, but he could smile as he shared that his daughter would be okay. It was only after hearing from others about the melding of Buddhism and animism in Laos that I began to comprehend the importance of this episode in the life of our cook.

This event clarified for me that Khampheng—along with most educated Lao—was trapped between two very different cultures and religions, a position supported by George Condominas *Laos: War and Revolution,* where he comments, "The *phi* are constantly present in the life of the Lao and govern many of their acts (if only because of the ability of the *phi* to inflict illness)" (15).

The scientific Western education of the *lycée* must have created enormous conflict within Khampheng. Very bright, she certainly was now struggling with the contradictions between her Buddhist-animist upbringing and revelations her education had provided. She seemed to be not so very different from many American young people who look upon their parents' Christianity as superstitious in the face of advancing technological wonders.

I felt twinges of deep concern over this, knowing that her daily life was caught up in the traditions and practices of her people, even as she exercised her training and curiosity in the search for better ways to care for her family and improve her own lot. It saddened me that the questions I asked her about Buddhist practices were inevitably answered in nervous laughter. It was not that I was being critical but that she was airing her own doubts.

I could see the disintegration of a long, honorable culture in her bewildered reactions, and I inwardly mourned the role that we Americans were often unconsciously playing in precipitating change in this small country and its people.

16
Saunas and Silkworms

Living overseas on a restricted travel post constantly challenged our ingenuity. We lived a tripartite life. The major obligation was to the mission and whatever job or position you had with it, employee or dependent. Whether you worked for the mission or not, there were obligatory meetings, social gatherings and events planned by the ambassador as well as other American officials at which your presence was expected if not required.

Often more rewarding were those relationships which formed a second facet to our lives. These were the bonds forged between Americans and the Lao themselves—bonds with servants and their families, Lao counterpart employees and their families, Lao children who attended the American or international schools, and families of students like Khamnouy or others we met in the course of our years in Laos.

Hugh Fincher, a USAID employee, teamed up with Xay Kaignavongsa, a talented Lao artist, to research Lao festivals and customs, spelling out in a remarkable little volume, *Legends of the Lao,* the ways in which festivals and holidays were celebrated and the traditions associated with them. In addition he shared literal translations of common Lao phrases that were descriptive of everyday practices, illuminating for us all the manner in which a simple language like Lao copes with complex new objects and ideas introduced by foreigners such as the French and the Americans.

A third challenge to our lives took over especially during those times when military restrictions kept us confined to Vientiane and caused social events to be curtailed. This was when we had to entertain ourselves concentrating on hobbies, skills and interests that would be both absorbing and recreating.

Our next-door neighbor put his energies into perfecting his sound system. He taped every record he could get his hands on and had four speakers. The Tijuana Brass thumped across his lawn during evenings that were not usurped by a limitless supply of Lawrence Welk, Bing Crosby and all the golden oldies and goodies. New speakers, more tapes and increased volume all alerted us to the times when this good friend was busy improving his audio system.

Fortunately we enjoyed his musical selections, and we often could hear an entire concert without flicking a switch. The neighbor on his other side, however, was not so pleased. He complained often about the sound level, and at times harsh words were exchanged. Neighbor John Stalcup was not one to be intimidated. When, even in our airconditioned bedroom, we could both hear the tapes and feel the reverberations of a full decibel rendition of Tijuana Brass, we knew that there had been a complaint registered and that the answer was to pull out all the stops.

John Rantala set to work to build a sauna. His Finnish heritage demanded this cultural luxury despite the hot and steamy late spring weather that was common to Laos. While I sweltered even in the airconditioned bedroom, John cheerfully brushed aside my remonstrances and explained that a two-person sauna would just fit across the back end of our carport.

He enticed Khamnouy as well as an assortment of neighbors into joining his building spree. Jack Huxtable was especially enthusiastic. In fact he was so intrigued that the next year when he was transferred to Ban Houei Sai, he contrived to get John up there to design a sauna for him.

At first I was hesitant to even mention the Km6 sauna to Khampheng, but of course she observed the activity and then utterly astounded us by telling us of the equivalent of a Lao sauna at a Buddhist *wat* on the Thadeua Road. We were eager to visit this *wat* and convinced both Khampheng and Souvanh to take us out there. On the way we shared that a Finnish sauna carries with it a mystique related to *sisu,* the spirit of the sauna, and that in Finland building the sauna was more important than starting on the house itself.

This Lao sauna was a bit more like a sweat lodge. It was housed in a small earthen building shaped like a low-ceilinged Quonset hut. We entered wearing simple cotton garments and sat on side benches, facing others who were also inhaling the swirling steamy atmosphere. At the far end of this hut was a huge cauldron, at least six feet in diameter, in which water laced with fragrant herbal leaves was gently boiling.

"Is it mint?" I whispered.

"No, I think it is eucalyptus, and perhaps guava leaves."

There were villagers and some monks on the benches, and if anyone was surprised to have two *farangs* share their moist reverie, they were much too polite to show it. We left half an hour later limp but savoring the physical and spiritual refreshment of the fragrant, steamy ritual.

As the neighbors began to learn of John's sauna, helping him to build and use it became a popular activity. Men who carved roads out of the jungle in outlying villages appreciated the camaraderie and relaxation of the sauna at the end of a week of hard physical labor. After a long time Khampheng confessed that she, too, was eager to try it and joined me late one afternoon. The cook, however, demurred, and it was several months before he was persuaded to take a turn.

Life in Vientiane was often confining, and we who were dependents, spouses who accompanied full time employees but who were not on the American payroll, searched for interesting ways to use our time and skills. Some taught at the international or the American school. Several of us volunteered to teach English at the Lao American Association. We also worked at the American Women's Club thrift shop, or at their amazingly current lending library. Our friend Jack had one of the more unusual extracurricular activities. He loved to water ski, a sport unknown in landlocked Laos. But Laos is bordered by the Mekong River, and when Jack was assigned to Ban Houei Sai as area coordinator, he had many transportation resources, including jeeps, helicopters and boats to carry out a variety of rural development projects in remote Houa Khong. He took the opportunity to rig up a long tow rope which dangled from a helicopter. The helicopter would fly low down a reasonably rock-free stretch of the Mekong River with Jack exuberantly sashaying back and forth on water skis, zigging around small obstacles, zagging with abandon to avoid small boats manned by bug-eyed native fishermen. His astonished riverside audiences clapped with laughter and delight. The sauna he and John built provided a relaxing way to unwind from this exhilarating sport.

It was Jack who indulged my extracurricular interest in seeing more of Laos. On one memorable visit to Houei Sai he arranged a helicopter trip over the Hmong poppy fields, pointing out to us how one spotted the opium-producing plants from the sky. This part of Laos was very hilly, and the foliage was thick. It was easy to believe that tribal groups living only a few kilometers apart had not met each other and that their languages and customs were very different.

"Say," he suddenly announced, "our project inspection includes a stop at one Lahu tribal village. You might as well come along." Within minutes our helicopter settled gently onto a small cleared patch of earth surrounded by small huts unlike the Lao stilt houses I was used to. Cautiously surveying us were two tiny women of indeterminate age. They were approximately four feet, nine inches tall and were very slender, dressed in loose, white cotton garments that reached the ground. Their straggly, graying hair framed faces bright with curiosity.

Jack spoke a few words they seemed to understand, and they herded me slowly through the center of the village while he and John disappeared in another direction. The village was deserted. We looked at the dismal one-room school where two small windows provided the only light and the benches were crude tree stumps. As we continued down through the village the women flanked me, speaking to each other across my chest, apparently arguing about something. The women chattered and examined me and chattered some more until one suddenly darted out a hand and grasped my breast firmly and squeezed. I was too astonished to even yelp. The hand pulled back, the two bright faces looked across my midrift and nodded, big toothless grins accompanying the action.

I burst out laughing. With my long hair pulled back in a ponytail, I resembled their men who wear their hair long and are usually dressed as I was, in a shirt and dark trousers. Satisfied by an indisputable test proving my gender, they now knew how to present me to the only male who was at home, their aging village chieftain.

Even during days of heightened military action and confinement, there was one acceptable escape available to us. We could go to Thailand, either to Bangkok on the commissary run, the plane that brought in American food and other unobtainable American goods for our use only, or we could schedule a trip to a tourist destination. Everyone on an overseas assignment travels abroad whenever it is possible. We each got a home leave every two years and an R&R in between. Travel expenses for these leaves were paid by the government, and although there were some mileage restrictions on the R&R, we could supplement the costs with our own money and go as far as time and interest would take us.

Many of us, therefore, took advantage of long weekends and made other excuses to travel to Bangkok or to the beaches of the Gulf of Siam. Pattaya was a favorite haunt of ours, and when we could, we joined colleagues in a three- or four-day revel on the white sands, enjoying fresh seafood and soft nights.

Getting to Pattaya involved taking a ferry across the Mekong to Nongkhai, followed by a long day's drive south in Thailand to a sharp left-hand turn that would point us to the beaches rather than into Bangkok. Driving the highway, the one I had seen from the plane on the day we entered Laos, was a nightmare. It was boringly straight, had only two lanes and if there were shoulders at all, they were of loose gravel. The road had been financed and in part built by the United States for military purposes. There was no such thing as a passing lane. Neither were there any sane rules of the road which was used mainly by truckers and suicidal drivers who often were high on drugs and who entertained themselves and each other by playing "chicken" when they drove. It was common to come upon horrendous accidents where neither player had yielded. Even we, in a passenger car, were not immune from danger. More than once we swerved into a field to avoid two trucks bearing down on each other, oblivious to any other traffic on the road. We were more than ready for a relaxing vacation when we arrived at our destination in one piece.

One memorable trip seemed to be proceeding as scheduled, and we knew we were approaching the left-hand turn that would take us toward the Gulf. There were no road maps to use and few signs to follow. Experience and memory were what a driver depended on, or a hastily scratched set of instructions gleaned from a friend before one left Laos. We made the turn and continued our long drive through very barren countryside, a stretch that seemed longer than I remembered. "Do you suppose we could have made a mistake?"

"Oh, no," John reassured me. "We're nearly there. I can smell the ocean."

Around the next curve we found ourselves at a dead end, in the center of a small village. Bewildered and tired, I climbed out, seeking advice from one of several bystanders. We had no common language nor did anyone understand "Pattaya" when I attempted to explain that it was the place we were trying to go.

Two of the men seemed quite agitated, and seeing an old map on the wall I mimed, "Can you show me on this map where we are?"

They could and did. We were eighty kilometers across country from Pattaya and about half a kilometer from the Cambodian border. The only way out was to return the way we had come. It was the *second* left-hand turn which led to the Gulf of Siam.

Not every American woman was free to pick up and take a short trip, and one of my friends developed her interest in fabrics when she learned of the silk-weaving project conducted by the wife of one of the prominent Lao generals. Unlike some of her compatriots who were known to spend entire days gambling, this charming and energetic Lao woman was busy researching the sources and development of sericulture and was teaching other Lao women the art of silk weaving. She used intricate and delicate patterns in home-dyed, natural colors. Her craftsmanship was outstanding and a visit to her work area both an aesthetic and a cultural treat. Her display room featured silk pieces of deep purple and violet hues interlaced with gold, magenta and other shades of soft pink or rose, brilliant green and gold patterns and a blue that automatically bespoke of royalty and people in high places. It was a treat just to go and browse among her looms and her finished pieces and to dream of places to wear creations that might be fashionable from this exquisite work.

My American friend took it upon herself to produce silk, beginning with silkworms on mulberry leaves and progressing through cocoons stewed in huge vats of boiling water. She could demonstrate the subsequent delicate art of threading out the silk created by this amazing process using very long, slender wooden chopsticks. I felt fortunate to be able to observe this process whenever I took her mulberry leaves from the tree in our yard as a supplement to her limited supply.

Toward the end of my stay in Laos I myself began to learn to weave. As I fumbled with a warp and woof, the endless knots and the simplest of patterns, I gained new respect for the process, and the weavers. I thought of the genesis of the thread, the dyeing, the intricate weaving and the patience required to prepare the looms. I thought of Boonpheng's mother and the loom under her stilt house in the refugee village where she wove cloths to sell in the market. She could not afford silks, but her work was nonetheless professional and as her only means of support for herself and her family of small children weaving was far from an avocation—it was her lifeline.

17
Embroidery and Opium

Some of our neighbors entertained themselves by taking shopping trips to Bangkok on the commissary run, or even quick runs to Hong Kong. John and I preferred to explore more of Laos and were fortunate to have an open invitation from Jack and Marge Huxtable to visit them in Ban Houei Sai. Three countries, Burma, Thailand and Laos meet at the bend of the Mekong River where Houei Sai is situated. When we could get away from Vientiane, a visit to a tribal area in any part of Laos was always a treat. To visit the famous "Golden Triangle" was doubly intriguing.

During one visit to the Huxtables Jack issued a spur of the moment invitation "to travel up the Mekong" with him on a school inspection that had sent us scurrying for sunglasses and hats. Ensconced in a small boat, headed up the river, we were soon inspecting both shores and were thrilled to find elephants at work in one area, lifting logs with their powerful trunks and hauling them up the riverbank to be graded and numbered. In this land of a million elephants these were the first we had seen.

Their activity, albeit picturesque, was also a poignant example of the rape of the teak forests in Southeast Asia. Enterprising and unscrupulous foreign merchants were often aided by greedy government officials who granted them permission to log the forests. Some of these lands belonged to the king. The laborers were paid pitiful wages, and the forests were irretrievably denuded. Millions of dollars were being realized from these valuable teak harvests, but neither the Lao people nor the Lao economy benefitted.

At the end of an hour's ride I stood on a dusty path in the center of a Yao village in northern Laos, watching the drivers of a long mule train tighten the hitches. There were more than thirty small mules, each laden with heavy burlap bags securely roped and tied. The path on which I stood was not more than ten feet wide and led past some dingy, sagging huts. On a low stool in front of one of these houses, metal-rimmed glasses perched on her nose, was a Yao woman. Needle and thread in hand, she was working intricate embroidery on a large piece of black cloth. The embroidery was a unique vertical stitch resembling a weaving stitch, one of the five traditional patterns used on the two matching panels of women's loose trousers. The colors were red hues, mainly magenta and pink, but she also was using blue and golden orange threads. The work was exquisitely complex, the setting starkly primitive.

Turbaned, wearing around their necks thick, round yarn sashes that resembled boas and were three to four feet long, the Yao, also known as Mien, are a tribal group thought to have originally come from southern China. They are unique among the tribal groups in Laos in that they have a written language.

Children playing in the dusty paths all wore small caps which identified them as belonging to this ethnic group. The caps were made of red and black cloth with bold patterns appliqued on the entire crown and red pompoms attached to the crown and often the sides. The children resembled bobbing apples as they ran and played together and were distinctively eye-catching when they accompanied their parents to another village.

"And what's in those bags?" I gestured towards the mules, which were being lined up to start on their journey.

In a low tone Jack stated that there was probably opium in the bags, although the drivers would tell us it was a less lethal agricultural product.

I was shocked. "Opium! Are you standing here telling me that you just watched a shipment of opium leave this village and head for the border?"

Jack, an agricultural worker for USAID, shrugged his shoulders at my innocence and explained that he had no authority to prevent this shipment. In fact, he continued, he didn't *know* it was opium, he just suspected there would be a large amount of the raw product intermingled with whatever else was being carried. It was common knowledge that mule teams were a major conduit for the opium grown in the infamous Golden Triangle. Branfman, in *Laos: War and Revolution,* claims that it was fairly common knowledge that General Ouane Rathikone, commander-in-chief of the Laotian Army, had as his main source of power, "his exclusive control over the opium trade from Northern Laos" (223). The general had direct connections also with the royal family, thus acquiring another source of power to be used when expedient.

As I was dividing my attention between the mule train and the Yao embroiderers, a young Yao woman came to the older woman seeking help with a square of black homespun perhaps fifteen inches in size, upon which she was practicing a variety of embroidery stitches. I learned that the young women are taught from the time they are six years old and practice their skills in this way before trying a larger piece. Her work also was delicate, intricate, and perfect. I asked if I could buy it, and she sold it to me for fifteen dollars. This was a fair price, but high for goods purchased in a remote village and demonstrated that these people had already learned how to apply Western principles of supply and demand, enhanced by the presence of the affluent foreigners in their midst.

As we stood watching the women work on their embroidery pieces I overheard an angry exchange among several small children and watched with interest as an adult moved to defuse the anger. Everywhere in Laos it was common to see strife turned quickly into agreement and smiles. I found that not only the Mien, but the Lao Loum, the lowland Lao, and the Hmong settle disputes quickly. Among some of the tribal groups serious conflict within the family is cause for the household to split up, to avoid further altercations.

Years later, as these people became refugees in Western countries, the tribal methods of solving problems had to be understood and used by social workers and resettlement personnel if they wanted to heal serious breaches between individuals and families with whom there were problems. The Western method of an individual talking with a counselor to solve a problem simply does not work with many of the refugees who have left Laos. A calling together of the family members involved in the dispute along with honorable and revered village elders is the acceptable method of mediation. Once this larger group decides on the course of action, the principals are bound by the solution on penalty of complete ostracization by the community.

The assignment given my agricultural-worker friend who had brought me to visit the Yao village was to find substitute crops for the opium so widely cultivated by all of the hill tribes in this area. The villagers had long since learned that the sticky substance painstakingly collected from opium pods was a cash crop highly valued by the strangers who came from faraway places. They also quickly discovered that it was easier to earn a living through opium culture than with vegetables which are perishable and hard to grow at the 3,000-foot-plus altitude required by opium poppies.*

**See David Feingold, "Opium and Politics in Laos," p. 332, in Adams and McCoy, eds.,* Laos: War and Revolution, *and, indeed, his entire chapter, for information on opium culture and distribution in Laos.*

Opium is the aspirin of Southeast Asian tribal groups. Older people with the aches and pains of arthritis or other disabling ailments find release and relief in the use of opium. Some do indeed become addicted, and if they do they are watched over and taken care of by others in the village. It is the Asian equivalent of having an American family member on pain medication. One seldom saw drug addicts on the streets of Vientiane or Luang Prabang.

The exception was a Hmong woman I took to be in her fifties who rode a bicycle around Vientiane and who sold crude silver jewelry to any American she could corner. Her rings and bracelets, hammered silver with designs etched into them, were very attractive, and I was a willing customer. The woman was very thin, her hair sparse and dull, her skin leathery and dry. She spoke in nervous, short twitches. I thought little about her addiction until I learned that she was only in her twenties.

Jack Huxtable had on another occasion pointed out to me that Lao officials apparently traveled with impunity both inside and outside of Laos, and he further revealed that most American employees in Laos assumed that many of these officials carried heroin in their attaché cases, refined in the mountain factories hidden in Laos and upper Thailand or Burma. After reading David Feingold's chapter in Adams and McCoy's *Laos: War and Revolution,* I came to the conclusion that I seemed to be one of the few people in Laos who didn't know that the hand-carried luggage of high officials was never inspected.

I was even more dismayed when I began to understand that at the same time as agricultural workers were being paid by USAID to try to persuade growers to change their crops, Air America was said to be flying drugs out of Laos and using the proceeds of their sale to finance the clandestine CIA war. Having heard the accusations made by both Americans and Lao close to this situation, I cannot claim to know the truth, but if mules were used in the villages, why not planes to transport it from the cities? Feingold also gives a comprehensive account of the role of American air support in the promotion and transport of opium trade in Laos, gratuitously pointing out that everyone else "involved with the political economy of Laos ends up involved with opium. . . . Why should it be any different with us?" (339).

Many of the men who worked in Laos when we did have consistently denied clains about any such activity, characterizing them as vicious and false accusations, and when I lived there I wanted desperately to believe them. The fact is that now, years later, the involvement of the United States in simultaneously promoting and suppressing drug production and distribution continues to be one of our country's most shameful activities. Far from changing our ways, we seem to have just changed locations. In recent years we appear to have substituted the generals of Panama for the Yao, and Panama City for Ban Houei Sai. In the matter of the suppression of drug trafficking, the United States is continually out-maneuvered and out-guessed.

I have been asked many times why the United States wasn't more successful in getting farmers to switch crops. It isn't that easy. Raw opium brings a much higher price than any other crop produced, and even when growers are willing to switch crops the soil, transportation and market conditions make it unrealistic. Feingold describes it in succinct ecological terms:

> Ecological limitations restrict the growing of poppies to fields above 3000 feet. Because of this comparative ecological advantage vis-à-vis the lowlands—an advantage shared by few other crops—and because of its high value per unit weight, opium is an ideal crop for regions whose access to markets is limited by steep mountain trails and transportation by human carriers and packhorses. [329]

Hidden behind all of this, of course, is the bitter truth that it is not the small grower who really benefits in any major way from drug trafficking. It is the government officials who are cut into the entire, intricate marketing process who keep this kind of activity viable. The American government has learned the hard way that trying to settle matters between drug lords and political overlords is a thankless, if not impossible, task.

We left the Yao village after a few hours, considerably more aware of the complexity of issues that face any kind of humanitarian-political-developmental efforts being made by an affluent nation to help solve the economic and political problems of a small nation. Might and wealth cannot always provide answers to the questions that are raised, and perhaps can seldom really identify with many of the grass roots issues that need solving.

This matter of being a member of a big, wealthy nation gnawed away at me as I traveled around Laos. As in the case of the huge irrigation project versus the installation of small pumps, I saw other instances of our glorification of bigness closing our eyes to basic, simple answers. The lack of electricity looked as if it were being solved by the building of a hydroelectric dam at Nam Ngum, but the electricity generated was slated to be sent into Thailand and only a very small percentage would benefit any Lao community. Roads, already mentioned, did not help farmers get their produce into the markets unless they just happened to be along a designated military route.

There were some ways, however, in which small problems were addressed by practical answers. One way the American Women's Club found to solve a persistent problem with limited funds was to underwrite the construction of what the Lao termed "watchers' sheds." These were shelters adjacent to hospitals, shelters in which the families of patients could stay.

For many years Operation Brotherhood, using medical personnel from the Philippines, had been staffing hospitals in the major population centers in Laos. The patient care system in an Asian hospital is a remarkable partnership between professional staff and the relatives of the patient. The hospital nurses and doctors provide medical care, but feeding and personal body care are the responsibility of the family.

As a result of this system, several relatives often accompany the patient to the hospital and live on the grounds where they cook his or her meals, do the laundry and provide simple patient care. In Luang Prabang the quarters for these family members were in ruins, a situation that was brought to the attention of the Social Assistance Committee. I made a trip to the hospital and confirmed the urgent need to reconstruct these shed-like facilities and proposed that the Women's Club provide funds for the materials and labor.

I saw these facilities in use later in my stay in Laos when I was asked to attend the dedication of a milk kitchen at the hospital, a second facility to which we contributed. This kitchen housed a supplementary feeding project which was a joint effort of the Lao and the Swiss Red Cross, with assistance from USAID. This latter group had alerted the Women's Club of Laos about this project, designed to prepare and provide milk for hospitalized and severely undernourished children. The facilities had been renovated to resemble a simple Lao kitchen, devoid of steam jets and huge stainless steel containers, yet providing equipment for sterilization that allowed local people to feel comfortable when they used it. The maintenance tasks for the equipment were easy to follow. The sterilized water in clean, sterilized containers would be used in the reconstitution of powdered milk under conditions seldom available to a village family. The uncontaminated milk was vital to a newborn.

As president of the American Women's Club, I was invited to attend the ribbon-cutting ceremony for this new milk kitchen. The wife of the local USAID official not only solicited my presence, but indicated that I was also expected to make a short dedication statement, preferably in the Lao language. Knowing that representatives of the Pathet Lao would also attend the ceremony, I labored hard over my speech.

I practiced my short presentation to the critical ears of several of my Lao friends and wrote pronunciation tips all over my page. At the dedication I stumbled over unfamiliar words and hoped the audience would be so pleased to see me in my best silk Lao *sinh* speaking their language, or trying to, that they would ignore or forgive my halting delivery.

I was much more nervous than I needed to have been on the day of the ceremony. The Lao in the audience beamed their approval of my efforts and crowded around afterward, *"Madame vow Lao* kaang *lai."* They were more than generous to suggest that I spoke Lao "*very* well," but I basked in the praise.

Flushed with the audience's generous applause, I toured the new facilities with the local hospital staff, the *chao koueng* (county official) and the *nai ban*, the local head of the village. The milk kitchen was a remarkable facility for this part of Laos, and I was proud and happy to have had a small part in making life a bit more bearable for these gentle, uncomplaining folk who were victims of a conflict not of their own making.

18
Sending Khamnouy to College

The decision to send Khamnouy to an American college seemed to be a natural outcome of our relationship with him. For months he had been a part of our household in one way or another, helping John with the bricking of a patio, housesitting when we went on R&R, introducing me to some of his friends and making sure we met his cousin, Loth.

Loth and Khamnouy showed up regularly to eat with us. Loth was also a student with a minimum of support toward his food and clothing, and once he discovered banana bread at our house he asked for a loaf a week. At the end of a visit he would tuck the bread under his arm and wheel off on his bicycle. Since the Lao do not have ovens in their homes Loth was probably the only student in Laos for whom banana bread became his daily breakfast.

Khamnouy's interest in all things practical became an irresistible tie to John. Here at last was a young man who sought to understand the principles of machines and of construction, who yearned to know how to make things and who was quick to absorb instructions. If John was not going to be geographically close to his own sons and able to badger them into helping him with projects, he could conscript this willing young Lao who so eagerly asked to learn. 'Nouy loved demonstrating the skills and the short cuts John taught him as they worked together. He obviously had an aptitude for working with his hands, and he didn't mind getting greasy or dirty.

The idea of sending him to an American university began to germinate when Khamnouy revealed to us that he was thinking about going to Thailand to one of the training schools that his Lao instructors had attended.

"No sir!" my husband exploded. "Khamnouy is not going to one of those schools. Why, when teachers get out of there they won't even touch a machine. Worthless." This was a harsh indictment and unfair when one considers the economic and social conditions out of which a trained teacher struggled in order to elevate his status beyond that of a common laborer. The concept of "hands-on" teaching was neither valued nor rewarded in the case of industrial arts instructors, which meant that graduates of the Thai technical training schools learned to theorize, but not to demonstrate.

I sympathized with John's frustration with the limitations of this kind of education and asked what he would suggest as an alternative to the Thai technical schools.

"I'd like to send him to a place like Stout. Now *there* he would really get good training." John had graduated from Stout Institute in Wisconsin when it was still a school dedicated to training men to work in the iron mines of that Midwest area. Now it was part of the University of Wisconsin system and noted for its excellence in the training of industrial arts teachers.

We began to talk about how to make arrangements to enroll Khamnouy in an American university, going over all the options, trusting that John's alumni status at Stout would carry some clout. We were prepared to be responsible for all of his expenses including transportation from Vientiane to Menomonie as well as tuition, room and board, and books.

I thought of those sub-zero storms in nearby Minnesota that our son Craig often wrote about and realized that Khamnouy would require a complete set of warm winter clothing. Perhaps there would be some cast-offs from family members to get him started. In any event, we needed a catalog and wrote off for it.

The three of us pored over the list of courses, accommodations and admonishments for applicants. Khamnouy's excitement was contagious as he plied John with questions about the campus and America and whether he would be near other members of the Rantala clan so that he would have family. I couldn't help wondering what his parents would think about all this and if they would have any way of imagining how far away Wisconsin is from Phone Xay, Laos. We asked Khamnouy what his parents would say when he told them he wanted to go to the United States to study.

"*Baw pen nyang.* Don't worry about it, they will understand." His eyes sparkled, and his whole body reflected the joyous anticipation of what was once an impossible dream. Could we send this young Lao away to America to school? We discussed it endlessly, sifting alternatives, working through problems, and at last found the answer. Yes, we could, and we were going to.

The next months were filled with application blanks and forms and efforts to discover what formalities the Lao government would require of us.

Stout was interested. In fact, Khamnouy was accepted as a freshman for the fall of 1974 based on the records of his junior year in the Fa Ngum High School. We were all elated. We had a year to plan for this, and we needed all of it.

Our first inkling of possible trouble came in the spring of 1974 during a stand-up cocktail party at the Australian consulate. I was chatting with one of the officials from the Lao Ministry of Education when he said in a deceptively casual manner, "I believe you and Mr. Rantala think you can send one of the Fa Ngum students to an American college."

I heard the skepticism in the "think you can" but did not at first understand it to be a reprimand and so cheerfully confirmed our plan, after which the man added, "He will, of course, need to get the approval of the Ministry of Education."

"Oh, and why is that, if he is a private student?"

"There is no such thing as a private student in Laos. The Ministry decides who will be sent abroad for higher education. We do not have high school students on such a list."

Not have him on a list? The smile froze on my face as I carefully inquired, "Are you saying that if the Ministry doesn't approve, Khamnouy will not be allowed to go to America, even if we foot the entire bill?"

An equally frozen smile matched mine. "I think you and Mr. Rantala should look carefully at the instructors with whom Mr. Rantala works. I am sure you will find an acceptable candidate."

With that the minister excused himself and left me raging and afraid. Not once in all the discussions we had held about sending Khamnouy to college had we seriously considered how our actions might be viewed within the Ministry of Education. Our American conditioning for seeing and solving problems had entirely blocked out the cultural and political difficulties inherent in this effort. It had never crossed our minds that private citizens would not be allowed to go to college as long as they could figure out a way to finance it.

I looked for John, extracting him from two Australian diplomats, and muttered, "Trouble, deep trouble. The MOE is going to block Khamnouy's application to go abroad to study." Hastily I capsulized the encounter I had just finished and watched John's face reflect the same anger I had felt. He squared his shoulders, thrust out his stubborn Finnish chin and said, "We shall see about that." We shortly left the party, too upset to engage in further small talk.

Everyone on the Hawaii team knew Khamnouy, but some seemed unconcerned that his educational plans might be aborted and advised us to heed the words of the minister and find another candidate. They were mildly sympathetic but not eager to "fight city hall" with us. This only hardened our determination. With some asperity we countered that we were not seeking to produce bureaucrats for the government of Laos. We wanted to encourage this particular young man whose aim was to get the best possible education that would equip him to return to Laos to help his people toward a better life. It did not seem an unreasonable goal.

Over the next weeks we built up a formidable arsenal of information about overseas studies. We held endless consultations, and we carefully planted information among the members of the USAID education section that would give them ammunition to use on Khamnouy's behalf. To our great relief some of the more important USAID officials let it be known among equally important officials in the Lao Ministry of Education that to block plans to educate this young man abroad would not be looked on with favor. It was a tense battle, but we won. Khamnouy would receive an exit visa.

As departure time drew close we began to think about an itinerary for his travels. With a thirteen-hundred-dollar travel scholarship awarded to him by the American Women's Club of Laos he could be routed to see some of the United States on his way to college. We pored over maps, calendar in hand, working out a trip that would help a young man from a Lao village grasp something of the vastness and potential of a country like the United States. Khamnouy's vibrant and inquisitive nature would stand him in good stead as he wrestled with luggage and schedules.

He would fly from Bangkok to Seattle and go by bus across the state of Washington to stay in Spokane with the parents of our daughter-in-law, Sally. From there he would go by bus to Minneapolis to be met by John's sister and her husband. After this visit he would spend some time with Craig and Sally in the cabin up in the Boundary Waters wilderness area of northern Minnesota.

Craig would see that he arrived in time for freshman orientation activities at the university. With the exit permit assured and air tickets on order, all seemed to be going smoothly. How wrong we were!

Khamnouy took his finals and left for Phone Xay to say goodbye to everyone in his home village. Two days later he had a call from the principal of the Fa Ngum school.

I picked up the phone and listened in frozen horror as Somsak stated coldly that Khamnouy had failed all of his exams. Stunned, I managed to gasp, "All of his exams? How can that be?" I knew that he had been at the top of his class in nearly every subject. The IVS English teacher had recently told me that Khamnouy was his best pupil. "It's not possible for him to have failed everything."

In icy tones the principal repeated, "I have the grades in front of me. All F's."

I put down the phone and groped for a chair, shaking violently. How could this have happened? What in the world was Khamnouy thinking of, to flunk everything? I must reach John. I must reach Khamnouy. I must notify the Stout campus, University of Wisconsin. I must pull myself together and think this through.

Reaching Khamnouy was not easy when he was off in a refugee village, but I brazenly called the USAID post at Ban Xon and asked them to please send someone up to Phone Xay to find Khamnouy. Yes, I assured them, it was a matter of life and death.

When John came home he was even more distraught than I. "But I monitored his practical arts exam myself. He and his partner finished first in putting together the machine that was their test problem. That one project alone counted for 60 percent of the mark, and they did it perfectly!"

"John, I'm going to talk with the English teacher. He's an American, an IVS volunteer. Surely he can tell us something about this."

The conversation with this young man confounded me even more. In a formal, neutral voice he simply said, "Khamnouy did not satisfactorily complete his course. It was necessary to fail him."

"What do you mean, didn't complete the course? Were there papers he didn't turn in? Did he miss an assignment? What are you saying? You told me a couple of weeks ago that he was the most promising student of English in the entire class. How could this happen? Did everyone in the class fail? What did you ask him?"

Indistinct mumbling on the other end of the line provoked me into yelling, "What's going *on*?"

"Sorry, I've nothing more to say."

I sat in silence, hugging myself in grief and misery until Khamnouy's call came through on the USAID line from up country. When I told him about the grades, he said in a tight, firm tone, "No! No, Mom, that's not possible."

"Maybe not," I said bitterly, "but two of your teachers have already confirmed it. I have no reason to believe the others will be any different. Oh, Khamnouy," I burst out, "how could you *do* it?"

"Mom, listen, believe me, I didn't fail, honest." 'Nouy's voice cracked with intensity and anger. "I didn't do it. I'm coming down. I'll come as quickly as I can." My thoughts were racing in every direction. Had 'Nouy been so confident of himself that he had simply goofed off during these last weeks and been totally unprepared for the tests? What other explanation could there be for total failure?

We have to notify Stout, I thought. We can't send him all the way to Menomonie only to have his grades follow and have him denied entrance to the freshman class. It would not be fair to have some other student turned away because we procrastinated in notifying the admissions office of these bad grades. Sadly I composed the letter, addressed and stamped it and took it to the American post office in the USAID compound. I turned away with gulping sobs in my chest reflecting the failure of all of our plans, sick at heart for myself, for Khamnouy, for John.

That evening Khampheng showed up after work. One look at her, and I burst into tears, the frustration and humiliation of all that had gone on that day overcoming me. In her response she came as close to criticizing me as any Lao had ever dared.

"Mom, Mom," she said. "Stop. Don't you see? They are jealous. The principal, Somsak, he's furious because you are sending Khamnouy to America to college rather than sending him, or at least one of his teachers. So he has decided to flunk 'Nouy. He told everyone to do it."

I looked at her in horrified disbelief. "Oh, Khampheng, he wouldn't do that. He *couldn't* do that. No principal can alter grades to suit his own whims."

"Don't be naïve," she retorted. "I have been telling Khamnouy he ought to pay his teachers to be sure he got good grades. I even offered him money. I didn't tell you about this because I knew you wouldn't approve."

"Pay his teachers for good grades?" My head whirled at the implications of what she was saying.

"That's the trouble," Khampheng continued. "He's stubborn, just like you. He said he wouldn't do it. Now see what has happened!" I was truly aghast at her revelation, and it showed on my face. Khampheng shrugged, giving me a look of pity and repeated, "I thought of telling you to do this, but I just knew you wouldn't."

"Khampheng, this is monstrous. You don't 'pay off' teachers in an American school in order to receive the grades you have earned!" I paced the floor, trying to comprehend the debacle facing all of us.

She shrugged again. "It's the way things are done here. You can't get very far if you don't bribe someone." I knew she was correct in her assessment and wondered how I could have ignored the possibility that this kind of payoff would affect our innocent desire to educate one young man.

"But what are we going to do? It's too late. They have the grades and they won't change them."

"Just don't pay any attention. Go right on with your plans. Didn't you say the university has already accepted Khamnouy? Well, let him go."

Was she serious? Could we really do that? I thought of the remark

Somsak, the principal, had made to me on the phone. "Too bad he won't be able to go to America now!" and this time my memory heard the crowing triumph in his words. He *did* plan this!

In all the confusion I had forgotten the letter, written and mailed to the registrar, University of Wisconsin, Stout. "Oh, my," I moaned. "I've already written Stout to tell them. I can't undo this now. What am I going to do?"

The postmistress at the U.S. post office in Vientiane was a friend. Next morning when it opened I was first in line. I rushed to the window and said, "I must talk with you. I've got to get back a letter that I put into the mail late yesterday afternoon."

Fortunately, mail did not go out every day, and I felt fairly confident that a letter posted in the late afternoon still lay somewhere in that post office, uncanceled, not yet processed.

We both knew the prohibitions against retrieving already posted letters, and she reminded me icily that if she tampered with the mails she could lose her job.

The anguish in my voice was clear. "I know, but honestly, this is life and death. The letter is addressed to the University of Wisconsin, Stout. It must *not* go out. I'll not breathe a word, Vivian. You've got to help me."

She gave me a long, calculating look.

"It's not for myself," I rushed on. "It's our Lao son, Khamnouy. His whole future is at stake. Please, please."

She softened slightly and agreed to keep an eye out for the envelope as she sorted the mail later that morning.

The call came just after lunch. "I've found the letter and have put it aside." In the late afternoon I went to the post office, and she handed me the uncanceled envelope, the letter intact. It would not travel to Menomonie. Khamnouy's future was not irretrievably damaged, and I hoped fervently that no one would uncover this unforgivable breach of post office routine. Neither of us ever mentioned the incident again.

It was not many days later that I was attending a USAID function and found myself face to face with the vindictive and unscrupulous principal. "Too bad about Khamnouy," he smirked.

"Yes, isn't it." I retorted. "He leaves tomorrow for Wisconsin." Leaving Somsak staring at me in ill-controlled disbelief I gave him the traditional Lao clasped-hand greeting, uttered, *"Puok en mai,"* until next time, and sailed out of the room.

Khamnouy's parents came to Vientiane for his departure. 'Nouy was scrubbed and shining in new slacks and shirt, a small carry-on in his hands. His mother, smiling and quiet in her lovely Lao woven *sinh;* his father tall and taciturn, awkwardly embracing his son once the plane was ready for

Sending Khamnouy off to college. (Left to right) John Rantala, Judy Rantala, Khamnouy, Tai Sivongsay, Piavong Sivongsay (Khamnouy's parents).

boarding. Standing together at the airport, we four sent him off to this new chapter in life, unaware that he would never again see Laos or that his parents would never again see him.

Khamnouy's first days in America were cushioned by a home visit in the state of Washington during which Khamnouy eagerly accepted every suggested "Would you like to see," leaving his hosts limp with fatigue when it was time for him to move on. His energy was boundless, and he looked forward to his arrival in northern Minnesota, perhaps the most exciting of all visits for him. He would at long last meet his American "brother" Craig and "sister" Sally. In his culture they were already as bonded to him as blood relatives, for, after all, weren't they family?

In the wilderness of northern Minnesota Khamnouy learned that the United States held more than vast spaces and big cities. Here were rivers and lakes, fish, trees, even squirrels! It felt familiar to him and his eyes sparkled at each discovery. Shortly after his arrival he begged Craig to lend him the shotgun and within a few minutes returned with a plump red squirrel swinging by its tail. Beaming in anticipation he announced, "We'll have it for dinner." Perhaps he didn't notice Craig's blanched face. Craig—who liked his hamburger very well done and seemed to have existed mostly on popcorn since he was a child—eat roasted squirrel?

'Nouy skinned it with care, marinated the meat and cut it in small strips which he toasted over an open fire. Eaten with rice and a hot sauce concocted as best the available ingredients would allow, it was a rare feast. Craig nibbled a piece, hoping that his stomach would not betray him when he tried to swallow. Sally found it palatable but just the idea of eating squirrel somehow failed to quicken her appetite. 'Nouy, oblivious to all this, enjoyed himself hugely and courteously took the roasted head, cracked it open with one thwack and politely offered Craig the first sampling of that great delicacy, squirrel brain.

That did it. Holding his hand over his mouth Craig fled to the safety of the front porch. 'Nouy, by now well aware of Craig's aversion, gave a hoot of laughter and dug in. This episode, reported in a letter from Craig, sent us into stomach-grabbing laughter as we pictured the three of them coping with roast squirrel garnished with hot sauce.

In addition to finding squirrels, Khamnouy was delighted to discover that there were Americans who knew about woodcraft and living in the forests, who fished from the lakes and streams and chopped wood and swam in the cold lake waters. This was life as he had experienced it in Laos as a small boy, and he loved it. Folks around the lake who were full-time residents found in Khamnouy a spark that lit fires of friendship between them. Archie Kirk, who ran a small resort and fishing service, loved to "talk story" after work, asking about Khamnouy's family and about life in Laos, a country he had never heard of until we had returned to the cabin on our first home leave. Mrs. Kirk found a willing consumer of home-baked cookies and went out of her way to keep Khamnouy supplied. They wrote to him when he went to college and asked about him whenever we saw them. It was from the Kirks' phone that we received the first news of Khamnouy's later illness.

All too soon the time was up, and by bus Khamnouy traveled nearly four hundred miles through Minneapolis to Menomonie and his introduction to American college life. Visiting him there in the fall of 1974, we found him the center of his dorm life with friends hardly letting him alone long enough to study. When they played tricks on him, hiding his books, tying knots in his clothes, swiping his towel when he went to the shower, he laughed ingenuously at his own naïveté. When he was prevailed upon to do errands, sent to pick up hamburgers, to drop off a late paper, to get the dry cleaning, he did them with such good grace and speed that teasing turned into respect and malicious pranks into affectionate horseplay.

His classmates taught him every swear word they knew, and when we visited him after a six month separation, he could hardly utter a sentence without embarrassingly fearful expletives spewing forth. He didn't know the difference, and the roommates thought it hilarious. I was shocked and John bemused. With some impromptu tutoring, however, Khamnouy came to honor our insistence that he use some substitute phrases and from then on tried very hard to clean up his language.

Everyone on campus seemed to know him. Not only was he friendly with other international students, but the faculty and staff, especially the director of the International Student Office, who helped him secure a scholarship, were well acquainted with him. He was enormously popular with the girls and complained to us that they followed him around and called him up to talk endlessly on the telephone or to ask him out.

"I don't know, Mom," he confided. "They don't let me alone. They're just friends. No one special. But sometimes three or four all come to take me out, and I don't know why they do." Assessing his handsome features, ready smile and sparkling eyes, I could understand why the girls were attracted to him, but I decided to let him work it out in his own fashion without any advice from me.

He apparently made out well enough, remaining popular all through his college days without being trapped into a steady relationship. He was a sought-after companion at holiday times, and letters from the parents of his peers told us about his Thanksgiving or Christmas visit, assuring us that he was a welcome guest. These glimpses of Midwestern home life were especially interesting to him because most of his classmates came from rural areas and on their farms he found an opportunity to perform daily chores and to learn more about how people lived in this, his new country.

He quickly adopted American customs. His hair was by now shoulder length, he lived in jeans, and he had succeeded in finding a used car to drive. But it was his first year Christmas cards that touched us most. On them the signature read, "Khamnouy R. Sivongsay." John's sister, "Auntie Bernice," was the first to bring this to our attention, and we rightly surmised that the "R" stood for Rantala. This was his way of letting us know that we had passed the ultimate test—he now considered himself to be a full member of the family—he was one of us.

19
Vang Vieng

In the fall of 1974 everything in Laos began to change. Khamnouy was off to America to begin college in Wisconsin. Souvanh, Khampheng's husband, was sent to southern France for training in finance and budgeting. The rest of us, including the servants, missed him and the animated conversations around the dinner table that their occasional visits had made possible.

Khampheng and Nono seemed especially at loose ends. Finding life at home confining, Khampheng began to come to the house regularly after work and often showed up on Fridays for the weekend. She became the daughter I had never had, and as we shared pieces of our lives with each other, a close, supportive relationship developed.

John and I were, thus, pleased when she one day said, "It is twelve years since I have been able to visit the village I was born in. Now the roads are open. Would you like to go up to Vang Vieng?"

Her parents had prudently taken her to Vientiane after Kong Le and the neutralists began to use this village as their headquarters. She was twelve years old and at her departure left behind two brothers and a village full of relatives. From their new city home, Khampheng had continued her schooling through to graduation from the *lycée*, and was now employed in a bank. Fluent in French and English, she supplemented her income by teaching LSL, Lao as a second language, to American USAID employees and their spouses.

In this spring of 1975 the political situation seemed to be improving. Americans were allowed to venture further on the roads leading out of Vientiane enabling us to secure permission to drive Khampheng to her home village.

Saying good-bye to Souvanh at Wattay airport in 1974 are Khampheng, Nono, John Rantala and Judy Rantala.

The prospect of a weekend away from Km6 and the usual repetitive activities galvanized us into action. After work on Friday afternoon we loaded the pickup truck and headed north, determined to make the most of our up-country adventure. John and I had chafed at being confined to a small geographical area with restrictions on where and how far we could drive. We were eager to see more of Laos and to meet village people. As we drove we plied Khampheng with questions and then laughed when she reminded us that her memories were dim and were those of a young child at best.

The road was virtually deserted. No cars or trucks passed, and we saw only one bus during our sixty-mile drive. The jungle was lush and thick and could have been hiding a platoon of rebel soldiers, but we really didn't care. We were in a holiday mood and felt invincible.

It was nearly dark when we arrived in Vang Vieng, yet the stark beauty of the setting was awesome. The evening sun was brushing the top of a sheer rock cliff which flanked one side of the village, an unexpected and dramatic background in otherwise flat terrain. The nearby river nourished lush vegetation as a background for the bamboo stilt houses scattered across the village. At that hour it was a picturebook panorama which we viewed in hushed appreciation.

We were hustled to the home of one of 'Pheng's brothers, Sithuk. He was expecting us and mercifully spoke surprisingly good English. This brother held the army rank of a major and had remained in the village because his political stance had led him to support Kong Le and to oppose the rightist military forces who defeated him and who were now in control of the government in Laos. Political differences like this within families were common and did not seem to create hard feelings. The Lao *"baw pen nyang"* (don't worry) attitude spilled over into politics, and kinship was strong once families were reunited.

The brother's home was large, in Lao terms. Not a typical stilt hut, but a fairly sizeable dwelling with a number of rooms and wooden floors polished by years of barefooted use. It wasn't too clear just where we would be sleeping, and Khampheng looked a bit nervous about our ability to adapt to the situation.

"We didn't come here expecting a hotel," we assured her. "We came to meet your family. We will make out all right wherever you put us."

The talk over supper, which included sticky rice, some smoked fish, and a curry with vegetables, was of the fishing trip scheduled for the following day. The brothers welcomed this opportunity to take a couple of days off to enjoy this most favorite of Lao activities.

"We will take Mr. John on a trip down the river, to fish and camp out." Always game for an adventure, John's face shone with anticipation. In a mixture of Lao and English they talked about gear, food and the logistics of the expedition. I would remain in the village and "do the rounds" by visiting the *"pi nong,"* the relatives who were eager to fuss over Khampheng.

Dinner over, we were ready to turn in for the night and embarrassed to have Sithuk and his wife insist that we take their bed. Our protests were brushed aside, and we soon snuggled under comforters which were most welcome in the cool of the night. We stretched out in luxury, grateful for rest after a long day.

Early morning found the household bustling with activity. Breakfast preparations, again on a toe-height charcoal fire, were nothing short of miraculous. The women scurried around preparing rice and eggs, washing fruit, making tea and coffee. Often they balanced a small child on one hip while moving an iron pot from the stove to a serving area.

The military connections of this brother were obvious in the number of vehicles and G.I. materials lying around. He was very much in charge. The men were packing clothes, discussing fishing lines, putting basic foods into packages and stowing things in the jeep.

Shortly after breakfast we all took off for the river where slender pirogues awaited the fishing party as other men from the village joined them. There were twelve men in all, several dogs and a lot of gear to be packed into the narrow Lao boats. They were skillful in stowing their packs and at last shouted that they were ready to take off. It was the last I was to see of John for two days.

Khampheng and I returned to the village and began our visits. It appeared to me that every small Lao house in the village held an aunt.

"Really, Khampheng, are all of these people related to you?"

She giggled, saying, "Most of them are *pi nong,* yes, and those who aren't knew me as a little girl so they consider me family."

It wasn't left to us to choose which homes to visit. As we sauntered through the village someone would come to the door of a small house and invite us in. We would join others seated on mats on the floor and be fussed over while the women exclaimed and asked questions. Lots of the questions were about me. My height always elicited comments, and the opportunity to quiz a foreigner was not to be missed. The villagers had been cut off from Vientiane, indeed, any other community, for much of their lives. They were entertained by my unsuccessful efforts to sit on the floor as daintily as they did and they plied me with cool drinks.

When lunch time came the auntie in the home we were currently visiting looked somewhat distraught and was, I realized, asking Khampheng what I could eat.

"Don't worry, Mom eats anything. She likes Lao food." I nodded in confirmation.

As a mat was being placed before us and small bowls readied for our lunch, one by one other village women slipped up the steps and into the room with a basket of sticky rice, a dish of meat or a curry, a plate of vegetables or some fruit. We cleaned our hands on a damp towel provided by the hostess and remained seated on the floor. The food was placed in the center of our small circle. Providing our lunch was the responsibility of everyone in the village, and these other women came with donations so there would be no danger of embarrassment for the women in whose home we happened to be just at lunch time. Women who brought the food did not join us, but neither did they leave. They needed to see for themselves if this foreigner could eat their food. As the tensions abated they began to talk and laugh and nudge each other, and I took this to mean that I had passed muster.

I gnawed on some very tough chicken wings, enjoyed a delicate vegetable soup and cemented everything together with the inevitable sticky rice. As the center of attention, I knew I would be judged by the deftness with which I managed my food, eaten only with our fingers. All the women watched me covertly, pretending indifference yet scrutinizing every move.

I wondered if a non–Asian woman had ever been a guest in that village and hoped I would uphold whatever standards by which they were judging me.

Following lunch we moved to yet another home until I pleaded with Khampheng for mercy.

"Enough already. These aren't *my* aunts, you know." Everyone was very solicitous of my welfare and obviously curious about me, but all of the conversation was in Lao, and Khampheng was so busy fielding questions she had little time to translate for my benefit. My smile seemed stuck on my face, and I felt the need to walk about a bit on my own. 'Pheng acknowledged my patience and agreed to release me from further visits for the day.

Unfortunately it had been late in the morning when I had begun to realize what the endless glasses of coconut water, produced on the spot by topping a fresh coconut, were doing to my digestive system. I started to sip my drinks ever so slowly, pleading quietly with Khampheng to find a way to relieve me of additional libations. She thought this hugely funny, but she was not the one who suffered stomach cramps and spent much of the afternoon within close range of a toilet.

When I was not otherwise engaged, I wandered around the village, watching women at their looms under their stilt homes, creating beautiful patterns in skirts and shawls. We had brought silk thread with us from the Vientiane market, a luxury the countryside did not afford, and the women accepted it with delight. They gladly showed me what they were working on and asked what sort of weaving I did.

For more than four years I had been observing Lao women at their weaving and had recently purchased a handsome rosewood loom on which I was learning something of the craft myself. When Khampheng found me later that day I was providing great entertainment for two women who were unsuccessfully trying to teach me to knot the warp threads with one hand.

"I'll never learn," I moaned. "I'm all thumbs."

To my surprise, she didn't know much about weaving, either. Her Vang Vieng relatives were shocked and vowed to teach her.

During that same afternoon I visited a small temple or *wat* in the center of the village. It was in bad disrepair, but there were offerings of food and incense and candles indicating that it was an actively used center of the village religious life.

In Major Sithuk's house that evening I sat quietly watching and listening to Khampheng exchange child-rearing ideas with Soudsada, her sister-in-law. We had left Khampheng's small boy in the care of his grandmother for the weekend, and she welcomed the opportunity to exchange child-rearing ideas with her cousins. She also talked about her life in Vientiane and brought them up to date on her work. The hours Khampheng had spent teaching me Lao paid off more readily during these home conversations, because the Lao was more understandable than that used by the other village women, and although I still struggled to speak the language, the joking and family banter all sounded very familiar.

The following day we returned to the river to meet the fishermen and to have a picnic. Trees shaded a natural landing spot on the rapidly flowing Nam Lick River. The children laughed and splashed in the water. The older folks arranged some of the food supplies and then hunkered down to talk and joke and await the return of the fishermen.

Disheveled and smiling, they showed up with wild tales of the fish that got away. Fortunately there were some that got caught, and these were promptly chopped up into a fish *lap*. This most typical of Lao foods also includes bean sprouts, chopped vermicelli, mint and red peppers. Knowing that Lao rivers are polluted and loaded with parasites such as liver flukes, I tried to substitute sticky rice and other foods for the raw fish concoction hoping I could camouflage my hesitation about eating their favorite dish. John helped the men grill small fish over an open fire as he expounded on the trip. Even he seemed somewhat surprised at the ease with which he had survived, adding, "We caught and ate a huge snake. Very tasty. Also we had plenty of fish to eat, smoked over the fire like this, and sticky rice." He paused. "There are a lot of strange noises in the jungle at night."

"Did you get any sleep?"

When I inquired further he was vague as to what animals might have been circling their jungle camp and complained, "The dogs barked most of the night and tore off to chase critters every now and then."

I looked at his grimy hands and face and suggested he might want to wash in the river before tackling the picnic fare.

He stood at the edge of the river, gazing down toward where they had gone and added, "I couldn't tell you where we have been, but it was real jungle. I felt as if we were a hundred miles from anything. The men sat up half the night singing and telling jokes, and we've had a great time."

John's tone of voice and the glint in his eyes told me the trip had been all he had hoped for and more, and I was relieved to have him back intact, braised snake meat and all. Sithuk and others came over to tell me what a good sport John was, how much they enjoyed having him along, and punctuated all this with a friendly slap on his back.

Lao picnics have a way of expanding themselves from what appear to be a very few containers and boxes into an endless display of foods. A bare piece of ground is covered with tatami (straw) mats and baskets of rice, pots of soup, dried meat, platters of cucumbers and mint, bean sprouts and red

Pirogue—typical Lao fishing boat—and John's fishing companions.

peppers are spread out, and suddenly there seems to be more food than can be consumed. This picnic gathered momentum as the beer flowed freely, voices grew louder, conversations more heated and the songs more raucous. Someone began to play the *khene* and soon men and women were dancing the graceful Lao *lamvong.* As dusk began to turn into evening, we gathered up the remnants, clambered into the jeeps and returned to the village, exchanging thanks for a wonderful day and gratitude for the peaceful surroundings that made our friendships close and deep.

Before we left Vang Vieng the following morning, we were taken to the medical dispensary which had been started in 1957 by Dr. Tom Dooley, who, in his book *The Edge of Tomorrow,* points out, "My mission was not to set up a permanent American outpost, but to establish something that the Lao themselves could carry on" (162). We found that this facility was still being staffed by the village medics and midwives he had trained. Woefully ill-equipped, it continued to serve as the center for all health care in the region and was shown to us with pride.

We said reluctant goodbyes to what was now also our extended family, promising to return soon. It was a promise we were not allowed to keep. Khampheng never saw Sithuk again, for he died in a re-education camp following the Pathet Lao takeover after she had fled to France.

20
The Beginning of the End

Now that Khampheng was so often with me, I begged her to teach me how to write the Lao language. All of the language teachers had shied away from doing this, admonished by someone in the USAID mission not to bow to the Americans' desires to learn to write Lao. The curls and squiggles of their language bear no resemblance to our romanized alphabet and are similar to, but not the same as, the Thai written language. We started with the basic primer, and like a first grader, I pored day after day over the first reader.

"Kaw, Khai, Kaw, Ki," a, b, c, d. As we went through each letter suddenly much of what she had formerly been trying to drill into my head became clear. I began to understand why the way I ended a word didn't sound right to her. It made a difference if I made a "d" sound where it should have been a "t." I could see it now, in the formation of the words I was learning to read, and I now heard it as well in all of our conversations. It was a joy to comprehend more fully this language I wanted so badly to learn.

Khampheng and I also now found time to devote to our determination to learn to weave. In every village in Laos I had found weavers busily at their looms. Most often they were set up under the stilt houses, where it was shady and where, also, an eye could be kept on the children while mother was at her loom. Lao weavers were skilled at their trade, and beautiful and intricate designs flowed from their nimble fingers. In the refugee villages the cloth was simple cotton, but in the towns they produced silk pieces using magnificent dyes.

I wondered aloud why Khampheng's mother had never taught her to weave. "I thought every Lao woman used a loom."

"Well, actually my mother isn't much of a weaver either," Khampheng confessed. "I don't really know why. Besides, when I was at school I didn't have the time."

"Then let's learn together," I begged.

Her mother had known an older woman in Vientiane who agreed to come to my Km6 house to give us lessons. This woman helped me select a beautiful rosewood loom which was set up on our screened porch. Twice a week we worked at our lessons, learning how to tie the threads for the warp and woof, pushing the shuttle back and forth. We learned to apply just the right amount of pressure and how to read simple patterns. It was a time for sharing confidences, for laughter and relaxation, and we began to develop our adeptness in this traditional craft of Laos. But it was not to be.

History caught up with both my language and my weaving lessons. All during the spring of 1975 there were major political upheavals. The recent evacuation of Saigon, which we learned about in those gut-wrenching photographs showing Vietnamese mobbing the helicopter airlifts from the roof of the American embassy, had lulled John and me into thinking that the Vietnamese Communists would be too busy rebuilding their own country to worry about what was happening in Laos.

Khampheng, on the other hand, was being warned by some of her friends that if she wanted to be reunited with her husband, who was studying in France, she needed to leave Laos as quickly as possible. Finally, in early May, she confided to me that she was trying to make arrangements that would enable her and her son, Nono, to fly to Paris.

Suddenly all of the Vietnamese began to exit Laos. Every major airline was booked solid, and Khampheng learned that it would be impossible to get an Air France booking to Paris. In desperation she made reservations on Aeroflot, via Hanoi and Moscow.

"Good grief!" I expostulated. "It is not only a horribly long trip, but they could yank you off at any one of those intermediate stops, and you would never get to France." Tales of students being shipped to Hanoi and Moscow were already feeding the rumor mill.

"I have no choice now. It's this or nothing. I must go." Khampheng was grim. She went to the offices that issued exit visas, and with her money and her passport she stood in line for two days. On Friday she got to within one person of the window when time ran out and the 4:30 closing bell rang.

On the other side of the window a former school chum saw 'Pheng standing there and hissed, "Slide your passport under the edge and come back Monday," slamming the window just short of Khampheng's trembling fingers.

The next day, Saturday, Khampheng announced, "I'm going to sell the Volkswagen."

The banks had been closed all week, and when I asked her where a buyer would get the money, she brushed my skepticism aside and pointed out that people had been hoarding their money for weeks and that someone would have cash.

Next we heard that Vietnamese people were being forbidden to leave Laos which meant the availability of airplane reservations on flights heretofore totally booked. Khampheng luckily secured a seat on an Air France flight to Paris for Tuesday night.

Monday at noon the phone rang. "Mom, I sold the car. I've got fifteen hundred dollars in Thai Baht. What am I going to do?" With the banks closed she had no way to exchange the money for either dollars or francs nor would she be allowed to take that much Thai money with her upon leaving Laos.

"Bring it to me. Do you need the cash now?"

"No. I'll need it more after I get to France."

"Then there's no problem. I can mail you a certified check drawn on an American bank."

"But I can't *get* the baht to you. I've sold the car!"

"Then I'll come to you." I drove to her home where she shoved a large bag full of the paper money into my arms. Her mother, hovering near us, was red-eyed at the prospect of losing both her daughter and her two-year-old grandson. As we talked, Khampheng asked if we could take her and the little boy to the plane the following night.

"Of course. What time shall we come?" We agreed on six as the pick-up time for her scheduled eight o'clock flight. We knew there would be many formalities to go through.

Stricken at the thought of Khampheng and Nono leaving, John and I nevertheless knew she was counting on us. I worried about her mother, wondering how that household would fare once Khampheng left. She had for several years been their main support and decision-maker. Since her father's death her mother had been increasingly dependent on her. The anguish in their eyes as mother and daughter parted was justified. It was the last time they saw each other.

It was after we picked Khampheng up the next evening that we discovered the flight had been delayed. There might be two or three hours to wait. We prayed that this was not a cancellation.

Khampheng went through the formalities, her exit permit intact, thanks to the friend in the passport office. Her tickets also were in order. We sat in the waiting room, entertaining small Nono as best we could. Each of us was mute under the enormity of the coming separation. On the surface Khampheng attempted to reassure us about being gone for only a year, but behind this glib prediction was the fear that darker days were upon us and that it might well be a much longer stretch.

On the previous Sunday evening John and I had been invited to have dinner with our chief of party of the Hawaii team. This man and his wife had a home on the edge of the USAID compound, and we had often been there for parties and Hawaii team gatherings. They had many Lao and Thai artifacts including some of the recently excavated *Ban Chiang* pottery, as well as *Kha* drums, Vietnamese ceramic lions and Cambodian weavings.

On Sunday afternoon the hostess had phoned to remind us of the dinner, remarking casually, "You will need to bring your own plates and utensils. We don't have enough to go around."

I had not realized it was going to be that large a gathering, but did not dwell on this advice. We were, therefore, totally unprepared for what faced us when we walked into their home. The house was bare, totally bare. The only remaining furniture was recognizable as the basic USAID welcome kit, a table and eight chairs. All of their own furnishings were gone. Rugs, furniture, paintings, lamps, artifacts, everything was gone.

I gaped at the barrenness and turned to my hostess who dismissed my unspoken question as if there was really nothing to remark on, saying, airily, "We are due to leave by mid-summer, so we've sent our things off early."

Sent everything off? Something was fishy here; why would they send even the bare necessities off early, including basic dishes and utensils?

"Something very strange is going on," I told myself. "We are not being told the truth." I wanted to drag John out and ask him some very pointed questions, but this was not possible. For the first time in Laos, I felt extremely uneasy.

As the evening wore on and people began to chat, a Lao guest, a member of the USAID Office of Education and a person I knew to be well informed about the Pathet Lao, casually began to outline a sequence of events that rendered us speechless. The rumors were, he said in an elaborately offhand manner, that by midweek the Pathet Lao would be in control of the city of Vientiane and would promptly see that all Americans left Laos. He outlined a day-by-day plan.

He so understated the whole scenario that we were tempted to write it off as fantasy, but watching others at the table, I saw confirmation and very little surprise in their eyes.

"What," I wanted to shout, "is going on?" How is it, I wondered, that our chief of party is totally packed out and has said not one word to any of the rest of us on the team? Or were only *some* of us considered to be members of this team?

For several days Americans in Laos had been frantically packing up boxes and standing in long lines at the American post office to mail them. Twice we had been called to meetings by the consular officer, who chided us for spreading unrest and rumors by so openly expressing our lack of faith in our own foreign policy that our long lines were jamming the area around the American APO. We were *not,* he said very firmly, to continue to do this. All was well. There was nothing to be concerned about. Don't panic.

Looking again around that denuded house, I bristled. "Ha!" I thought, "Don't panic!" I guess you don't have to panic if you have already sent your household goods out while assuring your co-workers not to worry.

I was so furious there was no room for fear. I was just murderously angry at being deceived and treated like some sort of expendable commodity. My admitted naïveté and the fact of a contract extension through December of 1976 had led both of us to believe that our days in Laos were guaranteed.

John caught the look on my face, and as soon as possible, we extricated ourselves, our plates and utensils, and headed for home. He, I realized, had been as stunned as I during the revelations of that social evening.

"Do you think what that Lao talked about is what will really happen?" I asked John.

"Don't worry, lovey, the American Embassy will take care of us. They don't like to have Americans become part of the problem. Try not to fret." If he had meant to be reassuring, he had utterly failed. The recollection of this evening was foremost in my mind as John, Khampheng, Nono and I sat in the Vientiane airport, waiting for the Air France plane to depart. It became increasingly difficult to find conversation topics. My heart overflowed with sadness.

At 10:15 the flight was called, and holding them tightly for the last time, we hugged our goodbyes, promising to write, to see each other in a year. It was, in fact, nearly six months before we were able to exchange letters and thirteen years before we saw each other again.

Khampheng, of course, was not the only Lao to have left. On the previous Thursday members of the American Women's Club had accepted an invitation to a morning coffee from the wife of one of the Lao generals. When I arrived for the ten o'clock coffee, I found myself milling around with other Americans, puzzled by the absence of our hostess. The servants informed us that we had no hostess. "Madame is not here. She is gone."

"Gone? Gone where?" How could she not be present for this occasion in her own home? And if she had to cancel, why had we not been notified?

Another American friend explained succinctly that the entire household had picked up and crossed the river to Thailand the previous day. In order not to arouse suspicion they had taken nothing with them. Ratnam, in *Laos and the Superpowers,* reports similar leave-takings as follows: "Then there was an exodus of thousands of Laotians of the middle and upper-middle classes, as also of the Vietnamese and Chinese nationals who made up the commercial middle class of Vientiane" (140).

On a later page he said, "On May 9, [1975], after consultation with Souvanna Phouma five Right-wing Ministers resigned. They left for Thailand soon after" (219).

The servants were left behind to explain. "Madame says she is very sorry she cannot give you coffee today." *Very* sorry. This prominent Lao family, in anticipation of the fall of their country to the Pathet Lao, had already transferred their funds out of the country to safer havens. They had relatives with whom they could stay in Thailand. Eventually, however, even they had to enter a refugee camp long enough to receive a number that entitled them to be processed as refugees and flown to the United States.

The morning after the disastrous revelations at the dinner party we had soberly assessed our own prospects. The families of the most prominent members of the Royal Lao Government had left; Khampheng and Nono were now on their way to join Souvanh; our own chief of party had packed out his entire household. How much longer would we be allowed to remain?

21
Last Days in Laos

Seven hours after Khampheng flew out of Wattay airport, at six o'clock the next morning, May 20, 1975, we received a telephone call informing us not to attempt to leave our Km6 housing area. The Pathet Lao had surrounded not only our living area, but were in command of the entire American USAID compound in town.

As I moved into the kitchen to heat water for coffee and tea, I hailed our neighbor who was passing by the door. "Joe, what's going on? What do you know?"

"I know that at midnight last night a group of Pathet Lao agitators, including some so-called students, took possession of the USAID compound."

The compound held the heart of the entire USAID mission in Laos. Consisting of a major administrative building, a commissary, a post office and adjacent offices, this was the nerve center of USAID. Its loss meant a crippling blow.

Gratuitously, Joe added, "Probably the worst part of all this is that those USAID personnel who have passports being processed by USAID now can't get them. They are locked up in that building and obviously cannot be returned to the Americans who will be needing them."

With that cheerful thought he continued down the street, leaving us to wonder how extensive looting of the commissary might have been. We knew that the Pathet Lao now had control of a major telephone system as well as any vehicles which might have been in the compound at the time of the takeover. We heard that two U.S. Marines had barricaded themselves inside the USAID building, and as far as anyone knew, they were still there.

The Pathet Lao agitators settled in for what became the end of the

USAID presence in Laos and the downgrading of this presence to mere representatives. It was a major set-back for U.S. foreign policy.

May 21 seemed to be about sixty hours long. USAID officials set up an operations center in the Km6 house of the acting director and allowed meager snippets of news to be filtered to us from time to time. Even in the emergency the American officials were able to maintain that incredible control of information that accompanies power. They eked out only the most skeletal information which they conceived to be necessary for those of us known as "dependents." Never did they so much as acknowledge the confusion, fear, frustration and eventually just plain boredom that overtook all of us who were trapped in our USAID-made dilemma.

It was a wonderful time to observe human nature. The woman who lived across the street had three small children. She was constantly flying in and out of our house with a late-breaking rumor: "I hear that all Americans have been placed under guard in town," or "They are going to evacuate women and children first. Well, that means we'll get to go right away because I have three kids."

She also warned us, "Better be careful about the water supply. You know they could easily poison it and get all of us." Another time she made a point of coming over to say, "I heard they are going to incarcerate the men but let the women all leave the country."

I had long since learned to filter her gossipy information through a severe test of probability. I knew her to be nervous and excitable, but even so, her ill-founded rumors made us all jumpy.

I gave more credence to the official words passed along from the temporary command post down the street. Even more informative were the occasional insights shared by our friend, Jack Huxtable, who had been evacuated the previous week from Ban Houei Sai, where he had been the area coordinator. Because of his excellent command of the Lao language, he was sent into town surreptitiously to listen to what was being said and done. His reports were the most current and much more interesting: "Americans who live in town are moving around as if nothing has happened. There are no house arrests." And later he was even more reassuring: "It's business as usual in town. The Lao don't know anything has happened. We in Km6 are the ones most affected because we live in this fenced compound. We are the most visible and obvious target. I don't sense that we are in any danger."

I asked if people in town, the Lao and third-country nationals, meaning Indians and Filipinos, were upset or anxious. Was there talk of a coup, or of military action or anything like that?

"No, they didn't seem surprised to see me walking around. The police in town paid no attention to me." He paused, "But I'll tell you one thing. Vietnamese and third-country nationals are leaving town as fast as they can get out. The road to Thadeua is crowded."

He was referring to the road that led to the ferry landings where one crossed the river into Thailand. For the past ten days the phrase "They have gone to Thadeua" meant that Lao folk were leaving the country.

This sobering news caused us to mobilize ourselves and start in earnest to pack our household goods.

Just then both servants arrived. The cook and the gardener confirmed that they had been allowed to enter when they had shown their IDs proving they worked at Km6. They said the guards at the gate were concerned about further "student" aggression. We were very skeptical about the reports of student activity. For one thing, there were not very many politically active students in Laos, and second, the few student agitators we heard about usually demonstrated against the Vietnamese and not the Americans. We knew of incidents recently in three other major Lao towns in which men calling themselves students had engaged in insurrectionist activities. We suspected these were well-trained Vietnamese cadre, hard-core agitators and not students at all.

As the day wore on, although many of us had our servants with us in our homes, we were advised to pay them off, including a three-month bonus, so that they would be free to leave and to insure them of their rightful wages. Payment was to be made in dollars or baht (Thai currency), not in the Lao kip which were rapidly becoming worthless. No one had access to banks which all had been closed for over a week. The admonition to pay in baht was an unexpected windfall for me.

I had a bagful of money given to me by Khampheng following the sale of her Volkswagen bug. Having been unable to convert the baht into hard currency, our deal was that I would eventually send her a dollar check which she could cash in France.

I called a friend and informed her, "I have baht to sell. Bring me an American check, and I'll sell you what you need."

One phone call did it. I was soon doing a brisk business in money changing. Baht enjoyed a firm rate of exchange, and there was no question about blackmarketeering this money. I simply wanted to get the fair exchange rate, and accepting U.S. bank checks was easier and safer for us all. I set aside enough baht to pay my own servants and for emergency money in Thailand and easily disposed of the remainder to grateful neighbors.

At ten o'clock that Wednesday morning Loth, Khamnouy's cousin, the banana bread–eating student who was a regular visitor, appeared in our house. Politically he was more willing to go along with the leftist government than either Khampheng or Khamnouy, and he was not fazed by the possibility of being sent to school in Hanoi or even Moscow. He and 'Nouy had often argued heatedly about all this, but it had not spoiled our friendship with him. He reached our house by climbing over the six-foot chain link fence that surrounded our house.

Loth's arrival destroyed any lingering illusions we had about the takeover being a minor uprising in a situation that would soon return to normal. He had come to claim our motorcycle. We had long since agreed that when we left we would sell it to him, and he had been patiently waiting for that time to come. There was absolutely no question in his mind but that we would shortly be out of Laos. He wanted the cycle.

"Loth, there is no way you can drive it out through the gate. They will surely demand identification."

"But Mom, you promised it to me, and I have money. I don't want to risk not getting it."

"We understand that," John intervened, "and we will not go back on our promise. At some point, I feel sure, we will be allowed out of Km6. When we are, we will bring it to your house. It's too risky for you to ride out on it now."

I shuddered. "Some people shoot first and ask questions later. Let's not be stupid."

We helped Loth back over the fence and waited. Luckily I didn't know then what I learned later on that same day as all residents were notified that anyone seen entering or leaving the compound by way of the fence would be shot!

We returned to the packing. For some time certain members of our American community had been shipping personal and household articles through the APO, and months later I learned that one couple had mailed all of their household effects through the American postal system! No wonder I had waited five hours when I had queued up to mail our photograph collection! John and I had agreed to attempt to send only those things we felt were irreplaceable. Besides, until today we really hadn't believed we would have to leave.

We had a whole house full of items that needed to be packed. Our Ban Houei Sai friends had been pulled out of their post a week earlier and housed down the street from us in a vacant home out of which the family had recently moved, leaving behind in the carport a great stack of cardboard boxes. The USAID warehouse was by now also in the hands of the Pathet Lao, which meant that no more boxes or packing materials of any kind would be available. We were ecstatic to have Jack offer us the leftover cartons—their Ban Houei Sai household effects had long since been packed and shipped down to Vientiane.

The day seemed to turn into one endless procession of boxes and packages. "Keep packing," my slave driver husband would bark whenever my spirits or energy flagged. He was incredibly creative about filling up odd spaces with our belongings and was working harder than I. We ripped up magazines, stuffed towels around sharp corners, filled cavities with clothing, artifacts and kitchen ware. There was no assurance that any American possessions would be allowed to leave Laos.

The hours crawled by, livened only by occasional pieces of information from our cook, another reliable source of rumors. Although his analysis and interpretation might vary from ours, his information was often more recent and more helpful than anything issued by the makeshift USAID headquarters down the street. Every hour or so I would circulate through the houses of our near neighbors to trade information, share a cup of tea and blow off a little steam.

I was not afraid. The Lao had always treated us with gentleness and respect. We had not experienced a single disagreeable incident during our four and one-half years in that country and it didn't occur to us now that this would change. As a matter of fact, we were much more apprehensive about the trigger-happy American vigilante types who were all for establishing armed patrols at night. Being shot by one of my neighbors seemed a very live possibility and not one I looked forward to. We begged the officials to clamp down on these suggestions.

During this day nearly everyone I spoke to recalled with considerable concern an incident involving a Cambodian ship in waters off the Thai coast that had been fired upon by Americans who were based in Thailand. Cambodia and Thailand were engaged in heated interchanges about this. Our fear was that the Thai might retaliate and close their borders to Americans, thus cutting off our only exit from Laos. There was no hope of escape through China, or Vietnam, or Burma, and Cambodia certainly wasn't an option.

I dug in the bottom of my closet for what I had always labeled my "evacuation shoes." In the unlikely event that we might have to walk considerable distances, I wanted to be sure to have sturdy and well-fitting shoes. There they were, ready for action.

The following day the grapevine informed us that the incident involving the Cambodian boat had been defused and that we were in no danger of being detained at the Thai border. The real question was how soon would Americans begin to leave?

22
Evacuation

On Thursday afternoon the first busload of American dependents left the Km6 compound for the airport, filled with mothers and children. Those of us not scheduled for this first departure went down to the school playing field where they had assembled, to wave goodbye and reassure each other we would be reunited shortly in Bangkok.

"Do you think the guards at the gate will inspect the luggage?"

"Isn't anyone going to help that woman with the four small children?"

"I wonder if the Lao people in town are hostile, if there will be any problem getting the bus to the airport?"

Most of us voiced concerns for which we had no answers.

There was no inspection at the gate, and as far as we knew they were safely delivered to Wattay airport.

American officials had arranged for Royal Air Laos, the local airline, to make special flights to Bangkok in as rapid succession as possible. With limited equipment and personnel, it meant that their scheduled daily runs had priority and special flights were fitted in where there were time and inclination. No telling how often or when flights might be made available. With no children in the family and a sound constitution, I did not expect to leave for another few days.

I walked through the streets to our house and returned to the packing which was considerably slowed down by a full-blown case of bursitis in my right arm. I had never had it before, nor has it afflicted me since, but at that time it was so painful I was restricted to doing everything with my left arm, favoring the painful shoulder as best I could. I plotted my eventual departure in the one suitcase I would be able to carry.

From time to time at Km6 the gates were opened by our captors. During these hours anyone could go into town or wherever they needed to go, but cars that were taken out were thoroughly searched, as were handbags and boxes or bags. We had no idea what they were looking for, and as we watched the process we concluded that the soldiers had no idea what to look for either. These were clearly Pathet Lao recruits brought into the city from the country who perhaps were seeing homes like the ones in Km6 for the first time in their lives. They were grim, silent and glowered at us no matter what was happening around them.

After that first busload of evacuees left Km6 the full drama of what was happening to us really hit. Outside of the Km6 fence were dozens of Lao who now were fully aware of the takeover and were hoping to get a glimpse of their American friends before it was too late. Many were in tears. They pressed against the chain link fence, calling out names.

"Have you seen Mrs. Betty? I want to tell her goodbye."

"Please, Ma'am, could you tell Mr. Dick that I am waiting here at the gate to see him?"

"I'm Miss Mary's secretary. Is she all right? Can you find her for me?"

Frantic to make contact, many were crying, afraid they would not see their American friends before we were sent away. Most of us did, indeed, leave without ever having a chance to say goodbye to friends with whom our associations had been mutually enriching. Many months later I learned that Souvanh's relatives had spent hours at the fence, hoping to see us. Others had left Laos themselves, even before we did, and caught up with us in Hawaii, or wrote to us from Iowa, Minnesota and Texas.

Once we felt assured that neither the Pathet Lao nor the Americans cared to precipitate anything other than an orderly withdrawal, our last hours in Laos took on a kind of black holiday atmosphere. Many were determined not to leave any of their imported liquor for the enemy, and the obvious solution for this was to drink it. Some seemed able to do this for several days running.

It also soon became clear that the guards at the gate were now instructed to prevent all duty free goods such as radios, electrical appliances, American-made bicycles and especially motorcycles from leaving the premises. Anything else in our possession also began to be fair game for looters or thieves. Most of us attempted to thwart the looting by bestowing upon our faithful servants an enormous variety of household goods. They in turn became very adept at smuggling out of the compound anything they felt they could either use or sell.

Clothing, bedding, towels, pots and pans, tools and small furniture items were especially coveted. There was a wide-open "secret" exit in the chain link fence through which at least half of Km6 was carried in about four days. It was easy to make arrangements to insure that most of the goods we wanted to share would actually get into the homes of our Lao friends.

The day when we were finally allowed to pass through the gate, we loaded my rosewood loom and the teak dining table and chairs into the pickup and drove out the gate to Khampheng's mother's home. She was overjoyed to see us, having stood for hours at the fence, unable to tell anyone who it was she wanted to reach. With a mixture of sadness and delight she accepted these gifts. Actually, the table wasn't ours to give away—it was a USAID table—but by this time it was clear that no American-owned furniture was going to leave Laos, so we rationalized that it was better to have it in the hands of a friend rather than an enemy.

We continued to pack. I discovered that my entire set of china would fit into a hollow cabinet that we had used as an end table. Since this was one of a pair we had brought from Pakistan, it was a precious memento. We harbored a hope that it and the dishes might someday find us in Hawaii.

Arrangements were being made between the takeover government and the British and Australians to lift cargo by helicopter out of the Km6 compound and transfer it to planes which would deliver it to a warehouse in Bangkok. Perhaps all the packing was not going to be in vain.

On Thursday, May 22, at two in the afternoon, Ah Chong phoned. "Hey you guys, the gate is open. Anyone can get out. You got errands to do?"

Did we! We had a motorcycle to deliver. John quickly grabbed his helmet, jumped on the cycle, revved it up, and as he whooshed out of the driveway yelled over his shoulder, "Follow me with the car."

I scrambled into the Datsun, keeping him in sight, and was relieved to see he was not challenged at the gate as I drove decorously behind him. The extensive search of the car—glove compartment, trunk, even chassis—revealed no hidden treasures. Eyes straight ahead, I drove through the gate and followed John to the small village area of Vientiane where Loth and his aunt were both amazed and delighted to see us.

As Loth counted out the kip for the motorcycle and I produced the papers that would certify that it was indeed his machine, I realized the aunt's heretofore unintelligible chattering concerned whether or not we wanted also to sell the car.

My Lao was not all that good, but I caught the gist of her queries and turned to John. "Loth's auntie is asking him if we want to sell the car."

"Hell, yes. It's not going to do us any good, and we can't take it with us. Sell it."

We began to dicker.

In spite of the fact that Lao banks had been closed for more than a week and the value of the kip was close to worthless, the American Embassy was exchanging Lao kip at the official rate of two hundred fifty kip to a dollar. This meant that we could ask for the true value of the car in kip and, at the embassy, exchange kip for their full value in dollars. It was a win-win situation. Auntie would have a car she could not possibly afford at the inflated prices, and we would have some cash in hand to start all over again in Hawaii.

We had been foresighted enough to pay the Lao import taxes on the car and thus have Lao registration papers which would provide her with proof of ownership.

I listened to her offers, trying desperately to convert her kip offer into American dollars at the embassy rate. She, of course, operating in true Lao style, wanted to bargain. That was fine with me, but time was of the essence, and I wanted us both to come out well. I mentally juggled kip and dollars, and we agreed on a price she could afford.

We then had to go to the American Embassy. It would be necessary to validate the sale, get a second set of official papers and, incidentally, reassure ourselves that it was still possible for us to exchange the kip at the official rate.

"We'll be back as quickly as we can. We have to be sure no one will accuse you of stealing the car. We don't want to cheat you."

Off we sped. With visions of red tape, excuses, and mass confusion confronting us, we were astounded to complete our business in less than an hour and return to the village. Auntie, Loth and I counted out kip which she had unearthed from hiding places in the house. The payment filled what I would have identified as a peck basket, and I stuffed handfuls of kip as best I could into my shoulder bag.

"Can you drive us back near the compound and our house?" Having disposed of both the car and the motorcycle we had no transport to traverse the three hot, dusty miles from home.

"Sure, get into the car."

Bumping over the road, barely missing chickens, trees, bicyclists and hedges, I realized that neither Loth nor his aunt knew much about shifting or steering American cars. They would have to learn on their own time. As we swerved about a small cart, missing it by about an inch, I responded to John's anguished look by advising him to close his eyes.

A quarter of a mile from our Km6 compound we agreed, "This is close enough. Better that we walk around the corner than drive up to the gate. The Pathet Lao might not like to see Lao and Americans in the same car." We quickly embraced.

"*Soke dee. Yu dee me heng.*" "Good luck. Long life."

"Puok en mai." "See you again." Not likely. Not bloody likely!

As I trudged down the dusty road toward the gate a frightening thought occurred to me. "John, what if they decide to look into my shoulder bag." They would get an eyeful of kip worth more than one thousand American dollars, and who knows what they would think about it! "If they make a move toward it I'm going to throw it over the fence and break and run."

"I hope they don't shoot," he commented, only half in jest.

There was no challenge at the gate, and I sauntered back into captivity, eleven hundred dollars richer. Not a bad afternoon's work! Of course we still had the problem of getting to the embassy to exchange the kip, and since we had returned too late to go on Thursday, there was no telling when the gate would open again. To our dismay, no one was allowed out of Km6 on Friday with the exception of those being evacuated who went on the bus to the airport. We kept packing to fill the time.

At 6:30 A.M., Saturday, May 24, the word came down the line, "The gate is open."

"John, take the kip and get down to the embassy. It's a lot of money, and we are going to need it."

Gulping his coffee, he was about to leave when the phone rang. It was one of our Hawaii team members. "I just left headquarters, and Judy's name is on the list of people departing today. This is not, I repeat *not*, official, but I thought you would like to know."

I gave John an anguished look. "If I leave before you return, I'll wait for you in Bangkok." My pragmatic solution belied the turmoil of my heart. John had already been asked to remain for a few days to help with the final duties. The decision that no pets could be taken with the departing evacuees meant that someone would have to put them to sleep, not a favorite job. Also, all of the portable, packed goods needed to be hauled from the houses to the school playing field. If they got out of Laos at all, it would be from this point. John wanted to keep an eye on our belongings as well as to help others. By this time "unessential" men—those who no longer had official duties to perform in Laos—were being scheduled to leave along with the dependent women and children.

I stayed close to the phone all morning. My shoulder throbbed unmercifully, and I couldn't help but wonder how John was faring. Surely he should be home by now. At 10:30 a neighbor phoned to report that a strike of Lao USAID workers had temporarily sealed the embassy. Because they had not been paid (all USAID payroll money was in the captured buildings), the Lao were demanding that wages be paid from embassy coffers. Joe said they had surrounded the embassy and refused to release those inside.

John was in the embassy. Was he all right? Was there any way I could find out? Would the strike become unruly? My experience with the essential calmness of the Lao people and their abhorrence of the use of force helped to convince me that although the unpaid workers were justifiably angry, they would not resort to violence.

I had no chance to verify my predictions. At 11:30 a USAID dispatcher loped through my front door and called to me as he went through the living room, "You're on the next bus. Be at the school in twenty minutes." He was out the kitchen door before I could ask any questions.

"Gee, thanks for the advance notice," I muttered to myself, heading for the bedroom to change into my going away clothes and my "evacuation" shoes. Even if I didn't expect a long trek there was no point in taking chances.

"Sakhorn, I'm leaving on the next bus. Make me a peanut butter sandwich. No telling when I'll have lunch, or where."

Stricken, the two servants stood at the kitchen door as I struggled with my suitcase, grimacing with the pain in that bursitic shoulder. We knew that it was not wise for Lao any longer to identify themselves with us or to call attention to themselves by carrying our bags to the bus. Sakhorn handed me a sandwich, carefully wrapped. Tears streaming down his face, he suddenly flung himself into my arms, "Please take care of yourself, Madame. I'll tell Mr. John where you are. Don't forget us, please don't forget us."

I too was crying. I hugged him as best I could and hurried through the door. My across-the-street neighbor happened to be getting into his car and offered me a ride to the school grounds, sparing me a ten-minute walk with a suitcase and a sore shoulder.

It was a relief to see friends at the gathering place. I was not only leaving without being able to be in touch with John, but I was also beginning to realize that I was leaving Laos forever. I looked desperately at the faces around me and saw reflections of my own grief and shock in them. Precious memories of cherished friendships flitted across tear-streaked faces. We fought to control our quivering chins, shared Kleenex and helped each other up into the waiting bus.

The bus ride to the airport was uneventful but unusual in that we took the most circuitous route possible. In fact we drove on lanes and roads I had never before traveled.

"They must be avoiding the middle of town, not wanting to provide cause for any incidents," my seat mate commented. It had never occurred to me that anyone in Vientiane would direct violence against departing Americans. In actual fact, most of the Lao people had no idea the Americans were being evacuated. Six months later in Honolulu I met the wife of the principal of the Fa Ngum school in Vientiane who told me that she herself had been unaware of all this.

"My sister worked for Royal Air Laos. On Thursday she came home for lunch at the usual time but said she had to hurry because she had another trip to Bangkok. When we asked her why, she surprised us by saying, 'It's for the Americans.'"

"What do you mean? What's for the Americans?"

"The planes. They are leaving. The Americans are leaving Laos."

This, said my friend, was the first hint they had had that Americans were being evacuated from Laos. She added, "We had no idea if it was your choice or our government's doing. But I got into my car, and I drove slowly to the airport."

Wattay airport had an elongated horseshoe-shaped drive that went past the entrance to the waiting area. Viengtha continued, "When I drove by the entrance I could see some of the Hawaii team members sitting there with their luggage. Then I knew it was true. You were leaving." She stopped a moment, looking very sad. "I didn't dare go in to say goodbye because I had no idea what was happening. I was afraid."

At that time she had thought she would never see any of us again, so the reunion in Hawaii many months later when she was en route to Iowa was a joyful one. We were both grateful to have one more chance to talk with each other and to provide some sort of closure to all of those years in Laos.

There were no hitches in my evacuation to Bangkok. The USAID authorities there were well organized to receive us. They had had very recent practice with evacuees from both Vietnam and Cambodia, and they were prepared for the emergencies they would have to face. Many people were without their American passports or official travel orders. There were bewildered women and tired children, and all of us faced uncertainty about the long-range as well as the immediate future. The reception crew coped well, and we were comfortably installed in a hotel within an hour of our arrival.

"The emergency USAID desk is in a room on the first floor. If you have no travel orders, check with them."

There were other admonitions posted in our rooms or in the hotel corridor: "Please don't try to telephone back to Laos. We will report your safe arrival. The few phone lines we have need to be kept open for official business."

"Please check with us first if you are inquiring about your spouse. We will try to help."

They also encouraged us to leave Bangkok as quickly as we could: "Others will be coming who will also need housing."

I listened courteously to this advice but stayed put. I would go no further until John was safely beside me. My plight somehow seemed much worse than his. What with the unexpectedly abrupt end to our tour in Laos, the uncertainty of our future and that terrible bursitis, I was unable to sleep. This, of course, aggravated the pain.

In Bangkok, to my relief, I was paired with the wife of a deputy USAID official which meant that without violating the phone restrictions, through her I could keep up with what was happening in Vientiane.

Monday morning at breakfast she looked at me and spoke her mind bluntly. "Why don't you get to a doctor? You look awful."

I felt awful. I was grey with pain, and it had been days since I had slept well.

"Where shall I go?" I hadn't a clue as to where to find someone who might help me.

Fortunately Bangkok had an English telephone book as well as one in Thai, and I was able to locate a doctor whose office was in a familiar location and whose specialty would enable him to treat me. A phone call put me in touch with a very pleasant sounding young man who immediately understood my problem and urged me to come in.

It may have been dumb to subject myself to a long ride on the public bus, but I had hours to fill and rose to the challenge of following his careful directions. The normality of being with people who were not in crisis gave me some perspective. I made the trip without mishap, shielding my aching arm from careless travelers as best I could.

One look at my shoulder and the young Thai doctor gave me a cortisone shot that he promised would help relieve the pain. "Give it a few days. If it is not better, come back." He had trained in both Thailand and in America and spoke good English. In addition, he was solicitous and competent, and the shot was effective. My arm stopped aching within a few hours.

The next day, Tuesday, John arrived. We clung to each other in relief and fatigue, happy to be reunited. He had spent all of the intervening time lugging cartons, boxes, crates and packages from Km6 homes to the playing field. He felt optimistic about our someday seeing our possessions again.

While I was separated from John and in Thailand I had been scrupulously careful not to use precious phone lines simply to hear his voice and was appalled to learn that a neighbor had called him.

"What on earth for?"

"You are going to find this hard to believe—when she called she said, 'John, I want you to do me a favor. Go over to my house and get my blowfish.'"

"Her *what*?"

"That was my reaction too," John spluttered. "Can you believe it? She telephoned to ask me to go to her house and take down a dried blowfish that was hanging from her porch ceiling. She wanted me to bring it to Bangkok."

I was furious. I had chosen not to tie up the phone lines selfishly to satisfy my own anxieties and she had blithely phoned *my* husband to instruct him to salvage a dried blowfish!

"What did you do?"

"Well, I went over to her house and found their servants there. They were very depressed and told me that they had been paid off in kip."

"Kip!" I interjected. "But it's worthless! We were all told to pay off in baht or dollars. And her husband is a foreign service officer!" My outrage matched John's.

"Her cook was in tears. She is Thai, you know, and she said she had no money, no job, nothing with which to buy food for her children. I was so furious, I marched through that house, opening cupboards and closets. I even broke open the tool room. I told the servants to take anything they could use or sell." A glint of grim satisfaction passed over his face. "The last time I saw them they were carting things off through that hole in the compound fence and looking much happier than when I first went over there."

We grinned at each other and agreed that we needed to take the next day off and use it for relaxation, swimming, perhaps even a movie, but first we told the woman at the USAID travel desk, "We want to fly to Hawaii as soon as we can, we really are not in the mood for sightseeing."

We phoned my family and John's sister to report our safety and spent the days until Saturday trying to unwind. The usual exotic offerings in Bangkok failed to tempt us for we were sick at heart at the precipitous end to our years in Laos.

We flew out of Bangkok on Saturday, May 31, and arrived in Hawaii almost five years to the day after we had departed. Neither of us had a guaranteed job, and in fact we had no place to stay. Good friends who were leaving for a vacation offered us their apartment, and we moved in. We were exhausted and had no clear ideas about where we would find jobs, but we were very glad to be safe, to be together, and to be home.

23
Captivity

Those Lao who, after the Communist takeover, did not get across the river and into a camp where it became possible to apply to go to France or to America, included people with large families, or no money, who had no contacts outside of Laos, or who had felt that some accommodation might be possible with the new government. Many simply were caught in the rapidity of events and had no opportunity to escape, even though they knew their lives were in jeopardy.

Such were the circumstances that led to the capture and incarceration of Khampheng's brother-in-law, Bounliane.* He was picked up by the police in July 1975, six weeks after his sister-in-law had left for France. He and his wife, Kongseng, had been on their way to the Buddhist temple to observe the anniversary of her father's death, the funeral rites John and I had attended. Suddenly soldiers stopped them and arrested Bounliane, taking him into the police headquarters in Vientiane. There were no American friends or colleagues to appeal to; all but a few had left Laos. Furthermore, no family member could be called on since three of his brothers-in-law as well as several friends were also either under arrest or being sought by the new regime.

Bounliane, a former captain in the Lao Army, was currently teaching law to recruits in the military police academy, hoping that the new government would continue the program even if it meant revision of the curriculum. He was shocked and dismayed to learn that the entire complement

**The information for this chapter has come from taped personal interviews held in 1990 with Bounliane Rajphoumy, who was at that time living in Alabama.*

of the school, seven hundred and fifty men, had been arrested on the same day as he. With no explanation regarding charges or action that might be expected, they had all been sent north to Xieng Khouang province where they had then been dispersed into small, scattered enclaves.

Bounliane had been able to keep track of the first months by systematically shifting small pebbles from his left to his right side every twenty-four hours. The total darkness of the cave in which he was imprisoned had eventually disoriented him to the point that he was no longer able to trust his counting, and he now had to ascertain the date from the occasional prisoner who joined him briefly.

He wondered if any other prisoner in the camp had been subjected to the isolation meted out to him in this program known as "re-education." There was little education going on in the solitary confinement of his cave, and he savored the rare times when another captive joined him and he could hear a human voice. These infrequent prisoner-companions knew nothing of Bounliane's prospects, but through them he learned that he had been there more than six months.

Initially the prisoners had been told they would be incarcerated for three months, and at first Bounliane had been allowed to stay with his men. Eleven days later, however, he and three of the former student recruits were called out and told there was going to be a big party. They saw that two butchered cows were indeed being roasted, and there were signs of other preparations for a celebration. Suddenly the party turned into a trial. Fifteen soldiers appeared and prodded the captives to stand before the crowd.

> We have caught four American running dogs. These men remained in Vientiane in order to complete the American plan, the CIA plan, to overthrow the Kaysone (Communist) government. They have been planning with the Americans to take over the country again. We have to kill these four people because they have been working for the Americans. Look at these American running dogs.*

Bounliane stared at the jeering spectators and judged that, while his accusers were Pathet Lao party members, the spectators were lackeys of the insurgent government, following the directions of whoever was currently in command. Tribal groups, with little loyalty either to the newly formed country of Laos, or to the Communists, had been unmercifully bombed by the Americans and had no love for anyone remotely connected to them. During the turbulent days of the Pathet Lao takeover many had hoped that the

**Direct quote from taped interview with Bounliane Rajphoumy.*

nationalist aspirations of the Lao might finally be realized. They had expected to be rid of all foreign domination, but in fact the leader of the insurgents, Kaysone, and the Pathet Lao were controlled from sources outside of Laos, and this Vietnamese influence became progressively stronger. The accusation that Bounliane and the other men were involved in a current American plan to overthrow the new government sounded plausible but was sheer fabrication.

Following the verbal scourging of the four men, their hands were tied behind them. Instead of enjoying the festivities and the roasted meat they were hustled out of the village onto a path that led behind a mountain. Were they to be executed out of sight of the villagers, their bodies left to rot?

Sporadic shots aimed over their heads by the soldiers did nothing to allay their fears. No one spoke beyond the grunts that accompanied jabs from the butts of the soldiers' guns as they prodded the prisoners over a narrow path. For five hours they walked and stumbled along the rough trail. It began to seem that instead of heading for annihilation they were being led toward a specific destination.

At six in the evening they came into a valley where Bounliane was surprised to see grass huts rather than the usual bamboo stilt homes. He looked around in dismay and noticed three people who were walking painfully toward a small stream behind the huts, dragging leg chains. He could not help but wonder, "Will I become like one of them?"

"You will be studying here." The soldier gestured toward the huts. "In these huts are enemies who were caught in 1968 from Nam Bak Kwah."

Despairingly, the four new arrivals calculated that for seven years the people had been imprisoned in this valley. Was a long painful captivity to be their fate also?

The grass hut to which the new arrivals were assigned was partitioned into two rooms. One of the rooms held nearly thirty people who were chained together, many of them very sick, and all of them emaciated and hollow-eyed. For three days no one came near the newcomers nor gave them any indication of what might happen next. Their imaginations presented them with terrible possibilities of torture, starvation, isolation, and even death. When they were eventually called out all that was asked of them was their name, rank and government position previously held. The questioning was repeated daily for two weeks until one by one they were handcuffed and their legs chained.

Bounliane had spent most of his first year in captivity separated from his men, isolated in a cave that was so small he could not stand, nor was there any light. He had wondered if he was in one of the caves that had for so long been used by the early Lao freedom party that pre-dated the Pathet

Lao, the people who had hidden from the French bombers and who had for years existed in cave communities, deprived of the daylight and cut off from communication with the outside world. (Marek Thee, the Polish commissioner, and chief of the International Control Commission to Laos in the early sixties, in *Notes of a Witness*, reports huddling for two days and a night in one of these caves in a Pathet Lao–controlled area while bombs rained down inches from the entrance. Although Percy Stieglitz describes Thee as consistently blocking all efforts of the ICC to investigate Vietnamese or Pathet Lao violations of the Geneva Pact [98–99], I find no reason to doubt the veracity of Thee's reported visit to the caves of Sam Neua. The existence of this vast network of underground rooms that housed thousands of soldiers and workers all during the French and American bombardments of this area is referred to several times by the tribesman whose letters are translated by Fred Branfman in *Voices from the Plain of Jars*.)

Banished to one of these caves, Bounliane worried about the effect of prolonged darkness on his eyesight. For the first week in the cave, given neither food nor water, he drank his urine in order to stay alive. Eventually allowed one meal a day, he couldn't stand, only sit or lie down and rarely had another prisoner to talk with. This confinement continued for a full year.

His reassignment in late 1976 to the huts was, if anything, worse. He was moved to a dark room constructed from the flattened sides of gasoline cans. There were no windows, and there was no insulation even of mud or straw, which meant that the room was scorchingly hot in summer and bitterly cold in winter. Some of the prisoners assigned to this space died from exposure. To protect his badly weakened eyes, Bounliane improvised smoked glasses to wear during the few precious moments he was allowed to go outside. At this time also, knowing that his diet was lacking in minerals and salt, he picked up rocks which he later tried to crush to powder, hoping that some of the minerals in the rocks would be utilized by his body.

Three years passed before any official spoke to or interrogated Bounliane. When the questioning did begin in 1979 it was repetitive and confusing. The interrogators told Bounliane they knew all about him, every move he had made, every plan leaked to him by the CIA.

"We know that you had plans to take over the Xieng Khouang area and that you have weapons hidden in many places. If you want to live you must take us to those caches."

The charges were totally without foundation, and there was no way in which Bounliane could lead them to hidden weapons. To make up a story and take them on false trails would surely be disastrous. Over and over they demanded that he find the weapons. Over and over he denied any knowledge of them.

Even more ridiculous was their assertion that, because in the early sixties he had been in the air force, he was now, fifteen years later, able and in fact about to fly T-28s to bomb their territory. That plane had not been introduced to the Thai and Hmong fliers in Long Cheng until after he had left the air force, so their accusation that he might bomb them by using American T-28s was another fantasy. The accusation would have been ludicrous had the captors not been so deadly serious and so persistent in demanding a confession.

"It's all a CIA plot," they repeated, seeking to link him to the all-pervasive influence of the American Central Intelligence Agency. (The history of CIA activity [in Laos] dates back at least to 1953 when President Eisenhower, writing in his memoirs, comments on the necessity to convince Americans as well as other Indochinese that there was a serious Communist threat in Southeast Asia. By 1954 John Foster Dulles was in the middle of the political fray, supporting Thai interests and decrying the neutralization of Laos by the 1954 Geneva Conference.

(The complexities resulting from the U.S. involvement in Laos through a Military Assistance Advisory Group (MAAG) which had been formed in the late 1950s certainly impinged on Bounliane's situation. By 1960 there was full-fledged CIA support of Lao right-wing forces through the formation of a Meo military force commanded by then Major Vang Pao.)

Bounliane denied all knowledge of any CIA plot. "I teach law in the Military Police school in Vientiane," he countered.

"Confess, or you won't see your family again."

"I don't have any information to give you. The things you are accusing me of I have never even thought about. I cannot tell you things that I don't know. I just want to return to my family. I am Lao. I want to be a good Lao citizen and serve my country."

Bounliane, an educated man who had twice been sent to the United States for training, was not overly impressed by the manner in which interrogations were conducted. The questions were repeated by rote, the guards were obviously rural, tribal people, co-opted by the Pathet Lao to guard and harass prisoners. They were so provincial they thought that Vientiane was another country. But they were also fierce and loyal and often cruel. One could not take their threats lightly.

Nighttime brought new horrors. They would wake him up in the middle of the night, and in spite of the chains on his legs, force him to drag himself to the fields beyond the village. Toying with the safety catches on their rifles, they gave him a shovel and told him to dig his own grave, because they were going to shoot him. "If you don't want to tell us the truth, you must dig yourself a good grave, because you will die here."

Years later, as he told me this story about his captivity, Bounliane gave a wry smile. "I dug myself a *very* good grave."

Sometimes during these evening interrogations they would brutally beat and kick him. They finally broke a rib which to this day has not healed properly. They would often shoot over his head, making him ponder what might provoke them to lower the gun a few inches.

The grisly night ordeals went on for more than a year following his move from the tin room to a room in a traditional Lao house where there were other prisoners. All during this time he wondered what had become of his wife and family and how he might get word to them.

The first inkling that he was alive reached his wife, Kongseng, through a Xieng Khouang man who, when he had occasion to travel to Vientiane, looked her up and told her that her husband was in "seminar" in his province. It was another two years before she was able to contact Bounliane through a cousin who worked in the Pathet Lao headquarters, but who sometimes traveled to the area in which Bounliane was held. The cousin offered to take a parcel to Bounliane and successfully smuggled in a small amount of tobacco and two hundred kip. Bounliane, a nonsmoker, used the tobacco for bribes and kept the kip to buy food. For a bit of tobacco a guard would allow the prisoners to buy bananas and other fruit from villagers to supplement their diet. "We had so little food we ate banana peels and all."

It was during Bounliane's sixth year in "seminar" that the restrictions seemed to become less harsh, allowing the guards to ease up on their harassment. He began to be allowed to go outside once a day and after several months was given permission to walk around the camp and also to perform simple duties. He now could see that he was living in a very primitive area where neither captor nor prisoner had basic tools or even eating utensils.

This was a part of Laos that had suffered heavy aerial bombardment, and that meant an endless supply of aluminum could be salvaged from the wrecked aircraft which littered the ground around them. Bounliane knew some simple blacksmith skills and informed the guards that he could make spoons from the aluminum. There would be a ready market for spoons in the nearby village, and he soon talked his captors into helping him find ash, a necessary ingredient for preparing the molds in which to make the spoons. He produced one spoon, then two, then five, and soon the prisoners were producing five hundred spoons a day which the guards marketed, making as much as fifty thousand kip on the enterprise. None of the money, of course, came back to the prisoners, but the villagers were soon expressing their respect by referring to their blacksmith as "uncle," and the relationship between captives and jailers gradually improved.

When animals were slaughtered for special occasions such as festivals like *Pi Mai* or weddings, the prisoners received only the hide of the animal. This they carefully dried and divided up into small pieces the size of an index finger. The dried morsels of hide were distributed to each prisoner and chewed to shreds. The men were always hungry, and daily, when they were released from their rooms, they rushed to the garbage dump to look for bones and vegetable peelings which could be washed in the river and boiled into a broth. Because they lacked minerals in their diet, some of the men followed Bounliane's practice and roasted rocks, pulverized them, mixed them with water and drank the residue, a makeshift mineral supplement.

Although she had been reassured that Bounliane was a captive, and alive, it had been several years since husband and wife had seen or talked with one another. When Kongseng received word through a friend that her husband was being held captive in Xieng Khouang, she used money she had been saving toward the day when she might find him, and in his sixth year of captivity paid ten bahts of gold as a bribe to get permission to visit him. She came to the camp and stayed about two weeks. During this time they took the chains off his legs, and even after she left they did not replace them, although he was still locked inside, and when allowed out was forbidden to move around except under guard.

By 1982 he had been a captive for seven years and had progressed beyond making spoons, having added the production of aluminum buckets, which he and a Hmong lieutenant colonel had learned to fashion and which sold for fifty kip. The Hmong helper also knew carpentry, and soon both men were making cabinets and beds.

"I also made hats out of bamboo. I knew how to catch fish and frogs and I grew my own garden. There was no point to having very much in a garden, because others would steal it, even my friends. I grew one plant of hot peppers at a time, and at night I had to take it to bed with me because it would have been stolen. I had one chicken, and I had to take it in at night too. I tied it to my bed."

Slowly, restrictions were eased, and at the beginning of the eighth year of captivity a Pathet Lao officer from Vientiane came to the camp. The officer was well educated and had been in Vietnam, Czechoslovakia and Germany. Because he was the officer in charge of the investigation bureau of the Central Committee of the Communist party, his presence in the camp was the occasion for a celebration.

The officer asked the chief of the camp to fetch Bounliane, and it became clear that he wished to invite him to attend the feast. As they sat together the officer said, "You are a very good man, Uncle. You have a good character. I have visited many of your seven hundred and fifty men and have asked about you. They still refer to you as *achan,* professor, and they obviously love and respect you. Because of your good character you will now be assigned to another job, away from here."

It wasn't clear to Bounliane why this endorsement merited a change of job, but he was pleased to find that the new assignment was in Phone Savanh where there were many people from other provinces. He continued his carpentry, using local wood to make closets, beds and tables. He still was not allowed to go to Vientiane, but Kongseng learned that he had been moved, and by again bribing members of the party, she was allowed to visit and to live with him for a month. After her visit, the prisoners were relocated to the mountains to a lumber camp and put to work felling huge teak trees. Under normal circumstances trained elephants were used to pull down the trees and to move them from the forest to the river where they could be rafted and floated to Thailand. In the area where the prisoners went there were no elephants and all labor was performed by the men, an extremely dangerous operation. Injuries were common, and it was only a matter of time before Bounliane became a casualty when a guide rope snapped, severely injuring his right arm.

Fortunately the arm was not broken, but he was in a hospital in Phonesavanh for a month, a hospital that had been built by prisoners who were in "seminar."

During this year it seemed as if restrictions were gradually being lifted, and all of the prisoners felt it was high time to be released. While living there Bounliane had become acquainted with the man who authorized the papers that allowed people to travel back and forth to Vientiane. Kongseng was able to send her husband three gold baht, which Bounliane used to bribe this man to forge the papers which would allow him to pass through the gate. Using a false name, he also bribed a driver for space on a truck and left the camp for Vientiane and freedom.

His destination was his village in Vientiane. The Lao people cluster in small villages within the confines of larger towns, and once Bounliane reached home he contacted the leader of his own village who encouraged him to find a job in Vientiane. A friend who was an agricultural worker had no work for him but found him a job in the Volvo repair shop. There his ability to speak both English and French was a great help to the Swedish mechanics who were training Lao apprentices. Utilizing his organizational abilities, Bounliane helped them set up a mechanics school and translated the Swedish Volvo manual into Lao and French. The workshop was very modern with new machines and the latest technology and provided a good living for him, Kongseng and their children.

Although it was now 1983, the Communist government was still arresting people, and the *Chao Khoueng,* a friend as well as the administrator of the province, sent word to Bounliane that former members of the Loyalist party as well as people who had been educated were again being picked up. He reported that Bounliane's name was on one of the lists adding, "You had better get out of Laos now."

Bounliane shrugged the information off. "I can't go yet. I don't have enough money." Escape was not just a matter of his leaving the country, but would involve taking his wife, three children and a nephew with him. However, when a friend in the police department, who also saw his name on a list, warned him that he would be captured by men who would "cut your neck off," Bounliane realized it was definitely time to move on.

"Go now, today, if you don't want to be captured."

There was no time to waste; he must be gone within twenty-four hours. The next morning he attended a party being given by the Volvo people at which they were recognizing new apprentices upon the successful completion of the mechanics course. Bounliane assured his employers that he would be there the following day to start the training for a new class and left when the party ended at noon. He rushed home to give the five members of his family enough money for the bus fare and left them to catch a public bus for Paksane, east of Vientiane, on the Mekong River.

Had he tried to leave Laos without these family members, they would have been interrogated, perhaps tortured and certainly jailed on suspicion of aiding the escape of a wanted criminal.

Bounliane needed transportation for himself, the public bus being much too risky, causing him to "appropriate" a motorcycle from a neighbor who carelessly left it unattended and who could not be warned or thanked.

At a prearranged spot on the Mekong River not far from Paksane, he paid fifteen thousand baht (two thousand dollars) to get himself, his wife, three sons and a nephew across the river. The timing was very tight, for his escape was known, and he was being sought. The Vietnamese were in his Vientiane home less than an hour after he had left. Ironically, the same policeman who had warned him of his imminent arrest had sold information about his escape plans to the authorities.

A cousin who had planned to escape with him delayed a few minutes too long and was rounded up by the police and held at a spot on the river where he expected to rendezvous with Bounliane. When Bounliane failed to show up the cousin was taken back to Vientiane and jailed, serving a six-month sentence. The policeman also was arrested because he had failed to produce the fugitive.

Bounliane made it to a different and safer place on the river after being warned by the resistance contact person not to trust the Thai who had been paid to help him at the river crossing. Employing clever subterfuge, all six members of the family evaded detection and crossed the river into Thailand.

Although they were now out of Laos, the family's future was far from settled. Only through the intervention of some American friends for whom he had previously worked was Bounliane able to obtain a job which allowed him to begin to round up other members of his family. They were all sent to the very crowded Nha Pho refugee camp to await the tedious process that would eventually allow them to go to the United States.

Frustration and tension were daily emotions at the Nha Pho camp as the family sought rice to eat, places to sleep and enough water to drink. Baths and clean clothes were almost unheard of, and the heat took its toll of everyone. Bounliane's sense of survival continued to stand him in good stead. He had contacted two Americans he had known in Laos who now worked for JVA, the agency that interviewed Lao refugees to determine their eligibility for immigration.

Bob and Mike Hearn both knew of Bounliane's escape and gladly employed him. They needed his linguistic abilities in interviewing other escapees. They were constantly on the lookout for Pathet Lao spies who posed as refugees in order to infiltrate the camps and assassinate people who had escaped their clutches in Laos. Attempting to ferret truth from fiction in the tales told by the never-ending stream of refugees was a difficult task, and they welcomed Bounliane's knowledge of people, his command of several languages, and his uncanny ability to assess the character and intentions of people he interviewed. At first the pay was only ten baht a day, fifty cents, but fortunately the authorities were able to increase this to twenty-five baht, and none too soon, for within three months a brother-in-law who had been in "seminar" for eight years also arrived, bringing three more teenagers to add to the family group.

Khampheng, who was in France, had put us in touch with Konseng and Bounliane and their family in Thailand, and we were actively exploring every available avenue seeking to help them join the Minnesota Lao families with whom we were closely allied. The size of the group was a major obstacle, because Minnesota landlords had successfully lobbied for housing ordinances that prohibited more than five people from living in a two-bedroom apartment, all that a refugee family, even with assistance, could afford. Under those regulations Bounliane's clan would have required three apartments, a financial impossibility for most sponsors. When an offer to sponsor the entire family of twelve to Atlanta, Georgia, came through, it could not be turned down. Our next letter from Bounliane had a Georgia postmark.

Starting over in America with ten teenage boys (two additional cousins were added before they left Thailand) has not been easy for this determined and resourceful man. The boys found being sent to school with youngsters half their age, assigned to lower grades because of English deficiency, just too humiliating. In spite of the language obstacle they learned enough English to get jobs and are now able to take advantage of educational and vocational training when time and financing make it possible.

"Would you go back to Laos?" I asked Bounliane as we wrapped up this long conversation about his captivity and his present situation in the United States. He looked momentarily pensive and then smiled. "But of course. My sons say they will never go back, but once I have my American citizenship, I would again like to see the land of my origins." His eyes took on a faraway look, and I envisioned him thinking of all the familiar, wonderful places he had known as a child, recalling the warm family ties and yearning for a renewal of the unique relationship that the Lao have to land and water and each other. I was not surprised to hear him continue, "I hope it will be possible to do something to help my country. After all, I *am* Lao."

24
The Refugee Pipeline

It was very hard to start over in Hawaii. Our hearts and thoughts were still with the Lao. We had not re-established contact with Khampheng, who was somewhere in France, and we had no knowledge of what was happening to our friends whom we had left behind in Laos. We heard vague rumors about re-education camps but had no real knowledge of who was taken to them or what happened in them.

Our anxieties were compounded by the fact that we had no home of our own. Neither of us had a job, or even a prospect of one, and John had picked up a rare disease in his last few months in Laos which made him listless and tired. His doctor really didn't seem to know what to do. In desperation I went with him for his appointment, and, remembering symptoms of friends back in Vientiane, I suggested, "Look up Tropical Sprue in your medical dictionary. Maybe that is what he has."

Her look of disbelief was not very reassuring, but she mumbled something that I assumed meant she would take this under advisement and scheduled another appointment.

When we returned later that week, with a perfectly straight face the doctor informed John, "You have a textbook case of Tropical Sprue." Fortunately the acknowledged cure for this ailment was a change of physical location and protracted rest which mean that John was already on his way to recovery.

Because the University of Hawaii had initially plucked John from a teaching job in Illinois in order to add him to the Pakistan contract team, they didn't feel any strong obligation to find a position for him. He was not tenured, and his thirty years of teaching in another state meant little to them.

For two months following our return to Hawaii we both applied for jobs and waited for interviews. I gratefully followed up on a one-year position offered by the East-West Center in Honolulu, my experience in Laos seeming to convince them that I might have some capacity to relate to Southeast Asian students. Although I would only be filling in for someone on a leave, at least it would give me a chance to re-establish myself professionally and let folks know that I was back in town and available for other positions that might open up. John was eventually offered a lectureship in vocational education graduate studies by the University of Hawaii College of Education.

In those first months after our return to Honolulu, the ability of the Lao to find us was nothing short of miraculous as a constant stream of refugees located us through letters and by phone and in person. We sponsored many of them, which meant assuming responsibility for assuring that they had housing, enough money for food and essentials. We helped them through the maze of health and educational tests required to get children into schools and adults into job training programs, and in general helped to ease their transition into the American way of life. We spoke to any church or civic group that would listen, urging them to open their homes and hearts. It was very clear that any Lao who had worked with or for Americans in Laos was in danger. Those who failed to escape, reportedly twenty thousand or more individuals, were rounded up and sent to "re-education seminars" in the north of Laos where some were held for as long as eleven years. Others simply disappeared or failed to survive the harsh treatment of their captors.

We slowly gathered up the threads of our own lives, and it was months before we re-established correspondence with Khampheng. She, Souvanh and Nono were typical of the thousands of Lao who were granted asylum in France, under provisions verified by Martin Stuart-Fox in *Contemporary Laos,* who reports that "until August 1975, under the terms of the Franco-Lao convention of 1954, Lao citizens required no visa for France." Many Lao had been educated in France as well as in the Vientiane-based *lycée* and spoke fluent French. Refugees in the camps in Thailand often applied to both countries and went to whichever country first gave permission.

Typical of her *"baw pen nyang"* philosophy, Khampheng had not bothered to leave us Souvanh's address in France, and we had not anticipated her need for a stateside address for us. We eventually found her through Souvanh's cousins, who were now in a Thai refugee camp.

Khamnouy, meanwhile, was doing well in college. We visited him briefly in the late summer of 1975, and he came to spend that Christmas with us in Hawaii. He was so Americanized we hardly knew him. His hair was shoulder length and his knowledge of American slang awesome.

He told us of getting to know Ted and Dorothy Foster who were related to a church in the town of Eagan, Minnesota. The members of this church, which was slightly south of Minneapolis and only sixty miles from the Stout campus, were aware of the need to resettle Indochinese refugees but had been told that for the time being the Vietnamese were being well taken care of. The social service agencies suggested they think about sponsoring some Lao, and atlases and maps of Southeast Asia were in sudden demand as the people attempted to find out about Laos.

We corresponded with the Fosters for two years before we met them, and at that time I quizzed Dorothy about how they got acquainted with Khamnouy.

"Ted and I were celebrating our anniversary and had gone to downtown Minneapolis for a late dinner. We stayed to dance and welcome in the New Year, and it was nearly dawn when we got home." She looked a little surprised at how the evening had fled by.

They returned home, quietly opening the door, and discovered their four children in the living room, talking with two young Lao. One of these men the Fosters knew. The other one, Khamnouy, they had never met.

"We didn't open the door until we knew who it was," their kids chorused. "Somchet is a friend who has been here before." Looking somewhat apprehensive they continued, "We didn't know the other person, but Somchet said he was okay, so we let them in."

Judging from the general dishevelment of the room and the puffs of popcorn scattered around, they had been enjoying games and snacks. Wrapped in quilts and still in their pajamas with a fire crackling in the fireplace, it was a friendly, cozy group.

"*Sabaidee,* Khamnouy. What brought you to our house tonight?" Ted thrust out his hand in greeting.

Khamnouy bowed over his clasped hands and flashed his famous smile. "I heard about you from my friends. I know you like Lao people, and I wanted to meet you."

Dorothy scrambled eggs, heated rolls from the freezer and made a large pot of cocoa. Khamnouy's eyes twinkled as he thanked her for his cup of "chocolate soup." The kids were sent off to bed, and Ted and Dorothy began to talk with their two guests. At this time they were looking for ways to organize other Lao students into an action group that could help new refugees, and as the Fosters shared ideas, they learned that Khamnouy had come to Stout through our efforts. We soon had a lively correspondence going between Hawaii and the Fosters' Apple Valley home.

"Khamnouy had an uncanny knack of knowing just when we were going to serve pizza and ice cream. He would show up just in time," Dorothy marveled in one of our early conversations with her. "He had *so* many friends. We couldn't wait to meet you, because he was always talking about you." In fact, it was the summer of 1978 before I had a chance to meet this remarkable family, following Souk's arrival and after Khamnouy's death.

It was to the Fosters that Khamnouy turned seeking sponsorship for this older brother. "Mom and Dad say Hawaii is not a good place for Souk to go," 'Nouy explained. "They say there are mostly only low-paying jobs, and it's very expensive to live there. Mom and Dad Rantala will help any way they can—they now are regularly sending Souk money for food and medicine." The evidence of our committed financial backing was welcome assurance for this family whose hospitality was often stretched beyond their limits. They agreed to look into sponsorship for Souk.

Over the next few months the Fosters worked with Khamnouy and the social agencies that dealt with Lao refugees, signing the necessary papers, assuring Khamnouy that his brother would get into the pipeline, confirming by their actions the incorporation of Khamnouy into the expanded Foster clan.

During that summer of 1976, 'Nouy found a job with a meat-packing plant in Minneapolis. The company liked his work and began to hire other Lao who resettled in or near the city. Entree into the work force through this company provided employment for over 50 percent of the Sivongsay family and countless other Lao they recommended to the boss.

John's job gave him several vacation weeks that summer, and we agreed that he should go to Minnesota to see his sister, his sons, and, of course, Khamnouy. I was envious of his opportunity to meet the Fosters, and be with Khamnouy and especially to have a vacation in our log cabin in the very northern part of Minnesota, but I needed to find a job if we were to continue to help this family resettle in America. I could not afford the luxury of a vacation at that time.

My one-year position at the East-West Center ended in September 1976, and while I was again applying for jobs and awaiting interviews, the State Department asked the University of Hawaii to send two of its vocational-technical education experts to consult with the government of Burma. John Rantala and Lawrence Zane were selected to help the Burmese government assess the feasibility of developing technical colleges. The universities of Rangoon and Mandalay were overcrowded and producing hundreds of graduates for whom no employment was available. Burma was very short of journeymen technicians in all fields and wanted to establish schools similar to Hawaii's community colleges. It was an opportunity not to be missed.

"What do you think they will do if I, too, apply for a visa?" I was itching to travel again and tired of hanging around waiting for a job to be offered.

My husband encouraged me to request a visa that would grant me the same number of days, thirty-five, that he would be there. We both knew that the Burmese usually issued visas for tourists that allowed only seven days because hotel and travel accommodations were so very limited.

"If I can go for only seven days, I'll skip it, but if they give me the thirty-five, I don't mind paying my own way." We left it at that, and I scoured the library shelves for anything I could find to read about this country which was virtually unknown to me.

We celebrated the arrival of my extended visa and agreed that I would schedule a little extra time in Thailand in order to visit the Lao friends who were now in the Nongkhai refugee camp. We would travel together as far as Bangkok, where the two men would continue straight through to Burma and I would change planes and head north to the refugee camp. Nongkhai is a small town directly across the Mekong River from Vientiane, and it now housed a huge refugee camp. Many of John's former students as well as Khamnouy's brother, Souk, were living there. It would give me an opportunity to touch base with a number of people we were planning to sponsor to the United States.

During the second week of December 1976, I changed planes at the Bangkok airport and headed north to Udorn. Very little seemed to have changed, and I welcomed the warning signs that heralded our landing. Below me the runways looked forlorn, overgrown, and deserted. Udorn airbase was the launching pad from which a high percentage of aircraft and accompanying troops, acknowledged and clandestine, had been catapulted into Laos. (Fred Branfman, writing in a chapter, "Presidential War in Laos, 1964–1970," estimated, "A conservative guess would be that at any given time there are some 50,000 American personnel involved in the air war in Laos. Udorn Air Force Base alone houses some 10,000 American airmen. In addition to ordnance, servicing, and logistic functions back at the base their tasks include [he lists nine major military operations]" (237). Branfman also points out that "Air America and Continental Air Services are based at Udorn," supplying equipment to military and paramilitary forces, rice and arms, and transport for army troops (239).

Now, in December 1976, nineteen months since Laos was taken over by the Communist Pathet Lao, Udorn was abandoned. A swaying set of steps led me from the plane into weeds, grass and dust. The futility of decades of American military and economic activity was summed up in this barren wasteland. I deplored the money that had been poured into this base, the effort, the spit and polish, the secrecy, the outrage. Dust to dust.

I walked gingerly across to the building that served as a passenger terminal, where the taxi drivers spotted me.

"Where are you going?"

"Nongkhai? Hundred baht."

"Don't be ridiculous. Twenty baht." It hadn't changed so drastically after all. Unreasonable taxi fares were hopefully put forth to trap rich foreigners who could fly to Udorn rather than take a bus or train.

I joined a group of Thai people who were bargaining for a taxi to Nongkhai, and we collectively negotiated a fifteen baht fare for each of us. Although the driver pretended to be outraged, he would get four times what he normally charged, and we all knew it.

Clutching our bags, we squeezed into a battered vehicle, and thirty minutes later we were dropped in the center of Nongkhai. Laos was on the opposite bank but might just as well have been half the globe away as far as present accessibility was concerned. My destination was the refugee camp in which Lao friends were currently "on hold," but first I must find a place to spend the night.

The small hotel that had been recommended was far from inviting. It was dingy, with chipped paint and furniture which listed to the right or left. I had to wait for someone to shuffle to the desk after slamming my hand on the bell.

Yes, they had a room. A dubious look at me. "Very noisy."

"Noisy, why?"

"Too many people have party next door at night."

Did he want my business or not? "Can I see it?" I hoped I hadn't picked the local brothel.

"Yes, yes."

Key in hand, I followed the man as he shuffled up a flight of stairs and down a very dingy hall. The room had two single, sway-backed beds, a concrete floor, and screening at the windows so covered with dust I couldn't see out. Well, I supposed no one could see in, either. At least there was a ceiling fan, although it was December, and perhaps I wouldn't need it. The sheets, dull gray, seemed clean. There was a blanket, and I could wad up some clothes for a pillow.

"It's all right. I'll take it." I hesitated as he started out of the room. "Will my clothes be okay? Will anyone steal them?"

He waved the key at me, giving me an injured look and adding, "Don't worry. Everything safe. No one take."

What alternative did I have?

I paid for the night and inquired about transportation to the refugee camp. I had come here primarily to touch base with Khamnouy's brother,

Souk, and his family. I also hoped to meet Phouvieng, Khamnouy's girl friend, and to find Souvanh's cousins, former students in the Fa Ngum schools.

On the previous day I had heard about the escape effort made by one of the Fa Ngum teachers. A brilliant, well-educated man, he and his wife and children had decided to swim the river. In the summer it was not wide and the current was slow. Five of them slipped into the waters and started across. They were spotted by a patrol, and gunfire burst over the river. The woman and all three children were killed. When he dragged himself out on the Thai side, the father was crazed with grief and shock. I heard that the Buddhist monks had taken him in and that he had been in a *wat* now for over a year. I prayed that there would be healing and peace for him.

The baht bus (fare, one baht, the equivalent of a nickel) dropped me at the camp gate where the barbed wire fences and evenly spaced watch towers chilled my soul. It looked like a Nazi concentration camp, not a refuge for harassed and stateless people. At the entrance there seemed to be little order, and I sought a Thai soldier, hoping he might help me.

"We'll call your friends on the loudspeaker. You wait." It was a long wait, and I had plenty of time to observe the bureaucracy of the camp—the cringing, abject queries of the refugees, the abrupt, officious responses of the Thai personnel—no great love was lost between these two groups.

"Mom, Mom!" I whirled around. Khantaly and her sister, Vilayvanh, embraced me in a bear hug, laughing and crying in their joy. Arm in arm they propelled me across a dusty field through groups of children playing with a makeshift ball and women washing clothes beside a single water spigot. I had a fleeting glimpse of rows and rows of gray, unadorned buildings as the girls ushered me to their room. These two young women were the daughters of Boun Hom, John's drinking partner during the *Pi Mai* weekend in Pakse.

Refugees in this camp lived in barracks that were elongated Quonset huts. Each barrack was divided into fifty rooms, and a family was assigned one room of less than ninety square feet. This group of Fa Ngum students had cleverly arranged for two adjoining spaces, marked off by woven mats and blankets. In this space were their kitchen, family space, storage for whatever clothes or possessions they had, and at night mats were rolled out for sleeping. Ten people lived here, and as I looked at the cramped quarters it was hard not to register the dismay I felt.

A shy, attractive Lao teenager was brought to me and introduced. This was Phouvieng, Khamnouy's girl friend about whom I had only recently learned—he had been uncharacteristically silent about the relationship, why I didn't know. She had gotten herself out of Laos to avoid being sent to Hanoi to school, and since she had no family in the camp, these friends had incorporated her into their household. She had large, soft, brown eyes, was neatly dressed, and a tentative smile hovered on her lips. We hugged each other as I assured her that Khamnouy was doing well in school and sent his love. My uncertainty about the depth of their relationship left me puzzled as to what she hoped to hear from me and what I might offer her in the way of reassurances.

All during these introductions people were rushing in and out, bringing in bowls, preparing food and laying extra mats on the floor. Vilayvanh enlightened me by revealing, "We're getting ready to give you a *baci*."

"A *baci!* How can you?" I blurted. "Where can you find the food, the flowers?"

"We want to celebrate your being here."

I was about to chide them for needlessly spending what money they had on something frivolous like a *baci,* when the significance of their decision struck me. This celebration represented a deeply ingrained cultural custom, but, more important, it was a defiant gesture in the face of all the uncertainty and deprivation that were part and parcel of their daily lives.

Many young people, all of them apparently former Fa Ngum students, began to gather in this tiny space, laughing, sharing news, greeting me with a polite *wai* of clasped hands. It was wonderful to see the teamwork and the close friendships, but the *baci* and the feast were almost more than my overflowing emotions could handle. Having already spent eighteen long months in this miserable camp, my young friends prepared a party complete with sticky rice, *sin heng* (dried meat), a curry of vegetables and chicken and platters of lettuce and mint. I had at least had the presence of mind to bring drinks with me from town. Orange pop.

We knelt around the *baci* bowl, a few green leaves and some paper flowers adorning the arrangement, white strings straggling off bamboo sticks. I was moved at the hope being expressed and the grit and stamina that helped it all come together. I was relieved that I also could contribute cookies and fruit I had picked up from the Nongkhai market.

"How's Dad?" My husband had been their teacher at the Fa Ngum schools as well as a family friend. They responded eagerly to questions I asked about their cousins, Souvanh and Khampheng, who were now in France. Their mother and Souvanh's father were brother and sister.

"They're okay. Nono (their three-year-old son) speaks French." It was hard to comprehend the adjustments that the small family must be making to adapt to living in France, far from relatives and barely able to survive financially.

"What about your father?"

"He and mother are still in Laos with our sister. When we get to America, we will get them out." The resilience and optimism they held about their future were catching. They felt sure they would eventually be released and would get to the United States, and I pledged to do everything I could to speed the process.

I shared gifts I had brought and showed pictures of Hawaii. As we later walked around the camp, I noted that the water spigots in the center of the camp were the sole source of water for all purposes, including laundry, baths, and cooking. As we paused to watch a soccer game on the dirt field, women with pitifully small bundles of firewood wearily stumbled by.

"They have to go as far as four hours away now to find wood," someone commented. "All the trees have been cut down." I could confirm this by just looking around at the treeless acres surrounding the camp.

I inquired of Phouvieng about Khamnouy's brother, Souk.

"We don't know where he is. We heard he is in the Hmong camp." A carelessly flung hand indicated an area which extended off in the distance. I would have to go there to try to find him, and I puzzled as to why none of these young people had tried to contact him.

In our conversations I was relieved to learn that money sent to them from the States actually reached them. We compared amounts sent with what was received, surprised to learn that nothing had been skimmed off. All of us who had worked with the Lao were receiving pleas for money to help supplement the meager food supplies provided by the UN refugee assistance program. John and I had sent moderate amounts from time to time, with no confirmation that anything had ever reached the hands for which it was intended. Apparently the postal system was still reliable.

In mid-afternoon I set out to find Khamnouy's brother. Khantaly's husband accompanied me to the adjacent area where Hmong tribal people stayed. "Why," I wondered, "did Souk choose to live here?" There were no barracks, only small huts jammed against each other—hovel might have been a more accurately descriptive word.

Souk, Chantalone and their three children, one a baby, looked up in amazement when we found them. We greeted each other with the traditional *wai,* but found hugs more expressive of our true joy.

"Sabaidee. Chow sabaidee, baw?"

The barrack the others stayed in seemed like a major hotel compared to the tiny, dark structure I now inspected. Too small to stand in upright, its only light came from the door. The deeper one went into it, the darker and smaller it became.

"Good grief! How do five of you manage to live here?"

Souk's familiar, embarrassed smile was an attempt to cover his obvious pain at having to receive me in such a dismal setting.

"Some of these are Sam Neua people." Souk's gesture encompassed the surrounding area. "I have worked with them, and they are my friends. I'd rather be here."

We visited until the shadows began to lengthen and I had to leave in order to find my way back to the hotel in Nongkhai before dark.

"I will visit you there, tomorrow," Souk promised.

"Can you get out of here?" I gestured toward the barbed wire enclosure. An outside pass didn't seem very likely to me.

"Not officially," his grin was shy, "but I am well known. I have been a teacher and have helped the camp officials. I have friends. Don't worry, Mom."

I spent a lonely evening in my hotel room which, with its peeling paint, sagging springs, and noisy neighbors, seemed obscenely luxurious. I lay awake for a long time puzzling over Khamnouy's reluctance to tell us about Phouvieng and the somewhat strained relationship between the two brothers that kept them both aloof, but also in touch. I sensed that I was dealing with certain cultural mores and inhibitions that I would never come to fully understand, and eventually I drifted into sleep. If, as I had been warned, there was a raucous party next door, I slept through it.

Souk did, indeed, find me the next morning, and we talked for hours as the stories slowly began to come out. Souk had been trained as an aircraft mechanic and maintenance worker and had at one time been sent to a Texas base to acquire those skills. Along the way he had also learned to pilot helicopters. After the fall of Laos he was still ferrying helicopters when he heard that all pilots were to be sent to Hanoi for "re-education." The strong anti–Communist leanings of his family would certainly mark him for harsh, if not fatal, treatment. He had to get out of Laos.

Chantalone, his wife, was never apprised of his plans. It would have been dangerous for her if she were interrogated. So it was that on a sunny Lao day, as she was hanging out her laundry, a helicopter flew over and dipped its wings.

"Wave to Daddy," she called to her youngsters, not suspecting that this really was Souk. It was a game she and the children played when any helicopter went over. The aircraft buzzed them once and flew on.

Souk was late coming home that night. In fact he didn't come home at all. By morning the police were there. Where was her husband? Did she know a helicopter was missing? What did she know? Had she helped her husband to escape?

Protesting her innocence, she herself wondered if they knew something that she didn't. It was days before Souk's parents told her that they knew of his plans and had, indeed, encouraged him to flee while he still could. Small comfort to this woman with three young children, one a babe in arms. What was to happen to her? Would she ever see her husband again? Would she and the children be able to get across the river?

Anger and frustration gave way to the more pragmatic considerations of how to cross the Mekong. When help appeared in the form of a neighbor, a citizen of Thailand who worked and lived in Laos, Chantalone was at first very suspicious. The neighbor told her he was going to leave Laos for good and said he could and would help her to escape. For some time she was very fearful of his intentions even though he had always been a good friend. Why would he now offer to help her? What was he expecting of her? Was this a trap of some kind?

The neighbor kept tendering his offer until she finally began to negotiate. The instructions were very exacting. She was to be at a certain spot on the Mekong River between one and two in the afternoon on a certain day. She was to bring the children, but no luggage of any kind. The neighbor would come with a boat, a plan her in-laws encouraged her to follow.

On the appointed day she washed clothes and hung them on the line to give the appearance of going about her daily chores. When she left with the children she did not close all the windows. Getting to the appointed spot meant going through a checkpoint, which she successfully passed, but when she reached the river, there was no sign of the neighbor. Fearfully, she waited for more than an hour, hoping not to rouse undue suspicion by remaining in the same place for too long a period. Still no boat. Had she misunderstood? Was he not intending to come after all? Was it the wrong day? The wrong hour?

Finally, despairing of finding her liberator, she passed back through the checkpoint to town and went to her in-laws. Yes, this was the right day. Perhaps something had delayed him. Go back. Back she went, fending off the queries at the checkpoint by saying that she was seeking a special medicine for one of her children and had failed to bring enough money the first time.

Shortly after she reached her rendezvous, the neighbor and his boat appeared. Gratefully, she welcomed him, urged the children on board—and stopped in her tracks. In the confusion and fearfulness of the return trip to town she had left the baby asleep with the grandparents. She would not leave the country without her youngest child. The boat must wait.

The owner of the boat was impatient and apprehensive, telling her it would be dangerous to wait, that she must go now.

"No, I must have all the children together. Wait for me."

Back to town she went, through the checkpoint, breathlessly into the family home, snatched up her still-sleeping daughter and by taxi went again to the river. "The doctor needs to see the baby before I can get the medicine," she blurted, swallowing her panic as the guards at the checkpoint drummed their fingers on the butts of their guns.

"Lady this had better be the last time."

"Oh, it will be, it will be," she silently affirmed.

Would her liberator still be there? Could they cross the river? Or had her unforgivable oversight of leaving the child behind ruined their plans?

The boat was there. She and the child joined the others, and they sped off, across the Mekong River to freedom.

It was hardly a glorious reception on the other bank. Chantalone had no idea where Souk was, or if he was even in Thailand. She had, of course, heard nothing that could possibly have endangered him or her. Now that she was out of Laos, she must find him.

For nearly all escapees to Thailand the first stop was a prison where the jailers extorted payment for their release. Often these exhausted and frightened refugees had no money at all. To be caught in Laos with Thai *baht* would immediately incriminate them. They had to try to reach friends or family in Thailand to ask them to raise the bail money and bring it to the jail. These were the initial requests American friends received from refugees who were former acquaintances and colleagues.

Jailing newly arrived refugees was not a policy of the country, but was, instead, a penalty imposed by unscrupulous minor officials who sought some benefits for themselves. With three small children, Chantalone was spared the jailing and was directed to the refugee camp in Nongkhai.

By this time the influx of refugees was in the thousands, and the authorities at the camp had a public address system over which they would list the names of family members seeking to find each other, or even someone they knew. For days after her arrival Chantalone asked the authorities to request that her husband, Souk Sivongsay, report to the arrival area. Several lonely days and nights passed as she waited. Was he in this camp? Would he hear the announcement? Would someone tell him, and if he wasn't in this camp, where was he?

Souk, already living about a mile from the reception center, was in the Hmong camp. In order to suppress his loneliness and guilt at leaving his country and his family, he had volunteered for any kind of service that would help a fellow refugee and was seldom within hearing of the loudspeaker. Finally, a neighbor, who had heard his name, sent him loping to the reception center.

The reunion for Souk, Chantalone and their three children was tearful, joyous, and the start of a long, hard stay among the thousands who were awaiting a new beginning to life. How little we in the West knew of the suffering and horror of being a refugee. As I listened to this first eyewitness account I had heard of the perils of trying to leave Laos to escape the new regime, I was grateful that the family was together, but recalled with shame the questions John and I had raised about the repeated requests for money that Souk had sent to us. His wife, he told me, had been hospitalized several times and would have been ejected from the hospital had one of our payments not arrived when it did. During the first winter of their reunion she had been close to death, and Souk had dug trenches, hauled water, and stood on patrol to earn a few meager *baht* in order to pay her expenses.

Souk was registered as a refugee and therefore had the all-important number that was a refugee's eventual ticket to release from the camp and transportation to the United States. Releasing refugees into the hands of American sponsors was not a rapid process. For more than a year we had been trying to make the arrangements that would expedite Souk's movement to Minnesota. We had agreed with Khamnouy's assessment that high-cost Hawaii would not be a good place for them to try to settle down, for skilled jobs were scarce and competition fierce among the large number of immigrants from Southest Asia, east Asia and the Pacific Islands for entry-level jobs. It would be better for them to be in middle America. Minneapolis was a major hub of airline activity and held the promise of Souk's eventual employment in that field (a hope as yet unrealized, seventeen years later).

Before leaving the camp and Nongkhai, I bought toys, food, and clothes for the whole family and pressed them into Souk's arms. "It's the least I can do. I wish I could take you with me, but you know that Dad and I are working constantly to speed your release. Don't give up hope."

From Nongkhai I took the train to Bangkok, laden with those special cooking pots used in the steaming of sticky rice. They had not yet reached American markets and were prized by Lao refugees and Americans alike who considered *caow niaow* a staple in their diet. The sight of a tall American woman with eight aluminum rice steamers strung together and slung over her shoulder provided enough conversation starters to cover the entire eight-hour trip.

25
Khamnouy Comes Home

The phone jangled me out of my final sleep. Six o'clock, Hawaii time. I fumbled with the offending receiver. "Hello?"

My husband's voice brought me instantly awake. "Khamnouy is sick. He's in the hospital."

Now I was really wide awake. "What do you mean, sick? When you called me from Minneapolis you said that he was fine."

"I know, I know. Well, he's not okay. He's in a lot of pain."

"Pain? From what? What kind of pain?"

Suddenly the enormous import of the phone call hit me. My husband was in our cabin in northern Minnesota, across the lake from a telephone and nearly four hundred miles from Minneapolis, where Khamnouy was working for the summer. Khamnouy was into his senior year at the Stout campus of the University of Wisconsin, Menomonie, sixty miles from the Twin Cities.

"Where are you calling from?" I asked.

"I'm at Kirk's." These neighbors across the lake from our cabin had the nearest telephone. "The doctor called here. He thinks it may be cancer."

The doctor? What doctor? Where *was* Khamnouy? For a moment I couldn't breathe. "Cancer," I whispered. Then I yelled, "Cancer! It can't be. He was fine. You told me you just had breakfast with him a couple of days ago. How can he be in the hospital? How does this doctor know what he is talking about?"

Frantically I searched for some means of eradicating the awful potential of what John had told me. I pictured this sparkling twenty-five-year-old young man who was like a son to us. Khamnouy, bright, charming, full of laughter and energy and ambition, whose college education we were paying for. No, not Khamnouy. He couldn't be ill. I must be having a nightmare. This couldn't be real.

"Honey," my husband said gently, "the doctor called today, and the Kirks came over in a boat to get me. Khamnouy went to the hospital late yesterday with severe pains. They were so bad he couldn't stand or sit up. He's having a lot of tests. The results won't be in for a couple of days, and one of them has to go to a lab in Boston. I'm going to Minneapolis, and I'll call you when I know more."

I could hear the fear and apprehension in John's voice, and I suddenly realized that he was reflecting the same incredulity and fear I felt. And I was not there to face all this with him. With them.

I talked to John again on Sunday. The doctor had confirmed his previous diagnosis: cancer of the liver. John told me, "I'm going to bring Khamnouy back home with me." I couldn't voice the questions. Does this mean they can't do anything for him? Is there no treatment, no help? When I hung up the phone, my throat was choked with fear.

Monday I dressed in a daze of confusion and headed for work. Crossing a campus road I came face to face with a good friend who cheerily asked, "Howzit?"

I might just as well have been a reservoir from which the plug had been pulled by that friendly greeting. Flinging myself into his arms, I let all the pent-up fear pour out in racking sobs. Finally I was able to gasp, "Khamnouy is dying."

Concern and tenderness were in my friend's gentle murmurs which finally helped me to regain a semblance of control as I shared the anguish caused by John's call, my sleepless night, and some of the hopes and dreams we both had for our might-as-well-be son. Hawaii friends understood the custom, often practiced, of giving a child to an aunt or a sibling who was childless, even to grandparents who now were without young people in their home. To be a "hanai" or adopted child was to be doubly loved, and John and I often marveled at how willingly Khamnouy's parents had placed their son in our care. He was our "hanai" son, given to us in trust to treat as our own.

And now it was Wednesday. Tomorrow John and Khamnouy would come home. I had gone to the store, and as I was replenishing the larder, I suddenly found myself wondering, "Will Khamnouy eat this? What does he like? Does he prefer rice? Will he eat bread? I began to reflect that, having been apart for more than three years, I had no idea which American food habits he had adopted. Further, I knew very little about how his cancer would affect him. Would he want to eat at all?

Khamnouy, Easter 1977.

Suddenly the reality of it hit me. This was the last night that would be like other nights in my life. Tomorrow everything would change; in fact, my life had already changed, and it now seemed very clear we would never again follow the familiar patterns John and I had worked out together in the two years since we had left Laos.

I was at the airport ahead of time. I couldn't help it. I fidgeted and paced. Sat down. Got up. Scanned the arrival board listings and sat down again.

August 1977. How would I feel when I saw Khamnouy? John was bringing him back to Hawaii where we could take care of him, but I had no clue as to what this might entail. I hadn't thought to ask how ill Khamnouy really was. When he went to the hospital he was in terrible pain. Could he walk unassisted? Should I have asked for a wheelchair? I didn't know anything about his condition. I cursed myself for being so slow-witted.

Through the waiting room windows I could see the Northwest Airlines plane taxiing up to the arrival gate. My heart pounded. "Dear God," I prayed, "let Khamnouy be able to walk off." This, my Lao son.

I waited as the passengers poured off. Lei-bearing greeters welcomed incoming travelers and bedecked them with flowers. Families eagerly embraced returning members, and I searched every face. There they were. I caught a glimpse of John and Khamnouy, coming slowly down the corridor. He can walk, I exulted. He's not as sick as I feared! Every nerve in my body was egging me on to find evidence that would deny, eradicate the words I had heard only a few days earlier over the phone—"Khamnouy is ill, the doctor says he has cancer of the liver."

I flung myself into Khamnouy's arms, careful not to squeeze too tightly, slipping my handmade flower lei over his head. "It's so good to see you. How was the flight? Did you eat? You must be very tired," babbling in my relief to see my men.

"It's great to have you home." I wanted to transfer some of John's anxiety to myself through the hug that I gave him.

I tried to ignore the lines of fatigue that showed on Khamnouy's face. How thin he had become. Thank God he hadn't lost the sparkle in his eye!

We took the transit car to the escalator and down to the luggage claim carousel. John's relief at being home poured over me, and the three of us held onto each other tightly.

"Sit down," he urged Khamnouy. "It takes a while for the luggage to come up." Suddenly we were surrounded with friends and flower leis brought by people from our church who had come to welcome Khamnouy. I had poured out my grief to them during the past Sunday service, and as they put leis over Khamnouy's head their concern brought comfort to all of us.

"I'll go get the car. Look for me outside when your bags come."

'Nouy struggled to rise, saying, "I'll come with you, Mom."

I observed the effort he was making to try to stand up and recalled words from the phone call John had made. "The doctor says he has maybe six months to live." I thought of my own struggles in these past six days to come to grips with the awful reality of terminal illness in this young man who wanted so desperately to be a credit to his family and his country.

I remembered the previous day, which had ended in my going down to the ocean and swimming, hard, for more than an hour, just to get some of the tension and hopelessness out of my system. I dragged my thoughts back to the logistics of baggage and the airport. "No, no, Son. You wait here.

I'm way across the parking lot. Too far." Good grief, was I making a mistake in assuming he couldn't manage it?

He sank down again, the relief in his face justifying my caution at not wanting to draw further on his reserves of energy as I went off to ransom the car.

Khamnouy had once visited us in Hawaii during a Christmas break and hadn't liked the sudden shift away from the bracing cold to the warm weather, which we had assumed he would really appreciate. He had become a northerner in his two winters in Wisconsin, and he missed the snow! Now, as we waited in the baggage area he again complained about the heat.

"It will cool down tonight." How bizarre to be talking about the weather in the face of the life and death issues already confronting us.

Friends helped us load the luggage, and within half an hour we reached our house. It was a relief to be home, and I busied myself trying to make Khamnouy comfortable. I was edgy and unsure of what to say, what to do. My arms wanted to hold him, but my mind told me to let him make the first moves.

Khamnouy solved this by suggesting that he take a nap. The trip had been tiring, and he wanted to rest.

It gave me a chance to talk with John, to give him an opportunity to pour out the anxiety and despair, to explain what arrangements he had been forced to make by leaving Minnesota so abruptly. He spoke of a rushed trip to his sister's home in order to leave Khamnouy's car in storage, followed by the two-hundred-mile dash back to the cabin to collect his clothes, secure the property, and report to the Kirks who themselves were very fond of Khamnouy, and who were also shocked at the news of his illness.

We clung to each other, seeking comfort for our weariness and anguish, hoping for a few hours of untroubled sleep before we tried to implement suggestions John had brought from the doctor in Minneapolis. Slowly we would adjust to being a family of three again.

The next day, as we were talking with Khamnouy, he expressed concern about the young Lao woman he had known in school, the one I had met in the refugee camp in Nongkhai nearly two years earlier.

Phouvieng was now living in France with relatives, awaiting Khamnouy's arrival. They had agreed to marry that summer, but 'Nouy had written very little about his plans, and I was surprised to learn that he had checked out of his college dorm and had taken all of his clothes and other belongings with him to Minneapolis. Furthermore, he already had reservations to fly to Paris. We would have to cancel those plans and rethink the next steps.

I had no idea how this young woman viewed her relationship to Khamnouy, nor what her expectations of the future might be. I had no way of knowing how she would receive the news of his illness. Certainly we would do everything we could to enable her to see him, but we wondered if she would want to be with him in Hawaii.

"She can come, you know. We'll be glad to help her with travel expenses."

Khamnouy's reaction was hard to interpret. He seemed to want to see her and not to want to see her—understandable ambivalence in the light of all that was happening. We listened to him talk about it, encouraged him to express his terror of becoming a victim of maudlin sympathy, and concluded that he really would like to see Phouvieng. We sent her a round-trip ticket between Paris and Honolulu.

In the meantime we shared the medical records from Minneapolis with an oncologist who agreed to accept this new patient. We were lucky that there would be medical insurance coverage for Khamnouy through the company for which he had been working in Minneapolis. The existence of that policy was in itself a telling vignette of the affection and respect which Khamnouy called forth in everyone who knew him. The day that he had left work and gone to the hospital in Minneapolis, the personnel director of the business for which he worked rushed to 'Nouy's hospital bed to get his signature on the company medical form that would entitle him to full coverage. This man could just as easily have ignored the whole matter, and perhaps he would have had he known the enormous costs that would be generated in the next seven months. As it was, all doctor, hospital and therapy fees were covered by an extraordinarily comprehensive policy, a fact for which John and I became increasingly grateful.

For the first few weeks, having Khamnouy with us was easy and fun, and he was in good spirits. The oncologist had prescribed chemotherapy, and one or the other of us would drive him to the clinic for treatment, giving us time for sharing the day's activity, talking about school, the future. Then the chemo began to get to him.

"Mom, something terrible is happening." I looked up from breakfast preparations one morning to see Khamnouy holding a fistful of hair. "It's all over my pillow, it's just falling out."

I swallowed and reminded him that the doctor had told us he would probably lose his hair. "It will grow back, you know, once the chemo ends."

"Jeez, Mom, I can't go around with no hair!"

I mourned with him the loss of his thick, black locks and laughed, wryly, when he began to wear a knitted cap on his balding head.

"You can't wear a wool cap in Hawaii. You'll die of heat prostration."

"What do you suggest? I can't go out bald!"

"How about a wig?"

"Are you kidding? Me? A wig? Come on, Mom, don't be ridiculous."

"Well it wouldn't hurt to look for one. To have it around, just in case."

The social worker at the hospital told us where to look, and together we found a black wig that 'Nouy sometimes wore, but he preferred the cap most of the time.

Phouvieng arrived in October, and although she was a very attractive young woman, she was also shy and obviously ill at ease in our household. Perhaps we had done the wrong thing to bring her. I searched for ways to help us all be comfortable in this very tense situation.

Her first night at our house she and Khamnouy lay head to head on the bisecting couches in the spare room, talking all night.

"I can't leave her there alone," Khamnouy confided. "She is terrified of *phis*. There may be bad spirits in that room."*

"The *phis*," I expostulated. "What makes her think there are some?"

"Listen," he said patiently and somewhat condescendingly, "you never know what strange spirits may be inhabiting a new space you go into. She's very worried. So I need to talk with her until she gets used to having a room of her own."

I could have kicked myself for being so insensitive. We had recently resettled a Lao family of six in a three-bedroom cottage, only to find that they all slept in one bed to protect each other from any unfriendly spirits lurking in this foreign place. It was a relief to know that Khamnouy was alert to her fears.

"Okay, if you say so. Do what needs to be done to reassure her."

It took only a couple of nights for Phouvieng to decide that the room was friendly, and after that she settled in quickly. She was cheerful and a wonderful help around the kitchen. She began to prepare Lao delicacies to tempt Khamnouy's appetite, and they sat together for hours laughing and sharing memories of happier days.

Toward the end of November, 'Nouy experienced a remission. After dropping to less than one hundred pounds, he began to gain weight. The sparkle came back to his eyes. His laugh rang with the mischievousness I had once known in Laos. He seemed to be getting better and better. It was such an enormous relief to allow hope back into our lives that we all became positively euphoric.

I had found it impossible to talk with either Khamnouy or Phouvieng about their marriage plans, and they had never raised the subject. I assumed they were much more pragmatic than I in assessing the realities and

**See discussion on the* phi *in Chapter 15 in this book.*

had in some way reached an understanding. It was clear that 'Nouy would in no way expect her to tie herself to him in his present condition, and I began to see signs on her part of a gradual releasing of expectations.

In December 'Nouy announced that he was going back to college. The mail had brought him information he had requested regarding spring registration at the Stout campus of the University of Wisconsin, and he was determined to finish up his final year. Because he had taken classes through two previous summers, he was a first semester senior. He looked and felt so well we could hardly believe our luck. The doctor warned us that this was probably only a remission, not a cure, and would not presume to guess how long it might last.

At this time Phouvieng announced that she had to return to France. Not only did she have a job there, but she felt that it would be better not to be hovering around Khamnouy day after day. We reluctantly agreed with her and made plans for her to depart at the end of December. Even though Khamnouy daily put on weight and regained lost energy, venturing out with Phouvieng to sports events and an occasional movie, there was a deep underlying sadness in these preparations that forecast the end of their relationship. I tried very hard not to even think about the unspoken implications. Through all of this Khamnouy was determined to conquer his illness. He did everything the doctors asked. He also begged his Lao friends to obtain special herbal medicines for him, and some of them wrote to Thailand for the small paper packets they brought to him from time to time.

In addition he had been working with a pastor-healer on a therapeutic course of visualization developed by Dr. Carl Simonton and his associates, which advocates the use of mental imaging to cure both physical and emotional illness. Khamnouy explained that he visualized rats as the "good guys," who were eating the tiny white cancer cells that were destroying his body. By picturing his healthy body he was trying to make the cancer go away. He devoted enormous energy toward willing himself to recover.

His spirit was an inspiration to us all. Everyone who came in contact with him became an instant fan. Our church friends welcomed him into activities, sent him cards and fruit, offered to give him a ride to his therapy when my work or John's prohibited us from taking him, and took him to shows and ball games.

The Lao community in Honolulu also rallied around. Many of these men and women had left Laos as refugees when we did, people we had known during our years there. Some had arrived in Hawaii at the same time we returned. Others had been processed through refugee centers and then sent on. They were a strong, loyal group of friends who advised us on the Lao way of handling illness and brought Lao goodies to tempt Khamnouy's appetite.

We issued an open invitation to the Lao to spend Christmas with us and make it a truly festive day. We learned Christmas carols together and then sang them lustily as everyone helped to decorate the big Christmas tree. There were turkey and sticky rice, turkey *lap* and delicious Vietnamese spring rolls wrapped in very thin rice paper, cranberry sauce and pumpkin pie and fruits. We laughed and talked, ate, sang and drank. It was a warm family day as dozens of friends dropped in to share greetings with Khamnouy.

As he shared hopes of going back to school our friends looked at me with question and doubt in their faces. I rolled my eyes, shrugged my shoulders and said, "Sure, why not? If you don't have goals, you can't reach them!"

Inwardly my heart ached. Would this remission last? Would he really be able to go back to school? I cursed the caution in the doctor's voice when we asked about the future.

One of the great benefits of using St. Francis Hospital was that a small hospice effort was beginning. The priest at the hospital became a close friend and encouraged me to attend the support group that met to help people who had someone in the family who was terminally ill. Sometimes Khamnouy went to this group with me.

Early in January we had together attended a special two-day symposium by a Dr. Rosenbaum, whose no-nonsense approach to cancer was both informative and very frightening. The next day Khamnouy flopped on our couch, his voice flat, almost expressionless. "Mom, I've been thinking about the group and those people."

"The people in the support group?"

"Yes, those people, and what Dr. Rosenbaum said at the conference. I've thought about it a lot." He was very quiet, then turned to look at me and said, "I'm going to die."

My heart seemed to stop, surrounded by a thick bed of ice. I wanted to scream, "No, no, 'Nouy, you are not going to die, not yet, I won't let you, I won't let you." Instead, with immense control, I asked very gently, "What makes you feel that you are going to die? What's happening?"

During the conference we had attended together the doctor had outlined in unequivocal terms the usual paths that various cancers take, including the kind that Khamnouy had.

"Look at me, Mom." He circled his bony wrist with his finger. "I'm so skinny. I can't go back to school. I can't get married. I won't have any children. I'm sick."

I thought I might suffocate in the images that flashed through my head of the remission he had been enjoying, the wonderful holiday festivities just past, his excitement about returning to school, Phouvieng's bittersweet departure.

His birth parents were never out of my mind. We had written Souk, his older brother who was still in a refugee camp in Thailand, to tell him of Khamnouy's illness and the diagnosis. We didn't know at this time where his parents were and if they knew about Khamnouy, but I sensed that they did. In fact, I wrestled constantly with the guilt brought on by our agonizing over whether he would have contracted cancer had we left him in Laos.

Our sense was that the seeds of cancer had been planted long ago either by the poor sanitation and nutrition rampant in Laos, or perhaps from the toxic conditions in soil and water that were caused, at least in part, by the wars that had been fought for so long in that country. Who really knows where this disease starts?

I ached for his mother, so far away and so impossible to reach with any kind of comfort.

I wrenched my thoughts back to our living room and the conversation I was having with Khamnouy. "I can't take it," my mind screamed. "He's telling you he is giving up, that he's not going to fight to live any more." I wanted to rush over to him and cradle him in my arms. I wanted to cry, to howl with anguish and rage. What kind of a world allows a twenty-five-year-old to discuss his own mortality and voice his fears about death? Imminent death.

"It's easy to get discouraged, isn't it?" I willed calm into my voice.

"I'm so tired, Mom. I'm a lot of trouble to you, and I can't do anything. I just want to rest. I don't feel like seeing anyone."

I had to agree that lately it did seem as if he tired awfully easily. "Yet you were doing so well," I blurted.

On my desk were three articles which had appeared in the local newspaper in which, using a pseudonym, Khamnouy was described, extolling the helpfulness of the kind of imaging our pastor-therapist friend had been using with him. It sounded like the success story of the century. The articles had appeared barely two weeks prior to this conversation we were now having.

"Don't give up, 'Nouy. Don't give up," I urged, fighting the lumps that were welling up in my throat.

He repeated, "But I'm a lot of trouble."

There was no mirth in my attempt at laughter as I repeated his words. "You sure are 'a lot of trouble.' You eat a couple of bites every few hours, and mostly you cook for yourself. You give Dad and me more pleasure than we can ever express, having you here, being able to do things with you and for you. It's a kind of trouble we're grateful to have." Would my heart ever beat normally again? What was happening to my voice?

Dear God, I prayed, please help me to help Khamnouy. Help me to say the right things to him now.

"Tell me what you feel like."

"Before, I felt good, strong. Then lately I got tired. Then I got this bad cough. It won't go away."

"Does it keep you awake at night?"

"Yes, I can't sleep at all. Just as I go to sleep, I cough, so I get up and try to drink something. But I still cough."

Is there fluid in his lungs *again*? I asked myself wildly. Is the cancer active in his lungs? Is it the fluid that makes him cough?

"I've seen you at night," I acknowledged. "We both seem to prowl around quite a lot."

He grinned a faint, lopsided grin and moved to another plane of thought.

"There are only two of us who got out. Goddamn it. Why does it have to happen?" There was real anger in his voice.

"Two of you?"

"Two of us from Sam Neua."

"You and that fellow you write to in France?"

"Yes, Phila. We came from the same village. We lived near to each other. You know, Mom, he's like my brother."

I knew that Khamnouy and Phila were the only two Sam Neua boys who had been accepted to study in universities abroad. To leave Laos for this reason had been an enormous achievement of which this former president of the refugee Sam Neua Students Association was justly proud.

And now he was going to die.

Dear Jesus, I prayed, how do I cope with this?

"Tell me about being a boy in Sam Neua."

As Khamnouy started to talk, his eyes softened with the memories.

"Our village was large, as villages go," he began. "We had a lot of houses. My father was almost never there. He was always working for the Royal Lao Government forces."

"You mean he already was a marked man because his loyalties were with the king and not with the Pathet Lao?" I supplemented.

"That's right. He was always off fighting, or mostly just being careful not to get caught by the Communists. Our family was big. My sister, myself and my two younger brothers."

"Your little brother must not have been born yet, and what about Souk?"

"He was so much older. He was already gone away."

"Gone where?"

"To Vientiane, to school. He kept writing to my mother and telling her to send me to him, that he would take care of me in school."

"You weren't very old, were you?"

"Yes, well, no. I was eleven on the day when my father came to get us, when we left Houa Thong. It was awful. We kids had been home with my mother and suddenly my father was there, and he said he had come to get us because the Communists would never let us go and he was afraid for us. We crept down through the village and by the river, and he helped us get away. We took nothing with us. We went and lived for a long time on a mountain."

"You lived on a mountain?" My surprise reflected that it was very unusual for ethnic Lao to adopt mountain living. Hill tribes such as the Hmong lived on the mountains, not Lao Loum like Khamnouy. (This family's unusual closeness to the Hmong explained why Souk had chosen to live in the Hmong area of the Nongkhai refugee camp rather than with the ethnic Lao.)

"Yes, on a mountain. It was very cold." He grimaced. "We never had enough to eat, and we had no blankets. It was pretty bad."

The talk about his early years had distracted us both from the beginning of this encounter, and Khamnouy snuggled down into his blankets and quietly dozed off. My own anguished heart was calmed also, and I tiptoed away, praying that we would both find at least a few hours of peace and rest.

26
The End as Beginning

In less than a week Khamnouy was back in the hospital. My job was very demanding at this particular time, and John's teaching schedule left him free only in the evenings to go to visit our sick boy. I sneaked in quick visits anytime I could get away, dashing to the hospital to spend a few moments attempting to cheer him up, trying to do whatever I could to make him a bit more comfortable.

The doctor felt that massive chemotherapy doses might arrest the cancer and buy time. I was not convinced, and my worst fears began to be realized as Khamnouy became even more miserably ill, not only with the cancer, but from the aftereffects of the chemotherapy. He looked so frail and tired. The days and nights were heavy with our concern and sorrow.

The nurse called on February 23 at 10:20 P.M. to report that 'Nouy's blood pressure was very low and that he was coughing up a lot of blood. She promised to call back in an hour. I spoke gently to my husband, who had been awakened by the phone call.

"Honey, I just have to go to the hospital. I want to be with Khamnouy."

"Do you want me to come with you?"

"No, you don't have to. You need your sleep. I just can't leave him there all alone. He must be so frightened."

"If he gets worse, or if you want me, call."

I donned slacks and a flannel shirt and drove to the hospital and went to Khamnouy's room.

Lying in bed, tubes attached to both arms and extra oxygen plugged in, Khamnouy was hollow-eyed.

With a lightness of tone that belied my heavy heart I leaned over his bed to say, "Hi, love, I've come to be with you for a while."

He responded with a wan attempt at a smile. "Good to see you, Mom. I feel awful."

"I know you do. Don't try to talk." I pulled a chair up to his bed, took his hand in mine and just sat with him. I felt certain it would be his last night. He seemed so pathetic. I didn't want to lose him, but I prayed for his release.

How we war with ourselves about death, I thought. One part of me screamed for more therapy, anything, everything. Help this boy! Fight for your life, Khamnouy! Another part of me begged for the release of death, an end to the pain and the struggle.

"But he was so well just a couple of months ago. Remember the remission. He can do it again." I was wholly unable to convince myself that he would ever get better.

"Be sensible. Look at the IV's, the plasma, the medicine," another part of me responded. "What does it take to persuade a doctor to cut off the life supports and lend a modicum of dignity to death?" my first self continued.

The nurse came in, glanced at us both and left. Hours passed. Khamnouy, accepting the comfort of our touch, fell asleep, and then I found myself talking to him, tears streaming down my face. "Khamnouy, my son, my dear son. Do you know how much I love you? Do you believe that if I could, I would gladly assume this terrible burden of pain and allow you to be free and healthy again?"

I wondered if he ever regretted the whole process that had brought him to America. Did we do something wrong? Would he not have developed cancer if we had left him in Laos? What about his mother and father? My tears fell harder. Here I was, not his natural mother, weeping for this lad—I who had encouraged him to leave his parents and his home in order to follow his dream of becoming a trained, educated teacher for his people. Could they forgive us? Would they blame us? How would we ever be able to compensate them for the loss of this vibrant, laughing son who brought such joy to so many? Where had we gone wrong?

"'Nouy, 'Nouy," I sobbed, "I just want you to know that if we had it to do all over again, we would do the same thing. I don't regret anything that we have done. I'm glad we met you. I'm glad we sent you to college. I'm just sorry this had to happen."

I felt a gentle squeeze of my hand. He had heard and understood. A sense of calm slowly wiped away the tears. I sat with him until the wee small hours and then, knowing that I too had a new day to face, crept home to my own bed.

Khamnouy didn't die that night, but he got worse. Two days later he was placed in intensive care, in isolation. We could visit him only by donning gowns and masks and by covering our feet with wrappings to keep his environment sterile.

He asked me to bring a Buddhist monk. While this request took my mind off his immediate condition, it sent me into a near panic. A Japanese Buddhist would hardly fit the occasion. I made frantic phone calls.

"Sengdao, do you know of a Buddhist priest who can speak Lao? Khamnouy is dying."

This close Lao friend told me that several Vietnamese priests lived in a house in the Salt Lake area of Honolulu and added, "Perhaps they also know about a Thai monk. Maybe one of them can help you."

The phone call to them was difficult because they spoke only halting English, but I finally got the message across. A young Lao man who was dying wanted a Buddhist priest. Would one of them come if I provided the transportation? Yes, the priest would come, and I found my way to the monk's house and ushered him into my car, hoping I would not insult him by requiring him to sit at my level in the car. I knew that a woman's head must always be lower than that of a Buddhist monk, but I did not know how to deal with this in an American automobile and hoped that the urgency of the mission would be understood and my rude behavior overlooked.

Visiting Khamnouy by this time was almost more than I could bear. The massive chemotherapy had blistered the inside of his mouth, his tongue, his throat. He was in terrible pain. I was so angry that I avoided seeing the doctor for fear of totally losing control over my emotions.

"I'm sure he has simply used Khamnouy as a guinea pig. The doctor knows he is going to die. So he figured he would experiment with this massive therapy, just to see what would happen."

John held my hand and said gently, "Now, now, love, talk like that will only make you more angry. I agree, they have gone too far, but we are not the doctors. There is always a chance of stumbling onto something that can help the next patient."

My husband's attempt to calm me down was not too successful. The monk and I went to the isolation unit where he donned the required sterilized garments over his saffron robe. A Lao friend had come to help with translation, and they entered the sealed room together.

I sat outside, reflecting that in all the time Khamnouy had been in America I had never known him to go near a Buddhist ceremony or seek a priest, but it was clear that with death only moments away, he was clutching for the reassurance of long-laid-aside practices from his childhood, and I prayed he would be comforted by the presence of the young Vietnamese monk, prayed that Khamnouy would understand that I had been unable to find a Thai or a Lao, that I had done my best. Each of us in our own way and our own language offered prayers for the comfort and release of our precious Lao son.

Later that afternoon Khamnouy died. His poor disease-racked body no longer had to suffer the indignities that medical science imposed upon him in the name of mercy.

His passing was a signal for the Lao community to gently mobilize their forces. There were many Lao in Honolulu who had come as refugees to Hawaii. A number of them were now settled in jobs while others were busy learning English in order to move beyond the American welfare system which had enabled them to make a new beginning in a new land. Most of them knew us and had visited 'Nouy both in our home and in the hospital.

Throughout the fall and winter I had become aware that their perception of illness and death was very different from mine. They were more attuned to the life cycle than I and as a result, less accepting of the hospital procedures. They were visibly uncomfortable with all of the life support measures and extraordinary lengths to which the doctors had gone to prolong Khamnouy's life. Now that he was released from all of this they were prepared to give him a proper Lao ceremony to help him into his next life.

John and I had enrolled Khamnouy and ourselves with a memorial society which provided for cremation within twenty-four hours of death. The Lao absolutely forbade us to do this. In their gentle but persistent way, they instructed us about what must be done to observe a proper Lao funeral for a young person who had died an untimely death.

"The body must lie in state so that we may pay our last respects to Khamnouy before cremation." They had explained to us that, according to their custom, he should be buried, not cremated, a requirement that was due to the nature of his illness which they saw as causing an "unnatural" death, yet they acquiesced to our wishes in this matter.

"All of us in the Lao community want to come to the funeral. You must permit us to make arrangements."

The mortician agreed to embalm the body, and we reached a compromise through which the Lao would take care of a service at the mortuary while John and I would prepare a memorial service over the ashes at the Church of the Crossroads. I was in a daze of grief and exhaustion and grateful to Khamnouy's friends for all they did to arrange a simple and dignified Buddhist service which allowed them to say goodbye to him in their own way.

Our entire community at the Church of the Crossroads in Honolulu attended a simple memorial service in which some of his history and accomplishments were reviewed and shared by the Reverend Gloria Kibbee:

> Knowing how much he wanted to return to the country of his birth to help his people, the finest memorial of his life would be that others carry out his dreams for an end to poverty and injustice and the establishment of peace in the world and especially in his homeland. . . . Let us comfort one another in the days and weeks ahead, for in that comforting we are sharing in the love that Khamnouy shared with us in his life. In the glory of that reflected love, may our own lives and deaths have deeper meaning and purpose—because the miracle of Khamnouy came our way.

This memorial service was held on what would have been Khamnouy's twenty-sixth birthday, in March of 1978. At the time it seemed like the end of all of our dreams of helping him to realize his ambitions for himself and his family. In fact, it was only the beginning.

We had hoped that Souk, the oldest brother, would reach America before Khamnouy died. Souk's path to freedom had been paved by Khamnouy and involved a process that would eventually allow every member of the Sivongsay family to emigrate to Minnesota. Try as we could, we had been unable to bring the two brothers together before Khamnouy left us in early March. Souk did not reach Minnesota until late spring.

Souk's arrival in Apple Valley started a pattern of immigration and settling-in that was repeated over a period of several years by successive members of Khamnouy's family. Khamnouy had learned about the Peace Reformed Church which was sponsoring Indochinese refugees and had begun to develop a comprehensive program to house, teach, retrain and launch newly arrived refugee families into mainstream America.

Shortly after Souk's late spring arrival he moved into the job his younger brother had left so precipitously when he became ill. The manager of this meat processing plant in south Minneapolis was so favorably impressed with the work of both of these men that they began to staff their entire operation with newly arrived Lao immigrants. The management was lavish in their praise of the hard-working Sivongsay men: "They are excellent workers, and anyone related to Khamnouy is guaranteed a job." This was good news for newcomers and proved to be a real stepping-stone for all members of the family in later days.

Once those left behind in Laos heard that Souk had arrived in the United States, they too began to make plans to escape to Thailand. A cousin, Khamphanh, the second family member to go, had been in the same camp in Nongkhai that Souk had left. Although alone and only fifteen when he escaped, Khamphanh determinedly lied about his age when he entered the refugee camp so that he would be considered old enough to be allotted food rations and a sleeping space with the other single men. He had been in contact with Khamnouy since he left Laos in July of 1976 and 'Nouy was working with the Red Cross to try to get permission for him to join us in Hawaii. Unfortunately, 'Nouy's death cut short the entire process, and with his sponsor in America now deceased, 'Phanh's case went back to the bottom of the list while we, not even knowing his name, had no way of contacting him. With typical Lao casualness, Khamnouy had merely referred to him as "my cousin." This did not help us find him.

"You know, Mom, he's all by himself in that camp." 'Nouy had been very distressed. Single people had difficulty getting enough food. "I'm mad at Souk because he doesn't help our cousin. How can he ignore his own family?"

None of us at the time realized the incredibly hard time Souk was having. His wife, Chantalone, had twice had to be hospitalized, and finding extra money for medicine and doctor fees was next to impossible. There had been no way Souk could spare money to help the young cousin.

As a result, we lost track of Khamphanh, but in 1981 he found his way through the refugee resettlement processes and arrived in Hawaii less than one hour after we were notified by a local social agency that he was expected—tomorrow! They had neglected to factor in the international dateline when they notified us, and it was only by chance that I phoned the airport to confirm the expected flight and discovered that "tomorrow's" plane was already in a holding pattern for landing at Honolulu airport. Khamphanh lived with us for a year before moving on to Minnesota.

On December 28, 1978, the same year that Khamnouy died, his next younger brother, Khamnai, swam across the river to freedom. He had not been sure just how to get himself out of Laos but knew it was time to go.

"What you can do is put your clothes in a plastic bag and swim with them," he was advised by a neighbor who had himself done this and then returned to Laos for his wife and children. Khamnai literally took the plunge just three days after his marriage. Mercifully, he was undetected.

His next challenge was to plot the retrieval of the remainder of the family. He and Souk raised two hundred *baht* per family member through us and our connections in the United States and searched for someone who was willing to risk crossing from Thailand to get them.

Eleven in the morning was the appointed rendezvous hour for the family members in Vientiane. Khambai, the newlywed wife, and Piavong, Souk's father, reported that they waited for four hours at the appointed place but the man did not show up. Khambai's mother was frantic with worry.

"Someone may know about your escape attempt and have had the man arrested. Now they will come for you, for all of us."

Crossing the Mekong River in those days was a truly death defying operation, and secrecy was difficult to maintain when there were so many people involved. A week after the first abortive attempt, Grandpa and Grandma Sivongsay, two of their daughter Mai's children, a cousin and Khambai again left the house, this time at six in the morning. They went first to Phone Penau where they were hidden in a gas station for four hours. Finally a man arrived in a taxi and took them thirty-five kilometers south to Paksane. "We must hide in the forest," he informed them, hustling them into the jungle.

"Don't cry, Mok. Mek, take care of your sister." Fearful and filled with apprehension, the adults soothed the small children, desperate to keep them from revealing the hiding place. From eleven in the morning until six in the evening, they huddled in the jungle, hungry and tired, imagining all of the things that could have gone wrong with this attempt to gain freedom. During that time two people from the town came out to bring them water and to instruct them to walk to the river when evening came. From dark until eleven at night they crept through the forest until they rendezvoused at the river's edge with twenty-four others. Six of these were escapees who had been directed to this place by guides from the underground resistance group which was loosely organized to help fleeing Lao citizens.

They stood in fidgeting groups or paced on the river bank, too nervous to sit during their wait. Would a boat really come? Would they successfully cross the river? What would they find on the other side? Hungry, tired and frightened, the small band of freedom seekers struggled to bolster their flagging spirits.

Through the darkness they detected the sounds of an approaching boat. Would it be their rescuer or would it be a patrol boat that would whisk them back to captivity? Should they let their presence be known or flatten themselves on the bank so as not to be detected? With great relief they heard themselves hailed by the Thai boatman who had been paid handsomely to ferry them. Quickly they squeezed into the boat and for thirty anxious minutes searched for a landing spot on the opposite bank. Again they had to wait, finally reaching the refugee camp at two o'clock in the morning.

Arrival at the camp did not mean security. The following afternoon they were all taken to jail and were forced to remain there for three days, then transferred to a second jail where they learned that Khamnai had stayed for a month while Souk sought bail money with which to buy his release. This added harassment was meted out by unscrupulous and greedy local officials who knew that desperate fugitives would pay anything to secure their foothold in a country where haven was offered to them.

The jail conditions were deplorable: a tiny cell with no water and so little space they had to sleep in shifts. No food was provided in the jail, and Khamnai was frantically scrounging enough rations to feed the eight incarcerated members of his family while at the same time seeking money with which to bail them out.

By securing their release, Souk was reunited with his brother and sister-in-law, but only for a short time—his authorization to leave for the United States came through, and he and Khamnai hastened to find quarters for their parents and the grandchildren before Souk left Nongkhai.

The mother of the children, Mai, had chosen to remain in Laos because her husband had been taken away to re-education camp by the Pathet Lao. She had no word of him and was unwilling to leave the country, fearing it would cut off all possibility of eventual reunion with him. How would he ever locate her if she left for America, a country so far away and so far beyond her ability to imagine that she rightly feared the loss of contact, should it ever be made?

Although Souk, once he arrived in the United States, could apply to have his parents join him, the other siblings would remain in the camp until their parents were processed and settled in America. According to American special refugee immigration regulations, it was parents who were permitted to apply for the reunification of the remainder of the family. It was a long and tortuous process that lasted nearly ten years.

27
Release and Reunion

All during Khamnouy's illness we had been trying desperately to speed up Souk's arrival in America so that the brothers might see one another, but this was not to be. In early May 1978, two months after Khamnouy died, Souk and his family arrived in Minnesota to start a new life. The meat packing company in which Khamnouy had worked offered immediate employment, and with halting steps the family began to adjust to living in the United States.

For Souk, who had twice been sent to Texas for aircraft maintenance training, the adjustment was not difficult, and his young children quickly began to learn English. Chantalone, his wife, also was eager to find a job and to be able to communicate with new friends and neighbors. The family quickly adopted many of the customs and patterns of their new home.

As with most refugees, Souk's goal was to reunite the entire family, and even as they struggled for subsistence living for themselves, they began the process which would allow their parents to come to the United States.

When the Americans had left Laos many families, including Souk's parents, moved down from the village and back into Vientiane where the government assigned them a small plot of land to cultivate. Backbreaking work was necessary to reclaim the soil in order to meet the quota of rice they were expected to produce. A system of cooperative agriculture was imposed by the Lao People's Democratic Republic which meant that the farmers could not keep the rice they grew but were given a monthly allotment by the central committee. It barely sustained them. The land cultivated by the Sivongsays was several kilometers out of town which meant a long daily trek, and it was a discouraging and mindless kind of drudgery for little reward.

Mai, the older sister, her husband Chanbounmy* and their children lived with the grandparents and also worked in the fields. At times the women were able to supplement the meager family income by selling some of their weavings.

Chanbounmy was also from northern Laos and had grown up in a time when constant turmoil and change marked his life. He had first served the Royal Lao forces when he was only thirteen, leaving sixth grade to take up arms and fight against the Communists. Alternating between military service and going to school became a typical pattern for him. When he had completed ten grades he was given a teaching assignment in a newly established elementary school in a rural area of Sam Neua. This school and several others were hurriedly organized by the Royal Lao Government in an effort to counteract Pathet Lao criticism that there was little concern for education. Chanbounmy was the sole teacher in a dingy, one-room, makeshift building with a dirt floor, poor lighting and hewn logs for seats. He had met and married Mai in 1962 when she was a refugee in Hua Mouang.

John and I had first met this couple in 1974 while at the refugee camp at Phone Xay where Chanbounmy was the principal of the school and served as our interpreter during the visit with Khamnouy's family.

For the three years since hostilities had ceased, Chanbounmy had lived and farmed with his wife's family, eking out an existence and carefully avoiding any activity that might attract the attention of the current government. In July of 1978, while he was working with his brother-in-law in the rice paddies, a police officer went to his home and told Mai, "We have a message for your husband and must find him."

"What is the message? I will give it to him when he returns from the fields."

"No. We must find him now. His brother needs him. Take us to him."

Suspicious, but not daring to defy them further, she led them to the rice paddy where Chanbounmy listened to the officer's story. There was something that did not ring true in all this, but concern for his brother won out, and Chanbounmy accompanied the officer into Vientiane. Mai too became uneasy about their real purpose and at a distance followed the officers who took her husband into Vientiane to the Government Center. She noted that his brother, Van Dy, was already there.

**The materials contained in this chapter were recorded on tape by the author in sessions with Chanbounmy Houangnakhone in 1990 in Eagan, Minnesota, where he now resides, and have been verified by him prior to publication.*

Both men were accused of political subversion and sentenced to jail on the spot, charged with treasonable political alignments during the sixties when they had alternately been teachers, foot soldiers and guides for the Royal Lao Army. To be arrested more than fifteen years later was both unexpected and frightening.

Within a few minutes additional prisoners were brought out and all of them loaded into trucks and taken to the Sam Khe jail, on the outskirts of Vientiane. At the jail all prisoners were interrogated and handcuffed, and the two brothers were separated, unaware that they would not see each other again for nine years. Uncertainty and confusion nourished the fear that marked these early days of captivity.

Mai had observed her husband's arrest and removal to jail and guessed that they would be taken to nearby Sam Khe. During the six months the prisoners were kept in that jail they were released from their handcuffs only when they were fed. At first weekly visits had been permitted from family members, but toward the end of December those who had visitor privileges were instructed to bring the prisoners warm clothing, and then all visits were cut off. It would be nine years before Mai saw her husband again.

Early one morning the prisoners were roughly prodded out of their quarters, lined up and had both hands and feet tied. "What's up? What do you think is going to happen to us?"

Their muttered queries brought kicks and blows from their captors as they were transported to Wattay airport where they were transferred into planes and tied into their seats. Hope and despair were mingled in their whispered speculations with one another.

"Someone said they are taking us to Sam Neua." Maybe they would go home.

"Why would they take us back where we have come from?"

"What will they do to us?" Rumors they had heard about "seminars" and "re-education" gave them little hope.

During their transfer to the north the men suffered from the pain of the shackles on their hands and feet and from the cold. Fear and uncertainty were constant companions.

Their last transfer was across a small river, and here the men were singled out by name. Chanbounmy found himself in a very dark cave-like room with no heat and no light. During the first three days there they were without food or medical care. He was later to compare notes with Bounliane and learn that they had both received very similar treatment.

Chanbounmy was in this cave for three years, receiving one hundred grams of food a day, living in a place with no lights. For one fifteen-minute

Piavong and Tai Sivongsay and granddaughter, Mok, 1984.

period a week he was allowed outside to wash his clothes, his weakened eyes causing even this bit of freedom to be a painful experience.

The years of incarceration in this windowless, dark space took both an emotional and a physical toll of the men. The hopelessness of their plight and their total separation from their families and from the outside world drove many to near madness. Limited space made all physical activity impossible, and as energy and morale sagged, the men became very depressed. Many became ill, and some died.

The psychological harassment of the prisoners was equally devastating.

"We know that you were a powerful leader in the army in Hua Mouang. Confess."

"How could that be? I was thirteen years old."

"Don't lie to us. We have records telling us that you engaged in subversive activities."

"You are wrong. I will not respond to these false accusations."

His refusal to verify their assertions eventually convinced his captors of his innocence, for after months of day and night interrogations they gave up and left him alone. He constantly asked newly arrived prisoners for word of his brother, Van Dy, but heard nothing.

In Vientiane, even before the disappearance of their son-in-law into the re-education camp, the elder Sivongsays, Tai and Piavong, had been formulating plans for their own eventual escape to Thailand. They had successfully convinced Souk to fly out of Laos and had later encouraged his wife to take their three children and cross the river by boat. Khamnai, another son, and his wife had been routed toward the southern part of Laos and then smuggled across the river, taking two of Mai's children with them. Mai's oldest son engineered his own escape.

Crossing the Mekong River as an escapee from Laos was extremely hazardous at best. Clandestine arrangements were made to be ferried by boat, and thousands of baht changed hands. There were many unscrupulous boat owners who took the money but didn't show up or, worse, turned their boatload of refugees over to the Lao police for an additional reward instead of taking them to the safety of the Thai side.

Less than a year after Chanbounmy's arrest the grandparents left Laos and entered a Thai refugee camp. There the authorities assigned them a transit or "T" number, the next step in a process that would eventually allow them to join Souk in Minnesota.

The whole family begged Mai to bring her two remaining children across the river and leave Laos by accompanying Tai and Piavong. "How will you manage without our help?" the grandparents demanded to know. "You must come with us."

"I can't go now. What if there is news of Chanbounmy? How would he find me? I will stay." Mai felt certain that her husband was alive, but no confirming word reached her. During the next two years she laid the groundwork for her own departure by contacting relatives and friends to ask their help in taking care of Chanbounmy if and when he should be released. At last, confident that when news of him surfaced, someone would contact the Sivongsay family in Minnesota, she too fled to a refugee camp in Nongkhai.

Mai's parents were by this time in the United States, and immigration regulations allowed parents in the United States to apply for reunification with any children who were still in refugee camps. In 1980 Mai and her two young children left Southeast Asia to rejoin her three older children who were at that time living with her parents in Eagan, Minnesota.

John and I visited the reunited family that summer and helped to welcome Mai at a huge *baci* held by the Lao and their American friends at the Peace Reformed Church. Referred to as *Poh Mee* (grandmother) and *Poh Tow* (grandfather), we were included as two of the approximately fifty members of the Sivongsay clan. Mai's classic round Lao face shone with tears of happiness as she spotted us and rushed over to *wai* and hug us. We exclaimed over how the older children had grown since that day in 1974 when we had first seen them in the muddy village of Phone Xay. We shared food and memories and came away from the *baci* with dozens of white strings tied on our forearms, promising protection from the spirits, good luck and good health.

As we celebrated, Chanbounmy, half a world away, had only recently been transferred with the other Sam Neua prisoners to that cave-like space where they were to be cooped up for three more long years. Not until 1983, when restrictions were eased and the men allowed to go outside to work in the forest, did Mai at long last hear that he was still alive.

Half-blind and badly undernourished, Chanbounmy was fortunate to have a friend in the village who hid scraps of meat and rice under his shirt, passing them along whenever he could. In addition, the prisoners learned to eat anything they could forage—roots, grass, snails, even banana peels.

The Sam Neua men had been imprisoned for five years before they were formally charged. Chanbounmy received a ten-year sentence, convicted of fighting against the Communists as a commander for the Royal Lao Army.

The sentencing did not prevent prisoners from moving about and working in the village. Although the villagers were hostile and sometimes brutal, the captives noticed that restrictions were being gradually removed and discipline lightened.

Chanbounmy had received word through a friend that his family was in America, and he kept his spirits up with dreams of fleeing Laos to be reunited with them.

His 1986 release, three years later, came as a complete surprise. He had no idea why they were letting him go seven years short of fulfilling his sentence. His unexpected freedom allowed him to concentrate all of his energy toward trying to get to Vientiane. Men whose families had fled the country were neither given passes to travel south of Xieng Khouang, nor were they entitled to a plot of land on which they could farm to sustain themselves. Villagers treated them harshly, often using them as slaves. In many ways freedom seemed little different from being a prisoner.

The major benefit of the release was the reunification of the two brothers. Cautiously they sought ways in which Chanbounmy could obtain permission to be reunited with his own family. Van Dy had met and married a woman in the village and was able to offer some help to Chanbounmy although he was not himself at that time considering leaving the country. That would come later.

"I must go to Vientiane to sell my house," Chanbounmy explained to the authorities. "Once I do that I will have money I can bring back to Muong Pao to start over. I am so poor now I can't contribute to the life of this village." He repeated all the party-line phrases that had been dinned into him day after day in captivity and led them to believe that he meant to return with the money in order to help the people.

He didn't mention that another brother had long since sold the Vientiane house and set the money aside for use at such time as Chanbounmy might be able to flee Laos. Some of this money had already been smuggled to him by officials who had permission to travel between Vientiane and Xieng Khouang province and who could be bribed. A former prisoner needed a very good excuse to obtain even a short pass to travel south, and applying to do this required endless red tape and patience.

Careful planning and judicious payoffs eventually secured a temporary pass for Chanbounmy to leave Muong Pao. He reached Vientiane on February 2, 1987, and learned from his sister-in-law's mother how to contact Mai and their five children who were with the rest of the Sivongsay family in the United States. He was the only family member remaining in Laos. He hastened to find a telephone.

Euphoric hysteria reigned in Eagan, Minnesota, when Mai picked up the ringing phone and heard her husband's voice for the first time in nine years.

"It's Daddy, it's Daddy." Tears of joy choking her, she passed the receiver around so that all the children could speak to and hear their father.

"Where are you? When will we see you?" The oldest son spoke only English, but his father recalled enough to understand and to be able to answer.

"I am in Vientiane on a twenty-day pass. I'm supposed to return to the north, and I am being constantly watched."

Our phone in Hawaii rang in the wee hours of the morning as Mek, the oldest daughter, cried, "Grandma Rantala, my dad is in Vientiane. He is all right. He is going to try to come to America." Astounded and relieved to know there was direct contact with this man from whom no one had heard for so many years, John and I shared in the rejoicing and assured the family they could depend on us for any help needed to reunite him with his family.

Money for Chanbounmy's escape was with Khambai's mother, who had elected to stay in Vientiane. Khambai, who was married to Souk's younger brother, had not convinced her mother to move to Minnesota. There were too many family members still in Laos with whom the mother did not want to lose contact.

After eighteen tense days during which he evaluated the possible ways to escape from Laos, Chanbounmy teamed up with a soldier whose home was in Thailand. Using the money saved for his escape, they boarded a bus to Thakek, south of Vientiane. Two days later, having successfully dodged the border patrols, they bribed the owner of a small boat at Se Bang Fai to ferry them to Thailand and freedom. While staying there with Lao soldiers who had regrouped on the Thai border, he again phoned his wife.

"I'm free. I'm in Thailand, and I'm okay. It has been very long since I saw you. I want to come to America. How can I do this? Please help me."

"You must enter a refugee camp and get a transit number." All the Minnesota members of the family reiterated that this was an absolute necessity.

Nine years of harsh treatment by soldiers, captors and other men in authority had made Chanbounmy extremely suspicious of regimentation, camps and regulations. He feared that entry into a refugee camp would be merely the first step toward recapture and return to seminar.

"No, I'm afraid I'll be sent back to Laos. I'm going to stay with the Lao soldiers." At this time no amount of pleading could change his mind. Family members talked with Indochinese refugee agencies, with each other and even with us in Hawaii. We all knew he had to follow the procedures required of every refugee and that, unbelievable as it might sound, it was not possible to bribe one's way around the red tape. There was no way to circumvent the established procedures.

"Dad," Souk asked in a phone call. "Is there someone you know who can help Chanbounmy get out of Thailand without going through the refugee camp? Surely surviving 're-education' is enough!"

Officials in the American Embassy in Thailand knew about Chanbounmy's recent escape. They had reliable channels of communication for keeping tabs on escapees who had been in the armed forces and had already helped hundreds who had been allied with American efforts to save Laos from Communism. They did everything they could to speed the reunification of escaped prisoners with their families, but they could not authorize a waiver of immigration procedures governing refugee departures. We shared this information with Souk, pleading, "You *must* convince him to go to a camp."

At the time of Chanbounmy's arrival in Thailand his sister-in-law in America was attending a conference featuring immigration lawyers. She had, for a number of years, been working with advocacy groups that assisted Lao to resettle, so attendance at this meeting offered a prime opportunity to talk with the attorneys about his case. Meanwhile, in Eagan, Minnesota, Dorothy and Ted Foster, who had sponsored other members of this family, now applied to Lutheran Social Service and also to Church World Service, pleading for speedy action to reunite Chanbounmy with his family.

The combined pleadings of family and the urgings of the officials helped Chanbounmy overcome his fears, and he entered a temporary refugee center. Hearing this, we in America erroneously assumed that release would be imminent—that he would have a "T" number and be on a plane almost immediately. All members of the family were so emotionally keyed up it was hard to concentrate on jobs or school. The waiting seemed endless and even a minor hitch was blown up into a calamity.

Obtaining his "T" number did not guarantee immediate release, and Chanbounmy spent two more anxious months at Nha Pho before being sent, on June 26, 1987, to the center from which all refugees were flown to America. Surely his authorization for transport would now be forthcoming.

For family members the days and hours of waiting had become nearly unbearable. John and I were as keyed up as the rest of the family. "It has been more than twelve weeks since Chanbounmy called from Vientiane, surely he is on his way by now." John turned to me and suggested that now, at the end of our summer in northern Minnesota, we stop on our way back to Hawaii to see our adopted Lao families. We fully expected to see Chanbounmy and were told that his departure from Thailand was imminent and that we *must* stick around to greet him.

With air reservations in hand and obligations awaiting us at home, we were unable to join their vigil, a decision that was justified when another unexplained delay kept Chanbounmy in the holding camp an additional week.

On September 13, 1987, word came through. Chanbounmy was cleared to leave Thailand. The suspenseful waiting among his family members was prolonged one last time, stretched to the limit. Instead of flying him across the Pacific, he was sent by the longest possible route—through Europe to Denmark, followed by a TWA flight to New York. There he once more changed planes, finally arriving in Minneapolis at 8:15 in the evening.

The Minneapolis airport was the scene of a tumultuous reception not only from the fifty members of his own extended family but from hundreds of additional well wishers and friends, Lao and American, who also crowded the airport arrival area for this emotionally charged occasion. The Minneapolis *Star-Tribune* featured his picture in their morning edition showing him being literally carried out over the heads of the crowd to his waiting wife. Exhausted from the trip and dazed by the size of his reception, he fell into Mai's tight embrace, ending a twelve-year effort to reunite the entire Sivongsay family.

From Hawaii John and I exchanged telephone calls with the folks in Eagan as we celebrated this reunion from afar. We relived the agony of our own last days in Laos: our sadness at leaving Lao friends and the schools on which John had worked so hard with the members of the Hawaii team. We recalled the hardships, the boredom and the disappointment suffered by members of the Sivongsay family who spent years in refugee camps both in Laos and Thailand, only to see their country taken over by the Pathet

Lao. We marveled at the progress each family group in Minnesota was now making as children advanced through the school systems, mothers struggled to learn English, and working members of the family moved up into better-paying jobs.

In a letter to his sister, John reminisced about Khamnouy who had been the catalyst for so many unforgettable experiences and for so much of our understanding of Laos and the Lao people:

> Khamnouy was the Moses of his family. He had a vision of a better life for his people, and with foresight and courage he led them through the wilderness. He climbed the mountain and saw the opportunities awaiting them all in the promised land. But God had other plans for him, and he was denied the chance to dwell with his family in the land toward which he had led them.

The realization of the struggle to make Laos free of outside domination has yet to be achieved by others who carry the same vision for their country that Khamnouy had. New leadership is developing both inside and outside of Laos. Hopeful, dedicated men and women speak of wanting to assist in the reconstruction of their country, to find ways to help Laos achieve economic viability in today's world and to preserve its unique culture. There are signs that the economy is growing stronger and that investment money is slowly being accepted by the present Lao government, yet there is a long way to go. As we watch for signs of new hope and talk with both Americans and Lao who speak wistfully of the good days we all knew in this small country, we offer the wish that so often was given to us, "Go well. Take care of yourselves. *Seun pai dee.*"

28
Reprise

I returned to Laos in May 1992, seventeen years to the month of my involuntary departure in 1975. Thai Airways was the carrier, and WaHay airport looked exactly as I remembered. A small, two-story structure whose sky-blue–painted exterior was spotted with age and neglect. There was only one small plane on the tarmac which was bordered, as before, by fields in which two lone water buffalo were staked and a single farmer hoisted a bundle of grass to his back and headed for a decrepit brown shack in the midst of parched rice fields. This was the hot season in Laos when the mighty Mekong River shrivels to a stream and dust storms rise on the rare occasions when there is a breeze.

Inside the building we form two straggling lines in front of a simple counter where an official carefully examines our documents and stamps an inordinate number of forms before returning our passports and motioning for us to continue into the main reception area. We bargain for a battered taxi and drive down the exit portion of the very long horseshoe-shaped entry road that looks just as it did seventeen years ago when I was driven up the opposite side to the departure area.

The road into town hasn't changed either—two-car width, bumpy, bordered with brown, dingy stores which offer, in this part of Vientiane, spare auto parts or occasional help with auto repair. It is a relief to recognize Wat Thai—the source of the Wattay airport name, and then to move around bicycles and Hondas and a few other vehicles.

Ah! There is something different. Where are the battered French Renaults that were so prolific still in the seventies? And how long have there been "tuk-tuks" in Laos? These three-wheeled motorcycle vehicles over which small passenger bodies sporting side benches have been fashioned are common in Thailand but not in Laos. Here six to eight slender Lao can crawl in through the back and sit knee to knee, clutching their market purchases in their laps. (In Thailand fewer people ride facing forward, the driver still in front of the body of the vehicle.) So, there are some changes after all (but only within the last eighteen months I am later told, when it began to be possible to import this new form of transportation which costs two thousand dollars and must, I surmise, be loaned out to drivers on some sort of franchise basis).

The taxi deposits my traveling companion and me at the Hotel Ekalath, recommended by a friend as "possible" and not as fancy or expensive as the Lan Xang Hotel, recently renovated to lure the hoped-for tourist trade. This hostelry certainly has seen better times. The tiled floor is cracked and has many missing squares, and the shower is rigged up in a claw-foot bathtub with hot water promised through a small wall gas heater. And there is a noisy but effective airconditioner, that's a new addition! We gratefully open the bottle of mineral water provided, abandon any thought of hanging up clothes when we find there are no hangers—and no long closets—and venture out to Rue Samsenthai, the main street.

The photo shop on the corner is where I had taken film to be developed in the seventies, but further down the way the shop formerly owned by a very shrewd Vietnamese woman who sold gold jewelry and gems of all kinds has been replaced by a state-sponsored health center, open to all and providing the people with on-the-spot health care and medications. Surely this is a product of the revolution, that event which, in December of 1975, turned the kingdom of Laos into the LPDR, the Lao People's Democratic Republic. There are now health centers such as this all over the country being aided by NGO's, non-governmental organizations, from France, Australia, Belgium and Japan. They offer medical supplies and training for doctors, nurses and medics through a cooperative effort with the Ministry of Health.

It is end-of-the-school-day time, and youngsters appear from all directions, each in the white shirt or blouse and navy blue skirt or shorts worn by every school child. Seated fore and aft of older siblings or a parent, they ride by us, two, three and four spooned together on motorcycles and bicycles.

Universal education is now Lao policy, another achievement of the LPDR, although we learn it is still the case that a student who has managed to complete ten grades of school is considered sufficiently qualified to begin to teach. Educational standards, therefore, are unfortunately low, and the schools that the French and Australian embassies run for their own children are not available to the Lao.

As the afternoon wanes we become aware that there are now street lights and that individual stores also have electricity, not the case when I was originally in Laos. I am told that the government is diverting electricity from the Nam Ngum Dam not only to Vientiane, but also to other cities including Luang Prabang. This is a major switch in policy for a facility built in Laos by the Japanese to provide electricity for Thailand.

Schools, health centers and electricity. I am impressed with the achievements of the maligned Vietnamese-directed Communist government over these past seventeen years. It is more than was left by the French or the Americans for all of the money poured into the country.

In fact, Vientiane has all the familiarity of my former days, and I realize that, given several years of drastic famine shortly after the revolution and reports of major neglect and hardship in the eighties, this country is on its way up. I see the change with my own eyes in the Fa Ngum schools which I had heard were never abandoned, but were in terribly bad repair, grungy and ill kept. We found the buildings spanking clean, in good repair, and four hundred uniformed students diligently plugging away at technical subjects in what is now a technical university in Laos. The Fa Ngum schools in other areas of Laos are, we are told, still secondary schools, but this one is using the expertise of Lao who have been trained in Russia, Hungary, Czechoslovakia and other eastern European countries. I am heartened by the appearance of the school and the direction of its training.

One major improvement in Vientiane is also a major disappointment. During this time *talat saow*, the morning market, burned. It had previously been a somewhat sprawling wooden structure that housed the meat and fish markets, surrounded by hundreds of small stalls which sold everything needed in the kingdom, from fresh produce to bedding and textiles to rubber slippers. A new *talat saow* is a show-piece reconstruction. The three buildings, two-storied, spanking clean and painted, styled in Thai pagoda lines and set in a huge open parking space, house hundreds of shops. But they are no fun to walk through. They are too orderly, too spacious, too commercial. I miss the rubbing of elbows, the vendor plucking a sleeve to offer a ceramic piece or a woven silk piece he assures me is "*ngam lai*," very beautiful. No one sidles up to offer an artifact reported to be smuggled in from the north which we both knew was probably manufactured in a nearby village. The market is sterile, and the food stalls, once such a challenge and a delight, are not even in these buildings. Instead we are assailed with an acre of t-shirts, gaudy manufactured clothing, shoes, and cosmetics with pirated Western labels. It's just not the same.

There is one major addition to the market. At least thirty stalls offer native weavings of all kinds—Hmong, Lao, Yao and Lisu handiwork—all

1992 version of *talat saow*, the Vientiane morning market.

are available and on display. In fact there are so many identical shops I begin to feel visually stuffed with more options than I can digest. There is so much I don't buy anything. And this plethora of shops also explains why the Hmong tribeswomen no longer squat on the sidewalk on Rue Samsenthai to embroider and sell their wares.

Ruefully I reflect that I am experiencing progress, and I find it depressingly uniform and unchallenging. This change appears not to be for the best, or maybe it is, and maybe the Hmong have more outlets for their handiwork than they previously had. Somehow it is all too up-front. Everything there is to see is spread out in endless array, and the thrill of discovery is missing.

It is the ride out the Thadeua Road that demonstrates the direction of the future of Laos. At Thadeua the old restaurant cum waiting area is a little more run-down, the tables a bit more scarred, the floor sagging more than I remember. This traditionally is the spot where ferries, large and small, move passengers and vehicles back and forth between Nongkhai, Thailand, and Laos, but here now the Australian government is building a bridge. This multi-billion-dollar engineering feat will feature a two-level span, and one day the railroad will cross into Laos. It will spell the end of much that contributes to the charm and the isolation of this small country.

In anticipation of this momentous linkage, property along the road we are driving on is skyrocketing. Forty thousand dollars for a house lot. Three hundred thousand dollars for an acre of land. Non-Lao citizens may not own property, but they can rent, and there are, as always, ways to get around the rules. The massive brick house-in-progress we pass is being built by a Chinese merchant—reaffirmation of the reports that with the exodus of the Russians, Chinese from Yunan and other southern Chinese provinces are moving in.

There will be clothing factories, wood-working shops, furniture-building industries and other export businesses developed in this area near the bridge which will, for the first time in history, provide easy transportation for bulk shipments to world markets. I wonder if low wages, exploitation of imported labor and the continued rape of the teak forests will shortly become major problems in Laos. And pollution—will there be a concern to preserve the present dusty, but nonchemically laden air? Which brings us to the present political situation. A kind of "*glasnost*" has come to Laos, too. In Vietnam it is called "*doi moi,*" and although my Lao contacts didn't label the change, it was very clear from a number of sources that sometime in 1989 the government began to relax some of its stringent procedures. For instance, between 1987 and 1991 seven new NGO's began work in Laos, supplementing the eight agencies that were firmly established, having been accepted mostly in the seventies and early eighties. All of these agencies work in partnership with various governmental departments and programs on health issues; maternal and child care; the training of health educators, teachers and agricultural specialists; irrigation and providing clean water. Five agencies of the UN are pouring hundreds of thousands of dollars into programs, although much of this money pays the greatly inflated salaries and living expenses of the UN staff. A Quaker friend recounted the experience of a group of local foreign women who are developing early childhood education programs and who requested ten thousand dollars from the UNDP for audio-visual equipment they could use in the 80 percent of Laos which is rural. "We don't consider requests for less than $500,000," was the reported reply.

Indigenous, trained personnel is the biggest problem for the present government. With the departure of the Russians and the loss of massive amounts of Russian aid, the LPDR is looking to France, Australia, the United States, Thailand and Japan for development and investment money. Young people ages twenty to forty who remained in Laos after the revolution were sent to Eastern Europe to be indoctrinated into Marxist-Leninist political theory and the Russian language. These Lao engineers, accountants, medical personnel and teachers now back home in Laos speak only Russian and Lao. They are not being hired by projects needing English-, French-, Japanese- and Thai-speaking personnel. I suspect that they are both frightened and frustrated. They are politically cut adrift and linguistically unwanted. Their skills are marketable *if* they can acquire the languages needed, but only in small, specialized projects are French and English being taught. At present there are no courses available to Lao children that will teach them the languages of development and commerce. A new kind of re-education is desperately needed, and soon, if this potential source of trained people is to be incorporated into the new Laos. But it must be started quickly and with considerable sophistication—a kind of deprogramming effort to rehabilitate a now politically incorrect generation.

"Please stay and teach English. You will easily be able to support yourself, and we need you." I am enjoying a bottle of Lao beer at one of the favorite haunts we all used to frequent at the end of the day where, in an open-air pavilion overlooking the Mekong River one could watch the crimson and orange interplay of the setting sun and unwind after a hot, busy day. The invitation comes from two young men who fled Laos in 1975, one to France, the other to Australia. They have both returned to stay, eager to help reconstitute their country through developing small entrepreneurial efforts that will enhance the economy and employ Lao people. They are two of twelve such returnees. As I listen to them it strikes me that a hundred such Western-trained young people with managerial know-how, fluency in English and French, and a love for their country can turn Laos around and help it into the twentieth century. When I share this observation with my Lao expatriate friends in America I doubt that they will receive it with much enthusiasm, certainly not those who spent years incarcerated in caves and prison camps in the north. Yet I am convinced that they, and perhaps only they, have the potential to rescue their country from another invasion by France, Japan, and the United States, this round in the name of development, which is too often spelled exploitation.

I listen to the sincere, half-hopeful invitation to stay, issued by these young men, and I am tempted to say I will find a way to help. It is hard to dismiss this naked admission of the need in this small country where one thing—the innate grace of the people—has not changed.

In my admittedly short visit I found among the Lao people what endeared me to them years ago and in fact is validated by everyone I know who has ever lived in Laos: the people continue to be peace-loving, nonconfrontational, generous and friendly. They have a capacity to adapt and to avoid becoming bitter or disillusioned or discouraged. Their buoyant sense of humor and sense of self-worth are as strong as I remember. I hope they can—I hope they will—preserve the freshness of spirit which makes this often overlooked small country a treasure-spot of human dignity and grace.

GLOSSARY

achan	professor, teacher
baci	ceremony of celebration, e.g., weddings, births, farewells, etc.
baht	Thai unit of currency
baw pen nyang	never mind, don't worry
bonze	Buddhist monk
caow	rice (also *khao*)
caow niaow	sticky rice
chao khoueng	administrator of a province
chow	you
hanai	Hawaiian term meaning to give a child to another person or couple to raise as their own child
khaophoun	thin rice noodle
khene	Lao musical instrument, a hand-held pipe organ (also *kaen*)
kip	Lao unit of currency
lai	many or much; lai lai, very much, a whole lot
lamvong	Lao couple dance, performed in a circle
Lao Loum	ethnic lowland Lao
lap	food mixture of chopped meat, herbs, rice noodles and bean sprouts
lycée	French public secondary school
nai ban	administrator of a village
ngam	beautiful, lovely
paa	fish
phi	spirit
phi-pop	evil spirit, possessed person
pi nong	cousin, relative
puok en mai	so long, see you again, until next time
saap	delicious

saap lai	especially good, most delicious
sabaidee	hello
seun	please
seun pai dee	goodbye, please go well
sinh	Lao woman's skirt
sin heng	dried strips of meat
talat	market
talat leng	evening market
talat saow	morning market
tip caow	basket in which sticky rice is served or carried
tuk lai	too expensive
wai	clasped hands (as in prayer) greeting of the Lao
wat	Buddhist temple or pagoda

BIBLIOGRAPHY

Adams, Nina S., and Alfred W. McCoy, eds. *Laos: War and Revolution.* New York: Harper and Row, 1970.

Branfman, Fred. *Voices from the Plain of Jars.* New York: Harper Colophon, 1972.

Dommen, Arthur J. *Conflict in Laos: The Politics of Neutralization.* New York: Frederick A. Praeger, Inc., 1969.

_________. *Laos: Keystone of Indochina.* Boulder, Colorado: Westview Press, 1968.

Dooley, Thomas A. *The Edge of Tomorrow.* New York: Farrar, Straus & Company, 1958.

_________. *The Night They Burned the Mountain.* New York: Farrar, Straus & Company, 1960.

Fall, Bernard B. *Anatomy of a Crisis: The Laotian Crisis of 1960–1961.* Garden City, N.Y.: Doubleday, 1969.

Lederer, William J., and Eugene Burdick. *The Ugly American.* New York: Norton, 1965.

LeBar, Frank M., and Adrienne Suddard, eds. *Laos, Its People, Its Society, Its Culture.* (Survey of World Cultures No. 8.) New Haven: Human Relations Area Files Press, 1960.

Ratnam, Perala. *Laos and the Superpowers.* New Delhi: Tulsi Publishing House, 1980.

Robbins, Christopher. *The Ravens: The Men Who Flew in America's Secret War in Laos.* New York: Crown Publishers, 1987.

Stieglitz, Perry. *In a Little Kingdom.* Amonk, N.Y.: M.E. Sharpe, Inc., 1990.

Stuart-Fox, Martin. *Laos: Politics, Economics and Society.* London: Francis Pinter, 1986, Boulder, CO: Lynne Rienner, 1986.

_________, ed. *Contemporary Laos: Studies in the Politics and Society of the Lao People's Democratic Republic.* New York: St. Martin's Press, 1982.

Thee, Marek. *Notes of a Witness.* New York: Random House, 1973.

Whitaker, Donald P., et al. *Laos, A Country Study.* Washington D.C. Foreign Area Studies; The American University 1971 (1985 fourth printing).

INDEX

AMERICA HAS A BETTER TEAM

To the Dietz family,
with my best wishes,

"I'm thrilled to see our story captured so well."

—LOU SPADIA,
Former president of the San Francisco 49ers

PUBLISHED IN SAN FRANCISCO

AMERICA HAS A BETTER TEAM

THE STORY OF BILL WALSH AND SAN FRANCISCO'S WORLD CHAMPION 49 ERS

GLENN DICKEY

INTRODUCTION BY
HERB CAEN

A TRIBUTE BY
MAYOR DIANNE FEINSTEIN

To Nancy and Scott, who have to put up with the absent-mindedness and grouchiness of a writer at work.

For information contact Harbor Publishing, 1668 Lombard Street, San Francisco 94123.

Printed in the United States of America.

Cover & Design: Design Office
Manufacturing Coordination: Peter G. Levison
Production: BookPack, Inc.
Production Director: Ray Riegert
Editor: Sayre Van Young
Typesetting: Kay Murray-Nears, Allen Hayward, Diane Valay
Paste-up: Beee Langley, Phil Gardner
Proofreading: Leslie Henriques, Kris Johnson
Consultants: Bruce LoPucki, Sam Lawson
Text Printer/Binder: Publisher's Press
Mountain States Bindery

Paperback/ISBN 0-936602-47
Cloth/ISBN 0-936602-48-1
Limited Cloth/ISBN 0/936602-49

ACKNOWLEDGEMENTS

My thanks go to Bill Alexander and Jack Jennings of Harbor Publishing, who realized seconds after Dwight Clark caught Joe Montana's pass against Dallas that there had to be a book on the 49ers.

Although much of this book is based on my own recollections and conversations with players and coaches, I also relied on written accounts to fill in information gaps. In that regard, I found Ira Miller's stories in the *San Francisco Chronicle* of special value.

Finally, my gratitude goes to Lou Spadia, who not only supplied me with information but has also personified the special spirit of the 49ers for so many years.

1981 NFL STANDINGS

AMERICAN FOOTBALL CONFERENCE

Eastern Division

	W	L	T	PCT.	PTS.	OP
*Miami	11	4	1	.719	345	275
#NY Jets	10	5	1	.656	355	287
#Buffalo	10	6	0	.625	311	276
Baltimore	2	14	0	.125	259	533
New England	2	14	0	.125	322	370

Central Division

	W	L	T	PCT.	PTS.	OP
*Cincinnati ...	12	4	0	.750	421	304
Pittsburgh ...	8	8	0	.500	356	297
Houston	7	9	0	.438	281	355
Cleveland	5	11	0	.313	276	375

Western Division

	W	L	T	PCT.	PTS.	OP
*San Diego ...	10	6	0	.625	478	390
Denver	10	6	0	.625	321	289
Kansas City ..	9	7	0	.563	343	290
Oakland	7	9	0	.438	273	343
Seattle	6	10	0	.375	322	388

NATIONAL FOOTBALL CONFERENCE

Eastern Division

	W	L	T	PCT.	PTS.	OP
*Dallas	12	4	0	.750	367	277
#Philadelphia .	10	6	0	.625	368	221
#NY Giants ...	9	7	0	.563	295	257
Washington ..	8	8	0	.500	347	349
St. Louis	7	9	0	.438	315	408

Central Division

	W	L	T	PCT.	PTS.	OP
*Tampa Bay ..	9	7	0	.563	315	268
Detroit	8	8	0	.500	397	322
Green Bay ...	8	8	0	.500	324	361
Minnesota ...	7	9	0	.438	325	369
Chicago....	6	10	0	.375	253	324

Western Division

	W	L	T	PCT.	PTS.	OP
*San Francisco	13	3	0	.813	357	250
Atlanta	7	9	0	.438	426	355
Los Angeles .	6	10	0	.375	303	351
New Orleans	4	12	0	.250	207	378

*Division Champion
#Wild Card for Playoffs
NOTE: San Diego won AFC Western title over Denver on the basis of a better division record (6-2 to 5-3).

AFC First Round Playoff
Buffalo 31, New York Jets 27

AFC Divisional Playoff
Cincinnati 28, Buffalo 21
San Diego 41, Miami 38

AFC Championship
Cincinnati 27, San Diego 7

NFC First Round Playoff
New York Giants 27, Philadelphia 21

NFC Divisional Playoff
San Francisco 38, New York Giants 24
Dallas 38, Tampa Bay 0

NFC Championship
San Francisco 28, Dallas 27

Super Bowl
San Francisco 26, Cincinnati 21

CONTENTS

NUMERICAL ROSTER

No.	Name	Pos.	Ht.	Wt.	Age	NFL Exp.	College
3	Jim Miller	P	5-11	183	24	2	Mississippi
7	Guy Benjamin	QB	6-3	210	26	4	Stanford
14	Ray Wersching	K	5-11	210	31	9	California
16	Joe Montana	QB	6-2	200	25	3	Notre Dame
20	Amos Lawrence	RB	5-10	179	23	R	North Carolina
21	Eric Wright	CB	6-1	180	22	R	Missouri
22	Dwight Hicks	S	6-1	189	25	3	Michigan
24	Rick Gervais	S	5-11	190	22	R	Stanford
27	Carlton Williamson	S	6-0	204	23	R	Pittsburgh
28	Lynn Thomas	CB	5-11	181	22	R	Pittsburgh
29	Saladin Martin	CB	6-1	180	25	2	San Diego State
30	Bill Ring	RB	5-10	215	25	1	Brigham Young
31	Walt Easley	FB	6-1	226	24	R	West Virginia
32	Ricky Patton	RB	5-11	192	27	4	Jackson State
35	Lenvil Elliott	RB	6-0	210	30	9	N.E. Missouri
38	Johnny Davis	RB	6-1	235	25	4	Alabama
42	Ronnie Lott	CB	6-0	199	22	R	USC
49	Earl Cooper	FB	6-2	227	24	2	Rice
51	Randy Cross	G	6-3	250	27	6	UCLA
52	Bobby Leopold	LB	6-1	215	24	2	Notre Dame
53	Milt McColl	LB	6-6	220	22	R	Stanford
54	Craig Puki	LB	6-1	231	24	2	Tennessee
56	Fred Quillan	C	6-5	260	25	4	Oregon
57	Dan Bunz	LB	6-4	225	26	4	Cal State-Long Beach
58	Keena Turner	LB	6-2	219	23	2	Purdue
59	Willie Harper	LB	6-2	215	31	8	Nebraska
60	John Choma	G-C	6-6	261	26	1	Virginia
61	Dan Audick	T	6-3	253	27	4	Hawaii
62	Walt Downing	C-G	6-3	254	25	4	Michigan
64	Jack Reynolds	LB	6-1	232	34	12	Tennessee
65	Lawrence Pillers	DE	6-4	260	29	6	Alcorn A & M
66	Allan Kennedy	T	6-7	275	23	R	Washington State
68	John Ayers	G	6-5	260	28	5	West Texas State
71	Keith Fahnhorst	T	6-6	263	29	8	Minnesota
74	Fred Dean	DE	6-2	230	29	7	Louisiana Tech
75	John Harty	DT	6-4	253	24	R	Iowa
76	Dwaine Board	DE	6-5	250	25	3	North Carolina A & T
78	Archie Reese	DT	6-3	262	25	4	Clemson
79	Jim Stuckey	DE	6-4	251	23	2	Clemson
80	Eason Ramson	TE	6-2	234	25	3	Washington State
84	Mike Shumann	WR	6-0	175	26	4	Florida State
85	Mike Wilson	WR	6-3	210	23	R	Washington State
86	Charle Young	TE	6-4	234	30	9	USC
87	Dwight Clark	WR	6-4	210	24	3	Clemson
88	Freddie Solomon	WR	5-11	185	28	7	Tampa

Injured Reserve: Ken Bungarda, Ricky Churchman, Phil Francis, Eric Herring, Paul Hofer, Pete Kugler, Ed Judie, Gus Parham, George Visger.

1981 RESULTS & ATTENDANCE

PRESEASON (2-2-0)						
(W)	49ers	27	at Seattle	24	(OT)	56,958
(L)	49ers	28	San Diego	31		41,667
(W)	49ers	24	Seattle	17		37,563
(L)	49ers	7	at Oakland	21		51,192
TOTAL ATTENDANCE						187,380
REGULAR SEASON (13-3-0)						
(L)	49ers	17	at Detroit	24		62,123
(W)	49ers	28	Chicago	17		49,520
(L)	49ers	17	at Atlanta	34		56,653
(W)	49ers	21	New Orleans	14		44.433
(W)	49ers	30	at Washington	17		51,843
(W)	49ers	45	Dallas	14		57,574
(W)	49ers	13	at Green Bay (Milw)	3		50,171
(W)	49ers	20	Los Angeles	17		59,190
(W)	49ers	17	at Pittsburgh	14		52,878
(W)	49ers	17	Atlanta	14		59,127
(L)	49ers	12	Cleveland	15		52,445
(W)	49ers	33	at Los Angeles	31		63,456
(W)	49ers	17	New York Giants	10		57,186
(W)	49ers	21	at Cincinnati	3		56,796
(W)	49ers	28	Houston	6		55,707
(W)	49ers	21	at New Orleans	17		43,639
TOTAL ATTENDANCE						872,741
POST SEASON (3-0-0)						
(W)	49ers	38	New York Giants	24		58,360
(W)	49ers	28	Dallas	27		60,525
(W)	49ers	26	Cincinnati	21		

A TRIBUTE

BY MAYOR DIANNE FEINSTEIN

On January 25, 1982, San Francisco outdid herself in sheer jubilation. At least a half million persons jammed downtown to cheer the triumphant 49ers on their return from Super Bowl XVI. San Francisco had seen nothing like it in terms of massive numbers of joyous celebrants since V.J. Day at the end of World War II. Some say the crowd totaled a million shouting and waving 49er fans. The city's 49er fever climbed with mounting anticipation as the team won game after game in its most spectacular season. It reached a high point in the play-offs with a mighty and unforgettable leap by Dwight Clark to gather in the winning touchdown over Dallas. And, of course, it soared to its apex in the great victory in the Super Bowl.

The 49ers, defying all odds, and in a tradition typical of San Francisco herself, rebuilt from the ashes of past defeats. They did so with determination, extraordinary effort and a calm sense of confidence. Their indomitable spirit gives pride to us all.

On behalf of San Francisco, I thank the 49ers for giving this city a splendid sense of hope and accomplishment. America has a great team ... and it is ours.

INTRODUCTION

BY HERB CAEN

"The World Champion San Francisco 49ers!"

It does have a certain lilt, that phrase. Thousands of us never thought we'd live long enough to hear it. Even now, when the fact that we are paramount in the world of professional football has sunk in, we find it difficult to believe. There is a fictional quality about the whole thing, a football version of "Damn Yankees," with a guy named Joe coming from out of nowhere to lead a young band of comparative unknowns to glory in the snowy January fields of Michigan.

A trip to the moon on gossamer wings? No, better. A trip to Pontiac, Michigan, to the Super Bowl in the Silverdome, there to defeat the Cincinnati Bengals on a day that will join some of the other legendary dates in the long history of Baghdad-by-the-Bay — January 24, April 18, November 11, August 15.

Reading backward from the final date, those great days would be the end of World War II in 1945, Armistice Day in 1917, the Great Fire and Earthquake of 1906, and the discovery of gold in 1848.

By wonderful coincidence, the 49ers discovered gold in the Silverdome on the very same date 134 years later — January 24, 1982. A powerful omen, and there were others. Quarterback Joe Montana's number is 16, the Super Bowl victory was the sixteenth of the season for the 49ers, and the game itself was Super Bowl XVI.

Not only that, it had been exactly 49 days since the 49ers

had met the Bengals for the first time, during the regular season, and had trounced them.

The team is young, it is solid, it will be together for years to come. Therefore, it may not be too wildly optimistic to predict that a dynasty was born that wintry afternoon in the unlikely setting of a depressed auto-geared city 30 miles from Detroit. Last year, it was the Oakland Raiders who won it all, a dynasty that had run its course and now faces the slow, agonizing task of rebuilding. For Bay Area football fans, it has been a remarkable two years, with the promise of more golden years to come. Make that scarlet and gold, the 49er colors.

"O ye of little faith!" I will confess that I was one of those who had almost given up on the Niners. Unlike the 49er faithful, who have stayed gallantly with the team through thick and thin, I only stuck through the thick — the exciting first years of the team, when we called ourselves the student body of "49er U.," wouldn't dream of missing a Sunday at old Kezar Stadium, and looked upon surrounding Golden Gate Park as our campus.

We were young, the team was young, and quarterback Frankie Albert, the demon bootlegger and quick-kicker, the most exciting player we had ever seen. In fact, his refreshing ad lib style would be exciting today, but let us not get off the subject. The years of Albert, Norm Standlee, Johnny "Strike" Strzykalski, Leo Nomellini, Bob St. Clair, Billy Wilson, Gordy Saltau, Y. A. Tittle, Hugh McElhenney, Joe "The Jet" Perry are enshrined in the hearts of us oldsters as among the best years of our lives.

Kezar itself was a dump, a madhouse populated almost entirely by maniacs, and yet, like so many things about San Francisco, it had a certain tacky charm. The seats were benches. The knees of the people behind you were constantly in your back, as yours were in someone else's. The "facilities" were laughably primitive. The stadium even ran the wrong way — East and West, rather than North and South — because the legendary Superintendent of the Park, "Uncle John" McLaren, who didn't want it there in the first place, insisted it be built in a manner that "would not disturb my beloved petunia beds."

Late in the fourth quarter, in came the fog and in came the sea gulls. If the day were clear, the sun would start setting just above the West rim of the stadium, driving the visiting quarterbacks and ends crazy. It was warm, corny, cozy, impossible and unforgettable — big league football in bush league surroundings, centered on a team of home-towners run by a home-town family, the Morabitos. We indentified like mad with those Niners.

When the team moved to Candlestick, some of us Original Faithful fell off the bandwagon, even though we admired the quarterbacking of John Brodie, the grace of Gene Washington, and, a bit later, the dramatic running of Paul Hofer. The seasons came and went, coaches came and went, new owners came, and a lot of us still went. "What have you done for the 49ers lately?" one asked me. "What have the 49ers done for me?" I replied after suffering through a couple of 2-14 seasons.

For a spell, the Niners became a joke. "They're called the 49ers because they never get beyond the 49-yard line. The original 49ers found gold, these guys can't even find the goal." We tried to be blasé about the whole thing. San Francisco is, after all, among the most sophisticated of cities. Unlike towns like Oakland, we said, we don't NEED winning football or baseball teams. We have the opera —in fact, we had the very best, Enrico Caruso, in 1906, when Cincinnati, the first major league baseball city, was a cow town.

We have culture, a major symphony and ballet, fine museums, incredible scenery, marvelous climate, the greatest pair of bridges, world-class restaurants and hotels — who cares if the Giants haven't been in the World Series since 1962, and that the 49ers haven't won a title in 36 years?

I remember writing something painfully lofty about "cities that have so little else going for them that they have to identify with their athletic teams. San Francisco doesn't need that. Our priorities are in line."

How wrong I was, and I suppose I knew it deep down inside all the time. The 49ers Super Bowl victory touched off the wildest, craziest demonstration since V-E Day, and the glow lives on. Some urban critics have called San Francisco "a city of losers," because of our high suicide rate and heavy drinking, and while these are still problems, that title now rings false. We still have major problems, to be sure, that a winning football team will never help to solve, but civic morale has been given a boost that makes San Franciscans feel a little prouder, a bit closer to one another.

The long era of "Wait till next year" is over.

The jokes have ended.

"The World Champion San Francisco 49ers!" are here to stay for a long time, and a new chapter in the ongoing story of Baghdad-by-the-Bay now begins.

HOW THE 1981 49ERS WERE BUILT

YEAR	NUMBER ACQUIRED	DRAFTED(21)	FREE AGENTS(17)	TRADES(7)
1973	(1)	Willie Harper (2)		
1974	(1)	Keith Fahnhorst (2A)		
1976	(2)	Randy Cross (2A) John Ayers (8)		
1977	(1)		Ray Wersching (FA '73 Chargers)	
1978	(5)	Dan Bunz (1B) Walt Downing (2) Archie Reese (5A) Fred Quillan (7)		1. Freddie Solomon (D2A '75 Dolphins)
1979	(6)	Joe Montana (3) Dwight Clark (10A)	Dwaine Board (D5 '79 Steelers) Lenvil Elliott (D10 '73 Bengals) Dwight Hicks (D6A '78 Lions) Eason Ramson (D12 '78 Packers)	
1980	(9)	Earl Cooper (1A) Jim Stuckey (1B) Keena Turner (2) Jim Miller (3A) Craig Puki (3B) Bobby Leopold (8)	Ricky Patton (D10 '78 Falcons) Lawrence Pillers (D11 '76 Jets)	2. Charle Young (D1 '73 Eagles)
1981	(20)	Ronnie Lott (1) John Harty (2A) Eric Wright (2B) Carlton Williamson (3) Lynn Thomas (5A)	John Choma (D5 '78 Chargers) Walt Easley Allan Kennedy (D10B '81 Redskins) Saladin Martin (FA '79 Giants) Milt McColl Rick Gervais Jack Reynolds (D1B '70 Rams) Bill Ring (FA '80 Steelers) Mike Shumann (FA '78 Dolphins) Mike Wilson (D9 '81 Cowboys)	3. Guy Benjamin (D2 '78 Dolphins) 4. Dan Audick (D4 '77 Steelers) 5. Johnny Davis (D2 '78 Buckaneers) 6. Amos Lawrence (D4A '81 Chargers) 7. Fred Dean (D2 '75 Chargers)

TRADES

1. Prior to '78 from Miami with Vern Roberson and two draft choices for Delvin Williams.
2. Prior to '80 for a 5th round draft choice in '83 from Los Angeles.
3. Prior to '81 from New Orleans for future undisclosed draft choice.
4. Prior to '81 for a 3rd round draft choice in '82 from San Diego.
5. Prior to '81 from Tampa Bay for James Owens.
6. Prior to second game of '81 for a 4th round draft choice in '84 from San Diego.
7. Prior to 5th game in '81 from San Diego for 2nd pick & option to exchange No. 1 picks in '83

1

A FRANCHISE IS BORN

As the San Francisco 49ers swept to their first Super Bowl ever, setting team records as they went, the entire Bay Area went 49er crazy. Songs were written about the team; bars sold exotic drinks for 49 cents; advertising campaigns for all kinds of products—T-shirts, cars, cameras, TVs—were linked with the 49ers. Posters, signs, and graffiti featuring team members suddenly appeared everywhere.

None of this was surprising, because the 49ers are an important part of the social and cultural environment of San Francisco. The 49ers *are* San Francisco, and vice versa.

For one thing, the team has never played anywhere else. The Chicago Bears started in Decatur, Illinois; the Green Bay Packers often play in Milwaukee; the New York Giants have played in Connecticut and New Jersey; the Los Angeles Rams started out in Cleveland and ended up in Anaheim.

But the 49ers have always played in San Francisco, first at Kezar and now at Candlestick Park, both stadiums unfortunate reminders of the city's inability to do anything quite right, a weakness of which residents are perversely proud.

The 49er name obviously recalls the well-known historic past of San Francisco. The team's initial logo—a drunken gold miner shooting off two pistols, one seemingly aimed at his head—is also a reminder of San Francisco's reputation as a town of serious drinkers.

"In the original picture," says Lou Spadia, who rose to

club president in the sixties, "there was a saloon in the background." The 49ers removed the saloon, but the image wasn't changed.

Until the 1981 season, the 49ers reflected San Francisco in yet another way: the club was usually entertaining but never entirely successful. In fact, all of the teams in the National Football League when the 49ers joined in 1950 won conference titles before the Niners finally did. Nine teams formed since 1950—Baltimore, Dallas, Denver, Kansas City, Miami, Minnesota, the New York Jets, Oakland, and San Diego—had won conference titles, while the 49ers struggled on.

In the late sixties, Spadia and Dick Berg, then the club's promotion director, coined the term "49er Faithful" to describe the fans who had stayed with the team through thick and mostly thin. The term had more and more of an ironic connotation as the frustrations continued on for the next decade.

The idea for a professional football team from San Francisco probably grew from a discussion in 1943 between businessman Tony Morabito and Bill Leiser, sports editor of the *San Francisco Chronicle.* Leiser told Morabito of Arch Ward's plan for a new football league to start after World War II. (Ward, the sports editor of the *Chicago Tribune*, originated both the baseball All-Star game and the NFL champions/College All-Stars game.)

Morabito, a self-made success who rose from an $80-a-month truck driver to become the owner of a successful lumberyard before he was 30, thought he saw the possibility of another financial bonanza with a local pro team. He reasoned that many of the servicemen passing through San Francisco, chief port of embarkation for the war in the Pacific, would later return as tourists or permanent residents, and would become enthusiastic football fans of a Bay Area team.

Leiser warned Morabito to be ready to lose a lot of money, at least at the start. Morabito, insisting he was prepared, soon proved his point. Though he originally made his partners in the lumberyard partners in the 49ers, when the 49ers opened in a bath of red ink, Morabito borrowed $100,000 to buy them out. For the next three decades, the 49ers would belong to the Morabito family—and friends.

Tony Morabito was an extraordinary man, with an emotional range that swept from love to hate and didn't miss any stops in between. To those he cared about, he was capable of almost unbelievably generous acts. He allowed his first quarterback, Frank Albert, and a friend, Franklin Mieuli, to buy parts of the club for nominal figures, an act which made both men wealthy in a fairly short period of time.

His treatment of Lou Spadia, who joined the club shortly after the end of World War II, was another prime example of Morabito's generosity. Spadia was doing a fine job for the 49ers. As a matter of fact, he was doing several — selling tickets, handling office paper work, acting as equipment manager. Morabito appreciated Spadia's hard work, and in time, gave Lou a chance to buy five percent of the club at considerably less than true value. It took a lot of scraping and borrowing, but Spadia managed it, and he held that stock until the DeBartolo family bought the club in 1977.

But to those he disliked, Morabito's anger could be awesome. Many of those he disliked were newspapermen. Many of those he liked were also newspapermen. Sometimes they were the same men—at different times.

Morabito had an ongoing feud with the San Francisco press. Though some feuds—such as the one he had with *San Francisco Examiner* sports editor Curley Grieve—were longstanding, most depended on what a writer had written that day. He had a list of writers who displeased him, and a writer could make a spectacular leap, from say tenth on the list to the top, with a particularly critical story.

But even those newspapermen who feuded with Morabito had many good times with Tony, and everybody who knew him grieved when he died of a heart attack during a 1957 game with the Chicago Bears. The players learned of his death at the start of the second half; behind 17-7 at the time, they played the last two quarters with an emotional fervor, tears running down the faces of many players, and turned the game around, winning 24-17. Afterwards, Frank Albert, then the coach, said, "If he was going to live, I would have been happy to lose by a hundred points."

* * * *

The San Francisco 49ers started play in 1946 in the new All-America Conference with one of the finest offensive teams ever, featuring Albert at quarterback, Norm Standlee at fullback, Alyn Beals at wide receiver, and John Strzykalski at halfback.

Their record in the AAC was excellent, too: 9-5, 8-4-2, 12-2, and 9-3, for an overall mark of 38-14-2. But they had the misfortune of being in the same league as the Cleveland Browns, then the best team in football. The Browns won the AAC championship four years running with the 49ers finishing second every time. In 1950, the Browns and 49ers were admitted into the established league; the Browns went on to win the NFL title.

The 49ers' move into the NFL was not as successful as the Browns: San Francisco finished 3-9 in its first NFL season. For the next three decades, the 49ers would field teams that were often entertaining — usually because of such offensive stars as Hugh McElhenny, Joe Perry, Y. A. Tittle, and John Brodie — but which had only occasional periods of success. And even the successful periods always ended in frustration.

There was, for instance, the 1957 season, for which the term "cliffhanger" could have been invented. Fooling around in practice, quarterback Tittle and wide receiver R. C. Owens developed the "Alley Oop" pass: Tittle would lob a high pass and Owens would use his great leaping ability (he had played basketball in college) to take the ball away from a defender. Done right, it was impossible to defend against.

Using the "Alley Oop" often in critical periods, the 49ers tied the Detroit Lions for the Western Conference title with an 8-4 record. In the playoff game, the 49ers led at halftime, 24-7, then surged to 27-7 with a field goal early in the third quarter.

And then they collapsed. The Lions stormed back to win the game, 31-27, and it would be 13 long years before the 49ers came close again. When they did—in the 1970-72 period—each season brought similar near-miss frustration.

The 1970 season was the best ever for the 49ers since joining the NFL: 10-3-1. They clinched the Western Division title with a smashing 38-7 win over their cross-Bay rivals, the Oakland Raiders. John Brodie was named Player of the Year, Dick Nolan Coach of the Year, and cornerback Bruce Taylor Rookie of the Year. But in the NFC championship game, the 49ers lost to the Dallas Cowboys, 17-10.

In 1971 the 49ers took another divisional title, this time with a 9-5 record. But for the second year in a row, in the NFC title game against the Cowboys, they were overrun 14-3.

In 1972 the persistent 49ers won their third straight division title only to be eliminated by Dallas in the first round of the playoffs, 30-28, perhaps an even more bitter defeat than to the Lions in 1957.

With 1:53 left in the game, the 49ers led Dallas, 28-16. Dick Berg, sitting in the stands with 30,000 buttons proclaiming "Super Bowl Fever," eagerly wanted to start distributing them.

"Not yet," said club president Spadia. "I remember 1957."

Dallas quarterback Roger Staubach took over for Craig

Morton and quickly threw a touchdown pass that brought the Cowboys close at 28-23.

On the ensuing kickoff, the Cowboys recovered an onside kick fumbled by Preston Riley (who never played another game for the 49ers). Again, Staubach took the Cowboys in for a touchdown, and the Niners were suddenly beaten.

That defeat seemed to take the heart out of the 49ers; next season they slipped to the bottom of their division with a 5-9 record.

The following dismal years—with 6-8 and 5-9 records—cost Nolan his job, and Monte Clark took over for the 1976 season.

Clark brought the 49ers back to a measure of respectability with an 8-6 record in 1976, narrowly missing the playoffs. But that decent year only set the stage for yet another incredible saga in the 49er story.

* * * *

After the death of Vic Morabito, Tony's brother, in 1963, the 49ers had been primarily owned by the Morabito widows, Jane and Jo.

Since the mid-seventies, the Morabito women had been anxious to sell the team. At one point, the club was almost bought by Wayne Valley, a former general partner of the Oakland Raiders who'd sold his Oakland interest because of a feud with Al Davis. In fact, Valley was so close to buying the Niners that Spadia had consulted with him before hiring Clark as coach.

But the ownership agreement for the 49ers included a provision which allowed minority owners a chance to buy the club before it could be offered to an outsider. Part-owner Mieuli tried to put together a deal, but it fell through. And by the time it did, Valley had lost interest, mainly because the asking price had risen from $12 million to $15 million.

It rose even further until the DeBartolo Corporation, for anywhere from $18 million to $23 million (depending on the accounting system used), bought ninety percent of the club. Mieuli retained his five percent, and Jane Morabito another five percent. Edward J. DeBartolo, Jr., was named owner, at 31 the youngest in the National Football League.

It was the end of an era, the first time the club had been owned by non—Bay Area residents.

Bay Area fans soon learned about the DeBartolo Corporation, founded in 1948 by Edward J. DeBartolo, Sr., and based in Youngstown, Ohio. It's the world's leading planner, builder, owner, and operator of regional shopping malls; the corporation also owns thoroughbred race tracks, hotels, industrial and executive office parks, a foreign trade zone and overseas shipping operation, the Pittsburgh Penguins hockey team, and the Pittsburgh Civic Arena. Net worth? It's estimated at between $750 million and $1 billion.

With the DeBartolos came Joe Thomas, a lifelong friend of Ed DeBartolo, Sr., and the man who had put the deal together—with the provision that he be named general manager.

Monte Clark, who had been an assistant coach at Miami when Thomas had been with the Dolphins, knew he couldn't work with Thomas; though offered a tax-sheltered $100,000 salary, he resigned.

Things didn't get better. Indeed, if Joe Thomas had drawn up a plan for disaster, he couldn't have done a more complete job with the 49ers. He did everything wrong.

Convinced that the San Francisco team needed to be completely rebuilt, he virtually gave away such quality veteran players as defensive end Tommy Hart and defensive back Mel Phillips. And his drafts were simply not good; not *one* player remains in the league from his first draft in 1977.

Trying to buy time, he traded for O.J. Simpson, whose legs were gone. O.J. did virtually nothing for the 49ers, but he cost the team second- and third-round picks in 1978 and a first-round pick in 1979—which turned out to be the very first pick in the draft that year.

Under Thomas's dismal misdirection, the 49ers went first to 5-9 and then to a league-worst 2-14. His first coach, Ken Meyer, was fired after one year. The second, Pete McCulley, lasted only nine games into the second season; then Fred O'Connor had a turn. It made no difference who coached; Thomas had all the authority. He cut the squad and told coaches who to play.

As the losses mounted, Thomas raged at the players, fuming into the dressing room to lecture them after losses. He fought with a sportswriter in a bar on a road trip. He alienated fans. When one fan put up a banner at Candlestick reading, "Blame Joe Thomas," Thomas had the guy ejected from the stadium. A group of fans formed an organization called "Doubting Thomases," with the express aim of getting rid of Thomas. It was a very ugly period in the history of the 49ers.

In the midst of all this, Edward DeBartolo, Jr., announced that Thomas's contract would be extended four years. It was a mistake, as DeBartolo admitted later, but an understandable one.

"I was looking for stability," he explained. "Because of all the turmoil, all the press criticism, I thought it was important to make a statement. If I had it to do all over again, if I could go back and think about it, no, I wouldn't have done it. I don't think now that it was the right thing to do."

DeBartolo's serious doubts about Thomas had begun before he made the contract announcement. "I hadn't really been happy about what was happening in the organization for several months." But he wanted to wait to make a final evaluation, without the emotion of the season intruding on his decision.

But when DeBartolo didn't sign the contract extension (the focal point of a later legal dispute with Thomas), Thomas knew he was in danger. Shortly thereafter, Thomas charged into the 49er dressing room after a loss to St. Louis and told the players, "If I'm going down the tubes, I'm going to take you with me."

He didn't last long enough to make good on his threat. DeBartolo fired him, less because of what the team was doing on the field than what was happening behind the scenes.

"Nobody felt at ease and comfortable within the organization," said DeBartolo. "*I* didn't even feel comfortable. You can't make an organization work that way."

One positive result came from the otherwise unpleasant situation: DeBartolo learned what he had to do. "I'm not afraid to admit I've made mistakes," he said, "but I think I've learned a lot."

He proved that with his next move: he named Stanford coach Bill Walsh as his new coach (and, a little later, general manager). Though it would take a couple of years for success, that decision started the 49ers on their way to the Super Bowl.

2

WALSH ARRIVES TO GREET DISASTER

In one way, Bill Walsh's career resembles a show business personality more than a football coach: he's an "overnight success" after more than 20 years of hard work in relative anonymity.

Like Vince Lombardi, Walsh didn't get a head coaching job above the prep level until he was 45, a damning indictment of the judgment of those who hire coaches. He was twice passed over in the sixties for a job he coveted, head coach at San Jose State, his alma mater.

Walsh was ready to quit football in 1968 when he went back to graduate school. In his spare time he coached the San Jose Apaches, a semi-pro team, and did well enough to catch the attention of the Cincinnati organization: he was hired the next year as an offensive coach for the Bengals.

At Cincinnati he coached a young Ken Anderson, an unknown from a small Midwestern college who become a star quarterback under Walsh's tutelage. It was widely expected that Walsh would become head coach when Paul Brown retired, but Brown passed over him to select Bill Johnson.

Walsh then left Cincinnati and went to San Diego, where he coached quarterback Dan Fouts to stardom. That, finally, got him his chance, and he was selected to coach Stanford in 1977; at 45, he was the oldest coach in the conference.

Two years later, after leading Stanford to successive bowl seasons, he was named coach of the San Francisco 49ers.

His failure to get a head coaching job much earlier in his career made him bitter at the time. Now, he is more philosophical. "This isn't like civil service," Walsh says. "You don't pass an examination to move up. As often as not, getting the right job is a matter of luck and timing.

"The NFL is opening up a lot now, but for a time, it was a very tight little circle. Jobs got passed around to the same people—and I wasn't one of those people."

Spending so much time in obscurity would have discouraged most men, killing their ambition. Men with the drive of Lombardi and Walsh only become more determined.

"I decided eventually that the way to succeed was to establish a reputation in one area," says Walsh, "and I did that with the pass offense, becoming known as the leading authority—or, at least, one of the best—in that field."

Now, Walsh feels that he benefited from all those years as an assistant, especially at Cincinnati under Brown, who he says had the most influence on his career.

"Paul and I are different men," says Walsh, "but I learned an awful lot from him. He thought of everything, to the point of determining where jocks should be hung. He told us, for instance, to always take ten minutes after a game before we talked to the press, so we could collect our thoughts and not just talk without thinking.

"I was determined that I was going to work as hard as I could at my job and not get in the business of campaigning for a head job and then being disappointed when I didn't get it. I feel I've improved as a coach just about every year. Certainly, I was a better coach my second year at Stanford than my first, and I think I've learned some things on the job with the 49ers, too."

The Stanford job made Walsh's reputation. After the first year, he was offered a multiyear contract (at $100,000 a year), to coach the Chicago Bears. He turned it down because he didn't want to go back to the Midwest. "I don't know why I even talked to them, when I knew I wouldn't take it," he says. "Sometimes you do things for your ego."

He also talked to the Los Angeles Rams, but Carroll Rosenbloom hired George Allen instead. Then, in one of the more bizarre NFL happenings, Allen was fired during the exhibition season. The episode worked out perfectly for the 49ers, however, because it meant Walsh was available the next year.

Those long years in the athletic wilderness had an effect on Walsh's personality. For sure, he is not at all the coaching stereotype of a bland, programmed man who talks only in jargon and cliches.

Walsh doesn't suffer fools gladly, and he admits that one of the hardest parts of his job is disguising his disdain for stupid questions, particularly those from television commentators. He has cut short post-game interviews for that very reason.

Walsh is a brilliant man, and he doesn't pretend otherwise. He is often impatient with those not quick enough to keep up with him, and his off-the-record comments about his coaching colleagues are candid and often caustic.

He has the politician's knack for manipulating large press conferences, often giving reporters good quotes, while revealing little of himself or his team. Walsh won't volunteer information at those sessions, and he'll answer questions only in the most literal sense. At the press conference announcing his selection as 49er coach, for instance, he was asked if he'd told Ed DeBartolo that he wouldn't come to the 49ers if Joe Thomas remained. He replied that Thomas's name had never been mentioned. That was literally true, but what he left unsaid was also true: he would never have worked for Thomas.

Because he's guarded in his comments to reporters he doesn't know or trust, Walsh is misjudged by many. One writer, for instance, wrote that Walsh's only interest seemed to be football. In fact he has many other interests, from travel to history. Last summer he sent me a copy of James Fallow's thought-provoking book *National Defense.* Needless to say, that isn't the kind of book most coaches read—unless they mistake it for a book on the Pittsburgh Steelers' game strategy.

Walsh took the job as 49er coach and general manager for three reasons: money, opportunity, and a break from recruiting.

Though no figure was ever released, Walsh's salary is probably triple what he was getting at Stanford, at least $150,000 a year. And, he has the chance to coach the best. "I felt I could be a better coach on the professional level than college," he says, a point he has certainly proved. Finally, there's no more recruiting. "I frankly don't know how much longer I could have done that. It was a lot harder the second year at Stanford than the first. It gets harder and harder, doing all that traveling."

Walsh stepped into a disaster. The 49ers resembled an expansion team after Joe Thomas's dismantling. Worse yet, Thomas, Monte Clark, and Dick Nolan had traded away an incredible number of draft choices. In the four-year period from 1976 to 1979, the 49ers traded away 20 picks! Sixteen of those came from the first five rounds, traditionally the basis for building a team. By 1980, not one of the players the 49ers received for those draft choices was still with the team.

For the morbidly curious, here's how the deals went:

—In 1976 the 49ers traded their own first and another first obtained from Houston for Vic Washington, plus Tom Owen, to New England for Jim Plunkett. Number three went to Dallas for Bob Hayes, who played one year. Number four went to the Giants for Norm Snead, a deal engineered by Dick Nolan the year before. The number five pick was traded for Al Chandler, a tight end who never played for the 49ers.

—In 1977 the first two picks went to New England as part of the Plunkett deal. Number three went to the Jets for defensive tackle Ed Galigher. Number five went to Buffalo for linebacker Dave Washington (a good deal, except that Thomas then traded away Washington!). Number eight went to Tampa Bay for offensive lineman Johnny Miller, who never played a regular season game for the Niners.

—In 1978 the 49ers lost their second- and third-round picks in the Simpson deal. Number five, and Tom Mitchell, went to Washington for wide receiver and punt returner Larry Jones. Number eight went to Washington for linebacker Joe Harris.

—By 1979 Thomas was gone, but his mark remained. The number one pick went to Buffalo in a continuation of the Simpson deal. Number three went to Seattle because of a trade Thomas had made for defensive back Bob Jury. Number four was also in the Simpson deal. Number eight went, because of another trade Thomas had made the year before, for offensive guard Steve Knutson of Green Bay.

It was a bleak picture, but Walsh had a long-range plan. The first element was to work on the players' confidence, and to show them that progress could be measured by something other than wins. At the start, it would have to be.

"Some people say a loss is a loss," Walsh said in training camp, "but I don't buy that. If I have to lose, I'd rather lose by one point than 30. I look for small things. I think it's better to have three goal-line stands, for instance, and then allow a score than to give up a touchdown on the first down. I think you have to look at this as a 16-game season that is followed by another 16-game season. You have to look for improvement."

That first year Walsh drafted for offensive help, figuring that he could install enough of an offense to partially compensate for defensive failings. Lacking his first-round pick, he went for James Owens on the second round. Owens had been a running back at UCLA but Walsh thought he could be turned into a wide receiver and that with his speed (Owens was a world-class hurdler), he would be the kind of deep threat that Cliff Branch was for the Oakland Raiders.

Owens, a disappointment, was eventually traded to Tampa Bay for fullback Johnny Davis two seasons later; but Walsh also drafted quarterback Joe Montana on the third round that year and wide receiver Dwight Clark on the tenth. That combination would eventually be a key factor in getting the 49ers to the Super Bowl.

Because San Francisco had the worst record in pro football, they got first crack at players released by other teams that first year Walsh headed the team.

And Walsh had a system for that, too. He would bring free agents into camp and work them out in a separate session at noon time. If he thought the new player was a significant improvement over what he already had in camp, he'd bring the player into regular drills. If not, he'd quickly let the player go.

Most of the players who came into camp that summer of 1979 never got past the first test. But occasionally, Walsh would come up with a gem: defensive end Dwaine Board and free safety Dwight Hicks both joined the 49ers that way.

The 49ers were an entertaining team in 1979, and quarterback Steve DeBerg set NFL records with most completions (347) and most attempts (578). But the Niners finished at 2-14 for the second straight season, a crushing disappointment to Walsh.

"I really thought we could come in and make a big difference that first year," he said later. "We had done it at Stanford."

What was the difference?

"In college you can literally outsmart people," he said. "We had nothing on defense at Stanford that first year, but we would load up against the run until we stopped that and force teams to throw the ball, and they were generally inept at that.

"And then when we played LSU in a bowl game, well, we were flabbergasted at the way they would telegraph their plays. They ran them the same way all the time, so we knew exactly what they would do.

"But you don't get that kind of break in the pro game. Teams don't give anything away, and when teams are physically superior to you, they just keep pounding away until you break."

Before the 1980 draft Walsh made two key decisions. The first was to trade his number one pick. The 49ers had the second pick, behind only Detroit, in the first round, and Walsh could have drafted BYU quarterback Marc Wilson, whom he liked. But the 49er coach felt he needed more help at other positions, and that it was better to get two quality athletes instead of one. He traded that pick to the New York Jets, who drafted Lam Jones with it, in exchange for the Jets' two first-round picks; Earl Cooper, a running back, and defensive lineman Jim Stuckey were selected with the picks from the Jets.

Walsh's second decision was even more important: he decided the 49ers had to build defensively first, and the next two drafts concentrated on defensive players. In 1980 he got Stuckey, linebackers Keena Turner, Craig Puki, and Bobby Leopold, strong safety Ricky Churchman, and punter Jim Miller.

The 49ers still had some conspicuous weaknesses—sensitive people covered their eyes when the 49ers secondary tried to defend against a pass—but the improvement that Walsh was looking for was there.

Before the start of his second season, Walsh approved the slogan "Roaring Back," knowing full well that he would look ridiculous if the 49ers stumbled again. "I thought it'd be good for the players to have something to point for," he said. "Still, I thought of 'Roaring Back' as maybe something like 8-8. I didn't think we'd be in the Super Bowl."

The 49ers might even have reached Walsh's modest second-year goal. They started out well, taking three out of four exhibition games, including a whopping 33-14 win over the Oakland Raiders, who would go on to win Super Bowl XV. They won their first three games of the regular season, from New Orleans, St. Louis, and the New York Jets.

But in that third win, Dwaine Board was injured and declared out for the season. "I would rather have lost the game and kept Board," Walsh told me the next day. He knew, with Board gone, that the 49er pass rush would disappear, and the weak secondary would be exposed.

Atlanta ended the 49ers' three-game streak with a 20-17 win the next week, and then Los Angeles thrashed the Niners, 48-26. The worst was yet to come: Dallas totally manhandled the 49ers, 59-14, the next week, and running back Paul Hofer was knocked out for the season with a knee injury. Hofer had been the 49ers' primary offensive threat with his running and pass catching. Walsh called Hofer and Board his two best athletes, and in the span of three weeks, both had been lost.

Without Board and Hofer, the 49er season was doomed. They went on to lose eight in a row before finally beating the New York Giants, 12-0, in the twelfth game of the season. They finished the year at 6-10, a big improvement over the consecutive 2-14 seasons but hardly what the Faithful had expected when the team got off to a 3-0 start.

Still, there were some positive signs, and it didn't take a lot of searching to find them. For starters, Joe Montana had emerged as the number one quarterback, which pleased Walsh; he hadn't been sure Montana could develop that rapidly in only his second pro season.

DeBerg had a good arm and grasped Walsh's complex system well, but he wasn't mobile enough to scramble out of trouble. Worse, he had a tendency to throw critical interceptions, a fatal flaw for the 49ers because Walsh's system is based on controlling the ball through passing. All his quarterbacks—Ken Anderson and Dan Fouts in the pros, Guy Benjamin and Steve Dils at Stanford—had been taught not to throw high-risk passes. DeBerg could not seem to learn that lesson.

Montana, by contrast, was cool under pressure, probably because he had played at Notre Dame, where the pressure is always on. He seldom threw the pass interception which took the 49ers out of a game. Moreover, his mobility enabled him to gain a second or two of extra time, often enough to complete a pass.

Another positive sign that year was the 49ers rebounding in the homestretch of the season. Though they had nothing particularly to gain, they won three of their last five games.

One of their successes came against a potential playoff team, New England. The 49ers' 21-17 win knocked the Patriots out of playoff consideration and was the first time under Walsh that they had beaten a winning team.

The 49ers also nearly beat another playoff team, going down to the wire on a muddy, miserable day that ended the season before losing to Buffalo, 18-13.

But perhaps the most significant game of all was the fourteenth of the season, against New Orleans at Candlestick. The 49ers were trailing, 35-7, at halftime and seemed well on their way to one of the worst shellackings in their history. Instead, they pulled themselves together to outscore the Saints, 28-0, in the second half; in overtime, a Ray Wersching field goal beat New Orleans, 38-35, in what is officially termed the best comeback in NFL history.

That kind of character would make the 49ers champions in 1981.

3

HOW DO ROOKIES GET SO SMART?

Perhaps it was an omen when the 49ers were able to draft Ronnie Lott in the spring of 1981.

Bill Walsh had had no trouble identifying the area to strengthen for the 1981 season—the defensive backfield. It was just as easy to identify the backs who could help him: USC's Lott or UCLA free safety Ken Easley. Easley had the greater collegiate reputation, but given the choice, Walsh wanted Lott because the former Trojan could switch from his collegiate safety position to cornerback, the 49ers' weakest position.

But it seemed both Lott and Easley would be drafted before the 49ers' chance came up. Easley's agent tried to discourage other teams from drafting Ken by sending out letters saying he wanted to play in San Francisco and wouldn't report to another team. The tactic didn't work; Easley was drafted by the Seattle Seahawks.

That left only Lott, and Tampa Bay would probably pick him, just ahead of the 49ers. But the St. Louis Cardinals, expected to draft Pittsburgh's Hugh Green, surprised everybody by picking Alabama linebacker E.J. Junior. That left Green on the board, and Tampa Bay grabbed him.

Almost immediately, the 49ers announced they would draft Lott.

That was just one of two key moves the 49ers made in the off-season. The other was the acquisition of Jack Reynolds, a 34-year-old middle linebacker.

Reynolds had been a great player for the Los Angeles Rams, appearing in the Pro Bowl as late as January 1981, but the Rams had become disenchanted with him. They considered him a liability on pass defense because he'd lost a step of speed; Reynolds came off the field in obvious passing situations. He was also asking more money than they wanted to pay, and so the Rams released him. Very soon, the 49ers signed Reynolds as a free agent.

"A lot of us thought that was a mistake," said John Ralston, then working in the front office. "We figured we were building with youth, and what did we need with a 34-year-old linebacker? But, we were wrong, and Bill was right. Reynolds gave the team just what they needed in certain areas."

Certainly Reynold's physical ability alone was a plus. A sure, punishing tackler, he led the team in the 1981 season with 117 tackles, 28 more than any other player.

His attitude, though, was even more important. He looked at game movies almost more than the coaches, taking home reels of film to run on his own projector. His experience enabled him to position the 49ers perfectly on the field, and he acted almost as a coach with the younger players. His enthusiasm rubbed off on the others. "He's our Pete Rose," said Walsh.

As he had in 1980, Walsh concentrated on defensive help from the 1981 draft. (Incidentally, Walsh depends heavily on draft information supplied by John McVay, director of football operations, and college scouting director Tony Razzano and his scouts, but the final decision on who to pick is Walsh's.)

The first five picks in the draft—and six of the first seven—were defensive players. Four of the first five picks were defensive backs: Lott, Eric Wright, Carlton Williamson, and Lynn Thomas. "We didn't think there would be any good defensive backs coming out for the 1982 draft," explained Razzano, "so we had to get everything we could out of this draft."

The rookie defensive backs didn't have the luxury of a gradual break-in. Walsh started Lott, Wright, and Williamson from the beginning, though Lott's debut was delayed somewhat because he didn't sign until after the start of training camp. Moreover, Walsh declared that he expected the defensive backfield to be "the strongest part of our team."

Others scoffed. Newspaper writers were quick to point out that, in the first two exhibition games, the rookie backs played so far off the receivers (to prevent deep passes) that they couldn't defend against short- and medium-range passes. Defensive coordinator Chuck Studley, who had been an assistant with Walsh in Cincinnati, admitted he was "scared to death" at the idea of starting three rookies (four when Thomas was used in a five-back formation in obvious passing situations). Studley tried to make the rookie backs less vulnerable by dropping linebackers in pass coverage on every play, instead of using them to occasionally blitz.

But Walsh was proved right. The rookies played so much that they gained experience far more quickly than they would have normally. By the time the season was one-third over they were playing like veterans and, yes, the defensive secondary was the 49ers strongest point.

The exhibition season generally pleased Walsh. Though he, like everybody else, was concerned about a weakness at running back, he was encouraged by the great improvement on defense. That, in turn, took pressure off the offense because the 49ers didn't necessarily have to score five touchdowns to win a game.

Walsh knows, as do all followers of the game, that though you can compensate somewhat for your offensive weaknesses, the opposing offense, because it starts the play, can always find a defensive weakness.

"We've got nine good linebackers in camp and will only keep seven," noted Walsh. "We've got eight good linemen and can only keep six. For the first time, we're letting players go who could play somewhere else."

Because of travel costs, the 49ers confined their 1981 exhibition season to the West Coast, playing Seattle twice, San Diego, and Oakland. Walsh was pleased when his team beat Seattle twice.

"You have to remember that they humiliated us just two years ago [a 55-20 Seattle triumph]," he said. "This shows our progression—and, to be honest, their regression."

But unfortunately what impressed most people was the 49ers' 21-7 loss to the Raiders in the final exhibition game. The 49ers seemed inept on offense against the reigning World Champions. Walsh insisted that he had seen some positive aspects to the game, obviously referring to the defense. One columnist, though, thought Walsh had "flipped his noodle."

* * * *

In the first four games of the regular season, the 49ers played much as they had during the exhibition season, showing flashes of brilliant play but never displaying the consistency a champion needs.

Their first game was in the Silverdome in Pontiac, and the Niners gave no sign that they would be returning four-and-a-half months later for the Super Bowl. Billy Sims scored a touchdown with just 18 seconds remaining to give the Detroit Lions a 24-17 win in a game filled with errors by both sides.

Paul Hofer didn't play because Walsh didn't want to risk Hofer's knee on the artificial surface. (As it would turn out, Hofer played little all year and eventually re-injured his knee, apparently ending his career.)

To partially compensate, Walsh used ten varied backfield combinations, including one fullback and three wide receivers, and three running backs with two tight ends. Nothing worked very well.

The 49ers bounced back to beat the Chicago Bears, 28-17, in their home opener at Candlestick. Joe Montana had his best game yet, completing 20 of 32 passes for 287 yards without an interception, and throwing three touchdown passes.

The game was as much a Chicago loss as a San Francisco win, though. Walter Payton lost two fumbles and his team made so many errors that Bear coach Neill Armstrong lamented, "We saw ourselves self-destruct."

Happily for 49er fans it was the other team that beat itself this time, but that pleasant feeling lasted only until the following Sunday when the Falcons demolished the 49ers, 34-17, in Atlanta.

The game, even more lopsided than the score, was a particularly painful loss to Walsh because the many 49er errors—including a Montana interception returned 101 yards for a touchdown by Atlanta's Tom Pridemore—were reminiscent of the bad play of the seasons before. "We're too good a team to play like that," said Walsh.

The loss was especially painful because the obvious difference between the teams at that point was in the running offense. As the *Chronicle's* Ira Miller, the most knowledgeable of Bay Area pro football writers, pointed out, the 49ers could have drafted either or both of the Falcon running backs, William Andrews and Lynn Cain.

Again, the 49ers bounced back the next week to even their record with a 21-14 win over New Orleans at Candlestick. But again, the win came less from what the 49ers did than from what the other team failed to do.

The Saints outgained the 49ers by 99 yards, but one receiver, Rich Caster, dropped a pass in the end zone when no one was near him. Another receiver, Wes Chandler, tipped a pass

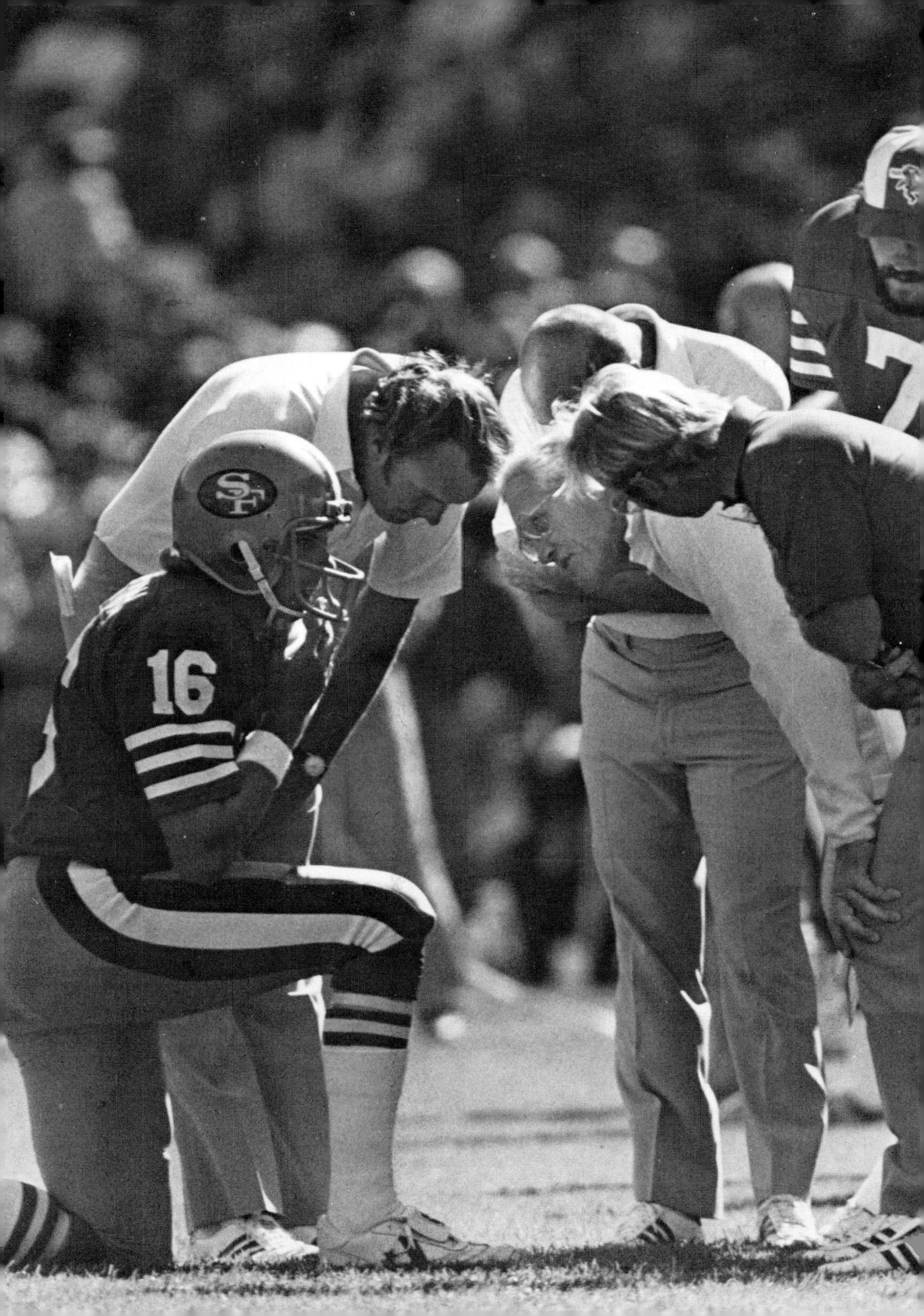
SF
16

(overleaf) Joe Montana huddles with coaches as reserve quarterback Guy Benjamin listens. Hugh McElhenny, shown about to stiff-arm a would-be tackler, and John Brodie (above), fueled the high-powered offense in the 50s and 60s. Frankie Albert, hit by a Cleveland lineman just after releasing a pass, was the star of the first 49er team. Tony Morabito founded the 49ers and owned them until 1957. Joe Thomas (upper right) almost ruined the 49ers during his two years as general manager in 1977 and 1978. Monte Clark (bottom right) brought an interlude of success in 1976.

(top left) Dwight Clark slips and falls, and then watches helplessly as Joe Montana pass that was intended for him is intercepted in Cleveland game. The 49ers were driving toward what would have been a clinching touchdown before this play. They wound up losing to the Browns, their only loss in the last 15 regular season and playoff games. (bottom left) Freddie Solomon shows the fine art of pass catching as he catches a ball with the fingertips of one hand behind the Dallas defense in the NFC championship game. (right) Dallas defensive end Ed Jones stretches out to an eight-foot plus barricade, showing why he is nicknamed "Too Tall Jones" in the NFC championship game, but somehow, 49er quarterback Joe Montana gets the pass by Jones for an important completion.

E. JONES

(top left) Pulling guards Randy Cross (51) and John Ayers (68) lead Lenvil Elliott around the right side against the New York Giants in the playoff game. (bottom left) Ricky Patton slips through hole created by blocking of Keith Fahnhorst (71 on left), Fred Quillan (on ground) and Johnny Davis (on right) in Houston win. (right) Dwight Clark and Raider defensive back Ted Watts reach for long pass, and Raider safety Burgess Owens also tries.

WATTS
CLARK
87

74

(left) Defensive end Fred Dean brings down Los Angeles running back Mike Guman after a short gain in second game, won by the 49ers, 33-31. (top right) 49ers middle linebacker Jack Reynolds pushes by a defender to make a tackle against the Giants in title-clinching victory. (bottom right) Ronnie Lott shows why the 49ers made him their No. 1 draft pick with this spectacular interception while falling.

(left) 49er tight end Charle Young and the Ram's Nolan Cromwell battle for a Joe Montana pass. (top right) Another look at Young as he signs autographs in the Candlestick parking lot after a 49er win. (bottom right) Paul Hofer slants through a good hole in the Atlanta defense as defensive back Tom Pridemore comes up to make the tackle.

(top left) Keena Turner brings down an Atlanta runner as Carlton Williams prepares to help. (bottom left) John Ayers, his cheeks puffed out, shows the 49er intensity as he prepares to block a Bengal defender in 21-3 regular season win over Cincinnati. (right) Unofficial 49er cheerleader Wayne Tarr, dressed appropriately for the Christmas season, prepares to lead the 49er fans in a cheer during the Houston game, last of the regular season home games.

GO

THIS BUD'S FOR YOU.
49

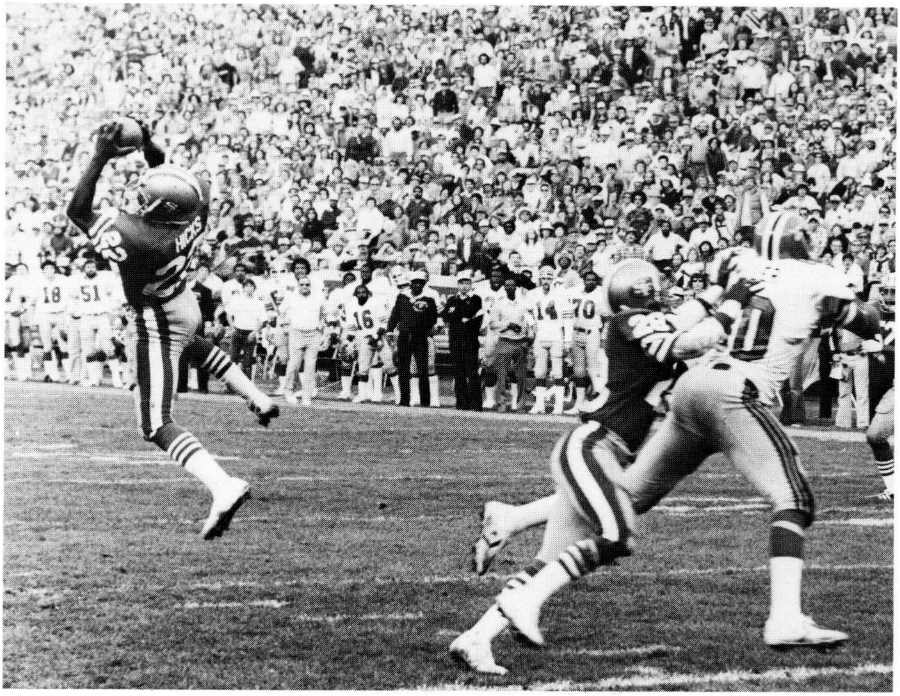

(left) Earl Cooper, who led the NFC in pass receiving in the 1980 season, shows why as he prepares to haul in a Joe Montana pass. (top right) Dwight Hicks leaps high to make an interception against Atlanta, as Lynn Thomas (28) prepares to defend the pass that never got that far. (bottom right) Dan Bunz draws a bead on Pittsburgh running back Frank Pollard.

BIKE
21
21

that was intercepted by Ronnie Lott and returned for a touchdown. "That was a 'gimme'," said Lott after the game, and much the same could be said for the 49ers win.

Walsh had enjoyed a largely admiring press for his first two seasons, but some writers were beginning to criticize him at this point, which he felt unfair.

"I thought we had shown definite improvement," he said later. "We had won three of our last five games in the previous year, we were 2-2 in the exhibition season and barely lost one of those games to San Diego, in the last minute. The worst we were in the regular season was 1-2, so we weren't playing bad football.

"But I kept hearing how dull we were, and I knew some people were licking their chops, ready for us to fall. If we had, if the players had become disheartened by criticism, I don't know where we would have gone from there.

"I thought to myself, 'Give us a chance. Give this city a chance. San Francisco needs a team it can be proud of. Don't tear us down.' "

Very soon, though, his worries would be erased. The 49er season was about to turn around for two reasons: Fred Dean and the game against the Washington Redskins.

Dean had been a Pro Bowl defensive end for the San Diego Chargers, a fearsome pass rusher who helped disguise the Chargers' weakness in the defensive secondary. But he had been locked into a contract that just didn't compensate him fairly for his ability, and he finally refused to play for the Chargers any more.

The 49ers obtained him for a second-round draft choice in 1983, and the option of exchanging first-round positions in 1983. "NFL games are often won with a fourth-quarter pass rush," said Walsh. "That's where Dean is so valuable. If you're protecting a lead and the other team has to throw, he's all over the quarterback."

Dean reported to the 49ers but, because it took some time to work out his contract, didn't play in the next game against the Redskins. He would prove to be a very valuable addition in the weeks to come, but he wasn't needed in this one.

The 49ers simply smashed the Redskins, 30-17; at one point, they were up, 30-3. This was easily their most impressive victory of the season so far, especially since it happened on the road, where the 49ers had lost 26 of their previous 28 games.

The defense played especially well, and Dwight Hicks became the first 49er defensive player to score two touchdowns. In fact, Hicks, outgained the running backs and receivers on both sides of the field with 184 yards on two interception returns and a fumble recovery and run.

The loss dropped the Redskins to 0-5, and it seemed the 49ers had just beaten another bad team. But the Skins were a much better team than their record (which they proved by going 6-5 after that terrible start), and Walsh later regarded that game as the key to the 49er season.

"Washington had been moving the ball well all season [they were leading the NFC in yardage at the time]," said Walsh, "but they had been beating themselves with mistakes. It seemed they were about to break out.

"The attitude of the Washington media that week was, 'Now we've got a team we can beat.' We were playing on the road, in a hostile atmosphere. Then, we came out and just blitzed them! It was a real maturing process for the team."

All of which was fine for the moment, but the next week the 49ers would tangle with the Dallas Cowboys at Candlestick. The last time the teams had met, the Cowboys had won, 59-14. And that would be only the start of the toughest stretch of the 49ers schedule: in a seven-week span they had to play Dallas, Los Angeles twice, Atlanta, Pittsburgh, and Cleveland. Ouch!

4

DOOMSDAY FOR DALLAS

As usual, Bill Walsh was guarded in his comments at the press conference before the Dallas game. He described the Cowboys as a great team, certainly no exaggeration, and implied that his team was not yet in that class. "Are you suprised that you're 3-2?" asked one writer. "No," said Walsh. "We're good enough for that and we've played well enough to be 3-2. I would be surprised if we were 5-0."

When I talked to him later in his office, he was considerably less circumspect. I asked if he seriously thought his team could beat the Cowboys. "Yes," he said. "The one thing we [the coaches] have to worry about is that we don't start worrying about having to out-think the Cowboys. We're good enough now to stay with them physically."

The players, too, were confident. The atmosphere in the dressing room before the game was quiet and relaxed. Offensive tackle Keith Fahnhorst, who had been through the bad years, could spot the difference now. "We all felt we were going to win," he said.

The fans were ready, too. The game was a sellout, and the fans came early and stayed late.

They saw a game that some thought might have been the biggest victory in the history of the franchise; certainly it was the biggest to date under Walsh. The 49ers not only won the game, they dominated in every aspect.

The 49ers took command from the start, driving 61 yards

for a touchdown after the opening kickoff, with Joe Montana passing to Fred Solomon for the score.

When the 49ers got the ball back after a punt, they went 68 yards for another touchdown. This time Paul Hofer went in from four yards out. Hofer wound up as the 49ers leading rusher for the day with 40 yards on 11 carries.

Solomon figured in two key plays on this drive. On the first, he hit Dwight Clark for 25 yards on a pass off a threatened reverse. Solomon had been a quarterback in college and, though he couldn't pass well enough to be a pro quarterback, his ability was a genuine plus on a play like this.

Freddie was at the other end of a key pass later in the drive, when Montana scrambled away from a blitz and hit Solomon for 26 yards.

Still in the first period, the 49ers scored yet again. This time, the Cowboys were on the three after a San Francisco punt, and Jim Stuckey tackled Dorsett for a two-yard loss on first down. Then one play later, the 49ers got their only real break. Danny White passed to Drew Pearson, who fumbled at the six. The ball would have gone out of bounds but it hit the foot of line judge Dick McKenzie on the sideline and bounced to the 49ers Ronnie Lott, who recovered on the four. Four plays later, Johnny Davis scored from the one.

That made it 21-0 at the end of the first quarter, and the fans gave the home team a standing ovation as they changed ends of the field. The Niners went up 24-0 on a Ray Wersching field goal in the second quarter; finally the Cowboys scored, to make it 24-7 at halftime.

Now the 49ers had only one worry: that they would relax and the Cowboys would come back.

"After the Washington game," said Fahnhorst, "Hacksaw [Jack Reynolds] and I agreed that we've got to learn to bury a team when we've got a chance to. We can't let up."

On the second possession of the second half, the 49ers showed they had learned their lesson well. Clark took a ten-yard pass from Montana on the right sideline, made a move to get away from rookie cornerback Eversen Walls, and then beat safety Michael Downs and linebacker D.D. Lewis to the end zone for a 78-yard touchdown.

And the 49ers weren't through. Two plays after the ensuing kickoff, Lott returned an interception 41 yards for still another score. Wersching's kick made it 38-7 and the 49ers were coasting to their eventual 45-14 win.

After Lott's touchdown, Dallas coach Tom Landry took

quarterback Danny White out of the game to avoid the chance of injury at a meaningless point. Landry had conceded.

Actually, Landry had virtually given up much earlier. Asked after the game if he had thought the Cowboys would come back in the second half, Landry shook his head. "Most games that start out that way," he said, "end up as lopsided games, if you're playing a good team. The 49ers are a good team."

The details from that game are incredible. The first two times the Cowboys had the ball, they ran off three plays and had to punt. The third time, White fumbled on second down. The fourth time, Lott intercepted a pass on first down.

The 49ers led by 24-0 before the Cowboys even made a first down! Dallas crossed the 50-yard line only once in its first 13 possessions. Tony Dorsett, the league's leading rusher at the time, was held to 21 yards in nine carries, third lowest total of his five-year career; that game probably cost Dorsett the NFC rushing title. White passed for only 60 yards before he came out.

Walsh had worried about trying to outthink the Cowboys, using trick plays, but it was the Cowboys who had to resort to a flea-flicker and an end-around in desperation.

The statistics reflected the lopsidedness of the game: the 49ers had 23 first downs to 10, ran 80 plays to 53, and they gained 440 yards to only 192 for Dallas.

It was the biggest winning margin for the 49ers since 1974, when they had beaten Chicago 34-0, and the Cowboys' biggest losing margin since 1970.

There was no question that the 49ers had caught the Cowboys on one of those low days they sometimes experience during a season—nobody, after all, is really 31 points better than Dallas—but that didn't alter the significance of the win. In some games young teams find themselves, discovering just how good they can be, and the Dallas game was exactly that for the 49ers.

Nor was it a fluke. The 49ers won with good, solid football on both sides of the scrimmage line, and the only real break they got was the recovered fumble before their third touchdown. Considering their dominance throughout the game, and the score, it's hard to see how that fumble had much effect on the outcome.

"The thing a lot of people forget about Bill Walsh," CBS commentator and former coach Hank Stram told me later, "is that he's a sound fundamental coach."

"Since the rules have been relaxed to help the offense, a lot of coaches have opened up their offenses to take advantage of that, but they forget that their teams still have to block and tackle well. Walsh has never forgotten that, and that's been an important difference for him."

Probably the most encouraging aspect of the Dallas win was the dominance of the 49er defense, which really came together against a great team. Dean's presence made a big difference. He sacked White three times in the first half alone; for the game, he had four sacks. The first time the 49ers unveiled their new 4-2-5 defense with Dean, he sacked White.

Dean was so overwhelming in his first 49er game that he forced a change in the thinking of defensive coordinator Chuck Studley.

The basic 49er defense had been the 3-4, in which the defensive linemen are primarily expected to hold their ground; linebackers make most of the tackles. Former 49er defensive end Cedrick Hardman, who dislikes the 3-4 defense intensely, told me one time, "You need Clydesdales for that formation."

Hardman obviously regarded himself as a thoroughbred. Dean is too, and Studley didn't use him in the 3-4. Dean played only when the 49ers went to a 4-3, or any other defense aimed primarily at stopping the pass. When Studley saw how effective Dean was, he modified his defensive strategy to include more 4-3 defenses, giving Dean more opportunity to play.

Dean is incredible. He's so quick off the ball, it sometimes seems he's offside! Although only 228 pounds, he has enormous upper body strength and can't be manhandled by the largest of offensive linemen. Basically, he combines the quickness of a linebacker with the strength of a lineman.

His muscles come naturally, from a youth spent doing heavy manual labor. He shuns even the normal exercises done by players. "Any time I think of doing exercises," he explained, "I lie down until the feeling goes away."

Even without Dean, the 49er secondary had been playing very well. With him harassing and sacking the quarterback, the secondary became awesome, especially Ronnie Lott.

The rookie cornerback, who played safety when the 49ers added a fifth defensive back in passing situations, was playing an aggressive defense, staying tight on his man to break up passes or make interceptions and tackling with an awesome ferocity if the receiver did catch the ball.

As the 49ers knew when they drafted him, Lott is a super athlete. In high school he played shortstop on the baseball team and point guard on the basketball team, and in the one year (his junior year) he played basketball at USC, he made the varsity.

In high school, he was strictly an offensive player, first as wide receiver and then quarterback. He didn't play defensive back until he came to USC, but his background on offense has probably helped make him a defensive star. He's the right man in the right place at the right time.

The rule changes in 1978 in the NFL, forbidding defensive backs to bump a receiver more than once and allowing offensive linemen to use their hands in blocking, opened up the pass offense (which was, of course, the intent) and drove a lot of defensive coaches and defensive backs crazy. Speed and athletic ability became far more important than strength; the rule changes have forced an attitude change, too. Defensive backs can't play passively. They must be aggressive, willing to give up an occasional touchdown in exchange for a gambling, critical interception that can turn the game around. That's exactly the way Lott plays.

"Look," he says, using a colorful analogy, "we're playing with a loaded revolver back there, but you got to keep reloading it and play the game. If you don't, somebody's going to reload it for you and put bullets in all six chambers of that sucker, and it's going to go off all the time. I think defensive backs are starting to do that. I think the trend is starting to turn."

Meanwhile, Lott was receiving the ultimate compliment: opposing teams were throwing mainly to the other side, no longer willing to risk many passes on his side. That put more pressure on Eric Wright, the other rookie corner, but Wright was playing well, too, though not quite at the same level as Lott.

The decisive win over Dallas also showed the maturing of quarterback Montana and wide receiver Solomon.

Montana had been consistently downgraded by many in pro football, supposedly because he lacked a strong arm. To Walsh, that was nonsense.

"I can't find any negatives about Joe Montana's arm," he said. "People who say it's only an average arm are mistaken, and they always will be. Because his delivery is not a flick of the wrist like Terry Bradshaw's, they think it's not strong.

"He throws on the run while avoiding a pass rush, and he doesn't have to be totally set. He's not a moving platform like some others who are mechanical and can only do well when everything is just right. Joe performs just as well under stress."

Montana showed what Walsh meant against the Cowboys, completing 19 of 29 passes for 279 yards and two touchdowns, and consistently making the big play.

He was helped by an outstanding performance from the 49er offensive line, particularly Fahnhorst, who blocked Ed (Too

Tall) Jones so effectively that Jones might as well have stayed in Dallas. But even when Montana was under pressure, he often scrambled out of trouble to pass for an important completion.

Solomon, who caught his fifth touchdown in six games, joined the 49ers (in a trade by Joe Thomas) before the 1978 season; he came with a reputation for great talent but no discipline. At the back of his mind, he still thought he could play quarterback and sulked because nobody else agreed. In a game late in the disastrous 1978 season, Solomon got his chance when both 49er quarterbacks were hurt in the game. That humbling experience finally convinced him he belonged at wide receiver, and his improvement dated from that point.

Even so, in Walsh's first year Solomon made some spectacular plays but wasn't a dependable performer. When the 49ers needed a big catch late in the game, he wasn't the one to make it.

By 1981 that had changed. He was making big plays consistently. "He should be in the Pro Bowl," said Walsh. As late as 1979, Solomon was taking snaps from the center in practice so he could play quarterback in a pinch. No longer; he was too valuable now for Walsh to even consider a switch.

The stunning Dallas win should have established the 49ers among the NFL's elite, but there were still doubters. The 49ers hadn't been featured on Monday Night Football since 1977, and ABC producer Bob Goodrich made the decision not to show any plays from the 49er-Cowboys game on the halftime highlights. Of course, the fact that Los Angeles and Dallas were meeting in a special Sunday night game the next week, and that the 49er win would take some gloss off the Cowboys, was purely coincidental. Of course.

Walsh blasted that decision at his Tuesday press conference. "We're not accepted nationally, obviously," he said.

"The football elitists, jockstrap elitists don't consider us in the comfort zone. There are power sources, influence sources in the National Football League, 45-year-old men who are football groupies who prefer that we not exist so they can hold on to their football contracts and associations or power groups.

"...It's obviously a business and they [ABC] need the Los Angeles—Dallas game to be a big game, to fight the excellent movies on Sunday night TV. It's obvious, it's blatant. In my opinion, it's a disservice to the public."

How could the 49ers fight that? Simply by playing well, Walsh suggested, and so they would, for a much longer time than anybody thought possible.

5

NO. 4, AND COUNTING

The problem with success in the NFL is that there's little time to savor it. The 49ers could be proud of their win over Dallas, but they still had a light workout on Monday, a heavy workout on Wednesday, a trip to Milwaukee on Friday, and a game against the Green Bay Packers on Sunday. The Packers hadn't been a championship team since Vince Lombardi had retired, but that made little difference: they were still capable of winning on that well-known "any given Sunday." A loss to the Packers would wipe out the win over Dallas; it would be like a tennis player breaking his opponent's service and then losing his own.

The 49ers were aware of that. Right guard Randy Cross started thinking about it only a few hours after the Dallas game, amidst congratulations from fans as he was trying to eat dinner in a Peninsula restaurant. The fans were ecstatically telling him, "You're going to the Super Bowl," but Cross wasn't buying. Not yet, anyway.

"It's great to be excited," he said, "but you've got to be realistic about it. As good as we've looked at times in the last two weeks, it doesn't take a genius to remember how good we didn't look against New Orleans, three games ago, so we're not exactly incapable of our own little miscues."

The 49ers knew from recent and painful experience how easy it was to let down. Just a year ago they had upset New England and then came out thinking of where they were going to spend Christmas the next week against New Orleans. The Saints, who had lost 13 in a row, stormed to a 35-7 halftime lead before the 49ers recovered to mount that spectacular comeback for a 38-35 overtime win.

Against the Packers the year before, the 49ers had squandered a 13-0 lead and lost 23-16. The Niners wouldn't be overconfident this Sunday, and Cross was optimistic because he liked the spirit of the team.

"We have *real* enthusiasm," he said. "Not just guys jumping up and down. You felt like giving them all pom-poms. We've got guys who have something to be enthusiastic about."

It was a little difficult to maintain that enthusiasm when the 49ers played the Packers in Milwaukee that gray and nasty Sunday. Rain started falling in the first quarter, making the grass turf slick, and winds gusting up to 40 mph made any pass longer than 15 yards a real adventure.

But the 49ers, meeting a new test every week, showed that they were capable of beating a mediocre team on a bad day, one of the important attributes of a good team.

Bill Walsh would term this a tactical win for the 49ers. Because the defense was playing so well and because weather conditions were terrible, he called a conservative game—so the offense wouldn't give the Packers a chance at an easy score. (Walsh calls all the plays, though quarterback Joe Montana has the right to change them at the line of scrimmage.)

The 49er offense produced just enough at the right times. Their first score came right before the end of the first half when, trailing 3-0, the 49ers marched 71 yards before settling for a Ray Wersching field goal.

In the third quarter, the 49ers had the wind at their backs; they knew they had to score in that quarter because the Packers would have the wind advantage in the fourth quarter. Johnny Davis climaxed a long drive with a short touchdown, from only inches out.

The third high point for the offense came in the last quarter, when they used up over seven minutes with a drive that finally ended with another field goal. In that fourth quarter, the 49ers had the ball more than twelve-and-a-half minutes, effectively negating the Packers' wind advantage.

Quarterback coach Sam Wyche said Montana, who completed 23 of 32 passes, had played his smartest game yet as a 49er, calling audibles to adjust formations and counter the Packers' defensive tactics. "A lot of little things that we've been stressing all year are starting to pay off for us now," said Wyche.

But this was primarily a defensive win for the 49ers. Defensive coordinator Chuck Studley, as imaginative on his side of the scrimmage line as Walsh is on the offensive side, came up with a new defense, using the 3-4 but putting Fred Dean in as a weakside linebacker alongside Dwaine Board. The idea was to have both Dean and Board, the 49ers quickest linemen, rushing from the same side to pressure Green Bay quarterback Lynn Dickey.

The Packers countered by using four wide receivers and double-teaming Dean, but that only left room for Lawrence Pillers to rush from the other side. Pillers sacked Dickey three times and twice nailed running back Harlen Huckleby for losses on running plays.

When it was all over, the 49ers had won their fourth straight, the longest winning streak since 1976, and were a game ahead of Los Angeles in the NFC Western Division—and the Rams were coming to town.

6

THE PERILS OF PAULINE

San Franciscans like to think of the 49ers-Rams series as a great rivalry, yet, historically at least, that's stretching a point. "Rivalry" implies that either team could win, but somebody had forgotten to tell the 49ers.

The 49ers hadn't beaten the Rams in San Francisco since 1966; their last win in Los Angeles had been in 1976 when they pitched a 16-0 shutout. Only four players remained from that 49er team: Keith Fahnhorst, Randy Cross, John Ayers, and Willie Harper.

Even when Dick Nolan's teams had won three straight divisional titles in the early seventies, they had beaten the Rams only once in six games. Overall, the Rams-49ers series stood at 41-19-2. Some rivalry.

But this time, the Rams looked ready to be taken. They were struggling a bit at 4-3. Injuries had hurt them, particularly in the offensive line; the Rams' strength always had been in their ability to control the line of scrimmage, and they could no longer do that. Quarterback Pat Haden had problems throwing long, and, at 5-feet-10, in seeing over the heads of defensive linemen who sometimes loomed nearly a foot taller.

Other deeper and off-field problems bedeviled the Rams. Georgia Frontiere, who had inherited the club when Carroll Rosenbloom died, was setting the women's movement back 50 years with her inept interference in what had been a model NFL operation. Her meddling had caused ace personnel director Dick

Steinberg, who had selected many of the Rams' top players in the draft, to move on.

She had stripped much of the authority from Rams' general manager Don Klosterman, who now had to get final approval on everything from Frontiere. Her stranglehold on the purse strings had been a primary factor in the loss of Vince Ferragamo, on the verge of becoming the best quarterback in the NFL, to Canada.

On top of all that, the Rams had had problems with their veteran players ever since rookie defensive back Johnnie Johnson had been signed to a huge bonus and salary in 1980; that seeming over-compensation had been a factor in the departure of Jack Reynolds.

A bizarre episode earlier in the year, when the club had tried to cut defensive end Fred Dryer, was also causing repercussions. Sometimes a star player negotiates a "no-cut" contract, which simply means he still gets paid even if dropped from the team. Dryer's contract went further: it specified that he couldn't be dropped from the team without his permission. When the Rams first tried to cut Dryer, he calmly reminded them of that clause. So they kept him around for a time, but doing nothing. Finally they cut him again; Dryer sued and joined CBS as a color commentator. Great for team harmony.

Forty-Niner fans sensed the kill, and their sizzling young team was a slight favorite. It was the hottest ticket in town; fans who had had no trouble getting tickets for the A's-Yankees' American League baseball playoff earlier in the month learned to their dismay that they'd have to watch the 49ers and Rams on television.

An added factor for this game, and one that became more and more important as the season went on, was the field. A two-day Rolling Stones concert at Candlestick preceded the game, and the turf had been badly torn up. The Candlestick field, never a good one, had become probably the worst natural-grass field in the league.

For the rest of the year, no runner would gain as much as 100 yards in a game at Candlestick. At all the remaining home games, members of the hard-working maintenance crew—the "Sod Squad"—would race out at every timeout and hurriedly replace the divots, some of them a foot long.

Everybody seemed to be running in slow motion on the field. Problems were especially noticeable at the south end, the infield during baseball season. Runners who tried to make sharp cuts there found their feet flying out from under them. Field goal kickers often as not fell down on their follow-throughs.

But, though this bothered the players, it didn't faze the spectators. No one who got a ticket to this game regretted it. The game wasn't one of spectacular plays, but it was excruciatingly exciting and a real test for weak hearts.

The 49ers got off almost as fast as they had in the win over Dallas, scoring twice in the first period on Joe Montana passes, the first a 14-yarder to Fred Solomon, the second a 41-yard strike to Dwight Clark. But this wasn't to be the lopsided contest the Dallas game had been.

The Rams came back in the second quarter as Frank Corral kicked a 25-yard field goal (his only successful field goal attempt in five tries during the day) and Mike Guman scored on a two-yard plunge to cut the Niners' lead to 14-10.

The 49ers retaliated with a 42-yard field goal by Ray Wersching, set up by a thrilling 50-yard strike from Montana to Earl Cooper just before halftime. Then Wersching did it again, this time from the 18, to make it 20-10 in the third quarter.

About that time a huge roar went up from the stands: it had just been announced that the New York Giants had beaten Atlanta, 27-24, knocking the Falcons back to a 4-4 record. Playoff talk had been downplayed by Bill Walsh and the Niners, but the fans knew what Atlanta's loss meant, and so did the players.

"We saw that score and we knew we couldn't let up," said Fahnhorst.

They didn't, although they had to survive a fourth quarter of incredible tension to win the game.

The Rams closed the gap to 20-17 with a touchdown late in the third quarter coming on a 16-yard pass from Haden to running back Wendell Tyler.

That set the stage for a nerve-racking test of the 49ers' courage. Many key games and events were part of their march to the Super Bowl, but in the fourth quarter of this game the 49ers proved beyond doubt that they belonged in the NFL's elite.

Five times in a row the 49er offense was unable to get a first down and had to punt. Five times in a row the Rams got the ball in good field position, three of those times inside San Francisco territory.

It was like the "Perils of Pauline." Each time the Rams got the ball, it seemed this would be the time when that Los Angeles locomotive would finally run over the 49ers. But each time, some Niner would come up with a big play to frustrate the Rams once again.

That somebody, oftener than not, was Fred Dean. More

and more, Dean's value to the club was becoming obvious. "He's one of those players like Ted Hendricks and Ronnie Lott who just have the ability to make the big play," said Walsh.

It's probably a matter of personality as much as physical ability. There are players who love the spotlight, and they get it by making the big play when the game or championship is on the line. Reggie Jackson hits home runs in the World Series; Hendricks blocks a field goal to win a game. And Dean makes the key quarterback sacks. "I feel I can get to the quarterback anytime I really have to," he says, and his play often supports that contention.

When the 49ers traded for Dean, Walsh noted that his chief value would be in protecting a lead in the fourth quarter, and there is no better example of that than what Dean did to the Rams in the fourth quarter of that October game:

—On third-and-five from the San Francisco 37 on the Rams' first possession, Fred Dean and Jim Stuckey combined to sack Pat Haden and force a punt.

—On third-and-five from the San Francisco 46 on the Rams' next possession, Dean's pressure forced Haden to the other side, where he was sacked by Lawrence Pillers.

—With just under three minutes remaining and the Rams at third-and-ten on the San Francisco 34, Dean sacked Haden again, forcing another punt.

—On the Rams' last drive Dean sacked Haden twice, for eight- and eleven-yard losses. A determined Haden kept the drive going with desperation passes until the Rams came up against a third-and-ten on the San Francisco 31, with 46 seconds left. Perhaps fearing Dean's rush, Haden called a draw play. Guman was stopped after four yards by...Fred Dean.

That forced Corral to try another field goal. For the fourth straight time Corral missed, sealing the 49er victory. Corral, who had kicked 10 of 12 before that game, blamed his performance on "the worst field I've ever seen." He was probably right about the field, but Wersching was kicking on the same field.

Dean's sacks were obvious, but less obviously, his mere presence in a 49er uniform forced the Rams to change their style and their game plan. Early on, for instance, they often threw on first down because Dean *wouldn't* be in the game. In passing situations, the Rams often ran, trying to counteract his effectiveness.

They even tried double-teaming Dean, which only opened up avenues for other 49er linemen. Doug France tried to arm-wrestle him, and on one play, Dean was literally tackled. But in the end, nothing worked when Dean really wanted to move on the quarterback.

There were other stars for the 49ers. Montana tied his career high with 287 yards passing and extended to 99 his club record for passes without interception.

But it was really a defensive victory, even though the 49ers yielded 401 yards, because they would not break in that critical fourth quarter.

"The good thing is that we're winning now and we're not playing that super, wide-open, blast 'em off offense," said quarterback coach Sam Wyche. "The defense is playing super."

The 49ers were obviously on a roll. They had won five straight and their 6-2 record was surpassed in the NFL only by Philadelphia's 7-1. More importantly, they had a two-game lead in their division over the Rams and Falcons, both at 4-4, and nobody else had that big a margin.

What meant the most, at least to the four players who had been on the team in 1976, was that the victory had come over the Rams.

"Dallas doesn't even compare to this," said Fahnhorst. "It's unbelievable. I'm not going to come down for five days. It's been a long, frustrating time for us."

Cross agreed. "This is a lot of satisfaction after all the knocks and all the bullshit we had to take for the last five years. It's just like a little bit of vindication. We've beaten two quote, unquote TEAMS. Now, we can't be criticized for just beating the little guys. That's a nice feeling."

And there were more of those nice feelings to come.

7

45 AGAINST 50,000

Football as coached by Bill Walsh is an intellectual exercise, but it's also a physical game—and that was the essence of the problem for the 49ers as they journeyed to Pittsburgh in the ninth week of the season, with their five-game winning streak on the line.

The Steelers, though not the team that had dominated the NFL in the seventies, still were a very punishing bunch, an apt reflection of the working-class city they represented. Highly skilled players like quarterback Terry Bradshaw and wide receiver Lynn Swann might dominate the headlines, but the real key to the Steelers' success was physical intimidation.

Normally coaches look only at game films from the current season, trying to pick up tendencies and note strengths and weaknesses of the team they are about to play. This week, though, Walsh looked at films of the Oakland Raiders' win over Pittsburgh the year before. He wanted to see how the Raiders had done it.

He wasn't looking for specific plays; the 49ers actually used only one play, a run that worked twice for five yards each time, that the Raiders had used. What Walsh was concerned about was style, and he learned that the Raiders beat the Steelers by hitting as hard as they were hit, disdaining fancy tactics.

Walsh decided the 49ers would have to do the same. "The coaches told us at the beginning of the week, 'We're going after them'," said right guard Randy Cross later. This would be no chess game.

Walsh also had to counter some psychological problems, one of them being simply that the 49ers were due for a letdown after five straight wins, especially coming off such an emotional victory as the one over the Rams. Psychologists claim a person who hits an extreme emotional peak cannot again reach such heights for eight days, making it a bit difficult for NFL teams playing games seven days apart.

For this confrontation, Walsh dealt with that problem by giving his players more work, including looking at extra game films of the Steelers. "They didn't complain," he said. "They wanted to look at extra films. Some even took films home."

The other problem was the fact that the 49ers were playing in Pittsburgh's Three Rivers Stadium, possibly the most hostile setting for a visiting team in the entire league. The Steelers played their best at home, particularly against National Conference teams. They were 15-2 at home against NFC teams since the merger of the NFL and AFL in 1970, and hadn't lost at Three Rivers against an NFC team since 1971.

Walsh used his historical knowledge to prepare his players for what they would face at Three Rivers. On Wednesday, two days before the team left for Pittsburgh, he recounted the lesson British troops had learned in Burma during World War II.

The British troops, he told his players, were retreating before the Japanese advance. Periodically, the Japanese would capture a few of the British troops and kill them. Finally, the number of troops down to perhaps a thousand, the British found themselves backed up against a mountain. They had no choice but to fight back.

The 49ers, Walsh said, were backed up against that mountain, and the Steelers were only part of the problem. "We're 45 against 50,000 [fans]," he told his team. "We have to fight back."

A bit melodramatic, to be sure, but the 49ers took it to heart. From the start that Sunday, they played as if they were fighting a war, and one they intended to win. They slugged it out with the Steelers, never giving an inch.

Strong safety Carlton Williamson was the chief warrior. In the second quarter, Steeler wide receiver Calvin Sweeney caught a pass in front of Williamson, and Williamson smashed him to the turf, a legal but very hard hit. Sweeney lay there for some time before getting up.

On the Steelers' next possession, Williamson blasted

another Pittsburgh wide receiver, John Stallworth, and again, it was some time before Stallworth got up.

Ironically, the scouting report on Williamson as a college senior was that he wasn't much of a hitter. The 49ers hadn't believed that then and they certainly didn't believe it now. Neither did the Steelers. Receivers had already learned to brace themselves for brutal tackles by Ronnie Lott; now they had to be just as aware of what would happen when they caught a pass in Williamson's territory. A receiver who's thinking of how hard he's about to be hit has a difficult time concentrating on the pass being thrown his way.

The 49ers were so aggressive that fights broke out early in the game. Walsh didn't apologize for that.

"We had to be physical to survive," he said. "The fights were not ragged, cheap shots. They were hard-hitting plays where we would not back off, and neither would they. That's a good sign.

"The fights showed up early. I interpret that as positive. It means we played head-to-head from the start and didn't resort to fighting when we were behind. The fights were more important in the early part than scoring. We established ourselves on the field."

The 49ers also established themselves on the scoreboard, breaking a scoreless tie with ten quick points just before the half.

The first score was set up by an Eric Wright interception, which gave the 49ers the ball on the Pittsburgh 46. Seven plays later, the 49ers were in the end zone.

The touchdown came on a five-yard pass from Joe Montana to Charle Young, but the key play was a 23-yard pass from Montana to Dwight Clark earlier on the drive. Clark admitted later that he had had his own kind of problem preparing for the game. "When I was in high school, these guys were my heroes—Bradshaw, Stallworth, and Swann. I was trying to get that out of my mind and not let them intimidate me. But after I got out there on the field, I saw that we're as good as those guys."

Ray Wersching added the PAT to make it 7-0, and he hardly had a chance to catch his breath before he was back in action. Williamson recovered a Frank Pollard fumble on the Pittsburgh 37. Two plays later, Montana scrambled eight yards to the 28, and then Wersching kicked a 45-yard field goal with just three seconds left on the clock.

The Pittsburgh fans were booing their heroes as they left

the field at halftime, down 10-zip, but those boos rapidly changed to cheers as the second half began.

Montana had extended his club record of passes without interception to 122 when the streak was broken in shocking fashion: Mel Blount intercepted on the sidelines and scrambled 50 yards for a touchdown, with just 4:24 elapsed in the third quarter.

Less than four minutes later Montana threw another interception, this one to Pittsburgh middle linebacker Jack Lambert, who returned it 31 yards to the San Francisco 22. Bradshaw threw a touchdown pass to Jim Smith on the next play.

There was a reason for Montana's suddenly erratic play: he had injured his ribs badly the week before against the Rams, and the ribs both pained him and restricted his throwing.

Montana's ribs had not bothered him during the week, but warming up before the game and thinking about playing before friends and relatives from nearby, he started hyperventilating and his ribs started to hurt again. So much for Joe Cool. Montana, reluctantly had worn a flak vest to protect his ribs. "I hate to wear it," he said. "It's like saying, 'Here's a target; aim for it.' "

After the kickoff following the second Pittsburgh touchdown, the 49ers were set to start from their 11. If Walsh had thought his team was backed up against a mountain before the game, how about now? They were down four points, the Pittsburgh crowd was going crazy, the Niners' quarterback was hurt, and they were deep in their own territory.

So all San Francisco did was drive 69 yards. Though their field goal attempt was blocked, that was less important than that the 49ers had shown the Steelers they couldn't, wouldn't be intimidated.

With only 10:46 left in the game, the 49ers got the break they needed: Williamson intercepted and returned the ball 28 yards to the Pittsburgh 43. From there, the 49ers simply hammered in for the winning touchdown. The key gainer was a 23-yard Montana-to-Solomon pass; Walt Easley went in from two yards out, and the Niners were up, 17-14.

(Easley, who went to West Virginia University, 75 miles from Pittsburgh, was one of three key 49ers who had once played ball close to Three Rivers Stadium: Montana is from Monongahela, a small town in southwest Pennsylvania, and Williamson played college ball at the University of Pittsburgh.)

The 49ers didn't have the game clinched yet, not with five minutes remaining and the Steelers with the ball. Pittsburgh mounted one last drive, using up three minutes to get to the San Francisco 34, where they had third down and one yard to go.

Probably the most curious play of the game followed. It seemed almost certain the Steelers would run the ball. If they failed to get the short yardage on third down, they would still have another down to try. The Pittsburgh offensive line is often considered the best in the league, and it was inconceivable that they couldn't make enough room for a Steeler back to get one yard in two tries.

But Bradshaw thought he saw something in the 49er secondary. Changing his call at the line of scrimmage [and almost getting a delay-of-game penalty in doing so], he faked the run and dropped back to pass.

Bradshaw wanted to hit running back Frank Pollard coming out of the backfield. Pollard was the responsibility of free safety Dwight Hicks, who was lined up as a linebacker in the short-yardage defense.

But as Bradshaw set to pass, Hicks saw a crack in the offensive line. With the gut instinct and quick reactions of a great athlete, he took off. "There was nobody there to block me, and I knew Bradshaw would have to do something quick when I got there."

What Bradshaw had to do was dump the ball off to tight end Randy Grossman to escape a sack; Grossman was tackled by 49er corner Eric Wright for a two-yard loss. The Steelers went from two chances to make a yard to one desperation chance to make three long yards.

This time, the Steelers really did have to pass, and the 49ers came with their best rush of the day, forcing Bradshaw to throw an incomplete pass. The 49ers had their sixth straight win, 17-14, and one of their most satisfying.

It was fitting that a defensive back made the big play at the end because it was the secondary which dominated the game, even though the 49ers couldn't put on much of a pass rush against the great Steeler offensive line.

"Their secondary is the best I've seen all year," said Bradshaw. "I'm the one who looked like the rookie, not them."

Hicks, Williamson, and Wright all had interceptions, and Williamson, Wright, and Lott also recovered Pittsburgh fumbles.

"Our young defensive backs could very well be the best in football," said Walsh. "I don't think there's ever been a rookie backfield that played like this one in the history of the game."

The 49er numbers were mounting. Their six straight wins was the team's longest streak in a season. At 7-2 they shared the league's best record with Philadelphia and led NFC West by two games. Within a four-week stretch they had beaten three of the teams that had been among the most dominant in the NFL for a decade: Dallas, Los Angeles, and Pittsburgh.

Not bad for a team that wasn't good enough to be on Monday Night Football.

8

NO PRESTON RILEY THIS TIME

Around the league, people thought...well, they really didn't know what to think of the 49ers. Judged by conventional standards, the whole thing didn't make any sense. Who are these people, and why are they winning?

And *how* are they winning: field goal wins over Pittsburgh and Los Angeles, only a touchdown over New Orleans, just ten points over Green Bay? Were they really good or just lucky?

Bill Walsh thought he knew why the wins came so hard. "We don't have a dominant runner," he explained. "The teams that can control games are those teams with the runners who get 1200-1500 yards in a season. We don't have that kind of runner, so that's why you're seeing these 17-14, 20-17 games."

To the rest of the league, the 49ers seemed to consist largely of players nobody else wanted; there were, in fact 15 free agents on the roster. They had a quarterback who supposedly couldn't throw long, a wide receiver who had been a tenth-round draft pick because he had little speed, an offensive tackle who should be playing guard, and three rookies playing in the defensive backfield. Nobody had ever heard of such a thing.

Those who looked a little closer saw that the San Francisco 49ers were not a team that could be judged by conventional standards. For one thing, Walsh had an extraordinary ability to turn a debit into an asset.

There was, for instance, the case of the guard playing tackle, Dan Audick. Walsh's original plan had been to start Ken

Bungarda, a giant of a man who was being switched from defense to offense. Ron Singleton, the starter at left tackle the year before and the one weak spot in the line, had been released.

Bungarda, injured in the pre-season, was out for the season, so Walsh traded a draft pick to San Diego to get Audick, a reserve for the Chargers, who were deep in offensive linemen. (It was, incidentally, the first of three trades between the two clubs; the 49ers later got running back Amos Lawrence and, of course, Fred Dean. Because the teams are in different conferences and thus not directly competitive, the Chargers didn't worry that the trades might strengthen the 49ers, which they did.)

Audick is a fine lineman, but he lacks the size of the typical offensive tackle. Walsh predicated much of his quick-pass offense on the knowledge that Audick could not be expected to consistently hold out defensive ends long enough for long passes.

But, at the same time, Audick is faster than most tackles, so Walsh devised plays which called for Audick to pull out and lead the blocking on a run, usually the responsibility of a guard. That thoroughly confused defenses.

Another example of San Francisco's unconventionality: their running backs. Paul Hofer was the only 49er back who could do it all—run inside or out, block, catch passes. But Hofer's knee limited him to spot appearances and he was seldom an important factor.

The other backs were all essentially one-dimensional: Johnny Davis and Walt Easley could run up the middle; Ricky Patton was more of an outside runner; Earl Cooper was being used almost entirely as a pass receiver out of the backfield.

It's certainly a lot easier to gear an offense around a Tony Dorsett or Earl Campbell type of runner. But it's also easier for a defense to prepare for that kind of offense. With the 49ers, other teams never knew quite what to expect from the San Francisco running attack. A different back would be the key every week.

And that's exactly what it was for the rest of the 49ers, too. It was a *team*, not overly dependent on any one individual, with the exception of Joe Montana.

Every week, Walsh would tell his team, "Somebody in this room is going to win this game for us."

And each week it *was* somebody different. Against Atlanta, in the tenth week, it was two men, safety Dwight Hicks and tight end Charle Young, who were the key players, and each had an interesting story.

Hicks was one of the 49er free agents, a fact which always astounded Walsh. "I don't see how anybody could watch Dwight Hicks play and not think that he was going to be an outstanding player," said the coach.

But somebody had made a mistake on Hicks. Twice.

Hicks was drafted in 1978 by the Detroit Lions and survived until the next-to-last cut in training camp that summer. He then went to the Canadian League and played out the season.

The next summer he signed with the Philadelphia Eagles and made it until the last cut of that training camp. Discouraged, he went home to Southfield, Michigan (a suburb of Detroit), and managed a health foods store. He thought he was through with football.

But Walsh was desperate for secondary help that first season, and he called Hicks to give him a tryout. It didn't bother Walsh that Hicks had been cut by two teams; quite the contrary, in fact. "Sometimes," he says, "players who aren't quite ready will go through a couple of training camps and become much better players. The experience of playing against proven players is far better than anything they get in college ball."

Hicks was an immediate standout with the 49ers. The first year, playing in only eight games, he led the team in interceptions with five. The next year, in a full 16-game season, he intercepted four passes and was involved in 92 tackles, 54 of them unassisted.

Young, too, was a castoff, though of a different kind. He had started his pro career in spectacular fashion, catching 167 passes in his first three years with the Philadelphia Eagles and being named Rookie of the Year in 1973 and All-Pro in 1974 and 1975. He seemed the prototype tight end, with both speed and size.

But after his fourth year the Eagles traded him to Los Angeles. Nobody could figure why the Rams traded for him; once they got him, they almost never used him. He caught only 36 passes in three years while playing behind Terry Nelson, a tight end who would be flattered to be called mediocre. Before the 1980 season, the 49ers got Young from the Rams for a 1983 draft choice.

Young, an ordained minister active in youth work, is philosophical about his three semi-idle years. "I learned patience, to persevere, to cope and deal with problems. When a man can deal with the situation I was in with the Rams, it tells something about that man's character. Besides, playing so little for them probably added three years to my career."

No longer possessing the speed that made him a great deep threat early in his career, Young nevertheless became a valuable clutch receiver for the 49ers, and his teammates recognized his leadership qualities by voting him the Len Eshmont award in 1981 as the most inspirational player.

The 49ers would need everything they could get from Hicks and Young, and all the others, to beat the Falcons. Atlanta had been the last team to beat the 49ers, and the Falcons were still only two games back; a win would bring them within one game of the 49ers, and many observers thought that might be the beginning of the end for the Niners.

Once again the 49ers got off to a fast start, taking a 10-0 lead into the dressing room at halftime after Montana threw a 14-yard touchdown pass to Fred Solomon and Ray Wersching kicked a 48-yard field goal.

The Falcons cut it to 10-7 in the third quarter as Steve Bartkowski drove them 75 yards to a score. At that point, the 49ers seemed in trouble, even though leading; their offense had sputtered and the Falcons had moved so easily on their last drive that it was obvious they would score at least one more touchdown.

But the 49ers had been an opportunistic team, seemingly able to make the big play or drive when they most needed it, and they displayed that ability once again, quickly driving 76 yards in 13 plays.

They used everything in the drive, including reverses by both Solomon and Dwight Clark and a run-pass option by Ricky Patton, who chose to run.

On third down from the Atlanta three, Montana lobbed a pass high to the back of the end zone, giving Young a chance to leap high above the smaller Atlanta defensive backs to make the catch...which he did.

"We had three plays like that in the game plan," Montana said. "They call it a 'drift.' I ran to the right, and Charle runs along the end line from the right to the left and then back to the right."

At 17-7, the 49ers felt pretty confident, even though Ronnie Lott was thrown out of the game with 5:39 left when he slugged Atlanta receiver Alfred Jackson while San Francisco's Saladin Martin was returning his first NFL interception.

"I don't even know what happened," said Lott. Television replays clearly showed him hitting Jackson, and teammates thought he might have hit Jackson more than once, but it's entirely possible that Lott didn't know he had done it.

Lott undergoes an amazing transformation when he puts on a uniform. Away from football he is mild-mannered and soft-spoken, but he's a tiger on the field. Many players experience somewhat similar changes, but Lott's is extreme. It's almost as if he's playing in a hypnotic trance. That concentration is one reason he is a superior player, of course.

With just 2:23 left, the 49ers still held that 17-7 lead and seemed to be in control. That feeling didn't last long. Bartkowski, thought by some to be the best quarterback in the game, engineered a classic drive, taking the Falcons 76 yards to a touchdown in just six plays. More remarkably, taking just one timeout (plus the timeout at the two-minute warning), he used only 40 seconds on the clock. He passed 25 yards to Jackson for the touchdown, and Mick Luckhurst added the PAT to make it 17-14.

Everybody in the park knew what was coming next: an onside kick. It did—three times. The first two were nullified by penalties, one against each team. Luckhurst, a former soccer player who can kick with more precision than a kicker who's never known any sport but football, lofted another one down the west sideline. It was fumbled by the 49ers and recovered by the Falcons.

Shades of Preston Riley! Forty-Niner fans who could remember 1972 were convinced that the Falcons would sweep down the field and score, and that almost happened.

The Falcons advanced to the San Francisco 17, where they had first-and-ten with still 1:23 remaining, plenty of time for Bartkowski to work on the 49er secondary, crippled by the loss of Lott, their best defender.

It was the time coaches call "gut checks," when the butterflies start fluttering in the stomachs because the game is up for grabs. The 49ers of previous years had lost games just like this one, but not this team, not this year. The Los Angeles game, when the 49ers stopped those five fourth-quarter drives, had given the young 49ers the equivalent of a season's experience under great pressure. Nothing fazed them anymore.

Bartkowski went back to pass. He thought he had Junior Miller open, but Hicks came over from the middle, where he had been helping double-cover Jenkins, to make a game-saving interception at the three-yard line.

"I got a good look at Bartkowski, and he was following the primary receiver [Miller] all the way," said Hicks. "Because of the pass rush, he didn't have time to look anywhere else."

That last comment by Hicks was a telling one: once again the 49er defense was controlling the flow of the game, forcing the other team to do something it didn't want to do.

That had been true throughout the Atlanta game, in marked contrast to the first time the teams had met. In the first game, the Falcons controlled the ball with their excellent running attack and exploited the 49er defense with long passes.

In this game, though, the 49ers neutralized the Atlanta runners, who gained only 74 yards and averaged just 2.9 a carry, and their pass rush kept Bartkowski from throwing long. He was pressured so much that he started to go to quick, slant-in passes. They were effective at times, but that wasn't what he wanted to throw. Any time you can force a team to change from what it does best, you've taken a big step toward victory.

For the first time, 49er players started talking about the playoffs; Young even said they were concerned not just about making the playoffs but about getting a record good enough to play at home.

Their confidence was understandable. The win over the Falcons had pushed the San Francisco record to 8-2. Meanwhile, the Falcons and Rams, who lost to New Orleans, were three games back at 5-5. And the win had stretched the 49er streak to seven games.

When would it all end?

9

THE STREAK ENDS

Next week, to the Cleveland Browns on a gloomy, early winter day at Candlestick.

Perhaps it was a consolation to the 49ers that relatively few people saw this game. A violent storm had hit on Thursday of that week, drenching the Bay Area with near-record rainfall, and more of the same had been predicted for Sunday. As it turned out, though the skies threatened to loose buckets at any moment, just a few drops fell during the game. Only 52,455 fans defied the weather forecaster to come to Candlestick, the smallest crowd since the second home game, against New Orleans.

Nor was the game televised locally, an irony because former 49er quarterback John Brodie was working his first game involving the 49ers in his eight-year broadcasting career with NBC.

Brodie talks frequently with 49er coach Bill Walsh, and sometimes even drops by the team's Redwood City offices to look at game films. He has nothing but praise for Walsh and his organizational skills: "He knows exactly what he wants and how to go about getting it."

As a former quarterback, Brodie especially liked Joe Montana, for many of the same reasons that Walsh did. He thought observers who criticized Montana because he couldn't throw the ball from one end of the field to the other were missing the point.

"It isn't only the spiral a passer puts on the ball, or the

length he can throw it, or how he scrambles out of the pocket, or even the way he reads defenses," said Brodie.

"It's all those things, yes, but it's that other thing, the intangible. It's a feeling of command, maybe even a little arrogance. Montana has it."

Brodie was partial, because he had pushed Walsh to draft Montana in the first place—not that Walsh needed much of a push.

"I saw Joe Montana a couple of times with Notre Dame and clearly he was quality stuff," said Brodie. "Then at the CBS Hall of Fame dinner, I sat next to Montana. We chatted for perhaps 40 minutes and I was impressed by his attitude.

"I really wanted Montana to be a 49er and I talked with Bill Walsh before the 1979 draft. I wasn't telling him anything—he wanted Montana, too—and I think his enthusiasm increased as we spoke of Montana's cool. Bill thought Montana would be available in the second round."

Before the draft, Walsh went to the Los Angeles area (Montana had moved there two months before the draft) and worked Montana with UCLA running back James Owens. Walsh was impressed with them and wanted to draft both. What he knew (and Brodie didn't) was that he would draft Owens first.

When Owens was taken on the second round by the 49ers, Brodie made a quick phone call to the team offices to find out why Walsh hadn't taken Montana. Walsh admitted he was gambling that other teams hadn't rated Montana so highly. "I think we can get him on the third round," he told Brodie.

As he is so frequently, Walsh was right. On the first round, Cincinnati had taken Jack Thompson and the New York Giants had drafted Phil Simms. Walsh liked Thompson but had known he would have no chance to get him, because the 49ers had no first-round pick (gone in the O.J. Simpson trade). He also liked Simms, and he might have been tempted to go for him had Simms slipped through to the second round.

Another quarterback, Steve Fuller, was taken by Kansas City on the second round, but Walsh had no interest in Fuller. He had gone to Clemson to watch Fuller work out and wasn't impressed, but the trip hadn't been wasted. On the tenth round that year, he drafted the receiver Fuller had thrown to in that workout, Dwight Clark.

Nobody was interested enough in Montana to draft him, even though he lasted almost all the way through the third round. The 49ers had traded their own pick on that round but had gotten Dallas's third-round pick in another trade. That meant they had to wait until Dallas's turn came up in the round, just two from the end, but Montana was still available.

"All it took was seeing him in a mini-camp to realize he was going to be something special," said Brodie.

Montana wasn't something special on this day against Cleveland and neither were his teammates. The 49ers were emotionally spent, and it showed in their error-filled play.

Their problem was understandable. There is only so much the human psyche can take. The 49ers had won a club record seven in a row (the 1948 team won ten straight, but that was in the All-America Conference, and the NFL doesn't recognize AAC statistics), and most of them had been big games. In the last five weeks, they had beaten Dallas, Los Angeles, Pittsburgh, and Atlanta, and Los Angeles was coming up the next week.

The offense was especially flat, unable to score a touchdown for the first time since Walsh had been 49er coach. Five times in the first three quarters, the 49ers drove within the Cleveland 25-yard line and each time had to settle for a Ray Wersching field goal, coincidentally every one from 28 yards.

A sixth opportunity came with a Dwight Hicks interception that put the ball on the Cleveland 31; that chance was wasted when Montana threw three incomplete passes.

Everything seemed to go wrong for the 49ers. Montana was penalized for intentionally grounding when he threw the ball away to prevent being tackled in the end zone; the penalty gave the Browns a two-point safety, the same result that a sack would have brought. A Walt Easley run to the Cleveland two, which would probably have set up a 49er touchdown, was nullified by a 15-yard penalty when Easley slugged Cleveland cornerback Ron Bolton after his run. Fred Dean bruised his sternum and missed most of the fourth quarter.

With all that, the 49ers still had a 12-5 lead at the beginning of the fourth quarter and were in position to put the game out of reach of the struggling Browns when Niner Bill Ring recovered a fumbled punt by Dino Hall on the Cleveland 21. Even a San Francisco field goal might be enough, and a touchdown would certainly seal the victory.

On the first play, though, Montana threw to Clark, who fell on the slippery Candlestick turf. The pass was tipped by rookie corner Hanford Dixon and intercepted by Browns linebacker Dick Ambrose. That was the last opportunity the 49ers had to score.

In the broadcast booth, Brodie was telling his listeners, "Joe tried to make a great play out of a bad situation. He threw off balance. He doesn't do that too often. If he never did it, we'd all be bowing down to him."

Soon Hall redeemed himself by returning a punt 40 yards, and the game was about to turn around. With Dean, their best pass rusher, out of the game, the 49ers stayed in a 3-4 defense. Walsh had said the 49ers hoped to pressure Cleveland quarterback Brian Sipe with blitzes, but the tactic didn't work. Sipe eventually passed to Reggie Rucker for 21 yards and the touchdown that enabled the Browns to tie the game.

Rucker, a 12-year veteran, fooled 49er corner Eric Wright because he acted as if the pass weren't coming to him, waiting until the last second to put up his hands to catch it. "That's one of the finest plays by a wide receiver I've seen in some time," Brodie said. "He turned Wright around, and Wright couldn't react because he didn't know the ball was there."

The Browns had one drive left, and again, the 49ers felt the absence of Dean. The key play was a 38-yard pass from Sipe to Rucker on the first-and-twenty, a situation in which the 49ers normally use a 4-3 defense, including Dean. Without him, they were in a 3-4 and couldn't effectively pressure Sipe.

With 43 seconds left Matt Bahr kicked a 24-yard field goal, giving Cleveland the 15-12 win and ending the 49ers' streak. Ironically, Bahr had played for the 49ers earlier in the season, while Wersching was out with a pulled muscle. When Wersching returned, Walsh traded Bahr because he felt Wersching was the more reliable kicker. "Ray has just made so many pressure kicks for us," said Walsh.

It's a reasonable assumption that if Dean had not been injured, the 49ers would have won the game. In the first three quarters Cleveland passed for 72 yards; on the fourth-period drives, when Dean was out, Sipe passed for 93.

Still, Walsh was more concerned with his team's offensive failures. "Our failure to score is very obviously what cost us," he said. "We finally ran into a situation where we put too much pressure on our own defense. When one single touchdown beats you, obviously you have to improve."

But though the 49ers lost, they stayed three games ahead in the NFC West because both Atlanta and Los Angeles lost. Now, with only five games left, the 49ers had a chance to bury the Rams by winning in Anaheim the next Sunday. They'd be ready.

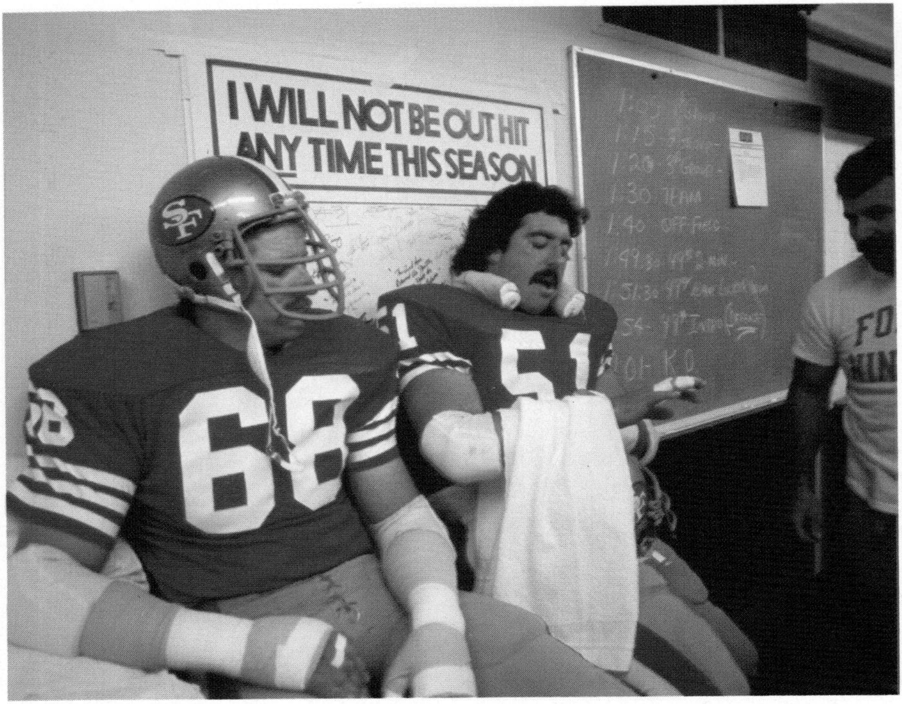

I WILL NOT BE OUT HIT
ANY TIME THIS SEASON

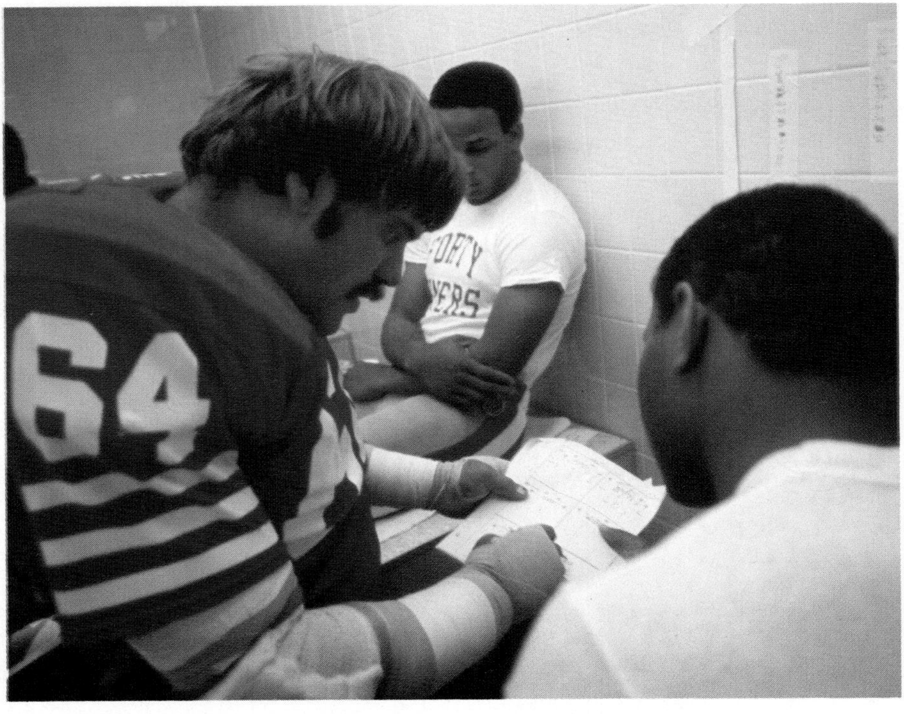

(Overleaf) Bill Walsh listens to assistants calling from press box. (top left) John Ayers and Randy Cross await the start of Super Bowl. (bottom left) Jack Reynolds advises Bobby Leopold as Ronnie Lott watches. (top right) Eric Wright sits quietly; cheerleaders look happy. (bottom right) Norb Hecker tells linebackers what Bengals will do.

(left) Joe Montana fades to pass in the Super Bowl behind blocking of Randy Cross, left, and Fred Quillan, right. (top right) Fred Solomon outduels Cincinnati cornerback Louis Breeden to make over-the-head catch. (bottom right) Dwight Clark is brought down after catching pass for good gain.

(upper left), Fred Solomon, John Ayers and Randy Cross lead Lenvil Elliott on a sweep against Dallas. (lower left) Solomon gains 12 on reverse that helped set up winning touchdown in NFC championship game. (right) Joe Montana scores the first touchdown on a quarterback sneak in the Super Bowl.

BREEDEN
34

49
FIELD JUDGE
6

(left) Earl Cooper leaps high in joy after scoring touchdown on Joe Montana pass in Super Bowl. (top right) Charle Young is upended after catching pass in Super Bowl — but he hangs on to the ball. (bottom right). The 49er defense stacks up Cincinnati's Pete Johnson at the goal line in third quarter.

WERSHING
14

(left) Ray Wersching kicks clinching field goal in Super Bowl. (top right) Jack Reynolds makes tackle against Giants in playoff. (bottom right) Fred Dean closes on Dallas QB Danny White in championship game.

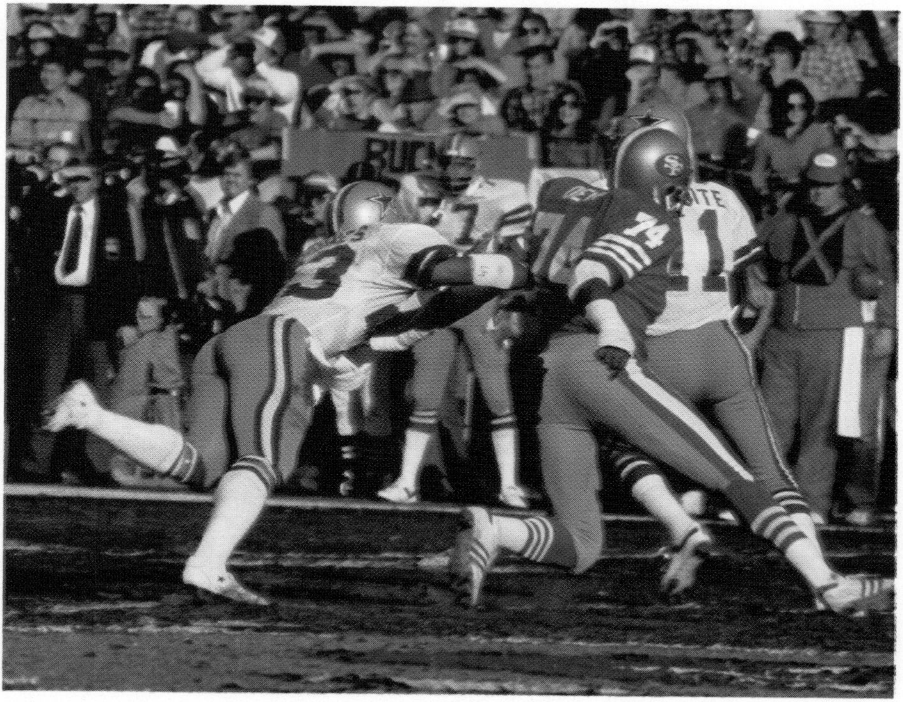

(top left) Archie Reese makes key quarterback sack of Ken Anderson in Super Bowl. (bottom left) Eric Wright intercepts Anderson pass in closing minutes. (right) Ronnie Lott and Dwight Hicks leap high in celebration as the 49ers win the Super Bowl.

42
22

68
16

(left) Charle Young signals touchdown after Joe Montana sneaks over in Super Bowl. (top right) NFL commissioner Pete Rozelle hands Vince Lombardi Trophy to 49er owner Ed DeBartolo Jr., as Bill Walsh claps. (bottom right) Forty-Niner fans show their feelings. (overleaf) Fans throng Market Street for 49er parade.

PRISE BANK
RST
ENTERPRISE
BANK

10

RAMS FALL AGAIN

The Los Angeles Rams were having a quarterback controversy. That was hardly news; the Rams *always* have a quarterback controversy. In the fifties, it had been Bob Waterfield and Norm Van Brocklin, and then, Van Brocklin and Billy Wade. More recently, it had been Pat Haden and whoever else was there: James Harris, Ron Jaworski, Vince Ferragamo. Now, it was Haden and Dan Pastorini, formerly of the Houston Oilers and Oakland Raiders.

The first Ram quarterback controversy didn't really hurt the team because the coach could choose between two quality players. What difference did it make if he sent Waterfield or Van Brocklin in to throw that 80-yard touchdown pass?

But Haden and Pastorini weren't in that class. Each had significant weaknesses.

Haden was smart, a Rhodes scholar in fact, a good leader and a good athlete, but because of his size he had been fighting an uphill battle since he joined the Rams.

In an off-season conversation a couple of years ago, Haden demonstrated to me that, with his straight overhand throwing style, he actually released the ball only a couple of inches lower than taller quarterbacks who threw with a three-quarters or sidearm motion.

But the question was less whether Haden could throw over defensive linemen than if he could see over them. True, Johnny Unitas was only a couple of inches taller than Haden, but he had played in an era when the linemen weren't so tall. Fran Tarkenton, perhaps just an inch taller, had been a scrambler who had rolled out so he could see downfield. Haden was more of a classic dropback passer and a good one; John McKay had called him the best college quarterback he had coached.

Pastorini had everything Haden lacked physically. He could throw the ball accurately and as far as any quarterback in the game. He had the size scouts look for in a pro quarterback, and he was a courageous player who had played with injuries throughout his career. But Pastorini was a very erratic personality, often in trouble. He had fought with a sportswriter, he had run his car into a tree, he had been hurt racing a speedboat.

Pastorini had been released by Oakland earlier in the year for unexplained reasons, though some thought it was because he had told Oakland owner Al Davis that he wasn't willing to be a reserve behind both Jim Plunkett and second-year quarterback Marc Wilson. Others thought it was because of his off-field behavior. But Davis isn't a man who cuts players because of their actions away from the field. Davis obviously felt Pastorini couldn't help the Raiders, and Davis makes very few mistakes on player judgments.

Even with that background, though, Pastorini would be starting for the Rams against the 49ers. Rams coach Ray Malavasi felt he had to try something; the Rams were 5-6 and very close to being mathematically eliminated in the NFC West.

The 49ers had troubles of their own. Because of his bruised sternum, Fred Dean couldn't play, and the fourth quarter of the Cleveland loss had shown what a difference Dean's absence made to the 49er defense.

There were a lot of questions about the San Francisco offense, too. The 49ers, as Walsh pointed out, had been an opportunistic team on offense, scoring when they had to in every game but the Cleveland loss, but they'd gotten by with a minmum of production since the Dallas win. They had scored only two offensive touchdowns against Los Angeles, Pittsburgh, and Atlanta, a single TD against Green Bay, and none against Cleveland—only seven touchdowns in five games.

Clearly, they had been leaning too much on their defense, and their defense wouldn't be able to shut down the Rams this time, without Dean, as it had in the first game. Had the bubble burst?

It hadn't, but it took the 49ers three-plus hours and the most exciting game yet to prove that. The first game between the teams had been thrilling because of the incredible fourth-quarter tension and pressure of the 49er defense. This one was a wide-open offensive show, with enough spectacular plays to mount a lengthy highlight film. The lead changed hands four times; three times the game was tied, and first the Rams then the 49ers performed late-game heroics when all seemed lost.

The game started slowly, with Ray Wersching's 47-yard field goal for the 49ers the only scoring in the first quarter.

The tempo picked up considerably in the second quarter. First, Frank Corral kicked a 44-yard field goal to tie the game, and then the Rams drove 80 yards on 11 plays to take the lead. Pastorini hit running back Wendell Tyler on a 22-yard pass on third-and-seven for the touchdown.

The 49ers came back with an explosive drive, 74 yards in just five plays. Montana passed for 44 and 28 yards to Fred Solomon for most of the yardage, and Johnny Davis surged over for the last yard and the TD.

Before the half, the Rams came back with another 80-yard drive, this one taking 13 plays. A pass interference call against Saladin Martin gave the Rams a first down on the seven. Two plays later Mike Guman threw to Preston Dennard on a run-pass option for the touchdown. Corral's PAT gave the Rams a 17-10 halftime advantage.

That lead lasted only 18 seconds into the third quarter. Amos Lawrence caught the second-half kickoff on his eight, broke a tackle by Joe Harris at the 29 and another by LeRoy Irvin at the 34, and them outraced everybody for a touchdown.

This was the first kick return for a touchdown by the 49ers all season, and an especially gratifying one for Lawrence, who had been so close to breaking away in two other games.

Lawrence had been a late acquisition for the 49ers, coming to the team in September in a trade with the San Diego Chargers, who couldn't reach a contract agreement with their fourth-round draft pick. Though Walsh thought highly of Lawrence's future with the club, that late arrival had kept him from being used for more than an occasional play from scrimmage.

"He really needs a training camp," said Walsh. "He played in an entirely different formation [the I formation] in college, and it's been a tough learning experience for him here.

"Maybe if we had a simple offense, he'd be able to fit in better, but he's had to learn things week to week. He'll learn a few plays one week, and then have to go to another set the next week.

"Because he doesn't know the offense, we haven't been able to use him much. We couldn't be sure he'd be in the right place on a pass pattern, for instance, and in these close games, that could be critical.

"But, I think he can be a real help. He's not terribly elusive, but he's got quick feet and he kind of slides off tacklers. And I think he has a real potential as a pass receiver coming out of the backfield. It's possible that in a couple of years, maybe even next year, he could be the kind of guy who catches fifty, sixty balls."

Lawrence's return began the best stretch for the 49ers that November afternoon, as they scored 17 points without answer from the Rams.

The Niners next score came from Wersching, who kicked a 34-yard field goal after a long drive—with a 23-yard pass from Montana to Dwight Clark and a 14-yard run by Davis—had bogged down at the Los Angeles 17.

Then Ronnie Lott showed the mental awareness that, as much as his tremendous physical ability, sets him apart from other defensive backs.

"I try to pick up everything that happens on a football field," he says. "The body movements of other players, the way that they carry themselves. Football is a game of emotions. Everybody shows them. You can pick up what's going through people's minds."

On this occasion the Rams' Billy Waddy ran a semi-curl in front of Lott. Waddy was wide open, but Pastorini didn't see him. Waddy ran straight to Pastorini after the play had ended and before the Rams huddled. "I figured he was telling Pastorini about the play," said Lott.

Waddy was, and Pastorini came back to him on the next play. Lott was prepared; he cut in front of Waddy to grab the interception and returned it 25 yards for a touchdown.

It was Lott's third interception touchdown of the season, tying an NFL rookie record and equaling the 49ers' *career* record for interceptions returned for touchdowns.

"I don't want to just play a position," Lott says. "I want to make big plays. When you get the ball, don't be satisfied with that. You try to score. When you make an interception and don't do anything with it—that's nothing."

That interception caused Malavasi to change quarterbacks, and Haden came off the bench firing. He immediately drove the Rams 80 yards in nine plays to cut the 49er lead to 27-24. The key play was his 43-yard pass to Drew Hill, and he got the touchdown with a two-yard flip to Walt Arnold.

Wersching gave the 49ers a little more breathing room by hitting his seventh straight field goal, this one from 32 yards, with 4:50 elapsed in the fourth quarter.

The ensuing kickoff backed the Rams to their own ten, and then Haden started an excruciating drive which typified the entire game: sudden ups and downs, accompanied by nail-biting tension.

At least three times, the 49ers seemed to have the Rams stopped. And three times, the Rams came back. On third-and-18 from the Los Angeles 29, Haden hit Dennard on a 22-yard pass that gave the Rams a first down on the San Francisco 49. On third-and-five on the next series, Haden hit Tyler for a seven-yard gain for the first. And on fourth-and-three from the San Francisco 30, Haden hit Guman for a 14-yard gain.

A pass interference call against Willie Harper brought the ball to the one, and Tyler scored from there. Corral's PAT put the Rams on top, 31-30.

The tension-filled drive had consumed eight minutes. The 49ers had only 1:51 left, and the depressing turn of events would probably have beaten a lesser team. "The 49ers have never had poise before," recalled Jack Reynolds, later, who knew what it had been like in his days with the Rams. "I remember in '79, they had us on the ropes, but they couldn't put us away. A lot of times, they would have just folded their tent."

Not anymore. Now the 49ers had Joe Montana and Ray Wersching, two consummate clutch performers. From the time Wersching had joined the club in 1977 until the end of the 1980 season, the 49ers had won only 15 games, and his kicks had decided six of them at the end of the fourth quarter or in overtime. So far in 1981, his field goals had been the difference in four 49er wins.

Montana's trademark had always been his ability to bring a team back. At Notre Dame, he had done it six times during his career, the most spectacular being the Cotton Bowl in his senior year. Notre Dame trailed Houston, 34-12, going into the fourth quarter, but Montana's heroics produced a 35-34 victory, the winning touchdown coming on his pass to Kris Haines on the last play of the game.

He had done much the same with the 49ers, and had come to be known for his poise, especially in the last two minutes, the time that separates the great quarterbacks from the average ones. "Most quarterbacks lose control right around here," says

Walsh. "They're trying to think of everything, and they can't think."

Montana, in contrast, shuts out everything but the relevant issues. The crowd noise doesn't intrude. He doesn't panic. He sees everything on the field and makes the play. He seems as calm as most quarterbacks are early in the second quarter of an exhibition game.

This time, he knew he had to drive the team just far enough to give Wersching a chance to kick a field goal. "We knew that if we got within 50 yards, Ray would kick it," said Randy Cross.

The winning drive began at the 49ers' 20. Three short completions and one run got the 49ers to their own 42, where they had second-and-one with 1:09 left.

A Montana pass on second down went just off Clark's fingertips. On third down, he had to throw the ball away because his receiver, Solomon, was covered.

Fourth down. One yard to go. The game was on the line. Walsh called for a sweep, but the Rams put two safeties up on the line, a defense that had stopped the sweep effectively earlier in the game.

Montana changed the play, calling an audible for a play where right guard Cross pulls out to block the defensive lineman coming between left guard John Ayers and center Fred Quillan, and Paul Hofer rams into the hole. "I was scared," admitted Montana, but Hofer got two yards and the first down.

Three plays later, on third-and-five, Montana threw to Clark for 16 yards, giving the 49ers a first down on the Los Angeles 35. They were almost within field goal range now.

Then Montana improvised. Solomon and Clark were both on the left side, with Solomon flanked outside Clark. The quarterback thought the Rams' defense would be vulnerable if Clark ran ten yards deep and cut left. The 49ers hadn't run that play during the season and hadn't even practiced it since training camp, but Montana was right. Solomon cleared the area by going deep, and Montana threw to Clark at the 25, who then battled for five more yards.

Only 23 seconds remained, and the 49ers had just one timeout left. An incomplete pass stopped the clock. Earl Cooper got one yard into the center of the line. Montana let the clock run down to two seconds, so the game would end with the field goal attempt, and then used the Niners final timeout.

Montana came into the huddle and said, "This has to be perfect." It was. Cross, who snaps the ball for placekicks, put the ball back on line, Montana put it down, and Wersching kicked it through. The 49ers had won, 33-31.

It wasn't pretty, but it was a win, and the 49ers had beaten the Rams twice in the same season for the first time since 1965. The Rams, at 5-7, were out of the race, and the 49ers were only one win from clinching the divisional title.

"I'm in shock about what we're doing," admitted Reynolds. "I won't say we're for real. We're lucky, very lucky, but it has been a very pleasant experience, very gratifying. That drive showed we have real character and a backbone."

And Walsh had a word of advice for the losing coach. "Pat Haden is a great quarterback. I cannot understand the controversy."

11

THE 49ERS CLINCH

It had been nine years since the 49ers had won a division title, but when they clinched the NFC West with a 17-10 win over the New York Giants the next Sunday, they acted as if it were just another ball game.

Oh, there was a little ceremony as some players, led by Ronnie Lott, carried coach Bill Walsh off the field, but that ended after a few steps. Paul Hofer seemed to be the only player really hit by the emotion of the moment. "When those last seconds were ticking off the clock, it was a phenomenal feeling," he said. "To be able to watch the fans who have stuck with us for so long, and the guys who have been through the hard times—it was just great."

In the dressing room the players were quiet and subdued. Their post-game ritual was the same as always: they said a prayer, listened to a few words from Walsh, waited for the phone call from owner Edward DeBartolo, Jr., talked to the press.

There was no champagne, not even any beer; NFL rules prohibit alcohol in the dressing rooms, but more excited teams have been known to overlook that rule.

The 49ers were calm for a couple of reasons. One was that they had anticipated both their win, and the winning of a divisional title. They had, after all, been leading the division for most of the season and by a good margin much of that time. Only a complete reversal could have cost them the title.

But more importantly, for the first time they were allowing

themselves to think of the ultimate, the Super Bowl.

"I think everybody realizes how far we have an opportunity to go," said Keith Fahnhorst. "It feels good to have it wrapped up, but none of us are going to be satisfied with just the Western Division championship.

"The way it was right after the game, you'd have thought this was old hat for us, like it was the seventh time in the last eight years we'd won it."

Randy Cross observed that winning the division title after leading for so long was "almost anticlimactic," and added, "We've been winning and winning and winning. We've been hanging on for the whole year. Everybody outside of the team has been waiting for something to go wrong, but I think maybe we've proved something."

Jack Reynolds was the one 49er who was accustomed to winning; with the Rams, he had played on seven division winners in eight years. But Reynolds is the classic pessimist; to him, the glass is always half-empty. Teammates feel the more worried Reynolds is about an upcoming game, the more likely they are to win.

"We were very fortunate to beat the New Orleans Saints and we were very fortunate to beat the Chicago Bears," said Reynolds, "and those aren't two powerhouse teams. I don't know how we're doing it but as long as we're winning, that's all right."

Walsh was equally low-key. With tongue in cheek he told the media, "It appears we've won our division." Not everybody caught the humor in the remark; one columnist wrote some palpable nonsense about Walsh being worried about a jinx.

Walsh *was* worried about his running, even in victory. Montana had been forced to pass 39 times, far too many, because the 49er running game could do little against the defensively tough Giants. Indeed, Montana had the longest 49er run of the day, 20 yards.

"I think we're playing at close to one hundred percent efficiency week after week," he said. "That's almost unheard of in the NFL in recent years. But we don't dominate anybody because we don't have that big runner."

Even while savoring the championship, Walsh was thinking of what he could do to solve the running back problem the next year. Because of their record, the 49ers would be drafting low, and Walsh thought he might have to trade a couple of picks to move higher in the first round. "To be honest," he said, "I thought we'd have a fairly high drafting position next year. But I prefer this."

Still, though the 49ers treated the win rather lightly, the title was a considerable accomplishment. They were the first team in the entire NFL to clinch a division title, and they hadn't backed in. They had beaten their chief rivals, Los Angeles and Atlanta, when they had to.

Their ten wins equaled the best a San Francisco team had ever done in the NFL, and represented as many wins as the team had had in its three previous seasons combined! This year was only the second winning season since 1972.

Even the way the win over the Giants was accomplished was a good sign. This was precisely the kind of dull, patternless game the 49ers had lost so often in the recent past. This time they won it.

Because of the importance of the game, there was apprehension in the 49er locker room before the players came out, but that didn't show in the early play. As had been true so many times this season, the 49ers got on the board first and never trailed thereafter.

The first touchdown came after Dwight Hicks returned an interception 54 yards to the New York 15. It was slow going for the 49ers from that point, but Johnny Davis finally pushed across from the one on the drive's seventh play.

Another break, this one a Keena Turner recovery of a fumble by Giants running back Rob Carpenter, set up the second San Francisco touchdown. The 49ers started on the New York 40 this time, and Montana's 20-yard run on a quarterback draw produced the touchdown.

Montana's run was the longest for a 49er since the second game of the season and the third longest of the year, a telling indictment of the San Francisco running attack.

That lack of a running attack kept this game from being the blowout it really should have been. A minute later, Carlton Williamson recovered still another fumble for the 49ers, and a touchdown, maybe even a field goal, would have wrapped up the victory against a Giants' team long on defense but short on offense.

But the Giants stiffened this time. The 49ers got no points out of this possession, and the game was a struggle from that point.

Just before the half, Joe Danelo boomed through a 52-yard field goal to make it 14-3 at halftime. A scoreless third quarter followed, with neither team being able to move the ball with any consistency.

Then, on the first play of the fourth quarter, Rob

Carpenter scored on a three-yard run that capped a 76-yard drive for the Giants, drawing them to within 14-10 after Danelo's PAT.

But all season the 49ers had been able to come up with a sustained scoring drive when they most needed it, and now they did it again, saving a win that seemed in jeopardy. Joe Montana calmly took his team from the San Francisco 22 to the New York one, using up seven minutes in the drive.

At the 23 they faced a fourth-and-one; Walsh went for the first down, which Davis got, gaining two yards. But when the 49ers came down to fourth down again, this time on the one, Walsh went for the field goal. A delay-of-game penalty pushed the 49ers back five yards, but reliable Ray Wersching boomed a 23-yarder.

That forced the Giants to try to play catchup, which they don't do very well. New York got the ball three more times...and failed to make a single first down.

Finally, Williamson intercepted a Scott Brunner pass to end the game and clinch the divisional title for the 49ers. The fans, who had been waiting a long, long time for this moment, poured out of the stands, onto the field, singing, dancing, screaming their joy. Most of them seemed to have pennants, banners, or signs of some description, and the party on the field and later in the parking lot probably went on longer than the game itself.

The fans were deliriously happy.

Even if the players weren't.

12

REVENGE FOR WALSH

Not the least of Bill Walsh's coaching abilities is his knowledge of which psychological buttons to push in getting his team ready to play.

His approach at Stanford was an intellectual one. He knew his players were more intelligent than the average, which meant they could absorb his system quickly, but were likely to become rapidly bored by the repetitious football drills. So Walsh made his practices short and snappy, a model of economy, to lessen the boredom factor. He challenged his players to learn a system of far more complexity than anything they had known before. And he treated them like adults, not just football robots. His approach worked perfectly.

With the 49ers, he was dealing with players who were less intelligent and less sophisticated than those at Standford (with some obvious exceptions). He had told me when he took the job that he thought it would take three years to install a system he had essentially installed in a year at Stanford—and this was the third year.

He had adjusted his approach accordingly. He played heavily on the underdog theme, as in the preparation for Pittsburgh, for instance. If an opposing coach said anything that could be construed as denigration of the 49ers, it went up on the walls of the locker room at Redwood City. That infuriated some football writers, who thought of it as a high school tactic, but it wasn't aimed at writers.

As the 49ers prepared for Cincinnati, Walsh didn't have to worry about psychological ploys. His team knew what had to be done. "The players know that he wants this game bad," said Joe Montana. "I don't think it needs to be said."

But Walsh managed this time to con the Bengals, their coaching staff, and also some of the national media. He talked of how good the Bengals were, certainly no exaggeration. He talked of how much Cincinnati needed the game, which was also true. Though the Bengals had the same record as the 49ers—10-3—they were in a treacherous spot. If they lost to the 49ers, they could slip to only one game ahead of the Steelers, who had won three in a row, and they had to face the Steelers in Pittsburgh the next Sunday. Thus, a slight slump at this point and the Bengals could conceivably be tied with the Steelers.

Walsh also pointed out that the 49ers had clinched their title, and he implied that they might let down somewhat in the wake of that triumph. He added that he was looking for a spot to give playing time to reserves like quarterback Guy Benjamin and running back Amos Lawrence, who hadn't had much chance to play.

Walsh didn't say that he would start either player, or even that he would play his reserves a lot in this game, but some people leaped to that conclusion, the most conspicuous being Howard Cosell.

On ABC Radio's "Speaking of Sports," Cosell said, "Forty-Niner coach Bill Walsh says he'll play second-string players against Cincinnati. Because the 49ers have already clinched a playoff berth, that will give him a good excuse for losing, which the 49ers will do. It's wrong to play second-stringers. I know the Tony LaRussa theory—'Save your players and win when it counts.' The 49ers want to win in the playoffs, but it's still wrong."

That helped convince the Bengals that the 49ers wouldn't be at their best, but anybody who thought Walsh wouldn't go all out in this game didn't know the man at all.

Walsh was still resentful because he had been passed over for the head coaching job of the Bengals when Paul Brown had retired in 1975, even though he much preferred to be coaching and living in the Bay Area.

As offensive coordinator Walsh had been responsible for much of the Bengals' success from 1969 to 1975. He had been widely regarded as the heir apparent to Brown. But when the time came to name a successor after the 1975 season, Brown chose Bill Johnson, another assistant. The angry and disappointed Walsh left and joined the San Diego Charger staff.

Nobody ever knew quite why Walsh was passed over. Brown's one public statement, that he thought Walsh would want to return to California, was nonsense. Despite Walsh's admitted, and understandable, preference for California, his priority was a head coaching job on the pro level, which Brown fully understood. If all Walsh wanted was to return to California, he could have done that at any time by settling for an assistant's job, as he eventually did with San Diego.

Paul Brown is a curious man, capable of extremely vindictive actions. He harbors petty jealousies and smoldering anger. (In the book he did with Jack Clary, "PB: The Paul Brown Story," darts of rage fly off the pages.) It's possible that Walsh, unknowingly, did something that offended Brown. It's also possible, as some have suggested, that Brown thought Walsh was too scholarly to be an effective head coach.

It's probably more likely that just the opposite is true: Brown thought Walsh would be too *good* a head coach, which might cause people to forget how great a coach Brown himself had been.

There is no questioning the ability of Paul Brown, who's in the Pro Football Hall of Fame. He won on every level: high school, college, and pro. He took four straight AAC titles with the Cleveland Browns, and another three NFL titles and seven divisional titles. He turned the Bengals, an expansion team, into a division champion in three years; the Bengals were 11-3 in Brown's final season. During his 25 years as a pro coach, his teams won 213 games and lost only 104.

Paul Brown and his coaching innovations have had a tremendous influence on the game. He was the first, for instance, to use intelligence tests to determine a player's learning potential; to use notebooks and classroom techniques; to set up complete film clip statistical studies and grade his players from those studies. He was also the first coach to keep his players together in a hotel before a home game; others had done it only before games on the road.

Brown didn't want anybody to forget his contributions to football. The game is his life. The five years he spent out of football, after being fired by Cleveland owner Art Modell at the end of the 1962 season, were spent in La Jolla, California, the garden spot of the world. But Brown was miserable, a fish out of water, and he leaped at the chance to get back into pro football with the Bengals in 1968.

By selecting Johnson as his replacement, Brown could be

assured that his own legend wouldn't be tarnished. Johnson had some early success as a carry-over from Brown, but the Bengals went downhill so quickly that nobody could doubt that it had been Paul Brown's coaching that had made them successful: from 10-4 in Johnson's first year to 8-6 his second, and 0-5 in the portion of the third season he lasted before being fired.

As Johnson's replacement, Brown hired Homer Rice, a knowledgeable football man but one lacking the charisma a head coach needs; Rice was 4-7 in a partial season, 4-12 in his one full year.

Significantly it wasn't until criticism of the Bengals started to be directed at Brown, for dictating policy to his coaches and dominating the organization, that he finally hired a strong coach, Forrest Gregg.

Now Walsh was returning to Cincinnati, eager to prove to Brown and the Cincinnati fans that it had been a serious error to bypass him. His task wouldn't be easy. During their bad years the Bengals had been in a position to draft some excellent players, and many people in football thought Cincinnati was now the best team in the league. Their biggest star was quarterback Ken Anderson, whom Walsh had made into a top-flight pro player.

Anderson had played for small Augustana College in Illinois, where he had caught the eye of Brown's son, Pete, the personnel director. Another Brown son, Mike, then the assistant general manager, scouted him and was also impressed; then Walsh gave him a tryout and added his approval.

"He was a great, raw talent," says Walsh. "He was the biggest player on his team and the fastest."

The Browns grabbed Anderson on the third round in 1971, one pick before Atlanta; Falcons' coach Norm Van Brocklin was also set to draft the quarterback.

Walsh worked and worked with Anderson on the physical aspects of a quarterback's job, drilling him endlessly on such basics as dropping back into the pocket. Anderson had been a sprint-out passer in college but he soon became a classic pro passer, though he was often able to run for yardage when his protection broke down.

Walsh also worked on building up Anderson's confidence. One example came in Anderson's first pro year when he replaced starter Virgil Carter, who had hurt his shoulder, in a game against Green Bay. Trying to keep a drive going in the final seconds, the rookie quarterback was forced out of the pocket and tried to run for a first down. He came up short and the Packers won, 20-17.

As Anderson stepped into the locker room, he was met by Paul Brown. "Well, Anderson," said Brown, "there's another game you lost for us."

Walsh immediately took Anderson aside and talked to him for a long time to make certain Anderson's confidence wouldn't be destroyed, either by the game or Brown's remark.

Bob Trumpy, then a receiver for the Bengals and now a radio-TV announcer, noted another way that Walsh built up Anderson's confidence. "Walsh gave the receivers things to help Anderson," says Trumpy. "Even when he scrambled, there was someone for him to throw to. It was all set up. He always had a place to go."

"It's hard for me to describe Bill Walsh as a teacher," says Anderson, "because I think of him above all as a friend. We worked together and we spent time together off the field. We've kept in touch over the years. I guess the greatest things he gave me were solid, fundamental techniques and confidence in what I was doing."

Now Anderson would be trying to beat his friend, and vice versa.

The Bengals-49er game would be a tough, physical one. "It was emphasized all week long that we had to outhit them," said Randy Cross. "It was another of those games, like Pittsburgh, where you could feel that in the whole mood of the team."

The 49ers would force six turnovers—three interceptions and three fumbles—by a team that had a league and season low of 15 turnovers going into the game. Two of the fumbles were caused by jarring tackles by Ronnie Lott. And in the third period, Anderson was knocked out of the game with a bent toe after a dramatic sack by Bobby Leopold.

"Our team hits as hard as any in football," said Walsh.

The pattern of the game was established early. On Cincinnati's first possession, Anderson tried to pass to Isaac Curtis on third-and-seven from the San Francisco 43. Lott batted the ball into the air with his right hand and then caught it as it came back down.

After that, the 49ers drove 66 yards to score in 15 plays, with Montana throwing to Bill Ring for the final four yards. It was Joe's first touchdown pass in four games.

As with all the turnovers that followed, Lott's interception came when the 49ers were in a formation aimed at stopping the pass. Frequently the Bengals were forced into obvious passing situations, enabling the 49ers to control the game's tempo.

"All year we've been forcing teams to make turnovers," Anderson said as he left the stadium on crutches after the game. "Today we were forced to make them."

Sometimes the 49ers used their "nickel" defense (an extra defensive back in, a linebacker out). Sometimes they went further, adding a sixth defensive back to replace the second linebacker, because of tight end Dan Ross. "We weren't sure that we could handle Ross with a linebacker," said defensive coordinator Chuck Studley.

Whatever defense the 49ers played, they went after the Bengals. "We go out there with the idea of getting the ball for our offense," said Lott. "We've got an aggressive secondary. We're always looking for the ball. A couple of times today, if we were just looking to make the play instead of stealing the ball, they could have had completions."

Late in the second quarter the Bengals finally got on the scoreboard with a 30-yard field goal by Jim Breech, but it could have been worse for the Niners. One play before Carlton Williamson had knocked down a pass to Steve Kreider in the end zone, preventing a touchdown.

There was only 2:26 left in the half when the 49ers got the ball on their 20 following the Cincinnati kickoff—but that was Joe Montana time. Montana took his team 80 yards to score with just two seconds remaining in the half.

The key play of the drive came when Montana ran for 13 yards on a third-and-ten situation from the San Francisco 49; the 49ers got another 15 yards when the Bengals were called for unnecessary roughness.

The touchdown was a beauty. Dwight Clark was double-covered in the rear of the end zone but Montana was able to loft his pass over safety Bryan Hicks, and Clark kept his feet just inbounds for the touchdown.

The 49ers scored once more, midway through the fourth quarter, going 40 yards after Dwight Hicks recovered a fumble by Ross, induced by a Lott tackle. Montana ran for the final yard. Three touchdowns for San Francisco, one field goal for Cincinnati: 21-3.

In the Cincinnati dressing room, Gregg told the media after the game that he had noticed as early as Wednesday that the team was flat. He had known, he said, that the Bengals wouldn't play well.

"Can you believe that nobody asked him *why* they were flat for such an important game?" Walsh asked me later.

No.

Walsh had a lot to be happy with, and he flashed a big smile at reporters after the game. "I think it was a hard-fought game and the better team won," he said. "It was a pleasant victory, in particular for some of us who have represented the Bengals in the past."

The 49ers had won without star wide receiver Fred Solomon, out with a bruised kidney. They had gotten a big day from running back Earl Cooper, who had rushed for 57 yards in the second half, a major factor in protecting the lead. "Earl would be one of the premier runners in the NFL if he could run on artificial turf all the time," said Walsh.

Their 11-3 mark was the best in the NFL, and they were assured of hosting at least the first playoff game: the "home swamp" advantage, the *Chronicle*'s Ira Miller called it.

Significantly, the 49ers' most impressive wins had come over the two strongest teams they'd faced, Dallas and Cincinnati. Against the Bengals, the 49ers' defense had held the league's second most productive offense to a field goal. The Bengals, in fact, had gotten no further than the San Francisco 35 in the second half, until the final two minutes, when the game was out of reach.

And, yes, Howard, Bill Walsh did play his reserves—in the final six minutes.

13

THE NFL'S BEST RECORD

The year before, the 49ers had been playing for pride going into the final two games, trying to salvage something from a disappointing season.

This year they were playing for pride, too, but of a quite different sort: they wanted to finish with the best record in the league. Considering they had the worst record just two years before, such a turnaround would be an almost unparalleled feat, though the Chicago Cardinals had once done it. They came from the NFL's worst record (1-9) in 1945 to the best (9-3) in 1947.

For the Niners, the more practical matter of field advantage was also involved. If San Francisco won their last two games, they were assured of the home field for both the playoff round *and* the championsip game, assuming they won the playoff game. If the 49ers finished at 13-3, Dallas was the only team that could equal that record, and the fact that the 49ers had beaten the Cowboys in the regular season would be the tie-breaker in deciding the game site.

Playing at home would be an advantage because of fan support and the fact that the players' lives and practice schedules would not have any unusual disruptions. The field itself, getting more and more beat up, wasn't an advantage. Indeed, there were times when coach Bill Walsh thought it was a disadvantage.

"We have to play on it ten times a year," Walsh noted. "Other teams only have to worry about it once.

"There's nothing we can run that other teams can't, and it really restricts us. People look at our team and say, 'Where's your running? Where are your offensive statistics?' Well, a lot of that is the field, because there's really so little you can do. You can't run wide, you can't cut sharply."

It wasn't supposed to happen that way. "I had meetings with the people in charge before the start of the season," said Walsh. "The engineers were there, too. They had all the plans laid out and it was supposed to be a great field. Obviously, it didn't turn out exactly that way.

"I'm sure the people living a quarter of a mile away have better lawns. Maybe we should call them in and have them plant the field."

* * * *

The biggest play of the game against Houston came on the 49ers' first play from scrimmage, when Earl Cooper caught a screen pass, knocked over a couple of defenders, and bolted 41 yards. Though the play was wasted because the 49er drive was eventually stopped on fourth down at the Houston one, it was a sign that Cooper was playing back to his rookie year form.

Cooper had been the first draft pick the year before, and Walsh had made some extravagant comments about him, comparing him to Chuck Foreman as a combination runner-receiver.

It seemed that Walsh was right when Cooper rushed for 720 yards, on a 4.2 average, and caught 83 passes to lead the NFC and set a club record as a rookie.

But everything had gone wrong in 1981. At his best, Cooper was not a powerful inside runner, despite his size. He needed to be able to get some running room to make his gliding style effective. In 1981, he seemed tentative in his movements, and he was often tackled before he really got going. He was being used less and less, and when he was in the game, it was usually as a receiver, not a runner.

"I think the field bothered Earl a lot," said Walsh. "He couldn't get the footing he needed. And, to be honest, the blocking wasn't always quite good enough, either. Our players would hold their blocks but they wouldn't blast anybody away. That kind of block was enough for a runner who really slammed into the hole, but Earl isn't that kind of runner. I think it helped Earl when we got Johnny Davis, because that took the pressure off him to run inside,"

But Cooper had been coming back gradually. The week before, he had had his best day. Against Houston he was even better, gaining 115 yards rushing and receiving, all the more significant because it was achieved on a sloppy field, not the artificial turf on which he excelled. Cooper's teammates gave him a game ball for the first time since the first game of his rookie year, and he credited Walsh for his turnaround.

"I think he handled it well," said Cooper. "He didn't make me go out and try to get it all back in one game. He put me in to run around end, or catch passes, just using me to get my confidence back."

Walsh had deliberately downplayed Cooper's problems, too, seldom saying anything for publication while encouraging the second-year back privately. It helped, of course, that the 49ers took off so spectacularly because that took attention away from Cooper's failures.

It meant a lot, Joe Montana felt, to have Cooper back in form. "When Earl was in a slump," said Montana, "it was pass automatically when he came into a game. We tried to disguise a lot of it, but it didn't work out. We'd bring Johnny Davis in at the goal line, and you could just follow Johnny and that's where the ball's going to be. That's the way it had been."

With Cooper playing well, the 49ers showed a more varied attack down by the goal line. Their three third-quarter touchdowns, after a scoreless first half, came on a two-yard run inside by Ricky Patton, a three-yard run outside by Cooper, and a two-yard pass to Dwight Clark, who caught five passes to give him a club record 84 for the season.

With the game well in hand, Walsh put in Guy Benjamin for Montana in the fourth quarter. Benjamin, with his first chance all season to pass, completed seven of nine and got the final 49er touchdown with a 27-yard pass to Mike Wilson.

Earl Campbell, held to just 45 yards in 18 carries by the 49er defense, got Houston's only score with a one-yard plunge with only 47 seconds left. Toni Fritsch's PAT was blocked by Dwaine Board, and the 49ers won, 28-6.

* * * *

Because Dallas had lost to the New York Giants the day before, the 49ers had already clinched the home field for the NFC championship game before they even took the field against the Saints in New Orleans on the last Sunday of the season. That made Walsh's primary concern avoiding key injuries, and took Montana out of the game after only 19 minutes. Joe had already thrown two touchdown passes.

The game wouldn't have been close except for two consecutive fumbled kicks late in the first quarter. Fred Solomon fumbled a punt; the Saints recovered on the 18 and went on to score. Amos Lawrence fumbled the ensuing kickoff (twice!); the Saints recovered on the seven this time and scored again.

The 49ers had a chance to score just before halftime, but Benjamin threw an interception that he later called "the stupidest play of my life." The play started as a screen pass; when Benjamin saw the Saints had the play covered, he tried to throw to Clark in the end zone, behind two defenders.

"I thought I saw something," said Benjamin, "but when you think, you don't throw it. You only throw it when you know."

But Benjamin later redeemed himself. After the Saints had taken a 17-14 lead with a third-quarter field goal, Guy took the 49ers on a seven-play, 79-yard drive in which he completed all three passes he threw, one of them against a blitz, for 48 yards. "I thought he moved the ballclub well," Clark said. "It's nice to know that if Joe should get hurt, we've got a capable quarterback who can come in."

Interestingly, Benjamin had played for the Saints the year before. "It was a fun game because I knew practically everybody on the field," he said.

Sloppy though it was, the win gave the 49ers some individual and team satisfactions. Clark caught one pass to raise his team record to 85, and he became the second straight 49er to win the NFC receiving title (Cooper won the previous year).

Their 13 wins were a franchise record, exceeding the 12 by the 1948 club, in the All-America Conference. Their sixth straight road win was another club record, and their six-game margin over second-place Atlanta was the third biggest spread in NFL history. Only unbeaten Miami (1972) and the Rams (1975) had had seven-game margins.

"We can take tremendous pride in having the best record in the NFL," said Walsh. "Regardless of what happens in the playoffs, that's a significant achievement."

14

GIANTS BAFFLED

Nobody knew Bill Walsh better than John Ralston did. At one time Walsh had been an assistant on Ralston's staff at Stanford. More recently, Ralston had worked as a front office assistant to Walsh with the 49ers, before leaving to pursue a chance to coach a team in the United States Football League, which was still on the drawing board.

And nobody was more amazed with what Walsh was accomplishing than Ralston.

"Everybody talks about the defense," said Ralston, "but it's the offense that's winning for them. Bill has done things with the offense that nobody thought could be done.

"Number one, he's put in a new game plan every week. We coaches have always thought that you had to drill players over and over before they could do anything, but Bill has run through things two or three times and expected players to do it right in the game.

"And they have. Oh, once in a while you see Joe Montana call a timeout because he's not sure exactly what formation they're supposed to be in, but by and large, they've run the offense as well as anybody could.

"The other thing Bill has done is to anticipate what defense the other team will be in and call the play to beat it.

"For instance he'll anticipate that the defense will be a 'five-under zone.' [Three linebackers and two defensive backs in shallow drops and two safeties playing deep.]

"He'll call for a guard to pull out, as if they're running a screen. The defensive backs see that and stay in tight, and a receiver like Dwight Clark will just slip through that first line of defense and be wide open.

"If the other team comes out in a man-to-man, he'll run picks, and again, a receiver will be open somewhere. I'm just amazed at the way he can anticipate."

This time Walsh's preparation would be for the Giants, who had beaten the Philadelphia Eagles in the wild-card playoff game, and he was planning something quite different from the first time the teams had met.

"I just hope it doesn't rain, because that would take away some of the things we'd like to do," he told me, as he outlined the basics of his game plan.

First the 49ers would try to throw deep early in the game. They hadn't done that against the Giants the first time, nor against other teams very often, and Walsh thought the element of surprise would work in his team's favor. The only concern was at left tackle, because Dan Audick was basically a guard playing tackle, but again, the element of surprise would help.

Second, the 49ers would pass to set up the run. Most teams, fearing the blitzing pressure of rookie New York linebacker Lawrence Taylor, had tried to "establish their running game" against the Giants. That conservatism played into the hands of the Giants, and was no doubt one reason the Giants had won four in a row since losing to the 49ers. Walsh would not make that mistake. "If the weather is decent, we plan to throw on 16 of our first 22 plays," he said.

Third, Taylor would have to be neutralized. "He has to be blocked like a lineman," said Walsh of the 245 pound Taylor. Since Johnny Davis was the only 49er back who could block Taylor on a blitz, the 49ers would try to seal off Taylor by blocking him with a lineman—guard John Ayers.

Defensively, the aim would be to stop running back Rob Carpenter. It had been the acquisition of Carpenter in mid-season that had sparked the Giants' drive to the playoff, and he had been the big factor in the Giants' win over the Eagles. Ironically, the 49ers had talked to Houston about acquiring Carpenter earlier in the year, but Houston's asking price at the time was too high.

"He reminds me a lot of [Mark] Van Eeghen of the Raiders," said Walsh, "but he's better."

The game a couple of days later took place just the way

Walsh had outlined it. His offensive game plan worked to perfection.

As he had said, the 49ers threw 16 passes on the first 22 plays. They passed when the New Yorkers least expected it, seven times on the first 12 first downs, for instance.

Montana threw long from the start. The first two bombs misfired, the first because he slightly underthrew Fred Solomon and the second because Solomon clipped. But eventually, Montana and Solomon connected on a 58-yard touchdown pass, and that kind of threat opened up the Giants' defense for shorter passes.

Taylor was neutralized because the 49ers never made the mistake other teams had of not putting anybody in front of him. "Taylor has been most effective when he's coming in from the split side," pointed out Hank Stram. "When the end is split and there's nobody in front of him, he's got a lot of room to go after the quarterback."

The 49ers often lined somebody up directly opposite Taylor—either Clark or one of the tight ends, Charle Young or Eason Ransom. Other times they had Ayers blocking him, and even if the play went to the other side, Taylor was blocked to keep him from pursuing the play.

As a result of the 49ers' strategy, the Giants were often forced to have Taylor drop back in pass coverage, where he was much less disruptive, instead of blitzing. When he did try to blitz, he was usually blocked. Montana was able to operate without worry about Taylor's harassment.

The other critical factor in the 49ers' offensive success was their ability to force the Giants into misreading plays.

"The 49ers throw so many different things at you," noted Stram, an admitted admirer of Walsh, "that it's really difficult to defense them. They've got different men in motion; they line up differently at times."

Some of the things the 49ers showed the Giants in the first half alone:

—Twice they faked reverses, which set up the real thing at a critical point in the second half.

—Montana faked a run to one side and then hit a quick pass to the other.

—On a play-action fake, Ricky Patton carried out his fake so well that he was tackled—at about the same time Solomon was catching a pass behind the Giant coverage for a touchdown.

—On a third-and-one situation, Walsh called on Earl Cooper, the least likely back to carry on a short-yardage situation, and Cooper slanted off-tackle and to the outside for 20 yards.

—Twice they lined up with two wide receivers in the backfield.

Sometimes the plays worked; sometimes they didn't. But they accomplished Walsh's main purpose: the Giants were constantly off balance. Their great linebackers were confused, often caught thinking pass when the 49ers were running, or vice versa. Forty-Niner receivers were getting wide open in the Giants' secondary. Clark was literally 20 yards away from a defender on one completed pass.

The Giants were so baffled by the 49er offense that the 49ers were able to score 38 points, a total exceeded only by their outburst against Dallas early in the season. In turn, they forced the Giants out of their game plan, which was to control the play with their defense and Carpenter's running. The Giants had to throw twice as often as they ran, and Carpenter was never a factor, with just 61 yards in 17 carries.

The only problem was the 49er defense was giving up points almost as easily, and sometimes more quickly, than the 49er offense was scoring. Suffering an obvious case of playoff nerves, the rookie defensive backs played like...well, like rookies. Mixups on passes that should have been short gains at best resulted in 59-and 72-yard touchdowns, and the Giants' second-year quarterback, Scott Brunner, passed for 290 yards, the most any quarterback had gotten against the 49ers all season.

Scott Brunner?

Once again the 49ers scored first, on an eight-yard pass from Montana to Young in the first quarter, but the Giants tied it up on the first of the bizarre plays by the 49er secondary.

Brunner threw a pass to Earnest Gray that should have been good for 12 yards. Carlton Williamson, in position to tackle Gray, took his eyes off the receiver because he thought the ball would be intercepted. It wasn't, Williamson missed his tackle, Ronnie Lott and Dwight Hicks collided, and Gray went 72 yards for a touchdown.

Then the 49ers hit a hot stretch that should have put the game out of reach. First Ray Wersching hit a 22-yard field goal on the first play of the second quarter. Amos Lawrence had returned the kickoff (following Gray's touchdown) for 47 yards to the New York 45, and Montana had set up the field goal with a 38-yard pass to the wide-open Clark.

Next, Montana hit Solomon on a 58-yard touchdown pass that was the best-executed play of the afternoon. The faking by

Montana and Patton was so good that blitzing linebacker Harry Carson, in position to sack Montana, turned around and tackled Patton instead.

Keena Turner recovered a fumble on the New York 41, and three plays later, Patton raced 25 yards for a touchdown, his second-longest run of the season. Wersching's PAT added to the 49ers comfortable lead, 24-7.

Then Joe Danelo's 48-yard field goal made it 24-10 at the intermission and, though the 49ers had trouble moving the ball in the third quarter and couldn't score at all, they would still have been safely in the lead but for another of those fluke plays in the secondary.

This time it was a gamble by Lott that misfired. Covering Johnny Perkins on a short pass, he was confused by the tight end's move. He tried for an interception and missed, and Perkins went 59 yards for a touchdown. Danelo's PAT made it 24-17.

'Twas a bad time for the 49ers. They had dominated play in the first half, but now their own mistakes had let the Giants back in the game. Given a half to study what the 49ers were doing, the Giants' coaching staff had finally figured a way to defense them, and the 49ers hadn't been able to move the ball with any consistency in the second half. With the Giants only a touchdown back, anything could happen.

Then the game started swinging back to the 49ers. First the erratic Danelo, who had been in a terrible slump for several games, hit the right upright with an attempted 21-yard field goal which would have pulled the Giants to within four points.

Moments later Solomon returned a punt 22 yards, deep into Giants' territory. But the 49ers started moving inexorably backward, not forward, and they faced a third-and-18 situation on the New York 41, well out of field goal range and seemingly unable to move closer.

And then Gary Jeter took a swing at 49er tackle Dan Audick in full view of an official. The resulting penalty gave the 49ers a first down on the New York 26.

"He was holding me," Jeter said later. "The play was over, and he kept pushing me downfield. All linemen hold, but he was holding the entire game."

Solomon went 12 yards on a reverse to the 14, the play that had been set up by faked reverses earlier, and Bill Ring got the final three yards two plays later.

Though both teams would each make another touchdown, for a final score of 38-24, the game was effectively over.

As if to underscore that point, the weather changed

dramatically. Only a light rain had fallen throughout the game, not enough to change the 49ers' plans, but a violent storm was about to hit the Bay Area, dropping as much as 12 inches of rain in 36 hours and devastating areas of Marin, San Mateo, and Santa Clara counties. For the next week, there would be only two significant topics of conversation in much of Northern California: that storm and the 49ers chances against Dallas.

15

THE REAL SUPER BOWL

Dallas. Forget what the NFL schedule said. "This is the *real* Super Bowl," said Lou Spadia, and thousands of long-suffering 49er fans would agree.

Everybody remembered that Dallas had beaten the 49ers in the NFC championship game two years running (1970 and 1971). Everybody remembered the miracle finish in the 1972 playoff game, when Roger Staubach had gotten two touchdowns in less than two minutes to stun the 49ers.

More than that, though, the Cowboys put off people with their arrogance. They were "America's Team," by self-design; one wonders what the vote would have been outside of Texas. When they were beaten, as they had been by the 49ers, it was because "Those weren't the real Cowboys out there today," or "They didn't beat the real Cowboys." What other team could dismiss a 31-point loss so easily?

"I'm tired of hearing that the *real* Cowboys didn't show up," snapped John Brodie. "They said that when we beat them, and they said that when the Giants beat them. How many players do they have on their roster, anyway?"

Though the Cowboys had their share of spectacular players (Tony Dorsett, Danny White, Tony Hill, and Drew Pearson), their image was that of a perfect franchise, and perfection is always boring. They did everything by computer, and computers are never wrong. (Actually, it had originally been the 49ers' proposal to start a scouting combine that utilized computers to organize the information, but the Cowboys' got the credit for it.) If a player didn't meet the Cowboys' physical and mental standards for a particular position, he wasn't drafted. Other teams' tendencies were broken down by the computer. Plays were rated on a percentage basis.

"Dallas has the personality of a video game," sniffed KNBR's Mike Cleary.

The local fans' dislike of the Cowboys was accompanied by apprehension. Dallas seemed to be reaching its peak at exactly the right time. The week before they crushed the Tampa Bay Buccaneers, 38-0. The Cowboys' pass rushers sacked Tampa Bay quarterback Doug Williams four times for 39 yards lost, forced him into four interceptions and two intentional groundings, and held him to ten completions in 29 attempts.

"There's no way anybody could have beaten Dallas today," said Williams. "We didn't have a chance, and I don't know if any other team would have either."

"I guess you could say we were awesome," said Cowboy linebacker D. D. Lewis.

That lopsided win added to the Dallas mystique, as did the contention that the Cowboys were at their best in the playoffs. In fact, at the two highest playoff levels they had lost as many as they had won; they were 5-4 in championship games, 2-3 in the Super Bowl.

Forty-Niner fans were edgy, too, because their team had beaten Dallas, and badly, in the regular season. Traditionally, the Cowboys revenged themselves in the playoffs for losses during the year. In 1980, for instance, the Rams had beaten the Cowboys, 38-14, in the regular season; in the playoffs Dallas smothered them, 34-13.

None of this bothered either the 49er coaches or players; they were confident they could win.

"We think we'll win because we have a better team," said quarterback coach Sam Wyche, a few days before the game. "We're very confident. We might beat them by two touchdowns."

At the press conference for head coaches Bill Walsh and Tom Landry the Friday before the game, one reporter asked Walsh why he would have confidence going into the game.

"I really wanted to tell him, 'Well, we beat them, 45-14. Why shouldn't we?'" said Walsh later. "We felt confident because we had played Dallas before and played very well against them. We had a formula as to what they do in moving the ball; defensively, too, we felt we had a good grasp of how to deal with them. I felt we were a quicker team than they were."

After the game, Wyche and offensive line coach Bobb McKittrick explained the reasons for their optimism.

"Our guys were playing good, and we felt like we could outplay them again," Wyche said. "I really felt good about the way our guys were playing, the way we would pass protect, which we did. I still think they have a good team, but I just thought that our guys were playing at the top of their game. The offense felt good about how we matched up against their defense."

"I felt we ought to get four touchdowns against them at least," McKittrick added. We knew it would be tougher than the first time, but we also knew they were going to line up the same way and that they were going to use basically the same pass coverages. Because of what we felt were weaknesses, we thought we could move the ball on them."

The players felt that confidence from the coaches. "You could hear it in the way they were talking," said Dwight Clark, "and the closer the game got, instead of getting more uptight, Bill and Sam and all the rest of the coaches seemed to get more confident and more loose about the game, like they knew we were better, and they knew we should win."

Walsh, though, made only one public prediction: "It will take four touchdowns to win this game." He was exactly right.

* * * *

It wouldn't have been a 49er game without at least one surprise, and Walsh's surprise came early, when he started Lenvil Elliott at running back.

Elliott started his career in 1973 in Cincinnati when Walsh was still an assistant there. Though never more than a spot player for the Bengals, he'd been a dangerous runner with good speed and an excellent pass receiver.

Released by Cincinnati after the 1978 season, he'd been picked up by the 49ers and had played well for them, again as a spot player. In 1980, he averaged 4.5 yards a carry in gaining 341 yards, and caught 27 passes for 285 yards.

But Elliott was coming off knee surgery, and he was 30 years old, playing a position which few had played beyond age 27 or 28 in the NFL. He had lost most of the speed that had distinguished his early-career play.

He was cut in training camp, when the roster was pared to 50, but that had been a tactical maneuver; Walsh reasoned that other clubs wouldn't pick up a 30-year-old running back, so Elliot would be available later if needed. After the first game of the season, he was re-signed and was active for five games. After a knee injury in mid-October, he was put on injured reserve.

"We kidded him a lot," said Randy Cross. "We told him he was going to sit back on a lake fishing for six or seven weeks. We said, 'We'll call you when the money games come.'"

Elliott went home to Cincinnati and kept himself in shape. Near the end of the season he returned to San Francisco and worked out with the team. When Paul Hofer went on injured reserve with a knee injury, Elliott was activated. Walsh used one of his "moves," so Elliott wouldn't have to pass waivers.

Walsh was starting Elliott because of his experience and his pass catching ability. If fans and writers were surprised, the players weren't. "We knew Lenvil had his legs back," said Hofer, "and we knew he'd do the job. He's very reliable."

* * * *

In pro football, the importance of a game doesn't guarantee excitement. Sometimes players and coaches are so tense and cautious in a big game that teams probe tentatively for weaknesses, trying nothing more daring than an off-tackle run. There's an outstanding example of that in Dallas history: the 1970 playoff game when the Cowboys beat Detroit 5-0. Yawn.

Nobody went to sleep at this game. God, what a game this was! For more than three hours, the 49ers and Cowboys attacked and retreated and attacked once again, the lead changing hands six times. There were spectacular plays, controversial calls, a gut-wrenching drive at the end, and finally, a catch by Dwight Clark that will forever be known as *The Catch* in San Francisco sports history.

The action was nonstop, starting in a first quarter that produced 17 points. The first score came when the 49ers drove 63 yards in eight plays, almost all of it coming on Joe Montana's four-for-five passing, for 60 yards. Montana hit Elliott for 24 yards to the Dallas eight, and then connected with Fred Solomon in the end zone for the touchdown.

Dallas countered with a 44-yard field goal by Rafael Septien, and then got a big break when Mike Hegman recovered a fumble by Bill Ring (caused by a resounding Bob Breunig tackle) on the San Francisco 29. Two plays later Danny White hit Tony Hill for 26 yards and a touchdown.

The 49ers weren't deterred, marching 47 yards in four plays in the second quarter to retake the lead. The drive-concluding touchdown came off of brilliant individual efforts by both Montana and Clark.

Clark put on a couple of moves that left Dallas defensive back Dennis Thurman spinning around and heading in the

(left) Eric Wright intercepts a pass against Pittsburgh and looks for running room. (top right) Walt Easley slips through a tackle, also against Pittsburgh. Johnny Davis protects the ball as he rams for short yardage against Green Bay.

(top left) Forty-Niner fans wait at Candlestick in the wet, cold weather to buy tickets for the NFC championship game. (lower left) Fumble! The ball pops loose in the playoff game against the Giants, and Bobby Leopold is there to make a critical recovery to set up an early score. On the sidelines, Archie Reese cheers as the clock winds down in the championship game. The 49ers have won, and the Super Bowl is the next stop.

78

(top left) Randy Cross prepares to block in the NFC championship game. Cross had the best year of his career and made the Pro Bowl game because of his contributions to the 49er season. (bottom left) End of the road! Forty-niner defensive end Jim Stuckey is about to nail Los Angeles running back Wendell Tyler after a short gain. (right) Ray Wersching is deep in contemplation during a Silverdome workout before Super Bowl. Placekicking is all concentration and ritual, and Wersching has several superstitious routines. The most obvious is the fact that he never looks at the goal posts when he comes out for a kick, depending on holder Joe Montana to line him up properly. It all works: Wersching is one of the game's best clutch kickers.

FORTY

16
16

(left) Joe Montana seems to be praying as he stands on the sidelines, but Joe's contributions went far beyond praying during the Super Bowl season. (top right) Charle Young is sent flying by a tackle after catching a pass in playoff game against the Giants. It's a hard way to earn a living. (bottom left) Carlton Williamson is concentrating on the ball as Dallas receiver tries to get there first.

(top left) Dan Audick prepares to make a block in the Atlanta game. Audick, at less than 250 pounds, is really more suited to playing offensive guard, but he filled in at tackle admirably during the season, using his quickness to compensate for lack of bulk. (bottom left) Lawrence Pillers closes in on Green Bay quarterback David Whitehurst, who is trying to run after failing to spot an open reciever. (right) Barefooted punter Jim Miller had his ups-and-downs, but he kicked magnificently in the Super Bowl, outkicking Cincinnati's Pat MacInally, considered the best in the game.

SF

(top left) Keith Fahnhorst shows intense determination as he prepares to make a block. (bottom left) Dwaine Board is just a step away from sacking Los Angeles quarterback Pat Haden. (right) Archie Reese shows why he is such a force in the middle as he swats down a pass from Tampa Bay quarterback Doug Williams. (overleaf) Forty-Niner owner Ed DeBartolo Jr. talks on the phone during a timeout in game. (last page) The 49er cable cars wind their way through the Market Street crowd in victory parade the day after the Super Bowl. An estimated half-million people showed up to cheer the 49ers, and the crowd was so large that the parade route had to be altered; the cable cars could not get through.

REESE
78

DAN AUDICK

JOHN AYERS

GUY BENJAMIN

DWAINE BOARD

DAN BUNZ

JOHN CHOMA

RICKY CHURCHMAN

DWIGHT CLARK

EARL COOPER

RANDY CROSS

JOHNNY DAVIS

FRED DEAN

WALT DOWNING

WALT EASLEY

KEITH FAHNHORST

WILLIE HARPER

JOHN HARTY

DWIGHT HICKS

PAUL HOFER

PETE KUGLER

AMOS LAWRENCE

BOBBY LEOPOLD

RONNIE LOTT

SALADIN MARTIN

MILT McCOLL

JIM MILLER

JOE MONTANA

RICKY PATTON

LAWRENCE PILLERS

CRAIG PUKI

FRED QUILLAN

EASON RAMSON

ARCHIE REESE

JACK REYNOLDS

BILL RING

MIKE SHUMANN

FREDDIE SOLOMON

JIM STUCKEY

LYNN THOMAS

KEENA TURNER

RAY WERSCHING

CARLTON WILLIAMSON

MIKE WILSON

ERIC WRIGHT

CHARLE YOUNG

BILL WALSH

CAS BANASZEK

NORB HECKER

MILT JACKSON

BILLIE MATTHEWS

BOBB McKITTRICK

BILL McPHERSON

RAY RHODES

GEORGE SEIFERT

CHUCK STUDLEY

AL VERMEIL

SAM WYCHE

SINCE 1852
WELLS FARGO BANK

wrong direction as Clark raced uncovered to the middle of the end zone.

Meanwhile Montana was being doggedly pursued by Too Tall, who finally grabbed the 49er quarterback around the ankles. But just at that moment Montana spotted Clark; as he was going down, Montana lofted a soft pass that Clark gathered in for the score.

The Cowboys came back, with a big assist from the officials. Starting on his own 20, White moved his team to the 37; from there he completed a sideline strike to Tony Hill right in front of the 49er bench at the San Francisco 47.

"He was clearly out of bounds," said Walsh later. "It wasn't even close. He was standing next to me when he caught it."

What followed was even worse, a call by side judge Dean Look that would have been the subject of bitter controversy if it had decided the game, as it appeared it would until the very end.

Then White tried to hit wide receiver Drew Pearson on a long pass down the right sideline. Lott was in perfect position and intercepted the pass, but Look threw his handkerchief and called pass interference, giving the Cowboys a first down at the Niners' 12.

As television replays clearly showed, it was Pearson who was doing the bumping, not Lott. Coming from behind, the Cowboy receiver was climbing all over Lott trying to get to the ball.

Asked for an explanation of his call, Look said that the bumping had occurred upfield when Lott had first moved in front of Pearson. But the flag hadn't been thrown at that point; it was seconds later, when Lott made the interception, that Look called the penalty. And the ball was placed considerably further downfield from where Lott had cut in front of Pearson. Clearly Look had put together his explanation after the fact, probably after he had been told that the replays didn't show interference.

The Cowboys needed no more help after that, and Dorsett got the final five yards easily, sweeping outside for the score that put Dallas up 17-14 at halftime.

Nobody thought anything was decided at that point; now the 49ers had a turn. After Bobby Leopold had intercepted a tipped pass, San Francisco went 13 yards to score in four plays. It wasn't easy. Three plays brought the 49ers just short of the three-yard line. Walsh made his choice: go for the touchdown. The Cowboys were offsides, giving the 49ers a first down on the two, and Johnny Davis scored on the next play. The 49ers had the lead going into the fourth quarter.

Less than a minute into that final quarter, the Cowboys drew to within a point on Septien's 22-yard field goal. Lott was called for another pass interference penalty on the drive, this one a good call. Though it gave the Cowboys a first down on the San Francisco 12, ironically the call may actually have worked in the 49ers' favor. On third down in that series, Eric Wright knocked down a pass in the end zone and the play could have been ruled interference. To this observer, at least, it seemed nobody was going to call a third critical pass interference penalty against the 49ers. In the trade, that's known as "evening out." NFL officials are human, if just barely.

Midway through the period, another critical break occurred as Walt Easley fumbled after a hard Breunig hit, the Cowboys recovering on the 50. It was the sixth turnover for the 49ers (three interceptions and three fumbles), an incredible statistic for a team with only 25 turnovers in 16 regular season games.

The Cowboys covered those 50 yards in just four plays, Doug Cosbie taking White's 21-yard pass for the score. Septien's PAT made it 27-21, Cowboys, with 4:19 gone in the last quarter.

An exchange of punts left the 49ers pinned back on their 11 with less than five minutes remaining. It looked like the end. Nothing had gone right for the 49ers, not with six turnovers and a controversial pass interference call.

Owner DeBartolo had already given up. He was heading down to the dressing room to commiserate with his players. But on the field the coaches and players were still optimistic.

"Almost five minutes left and all our timeouts," Walsh said later. "I liked our chances. If we got as far as the 35, we'd go for it on the fourth down, no matter what."

"We knew, going into that drive, that they hadn't really stopped us yet," Cross said. "We stopped ourselves most of the time. It was so ironic to look up at the scoreboard and see the score, 27-21, because I just knew what the score had to be. I just knew it."

Montana had thrown three interceptions, two of them into coverage, but he wasn't discouraged either. "It was a very confident feeling in the huddle," he said. "We had to move the ball, and we knew we could."

The Cowboys played into the 49ers' hands by going into the notorious "prevent defense," playing six defensive backs. Coaches never learn, even as smart a one as Tom Landry.

The "prevent" works best when the offensive team has little time left and has to throw long; receivers going deep are always double-covered in that formation.

But the 49ers were hardly in that desperate a situation. They had plenty of time and thus, no reason to restrict their offense, which is geared to short- and medium-range passes. Because the Cowboys were playing only three defensive linemen, they wouldn't be able to put much pressure on Montana. A final important point: the "prevent" is vulnerable to runs.

The first play, a swing pass from Montana to Elliott, misfired when Elliott couldn't handle the low throw. The next, a draw to Elliott, went for six yards. "We had to slow their rush down a little bit," said Wyche.

A sideline pass to Solomon gained six yards and gave the 49ers a first down on the 23, and then the 49ers ran some more. First they swept right: Elliott gained 11 yards behind the blocking of Cross and John Ayers. Elliott ran the same play the other way for another seven yards. A Dallas offsides gave the 49ers a first down, and then Montana hit Earl Cooper for a five-yard pass at the two-minute warning.

Cross, who had been battling the flu all day, vomited on the field. "I'd thrown up on the sidelines twice before that," he said. "This time I couldn't make it over there." But there was no way he was going to leave the game.

On the sidelines Walsh and Montana talked about what play to call next, and Walsh decided on a reverse to Solomon. "I thought Dallas was a little tired and might have trouble reacting,"Walsh later explained. And he was right: Solomon went for 14 yards on the play.

Then Montana threw a sideline pass to Clark, against double coverage by Dallas corner Eversen Walls and extra back Benny Barnes. Walls had already intercepted two passes, but that didn't faze Montana. This time Walls just tipped the ball but Clark maintained his concentration and grabbed it for a ten-yard gain before going out of bounds.

There was a minute and a half left now. Montana hit Solomon crossing underneath the coverage for 12 yards and a first down on the Dallas 13, and then he called time with 1:15 left.

Cross looked across at the Cowboys and thought they had a beaten look. Probably it was just fatigue. The game had taken its physical and emotional toll on almost everybody.

But nobody seemed in worse shape than Niner Dwight Clark, who had lost seven pounds battling the flu that week. The game doesn't come easy for Clark. Lacking the speed of a receiver like Solomon, he's usually tackled as soon as he gets the ball, and he takes a terrible beating during the course of a game. That had been true again on this day, and he was spent.

The 49ers went for it all on the next play, with Solomon breaking free into the left corner as Mike Wilson helped screen off a defender with his move the other way. But Montana's pass sailed wide. Walsh screamed in frustration.

"I thought that was the championship right there," he said. "We were never going to get that open again. It had worked perfectly to get Solomon free in the end zone, and we missed it."

It was time to run the sweep again, and Elliott ran left for another seven yards. The 49ers took their second timeout, stopping the clock with 58 seconds left. The Cowboys went back to a normal defense, with three linebackers.

Walsh called the play that had given the 49ers their first touchdown and had been a key play all year, one of the first that they had put in during training camp at Rocklin. Solomon was to line up inside Clark on the right side and then cut to the right side of the end zone while Clark was cutting first inside and then back outside. Montana, rolling right, would look for Solomon first and then, if Solomon were covered, for Clark.

The teams lined up, the ball was snapped, and suddenly Too Tall Jones, the Cowboys' huge All-Pro defensive end, was chasing Montana. Solomon was covered; Clark had double coverage in the end zone. Just before Jones could bury him, Montana lofted a pass to the rear of the end zone. Jones thought he was putting the ball up for grabs. Nobody was open. Those watching thought he was just throwing the ball away. But Clark lifted his tired body in a leap that even he thought impossible and caught the ball, coming down just inbounds. The 49ers had tied the game.

A wall of noise came from the stands, a steady blast of sound which didn't abate until long after Ray Wersching had kicked his thirty-sixth consecutive point-after to give the 49ers a 28-27 lead.

In the press box, where writers are often cautioned by announcer Stu Smith to remember "The press box is a working area and no cheering is allowed," there were shrieks of joy and dismay, depending on where the writers were from. Stu Smith be damned; anybody who could have remained calm at that point was a robot, fit only to play for Dallas.

The play meant that Walsh didn't have to spring his last surprise: if the pass had failed, Walsh planned to run a sweep against the tired Cowboys on the fourth down, knowing full well that he'd have to be prepared for an avalanche of criticism if the run failed.

The game was not over yet. The Cowboys still had a chance to move into range for what could have been a winning field goal, and many thought they would do just that when White passed to Pearson for 31 yards to put the Cowboys on the San Francisco 44 with 38 seconds left.

But on the next play, Lawrence Pillers broke through to sack White, who fumbled as he was trying to bring his arm up to pass. Jim Stuckey recovered, and the 49ers were league champions for the first time in their 36-year history.

All week the 49ers said that to win they had to eliminate the mistakes they'd made against the Giants the previous week. They hadn't eliminated those mistakes, but they had still won.

"Six turnovers, and we still won," said Jack Reynolds, forgetting to be a grouch. "I don't know how we did it. With the number of turnovers we made, we should have been blown out. If we didn't make all those mistakes, it wouldn't have been that close."

Cross thought the conclusion was inescapable. "We're the better team," he said, and the statistics backed his contention. The 49ers made 26 first downs, a season high, and gained 393 yards; Dallas had 16 first downs and 250 yards.

But Landry wasn't convinced. "I don't think the 49ers are a better team," he said. "Sometimes in a game like this, it just depends on who has the ball last."

His players were in a somber mood, most of them just sitting on their stools in shock. "We all had visions of a winning field goal," said linebacker D. D. Lewis. "I was thinking of a lot of times we came back to win. We just came up one play short of getting into the Super Bowl. It's a blow, but I'm not about to hang my head down and be sorry."

"It was frustrating to sit on the sideline and watch the last 49er drive," said quarterback White, "but that's the way great games end up. I felt like going out on the field and trying to tackle somebody.

"You can't really say where we lost it. It was a matter of two great teams going at it. It's times like this that we earn our money. People think we're overpaid, but believe me, it's not any fun. No amount of money in the work would make me feel better.

"I learned you've got to play 60 minutes and take advantage of every opportunity. It's going to be a long time before we can do that again. This is one of those games you never get over."

In the 49er dressing room, Fahnhorst was remembering his pre-game nerves. "Joe had to talk to me. He'd won a national championship in college, so this was no big thing to him. I'd never won any damn thing. He calmed me down."

Archie Reese spoke quietly about his feeling of confidence. "It never came into my mind that we were going to lose," he said. "We overcame adversity because we played our hearts out, and we're going to need that to get ready for the Super Bowl."

But, as usual, it was the articulate Cross who best summed it up. "I knew we would win because I read it in my horoscope," he said, pointing to the neatly-folded newspaper in his locker.

His horoscope: "You feel positive and highly revved-up about a dream you've been pursuing."

16

A WORLD CHAMPIONSHIP

When the 49ers arrived by bus at their hotel in the Detroit suburbs the Sunday before the Super Bowl, they were greeted by a white-haired man in a bellman's cap and uniform.

"Help you with your bag, sir? Help you with your bag?" the man repeated to several of the players. It was several moments before the players recognized the "bellhop" in the darkness.

It was Bill Walsh.

Walsh had left San Francisco on Saturday morning, the day before the players left on their United DC-10 charter with "49er Liner" painted on the side; he was scheduled to appear at a Touchdown Club banquet in Washington, D.C., where he was honored as Coach of the Year. From there he'd flown to Detroit early Sunday, arriving before his team.

The sidewalk scene was a reminder of Walsh's love of a practical joke. The players had learned that much earlier, in the exhibition season. He'd sternly informed them before the first road game that he expected them to wear coats and ties on the plane because they were representing San Francisco. *He* showed up for that trip dressed in a general's uniform, while his assistants were dressed in jeans. For the rest of the season's road trips, the players dressed...shall we say extremely casually?

The bellman routine was also Walsh's way of letting the players know they could have a good time during Super Bowl week. It didn't have to be a grim experience, as it had been for some teams.

The Super Bowl is unique in American sports. There are other big events—the World Series, the Kentucky Derby, the Indianapolis 500—but none match the Super Bowl as a spectacle, nor do they equal the attention riveted on it by media and fans.

The World Series, the closest comparison one can make to the Super Bowl, is played in October when the pro and college football seasons are in full swing and pro basketball is about to start. As much attention as the World Series gets, there's still big competition for space on the sports pages.

The Super Bowl, in contrast, is played at a slow moment in the sports year. The only significant competition for attention comes from basketball and hockey, and neither comes close to having the broad base of fan interest of football and baseball.

The big game is played in late January, when everybody needs a pickup. The excitement of the holiday season is past, the weather ranges from bad to terrible throughout the country, and everyone is looking for some excitement. (The Super Bowl doesn't always provide a lot of excitement, but that's another story.)

It's a television game, much more so than the World Series, or any event other than a championship fight. Baseball has never televised well because its action is so spread out; split camera work helps, but it doesn't capture the essence of the game. Football televises beautifully; multiple cameras and instant replays often make the game seem more exciting at home than it is at the stadium. The time between plays is perfect for the use of replays and sometimes informative comments by the color commentators.

The media blitz during Super Bowl week is incredible. This year it would be even worse because the game was being played in snow- and ice-bound Pontiac (possibly the worst decision for a site since the 1980 Olympics were scheduled for Moscow); there would be no idle distractions for writers. "Nobody will be playing golf," observed Walsh.

The same stories would be written over and over; the same questions would be asked over and over, until athletes' minds were numb. There's some respite for team members during the World Series because games are played almost every day, so new plays and new decisions can always be asked about. During Super Bowl week everything leads up to a single game, and there are no new questions to ask. The players hate it, but having been on the other side many times, I can tell you that the writers hate it just as much.

How all this attention is handled can make a big difference to a team. The problem isn't so much the star players, more accustomed to a lot of attention, but the lesser players, who are not. During this particular week, a reserve offensive lineman named Allen Kennedy, who had hardly played all season for the 49ers, found that even he was being interviewed.

Some coaches had handled the media blitz effectively. When coaching the Oakland Raiders, John Madden simply included player interviews and press conferences as part of the daily schedule, not letting the players think of them as anything added. "I told them there were just certain things we had to do, so they might as well enjoy them. I always felt something couldn't be distracting as long as you knew about it."

Pittsburgh coach Chuck Noll seemed to take everything in stride too, though he drove the writers crazy because they could never understand the point of his stories. (Noll has a sense of humor so dry that only one other person in the world understands it, and that person hasn't been found yet.)

But some coaches did have trouble dealing with the attention. George Allen resented it, feeling that it took time away from his preparation. Bud Grant reinforced his image as a cold, emotionless man (an image which is quite distorted, incidentally, as anybody who has dealt with Grant in less frenetic circumstances knows), because he just could not deal with huge press conferences.

It's probably not a coincidence that Madden and Noll were Super Bowl winners and Allen and Grant were losers.

The media blitz started for the 49ers before they even left home, and not just in the sports section. Interviews, including one with Walsh's vivacious wife, Geri, appeared in the society columns; business writers were busy finding aspects of the 49er operation that they could write about. Walsh's customary Tuesday press conference even had to be moved out of the 49er offices to an adjoining building because so many media people showed up.

At that press conference the 49er coach was angered because his team would have to practice early in the morning. Since teams couldn't practice outdoors, they both had to schedule practices in the Silverdome; besides that, the television crews had to have time to work out their complex procedures.

A flip of the coin determined practice times and the 49ers lost; they would have to start practice at 9 a.m. and, worse, hold a press conference an hour earlier. Walsh was especially upset because the NFL had denied his alternative: practicing at the University of Michigan's indoor facilities in Ann Arbor. NFL executive director Don Weiss had told Walsh that the League had been through all this many times and they knew all the factors that had to be taken into account.

"Well, they didn't take into account the fact that one team is traveling across three time zones to the game and the other will be staying in the same time zone," said Walsh. "We'll be talking to the press at 5 o'clock by our body clocks."

The NFL decision on the press conference time was baffling even to writers, who would have much preferred a later hour, both because they would get more information after a practice and because they would be able to sleep later, not necessarily in that order of importance.

Possibly Walsh's anger was more tactical than real, a chance to persuade his players they were really the underdogs, despite the odds posting them as one-to-three-point favorites. He surely realized that the early practices would help the 49ers acclimate to the time change that much faster.

Walsh seemed even more relaxed than he'd been at the start of the season. "I can see the end in sight now," he said. "When you get to the end of the season, you don't have to be as guarded in your statements."

His press conference had run over an hour and a half longer than usual, because groups of reporters came up to talk to him after the formal part had ended. He still had an interview to do with Don Klein of radio station KCBS, but he seemed in no hurry to break away.

"It means that I'll have to stay later tonight to work on my game plan," he told me, "but you just have to accept that as part of the job. You don't want to let that force you to cut your work short. I can't let myself leave early without getting everything done. And I can't worry about it. Some coaches try to turn off the questions so they can get back to their work, but that only gets them more tense. If I have to stay five minutes longer at a press conference, I'll stay five minutes longer."

Walsh planned to do the bulk of his work before the end of the week, right there in Redwood City. "I'm sure we'll have the game plan in by the end of the week," he said. "We can't depend on getting a lot done back there, so we'll have to do it here. And, after all, this is what we usually have to prepare for a game — one week."

He didn't anticipate any special problems in preparing for the Bengals. "I don't mean that it will be easy to stop them," he said, "because they have a lot of weapons, but I don't expect any real surprises from them."

Walsh's approach, as well as his mind, seemed to give the 49ers an edge over the Bengals.

Everybody who wrote or talked of Cincinnati coach Forrest Gregg stressed the "discipline" that Gregg had instilled, and the way he ran a "tight ship." What they meant was that Gregg told the Bengals exactly what to do; the Bengals were not expected to act or think for themselves. That approach can work well during the regular season, but players who depend on it have a tendency to fall apart in unusual situations, a category which succinctly describes the Super Bowl.

Just such a collapse happened to the Philadelphia Eagles in the 1981 Super Bowl. They came into the game as tightly strung as Bjorn Borg's rackets; the relaxed and confident Raiders took them apart.

The 49ers were nearly as loose as the Raiders had been the previous year. "I'm not a drill sergeant," said Walsh. "Players know what they have to do, but I'm not hammering at them all the time.

"I really said nothing to get them up for Dallas. That sort of thing has to come from the players, and we're fortunate to have players like Charle Young who can inspire others. That's really why the Raiders won last year; they had a few players who could get everybody else up."

* * * *

In Detroit, CBS executives were grumbling because two obscure teams had made it to the Super Bowl. They would have preferred big-name teams, like the Cowboys and Steelers, or teams from the two big media centers, New York and Los Angeles.

Still, the 49ers were starting to become known as individuals. Joe Montana was the subject of a cover story in *Time,* and he shared the *Newsweek* cover with Cincinnati's Ken Anderson.

Dwight Clark, too, was frequently interviewed, partially because his girlfriend, Shawn Weatherly, had been Miss Universe. Though they both looked as if they came straight off a Southern California beach, they'd met while attending Clemson in South Carolina.

Perhaps the most interesting 49er, though, was right guard Randy Cross, who was showing up on most of the All-Pro selections. Offensive linemen tend to be conservative men, neat and orderly, accustomed to doing their job with little recognition. Most offensive linemen get noticed only for negative actions, such as penalties or missed blocks that result in quarterback sacks. Cross admitted he was no exception.

"I have very strong feelings about law and order," he said. "But I also have a strong interest in kids, particularly the underprivileged. They're the most helpless, along with the older people. There's nothing they can do for themselves, so there's got to be something done for them."

Off the field, Cross was a gentle, smiling giant of a man who preferred to talk and think about something besides football. His nature didn't change dramatically on the field.

"It's not a personal vendetta out there," he said. "I'm not interested in letting blood. Football is just something I do, and I happen to do it very well. They aren't paying us to get hurt. Our business is to play."

He seemed to have an excellent perspective on the Super Bowl. "I would hate to look back when I'm 77 and say that something in sports was the highlight of my life."

His teammates, too, seemed to be taking the game in stride. Clark, writing a daily "diary" for the *Chronicle*, was frequently kidded. "One night, they told me we had a team meeting — and no press. I said, 'OK, I'll leave my note pad at home.' Randy Cross told me I had to bring my press pass to get into the meeting. One of our public relations people made up a Pro Football Writers card for me. I don't mind the kidding. It's just part of keeping everything loose."

The difference between Walsh's and Gregg's approach was interesting. Gregg had an 11 p.m. curfew; Walsh's curfew was 1 a.m. Walsh allowed the married players to have their wives with them; Gregg didn't. Walsh even let his squad go to a Diana Ross concert on the Friday night before the game.

And when tables were set up to interview players at their hotels, the 49er tables had the players' names on them, while the Cincinnati tables only listed players' numbers.

Walsh was using every possible psychological ploy, starting with an "us against them" mentality because of the treatment the 49ers had gotten from the NFL (worse hotel than the Bengals, bad practice time, etc.).

When Fred Solomon was hurt in a practice collision with Ronnie Lott, Walsh allowed everyone to think the injury was serious by listing the receiver as "questionable" in the NFL injury reports, which means only a fifty-fifty chance of playing.

Solomon got an unusual treatment for his injury, a process perhaps best described as electronic acupuncture. Herb Berger, a salesman who's also a specialist in the field, treated Solomon. Berger is retained by the 49ers. "The 49ers are the only team in the NFL to use this method to speed up the healing process," he said.

He used a rectangular instrument which poked into Solomon's body much as an acupuncturist would put in needles, but Berger was cautious about calling it electronic acupuncture. "It's an electronic physical therapy instrument that incorporates certain acupuncture techniques," he said.

By any name, the treatment apparently worked. Solomon was listed as "probable" the next day, which meant he had an 80 percent chance of playing.

For all the talk about psychology, however, when looking back dispassionately at Super Bowl results, the better team had usually won. Only the New York Jets win in the third Super Bowl was still a real shocker in retrospect, and actually the Jets were a much better team than most people had ever realized.

Games that had seemed a surprise at the time — Kansas City's win over Minnesota, Pittsburgh's win in the Steelers' first Super Bowl appearance against Minnesota — weren't at all, in retrospect. Kansas City and Pittsburgh were clearly better teams.

So, who was the better team in this game? That proposition was debated endlessly. Hank Stram picked the Bengals. Sam Rutigliano, whose Cleveland team had beaten both the Super Bowl teams, thought the 49ers had an edge. I called Sid Gillman, living in retirement near San Diego, and asked his opinion.

Gillman, an assistant for the Eagles the year before, is the acknowledged master of the passing game. Everybody has borrowed from him, from Al Davis to Bill Walsh, though Gillman disagrees with Walsh's high percentage game; Sid prefers the bomb. "I used to kid Bill when he threw all those five-yard passes," said Gillman, "and ask him when he was going to lengthen out to ten yards."

Listening to Gillman is like attending a seminar on the passing game. Predictably, he thought passing would decide this game. "You're never going to see a big game decided by running," he said. "Our game has just changed so much.

"Usually, teams come out conservative because coaches are afraid to make a mistake—no matter what they say the week before. But I don't think that's going to happen this time.

"I know Bill: he'll come out throwing. If he's got 20 plays drawn up, probably 16 of them are passes. And I keep remembering the AFC championship game when Anderson came out in the second quarter and took Cincinnati downfield on practically nothing but passes. If they passed in that weather, God almighty, what will they do inside?"

So, who did he like? "What are the odds?" he asked. Told they were 2–3 points favoring the 49ers, he said, "That would be enough to swing me to Cincinnati if I were betting the game."

Elsewhere, writers were playing the match-up game, rating individual players and positions. Usually the Bengals came out ahead; they had faster receivers, better running backs, bigger offensive linemen. Only in the defensive secondary did the 49ers rate a clear edge.

But these "experts" were missing the point: football is a team game, not a collection of individual efforts, and a team's success depends on how well the individual players mesh. The 49ers always seemed to get the job done. Sometimes their offense fell off and the defense had to win a game; sometimes the defense had slipped and the offense had to play a great game. Whatever it took, the 49ers had had it for 14 of their last 15 games.

Their seeming weaknesses hadn't hurt them. Supposedly the Cincinnati running game was much better, for instance, but the Bengals had averaged only two yards more a game, though playing their home games on artificial turf, while the 49ers were playing in the Candlestick swamp.

And the 49ers were a much more difficult team to prepare for than the Bengals, because of Walsh's intricate game plans.

"We study their game films at least three times more than we do anyone else," said Atlanta defensive coordinator Jerry Glanville. "We thought they were running the best offense even before they were winning. We beat them a couple of times because they weren't very good then, but we were defending them wrong."

Glanville said the 49ers were difficult to defend against because their pass routes were so variable, and he thought it was essential to play zone defense instead of man-to-man (as the Cowboys had done) because the 49er patterns created such confusion in the defensive secondary. The 49ers' ability to cross receivers and screen (pick) defensive backs was especially important, he felt.

"Then somebody's wide open," said Glanville. "I can remember when they played the Jets two years ago. There wasn't anybody near the 49ers' receivers who could hit them with a rock. I love their offense. I love studying it and watching it."

* * * *

The day of the Super Bowl didn't start auspiciously for the 49ers; the bus carrying Walsh and half the team got stuck in traffic. The trip from the 49ers' hotel to the Silverdome was supposed to take 25 minutes, but instead took an hour and ten minutes. The team was expected to be on the field for warmups at 3:05, and those players who had come to the stadium in taxis were becoming somewhat concerned by 2:30.

Walsh was concerned, too, but he was determined not to show it, kidding with his players on the bus.

"I've never in my life been in that situation," he said, "where you're in traffic bumper-to-bumper, police can't clear out the cars, you can't see the stadium, and you're supposed to be on the field in 30 minutes. It takes the players 25 minutes to dress.

"I thought of telling everyone to get off and hold on to each other's arms, and maybe we could ski cross-country."

When the 49ers finally reached the stadium, at 2:40, Walsh was still loose — or pretending to be. "When he walked into the locker room," said Dwight Clark, "he was laughing and joking — like, did we think we were going to have to go without him? He wanted to know who was trying to take over."

Before the game the 49ers played the Kenny Loggins record "This Is It," at the suggestion of Joe Montana. "The song has a message," said Randy Cross. "You have a once-in-a-lifetime chance and, as the song says, 'This is your miracle.' You have to grab it."

The players listened to the song once and turned it off, thinking it was time to be serious about the game. Walsh came into the room and said, "Where's the music? Play that song again."

Walsh's approach paid off once the game began. The 49ers were relaxed and confident. Had they not been, they could have been undone by the very first play of the game, when Amos Lawrence fumbled while returning the opening kickoff, with the Bengals recovering on the San Francisco 26.

Ken Anderson went right to work, passing to Isaac Curtis for eight yards, running Pete Johnson up the middle for two, and throwing a quick strike to Dan Ross for 11 yards and a first down on the San Francisco five.

And then the 49ers' defense stiffened. Charles Alexander was stopped for no gain, and Jim Stuckey sacked Anderson for a six-yard loss. On third down Anderson looked for Curtis again, coming across the middle. Dwight Hicks had been helping double-cover Steve Kreider, but when Kreider broke to the outside, Hicks stayed in the middle. "I don't think Anderson saw me," he said.

As Anderson released the ball, Hicks stepped in front of Curtis and picked off the pass, returning it to the San Francisco 32. The air began to leak out of the Cincinnati balloon right there.

Just as Sid Gillman had predicted, both teams came out throwing. Montana threw on five of the first six 49er plays; with the Bengals looking for the pass, Joe went to the run. The Niners' first Super Bowl touchdown came at the end of a 68-yard drive with a quarterback sneak for the final yard.

That touchdown was significant on a couple of counts. It was the fifteenth time during the season that the 49ers had scored first; in the first fourteen such games their record was 13-1. The team that had scored first had also won thirteen of the previous fifteen Super Bowls.

Once again the 49ers had scored first because a Walsh strategem had confused the opposing defense. This time it was an unbalanced line, added to the game plan only the day before. "The 49ers caught the Bengals in the wrong defense a lot," noted Jack Faulkner, assistant general manager of the Los Angeles Rams and a former coach.

The 49er defense was bothering the Bengals, too. The 49er's used several different defensive formations, including one in which Fred Dean was lined up as a "rover," a linebacker free to move where the ball goes. The 49ers were also waiting until the last possible moment to shift into the defense they would use on a particular play; Jack (Hacksaw) Reynolds was barking defensive signals even as Ken Anderson was calling offensive signals for the Bengals.

Cincinnati turned the ball over again early in the second quarter, and again, the 49ers took quick advantage of the miscue. It began this way: a Pat McInally punt that got a great Cincinnati roll on the carpet backed the 49ers up to their own ten, and Jim Miller had to punt out of the end zone, after the 49ers had advanced only to the 12. His punt went to the Cincinnati 44 and was returned five yards.

Anderson marched his team down to the San Francisco 27. On second down he hit Chris Collinsworth at the five, but when Eric Wright tackled Collinsworth the ball popped loose, and Lynn Thomas recovered for the 49ers at the San Francisco eight.

Once again, though, the 49ers were deep in their own territory. Usually teams are hesitant to throw the ball in this situation because an interception would be so costly. The 49ers ran on the first two plays, Johnny Davis getting just a yard and Bill Ring two yards. But the beauty of Walsh's offense is that it is geared to use the pass as a means of *controlling* the ball. Run properly, it's a low-risk offense, with options available to the quarterback on every play. That means that Montana can throw in virtually any situation . . . including this one. On third down he rolled to his right and hit Fred Solomon for 20 yards and a first down. The 49ers were back in business.

In any system, it's important for a coach and quarterback to think alike; in Walsh's system, it's an indispensable attribute. In Montana, Walsh had a quarterback who saw the game as he did, an on-field extension of the coach's thinking.

Probably Walsh had realized that Montana could be this kind of quarterback for him from the start. He had taken great pains with Joe, making sure that the moment was right to use him. Though Steve DeBerg was the starting quarterback during Montana's first two pro years, Walsh would use Montana in situations where he could look good, down near the other team's goal line, so Montana could build up his confidence.

Walsh had never been enthusiastic about DeBerg because DeBerg wasn't mobile enough to escape the rush and couldn't get away from a tendency to throw high-risk passes — which usually resulted in critical interceptions. "I'd hate to think of my reputation depending on Steve DeBerg," he had told me at one point early in the 1980 season.

For a time in 1980, he seemed to waver between DeBerg and Montana, using first one and then the other. That created tension because the two quarterbacks were good friends off the field, and led some writers to think Walsh was being indecisive.

In fact, though, he knew exactly what he was doing. He knew Montana would be his quarterback, but he didn't want Joe playing before he was ready. He didn't want the fans booing Montana for mistakes caused by inexperience, or because his teammates weren't yet good enough.

DeBerg was left in long enough to get the boos; when Montana took over, the fans (and writers) were so happy to see a change made that Montana had a grace period. By the time the honeymoon was over, the 49ers were winning. Montana has never been booed by the home fans, and he may be the only NFL starting quarterback with that distinction.

Now Joe was moving his team downfield again, making the big play when he had to. Chased out of the pocket, he ran for eight yards on one play. Under pressure again, on third down at the Cincinnati 43, he rolled right and tossed one to Clark for 12 yards and a first down.

On first down from the Cincinnati 19, the 49ers ran a reverse with Dwight Clark and got a big break. Clark got hit in the backfield for a two-yard loss ("I tried to put on a move to get away, but I don't have many moves," he said), but Cincinnati linebacker Jim LeClair was called for a late hit. That moved the ball to the Cincinnati 11, where the 49ers had a first down. Television replays showed that LeClair was blocked into Clark and shouldn't have been penalized. The zebras strike again.

On the next play Montana rolled to his right and then looked across the field. Earl Cooper had run to the middle of the field and then cut to his left, and he was open for Montana's pass at the four, bulling his way into the end zone from there. Ray Wersching's kick made it 14-0 and the 49ers were rolling.

With just over four minutes to go in the first half, the 49ers went on the move again. Working the clock down so Cincinnati wouldn't have time to score, the 49ers hustled to the Bengals' five before faltering. Wersching kicked a 22-yard field goal to run the score to 17-0 with just 15 seconds remaining in the half.

All week long Wersching had been practicing squib kicks in the Silverdome. The practice paid off. His kickoffs had skittered along the carpet, taking erratic bounces, and the Bengals had had trouble handling every one. This time, Archie Griffin fumbled Wersching's kick, and the 49ers' Milt McColl recovered on the Cincinnati four.

Only two seconds remained in the half, enough time for Wersching to kick a 26-yard field goal (after the 49ers had been penalized back to the nine for illegal procedure).

The 49ers took a 20-0 lead into their dressing room, the biggest halftime lead any team had ever enjoyed in the Super Bowl. Assistant coach Sam Wyche wrote on the dressing room blackboard, "This game is not over yet." His words became almost frighteningly prophetic in the second half.

The Bengals came out smoking, eager to atone for their first-half mistakes, and the 49ers played like a team that was already counting the winner's share.

"We played the third quarter like everyone thought we would play all year long," said Jim Stuckey. "I think we lost our discipline in the third quarter."

Cincinnati took the opening kickoff, not fumbling this time, and drove 83 yards for its first touchdown — and the first touchdown for the Bengals against the 49ers, who had held them to a field goal in the regular season confrontation.

Only twice did the Bengals have to convert a third down on the drive. On the first one, third-and-four from the Cincinatti 41, Anderson passed to Kreider for 19 yards.

The second time was also third-and-four, on the San Francisco five. Anderson had faded to pass but saw that nobody was coming in from the right side of the 49er defense. He tucked the ball under his arm and ran across for the touchdown. Jim Breech's PAT made it 20-7.

The 49ers ran three plays and punted after their first possession, as they would do the first three times they had the ball in the second half. Now the Bengals had excellent field position, at the San Francisco 49. But the Niners' defense stopped them and forced a punt.

Once again, though, the 49ers went three downs and punted, and this time, the Bengals were ready to move. The big play came on third-and-23 from the Cincinnati 37, when Anderson zeroed in on his outstanding rookie receiver, Collinsworth, for a 49-yard gain to the San Francisco 14.

Three plays later, the Bengals had a first-and-goal at the San Francisco three, and the dramatic sequence that followed probably decided the game.

On first down John Choma stopped Pete Johnson after a two-yard gain, but the Bengals had three downs to make just one yard. "When you're that close," said Cincinnati guard Max Montoya, "if you've got any pride at all, you've got to get it in."

But the Bengals didn't.

On second down Anderson called an audible to change blocking assignments. Wide receiver David Verser was supposed to block a linebacker, but Verser didn't hear the signals because of the crowd noise. He didn't block anybody, and linebackers Reynolds and Dan Bunz stopped Johnson cold for no gain.

On third down Cincinnati offensive coordinator Lindy Infante, who calls all the Bengals' plays, gambled, calling for Anderson to throw to running back Charles Alexander, who was supposed to be just inside the end zone.

Alexander wasn't quite in the end zone when he caught the ball. "I thought I could run in," he said. But Bunz had come up quickly and made a jarring open-field tackle that stopped Alexander in his tracks, perhaps six inches from the goal line.

Everybody knew what was coming next. The Bengals' Johnson, listed at 249 pounds but probably more, and bigger than anybody besides Archie Reese on the 49ers' defensive line, would be carrying the ball. The only question was which direction.

Normally Johnson would have gone left, behind massive tackle Anthony Munoz, but the Bengals thought that might be too obvious. "We had just gone to the left," said Infante. "The decision was, instead, to run the same play, but to turn it around and run it to the other side."

Reynolds had it figured the same way. "The backfield was set up that way," he later said.

Johnson headed into the line, the human bowling ball led into the hole by Alexander, who was supposed to block. "I knocked Alexander back into Pete, and there was nowhere for him to go," said Bunz, who lost his chinstrap and broke the clamp on his helmet. The entire 49er defensive line, and linebackers Bunz and Reynolds, collapsed on Johnson, who fell just short of the goal line. Turned on his back on top of the pile, Reese squirmed and kicked with joy, and the Silverdome rocked with noise. The 49ers had held!

That goal-line stand should have been the clincher, but give the Bengals credit: they didn't concede. After the third straight three-downs-and-punt situation for the 49ers, Cincinnati was on the move again. From the Cincinnati 47, the Bengals moved down to the San Francisco four, helped by a pass interference call against Ronnie Lott.

From the four, Anderson hit tight end Dan Ross for a Bengal touchdown. It was one of eleven passes Ross would catch for a Super Bowl record, and the first of two touchdown passes, tying another Super Bowl mark.

Breech's point-after kick made it 20-14, and the 49ers seemed in serious trouble. The momentum was all with Cincinnatti and there was plenty of time left, more than ten minutes. The 49ers hadn't yet had a first down in the second half; the Bengals had had nine. In the first half, the 49ers had outgained the Bengals, 202-99. In the second half, the Bengals would roll up 257 yards to just 73 for the 49ers.

But all year long the 49ers had been able to make that one drive they had to make to win a game. On the sidelines, they knew what had to be done. "I don't think there was ever a moment of doubt," said offensive tackle Keith Fahnhorst, "but I was getting a little nervous. We had to cool them off and get something, get some momentum going."

In the huddle, one player said, "Think of it as the last ten minutes of your life and you've got to give it everything." Somebody else mentioned the difference between the winning and losing shares, but, as Clark said later, "Money is not the big motivator in this type of situation. No one will ever take away a world championship from me."

The drive didn't start auspiciously. Montana's pass was incomplete on first down, and offensive tackle Dan Audick was penalized for a false start on the next play. It was second-and-15 from the San Francisco 22, and you wouldn't have found many bettors eager to take the 49ers at that point.

Then Walsh called a play that had just been put in for this game. "I was supposed to make them think I was going long," said wide receiver Mike Wilson, one of the 49ers' 15 free agents. "I ran 25 yards down and then came back."

Montana dropped straight back as if he were going to throw deep, and then rolled to his right. On the move, he fired to Wilson on the right sideline, just in front of the Cincinnati bench, at the 44. Cincinnati coach Forrest Gregg and his players jumped up in rage when the official signaled a catch; they were certain Wilson was out of bounds.

That was the play the 49ers needed. Now Walsh could think of both the score and the time. He determined to run some time off the clock, and the 49ers went to a running offense. Montana threw on the first play after Wilson's catch, an incomplete pass; but Cincinnati's Ken Riley was called for pass interference and that gave the 49ers another first down. After that, the 49ers did nothing but run. They knew they had only to get a field goal to put the game effectively out of reach of the Bengals.

Finally, at fourth-and-five on the Cincinnati 23, it was time to call on Wersching, as reliable a kicker as any in the NFL. Wersching went through his usual superstitious routine. He resolutely refuses to look at his target, putting his hand on Montana's shoulder, and looking like a blind man, relying on Joe to line him up correctly.

There was no sloppy turf to worry Wersching this time. There were no variable wind currents in the covered Silverdome. Just the kick.

The snap from Randy Cross came back perfectly. Montana spotted the ball. Wersching kicked it. The ball sailed true through the goal posts, and the 49ers had a 23-14 lead.

The 49ers had run the clock down to just over five minutes, and Cincinnati's position was precarious indeed. The Bengals now needed both a touchdown and a field goal.

The Bengals were soon in an even deeper hole. On their first play from scrimmage after the kickoff, Anderson tried to hit Collinsworth but Wright stepped in front of the Bengal receiver at the Cincinnati 47 and ran the ball back 25 yards. For one fleeting moment, Wright almost gave it back. As he was tackled, he tried to lateral to linebacker Willie Harper, but he couldn't control the flip and the ball bounced loose on the carpet. But Harper finally recovered it for the 49ers.

Now more than ever it was important for the 49ers to run time off the clock and force Cincinnati to use its timeouts. Three running plays gained a first down. Two more resulted in a net loss of three yards. On third down Montana rolled left and gained seven — and he stayed in bounds so the clock wouldn't stop.

Close enough. On the fourth down Wersching came in to kick his fourth field goal, tying a Super Bowl record, from 23 yards out. 49ers, 26-14.

The Bengals got the ball back, starting on their own 26 after the kickoff, with no timeouts left. Anderson took his team smartly downfield to score in just six plays, the last one a three-yard pass to Ross for the touchdown. But surprisingly, Anderson didn't throw any passes to the sidelines to stop the clock; all his passes were into the middle of the field. That meant that the clock never stopped, and only 16 seconds remained when Cincinnati scored to make it 26-21.

On the kickoff the Bengals went for an onsides attempt, but Clark smothered the ball before any Cincinnati player could get to it. The 49ers ran one play, Montana falling on the ball, and Superbowl XVI was all over.

* * * *

In the 49er dressing room NFL commissioner Pete Rozelle, presenting the Vince Lombardi trophy to owner Edward DeBartolo, Jr., and Walsh, noted that, "This is the greatest turnaround in Super Bowl history, from 6-10 to Super Bowl champions."

Walsh took a phone call from President Reagan, whom he had met while in Washington to accept the Coach of the Year trophy from the Touchdown Club, and then told the press that the Super Bowl win was the "highlight of my life."

"This is a group of men who do not have great talent," he said, "but they have great inspiration. No one could take us this year."

The players showed their reaction in different ways. "We're world champs!" Lynn Thomas screamed across the room at Ronnie Lott. Keith Fahnhorst wondered, "What can we ever do to top this?"

The usually whimsical Charle Young was serious, perhaps for the first time. Young loves to put on writers, and turn interviews around so that he is the one asking questions. The first time we had met, he had told me that, judging from the way I was dressed, I should be a college professor who drove a Volvo. (I will never be a professor, but he was right about the second part of the equation.) When I wrote this year that the 49ers needed a tight end who could get deep, he came up to me in the dressing room the next week and thanked me for writing that. "It made me play harder," he said.

This time, though, there were no jokes, no put-ons. "I came from the basement, from not being able to play, to this," he said in wonderment.

Finally, Hacksaw Reynolds forgot for the moment that he is supposed to be the team's resident grouch. The man who had talked all year of the team's "luck" and doubted before each game that the 49ers could win, said, "We were obviously good, possibly great, and nobody can take that away from us."

Amen.

POSTSCRIPT

San Francisco has a reputation as a sophisticated city, but the reaction to the 49ers' Super Bowl win, during the game and after, certainly belied that.

The game itself smashed all records for television watching, with almost 2.6 million Bay Area TV sets tuned in to the game. "We claim with total confidence that the game had the biggest Bay Area audience ever for any program, sports or otherwise," said Andrea Hine of KPIX-TV, San Francisco's CBS outlet.

The ratings jumped as high as 55.7, with a 93 share during the critical third quarter. That meant that 55.7 percent of all the sets in the Bay Area were tuned to the game, and 93 percent of the sets in use were on the game. By comparison, the 1981 Super Bowl, in which the Oakland Raiders beat the Philadelphia Eagles, had a 50.7 rating and 82 share.

The telecast surpassed the two previous record holders, the 49ers' championship win over Dallas and the final installment of the serial "Roots."

Newspapers also benefited from the great interest. The *San Francisco Chronicle,* which has the largest circulation of any Bay Area newspaper, sold about 100,000 more copies than usual; the 625,000 copies sold represented the largest one-day sale in *Chronicle* history.

In the aftermath of the game, San Francisco became the scene of one continuous party. Traffic came to a stop in many parts of town, and areas such as North Beach, Union Square, and Union Street were closed off because huge crowds were milling in the streets. It was a scene reminiscent of the celebrations following the end of World War II, as people kissed and hugged total strangers.

As the celebrants drank more and more, the scene turned rough. Eventually there were 83 arrests, 125 people treated and released at city hospitals, and four police officers injured.

"It was not a riot," said a police spokesman, Sergeant Michael Pera, "but it was violent for a short time in some places."

The wildest scene was yet to come. The next day, after the 49ers returned home on their chartered plane, the city held a victory parade and virtually everybody came.

A tremendous throng overflowed Civic Center Plaza as the 49ers were honored on the stairs of City Hall. Ray Barnett, general manager of KCBS, which broadcast the 49er games for the first time in the 1981 season, was standing at the rear of the podium and couldn't believe what he saw. "People were standing in the trees, on the top of cars, hanging out of buildings. One security guard told me he hadn't even seen anything like that in the celebrations after the war."

"On behalf of the people of the city, we would like to say welcome No. 1," said Mayor Dianne Feinstein, presenting the players and coach Bill Walsh with the symbolic keys to the city. "We have the No. 1 owner in the country, the No. 1 coach in the country, the No. 1 quarterback in the country, and the No. 1 team in the country!"

Hours before the parade for the 49ers, people started gathering along the announced parade route. Businesses let out early, out of necessity. Bus lines were rerouted because Market Street was impassable. The Bay Area Rapid Transit system carried 213,745 passengers, breaking the previous one-day record of 201,555 set the day of an American League playoff between the Oakland A's and the New York Yankees.

Motorized cable cars took the players and coaches through the financial district, but when the motorcade tried to turn from Montgomery Street onto Market Street, a wall of people blocked the way. Hundreds of screaming fans rushed toward the cable cars, wildly grabbing at the players. The cable car engines began overheating because of the slow progress, and police decided to reroute the parade two blocks away.

Anybody selling 49er memorabilia was doing a great business; at one point, a T-shirt salesman on Powell Street had 30 people waiting in line.

Marsha Washburn, a fan who came from Stockton for the parade, said of the celebration, "It's like going without sex for six months and then finally getting it."

As with the celebration the night before, there were a lot of injuries and arrests: 30 people were treated at Mission Emergency and 14 were arrested.

The biggest problem was that city officials had grossly underestimated the magnitude of the celebration. The first projections for the parade assumed that only about 20,000 people would watch.

As soon as this parade ended, police and city officials began to plan for the possibility of another one next January. Police spokesman Michael Pera said that Market Street would probably be blocked off next time, so cars and people couldn't block it themselves.

"I think even if they win next year, you're not going to get the reaction we did this year," Pera said. "Next year, people will expect them to win."

REGULAR SEASON STATISTICS

Team Statistics

	49ERS	Opp.
Time of Possession	8:27:28	7:33:30
Total First Downs	317	280
By Rushing	110	113
By Passing	183	144
By Penalty	24	23
Third Down-Made/Att.	114/259	87/224
Third Down Efficiency	40.0%	38.8%
Total Net Yards	5484	4763
Avg Gain per Game	342.8	297.7
Total Offensive Plays	1106	1014
Avg Gain per Play	5.0	4.7
Net Yards Rushing	1941	1918
Avg Gain per Game	121.3	119.9
Total Rushing Plays	560	464
Avg Gain per Rush	3.5	4.1
Net Yards Passing	3543	2845
Avg Net Passing Per Game	221.4	177.8
Lost Att to Pass	29/223	36/290
Gross Yards Passing	3766	3135
Attempts/Completions	517/328	514/273
Percent Complete	63.4	53.1
Had Intercepted	13	27
Punts/Average	93/41.5	83/41.4
Net Punting Average	31.1	36.0
Punt Returns/Average	48/7.2	57/11.6
Kickoff Ret./Average	45/20.2	67/20.7
Intercepts/Avg Ret	27/16.6	13/22.8
Penalties/Yards	92/752	108/866
Fumbles/Ball Lost	26/12	36/21
Touchdowns	43	30
By Rushing	17	10
By Passing	20	16
By Returns	6	4
Extra Points	42/43	29/30
Field Goals	19/29	13/23
Safeties	0	1
Total Points	357	250
Avg. Per Game	22.3	15.6

SCORE BY QUARTERS	**1**	**2**	**3**	**4**	**OT**	**Total**
49ers Total	80	100	88	89	0	357
Opp. Total	40	76	55	79	0	250

Individual Statistics

INTRCPTNS	**NO.**	**YDS.**	**AVG.**	**LG**	**TD**
Hicks	9	239	26.6	72	1
Lott	7	117	16.7	41T	3
Williamson	4	44	11.0	28	0
Wright	3	26	8.7	26	0
McColl	1	22	22.0	22	0
Reynolds	1	0	0.0	0	0
Martin	1	0	0.0	0	0
Turner	1	0	0.0	0	0
49ERS	27	448	16.6	72	4
Opponents	13	297	22.8	101T	2

RECEIVING	**NO.**	**YDS.**	**AVG.**	**LG**	**TD**
Clark	85	1105	13.0	78T	4
Solomon	59	969	16.4	60T	8
Cooper	51	477	9.4	50	0
Young	37	400	10.8	29	5
Hofer	27	244	9.0	22	0
Patton	27	195	7.2	31T	1
Wilson	9	125	13.9	27T	1
Easley	9	62	6.9	21	0
Elliott	7	81	11.6	19	0
Ramson	4	45	11.3	16	0
Ring	3	28	9.3	21	1
Shumann	3	21	7.0	8	0
Lawrence	3	10	3.3	5	0
Davis	3	-1	-0.3	3	0
Peets	1	5	5.0	5	0
49ERS	328	3766	11.5	78T	20
Opponents	273	3135	11.5	67	16

RUSHING	**ATT.**	**YDS.**	**AVG.**	**LG**	**TD**
Patton	152	543	3.6	28	4
Cooper	98	330	3.4	23	1
Davis	94	297	3.2	14	7
Easley	76	224	2.9	9	1
Hofer	60	193	3.2	12	1
Ring	22	106	4.8	16	0
Montana	25	95	3.8	20	2
Lawrence	13	48	3.7	14	1
Solomon	9	43	4.8	16	0
Clark	3	32	10.7	18	0
Elliot	7	29	4.1	9	0
Benjamin	1	1	1.0	1	0
49ers	560	1941	3.5	28	17
Opponents	464	1918	4.1	29	10

SCORING	TR	TP	TRT	FG	PAT	SF	TP
Wersching	0	0	0	17-23	30-30	0	81
Solomon ..	0	8	0	0-0	0-0	0	48
Davis	7	0	0	0-0	0-0	0	42
Patton	4	1	0	0-0	0-0	0	30
Young	0	5	0	0-0	0-0	0	30
Clark	0	4	0	0-0	0-0	0	24
Bahr	0	0	0	2-6	12-12	0	18
Lott	0	0	3	0-0	0-0	0	18
Hicks	0	0	2	0-0	0-0	0	12
Lawrence	1	0	1	0-0	0-0	0	12
Montana ..	2	0	0	0-0	0-0	0	12
Cooper ...	1	0	0	0-0	0-0	0	6
Easley	1	0	0	0-0	0-0	0	6
Hofer	1	0	0	0-0	0-0	0	6
Ring	0	1	0	0-0	0-0	0	6
Wilson	0	1	0	0-0	0-0	0	6
TEAM	0	0	0	0-0	0-1	0	0
49ERS ...	17	20	6	19-29	42-43	0	357
Opponents	10	16	4	13-23	29-30	1	250

PUNT RETURNS	NO.	YDS.	AVG.	FC	LG	TD
Solomon	29	173	6.0	6	19	0
Hicks	19	171	9.0	4	39	0
49ers	48	344	7.2	10	39	0
Opponents	57	664	11.6	8	58T	0

PUNTING	NO.	YDS.	AVG.	TB	IN 20	LG	BLK
Miller	93	3858	41.5	15	14	65	0
49ers	93	3858	41.5	15	14	65	0
Opponents	83	3433	41.4	5	17	66	0

Kickoff Rets.	NO.	YDS.	AVG.	LG	TD
Lawrence ...	17	437	25.7	92T	1
Ring	10	217	21.7	29	0
Lott	7	111	15.9	20	0
Wilson	4	67	16.8	22	0
Jones	3	43	14.3	22	0
Hicks	1	22	22.0	22	0
Ramson	1	12	12.0	12	0
Patton	1	0	0.0	0	0
Davis	1	0	0.0	0	0
49ers	45	909	20.2	92T	1
Opponents.	67	1389	20.7	55	0

FGs.	1 -19	20 -29	30 -39	40 -49	50+	Total
Wersching	2-2	7-7	4-7	4-7	0-0	17-23
Bahr	0-0	0-2	0-1	2-3	0-0	2-6
49ers	2-2	7-9	4-8	6-10	0-0	19-29
Opponents ...	1-1	6-9	3-6	2-6	1-1	13-23

PASSING	ATT.	COMP.	YDS.	PCT.	AVG./ ATT.	TD	PCT. Td	INT.	PCT. INT.	LG	LOST/ ATT.	RATING
Montana ...	488	311	3565	63.7	7.31	19	3.9	12	2.5	78T	26/193	88.2
Benjamin ..	26	15	171	57.7	6.58	1	3.8	1	3.8	27	3/ 30	74.4
Easley	1	1	5	100.0	5.00	0	0.0	0	0.0	5	0/ 0	87.5
Clark	1	0	0	0.0	0.0	0	0.0	0	0.0	0	0/ 0	0.0
49ers	517	328	3766	63.4	7.28	20	3.9	13	2.5	78T	29/223	87.8
Opponents .	514	273	3135	53.1	6.10	16	3.1	27	5.3	67	36/290	60.0

PLAYOFF STATISTICS

Team Statistics

	49ers	Opp.
Time of Possession	52:45	1:07:15
Total First Downs	50	30
By Rushing	14	8
By Passing	30	18
By Penalty	6	4
Third Down—Made/Att	9/24	11/29
Third Down Efficiency	37.5%	37.9%
Total Net Yards	816	596
Avg. Gain per Game	408.0	298.0
Total Offensive Plays	137	121
Avg. Gain per Play	6.0	4.9
Net Yards Rushing	262	180
Avg. Gain per Game	131.0	90.0
Total Rushing Plays	65	54
Avg. Gain per Rush	4.0	3.3
Net Yards Passing	554	416
Avg. Net Passing per Game	277.0	208.0
Lost Att. to Pass	6/36	6/47
Gross Yards Passing	590	463
Attempts/Completions	66/42	61/32
Percent Complete	63.6	52.5
Had Intercepted	4	3

	49ers	Opp.
Punts/Average	8/39.1	10/41.1
Net Punting Average	35.3	34.5
Punt Returns/Average	4/11.5	6/5.2
Kickoff Ret/Average	11/18.2	12/19.3
Intercepts/Avg. Reg.	3/12.3	4/0.5
Penalties/Yards	21/251	13/100
Fumbles/Ball Lost	5/3	8/4
Touchdowns	9	6
By Rushing	3	1
By Passing	5	5
By Returns	1	0
Extra Points	9/9	6/6
Field Goals	1/2	3/4
Safeties	0	0
Total Points	66	51
Avg. per Game	33.0	25.5

Score by Quarters

	1	2	3	4	TOTAL
49ers	14	24	7	21	0-66
Opponents	17	10	7	17	0-51

Individual Statistics

RUSHING	ATT.	YDS.	AVG.	LONG	TD
Cooper	15	87	5.8	20	0
Ring	16	56	3.5	11	1
Elliott	10	48	4.8	11	0
Patton	7	32	4.6	25t	1
Solomon	2	26	13.0	14	0
Easley	6	15	2.5	5	0
Clark	1	6	6.0	6	0
Davis	2	6	3.0	4	1
Montana	6	-14	-2.3	2	0
49ers	65	262	4.0	25t	3
Opponents	54	180	3.3	13	1

RECEIVING	NO.	YDS.	AVG.	LONG	TD
Clark	13	224	17.2	39	2
Solomon	12	182	15.2	58t	2
Young	6	67	11.2	17	1
Patton	2	38	19.0	28	0
Elliott	2	29	14.5	24	0
Wilson	2	21	10.5	15	0
Cooper	2	11	5.5	6	0
Ramson	1	11	11.0	11	0
Shumann	1	11	11.0	11	0
49ers	42	590	14.0	58t	5
Opponents	32	463	14.5	72t	5

INTERCEPTIONS	NO.	YDS.	AVG.	LONG	TD
Lott	2	32	16.0	20t	1
Leopold	1	5	5.0	5	0
49ers	3	37	12.3	20t	1
Opponents	4	2	0.5	2	0

KICKOFF RTRNS	NO.	YDS.	AVG.	LONG	TD
Lawrence	6	148	24.7	47	0
Ring	4	52	13.0	17	0
Lott	1	0	0.0	0	0
49ers	11	200	18.2	47	0
Opponents	12	231	19.3	35	0

PUNT RETURNS	NO.	YDS.	AVG.	FC	LONG	TD
Solomon	2	25	12.5	1	22	0
Hicks	2	21	10.5	1	12	0
49ers	4	46	11.5	2	22	0
Opponents	6	31	5.2	0	13	0

PUNTING	NO.	YDS.	AVG.	TB	I20	LG	BK
Miller	8	313	39.1	0	2	52	0
49ers	8	313	39.1	0	2	52	0
Opponents .	10	411	41.1	1	1	51	0

FIELD GOALS	1 -19	20 -29	30 -39	40 -49	50+	TOTL
Wersching	0-0	1-1	0-0	0-0	0-1	1-2
49ers	0-0	1-1	0-0	0-0	0-1	1-2
Opponents	0-0	1-2	0-0	2-2	0-0	3-4

PASSING	ATT.	COMP.	YDS.	PCT.	AVG./ ATT.	TD	TPCT	INT.	ICPT	LG	TK/ LOST	RATING
Montana ...	66	42	590	63.6	8.94	5	7.6	4	6.1	58T	6/36	92.3
49ers	66	42	590	63.6	8.94	5	7.6	4	6.1	58T	6/36	92.3
Opponents .	61	32	463	52.5	7.59	5	8.2	3	4.9	72T	6/47	84.4

Defensive Statistics

NAME	TOTAL	TACKLES SOLO	ASSISTS	SACKS	PASSES INT.	PASSES DEF.	FUMBLES REC.	FUMBLES FORCED	KICKS BLOCKED
Jack Reynolds	17	9	8	0-0	0-0	1	0	1	0
Carlton Williamson	15	7	8	0-0	0-0	3	0	0	0
Archie Reese	12	7	5	0-0	0-0	0	0	0	0
Willie Harper	11	6	5	1-8	0-0	0	0	0	0
Ronnie Loft	11	8	3	0-0	2-32	2	0	0	0
Eric Wright	9	5	4	0-0	0-0	7	0	0	0
Dwight Hicks	7	4	3	0-0	0-0	1	0	0	0
Craig Puki	7	3	4	0-0	0-0	0	0	1	0
Bobby Leopold	7	4	3	0-0	1-5	1	1	0	0
Keena Turner	6	2	3	1-1	0-0	0	1	0	0
Lawrence Pillers	4	3	1	2-20	0-0	1	0	1	0
Fred Dean	3	1	3	0-0	0-0	0	0	0	0
Dan Bunz	4	2	2	0-0	0-0	0	0	0	0
Mike Wilson	3	2	1	0-0	0-0	0	0	0	0
Dwaine Board	3	1	2	1-11	0-0	1	0	0	0
Milt McColl	3	1	2	0-0	0-0	0	0	0	0
Amos Lawrence	2	2	0	0-0	0-0	0	1	0	0
Lynn Thomas	2	2	0	0-0	0-0	1	0	0	0
Jim Stuckey	2	1	1	1-7	0-0	1	0	0	0
Rick Gervais	1	1	0	0-0	0-0	0	0	0	0
Fred Solomon	1	1	0	0-0	0-0	0	0	0	0
John Harty	1	1	0	0-0	0-0	0	0	0	0
Ricky Patton	1	1	0	0-0	0-0	0	0	0	0
Ray Wersching	1	0	1	0-0	0-0	0	0	0	0

DIRECTORY

Management

Edward DeBartolo, Jr. .... President
Franklin Mieuli .... Limited Partner
Mrs. Victor P. Morabito .... Limited Partner

Administrative Staff

John McVay .... Director of Football Operations
Ken Flower .... Director of Marketing & Community Affairs
Keith Simon .... Business Manager
George Heddleston .... Director of Public Relations
Jerry Walker .... Assistant Director of Public Relations
Delia Newland .... Assistant Director of Publicity
Ted Glarrow .... Ticket Manager
Ken Dargel .... Assistant Ticket Manager
R. C. Owens .... Executive Assistant
Melrene Frear .... Controller
Roy Gilbert .... Film Director
Walt Porep .... Game Films Photographer
Michael Zagaris
Dennis Desprois .... Photographers
Michael Olmstead .... Entertainment Director
Chris Poehler,
Paul Potyen .... Band Directors
S. Dan Brodie .... Statistician
Chico Norton .... Equipment Manager
Don Klein
Wayne Walker .... 49ers' Radio
Greg Cosmos,
Ted Walsh .... Assistant Equipment Managers

Coaching Staff

Bill Walsh .... General Manager-Head Coach
Chuck Studley .... Defensive Coordinator
Norb Hecker .... Linebackers
Milt Jackson .... Special Teams - Receivers
Billie Matthews .... Running Backs
Bobb McKittrick .... Offensive Line
Bill McPherson .... Defensive Line
George Seifert .... Secondary
Al Vermeil .... Strength and Conditioning
Sam Wyche .... Quarterbacks
Cas Banaszek .... Assistant Offensive Line
Ray Rhodes .... Assistant Secondary

Scouting Staff

Tony Razzano .... Director of College Scouting
Proverb Jacobs .... Pro Scouting
Vic Lindskog .... Scout
Ernie Plank .... Scout
Warren Schmakel .... Scout
Neil Schmidt .... Scout
Billy Wilson .... Scout
Neal Dahlen .... Staff Assistant